# NASCLA CONTRACTORS GUIDE TO BUSINESS, LAW AND PROJECT MANAGEMENT

*Louisiana Contractors*
*12th Edition*

---

Supplemental forms and links are available at NASCLAforms.org using access code LA129354.

**National Association of State Contractors Licensing Agencies (NASCLA)**
23309 N. 17th Drive
Building 1, Unit 110
Phoenix, Arizona 85027
(623) 587-9354
(623) 587-9625 fax
Visit our web site:
www.nascla.org

**NASCLA Contractors Guide to Business, Law and Project Management**

*Louisiana 12th Edition*

*Revised June 1, 2015*

Previously published as *Construction Management Guide–Louisiana Edition, Business and Project Management for Contractors–Louisiana Edition and Contractors Guide to Business, Law and Project Management, Louisiana 9th Edition.*

Copyright © 1995, 1998, 1999, 2000, 2001, 2003, 2004, 2005, 2008, 2010, 2012, 2013, 2014 and 2015 by

National Association of State Contractors Licensing Agencies (NASCLA)
23309 North 17th Drive, Building 1, Unit 110
Phoenix, Arizona 85027

ISBN-10 1-934-234-79-6

ISBN-13 978-1-934234-79-2

All rights reserved. No part of this book may be reproduced or utilized in any form or by any means, electronic or mechanical, including photocopying and recording, or by any information storage and retrieval systems beyond that permitted by the United States Copyright Act without the express written permission of the copyright owners.

The information contained in this reference manual is being provided as a service to the construction industry. Although the information contained herein is believed to be correct at the time of printing, changes in laws and regulations occur regularly. It is the contractor's responsibility to review his or her activities with an attorney, accountant, and tax professional. The publishers do not assume, and hereby disclaim, any liability to any party for loss or damage caused by any errors or omissions in this publication.

This publication is designed to provide authoritative information in a highly summarized manner with regard to the subject matter covered. It is sold with the understanding that the publishers are not engaged in rendering legal, technical or other professional advice or service. If legal, financial, technical or other expert assistance is required, the services of competent professionals should be sought.

# INTRODUCTION

The construction industry is one of the strongest industries in America. To keep the construction industry thriving and to be a successful construction contractor, you must be knowledgeable in both your trade and managing a business.

Thorough business planning and good management skills are the keys to success in today's market. A solid business plan lays the foundation for your financial, marketing, and management strategies and helps you maximize your potential. Competition can be fierce in the construction industry. In developing a business plan, you analyze your market and competition and understand where you can gain an edge.

Good management skills entail applying knowledge from all aspects of the business to create a successful operation. Effective managers know how to win customers, satisfy employees, meet all legal obligations, and increase the bottom line. If this is where you want to take your business, this book can help you get there.

## About This Book

This book is organized into three sections. Part 1 focuses on planning and starting your business. This section will help you formulate a business plan, choose a business structure, understand licensing and insurance requirements and gain basic management and marketing skills.

Part 2 covers fundamentals you will need to know in order to operate a successful construction business. This section covers estimating, contract management, scheduling, project management, safety and environmental responsibilities, and building good relationships with employees, subcontractors, and customers.

Part 3 provides valuable information to assist you in running the administrative functions of your business. Financial management, tax basics, and lien laws are covered. Effective management of these areas of business is vital and failure to give them proper attention can cause serious problems.

### Part 1: Getting Your Business Off the Ground

- ✓ Chapter 1 covers tips for writing a business plan and discusses key characteristics of entrepreneurship. A sample business plan is provided in Appendix B and at **NASCLAforms.org** using access code **LA129354**.
- ✓ Chapter 2 describes each type of business entity and summarizes their advantages and disadvantages.
- ✓ Chapter 3 reviews the licensing process and the requirements for getting a license.
- ✓ Chapter 4 discusses insurance and bonding options to protect your business against unmitigated risk.
- ✓ Chapter 5 is your business toolbox with tips on time management, delegation, business ethics, and technology. It also provides information on resources available to assist small businesses.
- ✓ Chapter 6 helps you execute your marketing plan through promotional materials, public relations and effective selling skills.

## Part 2: Fundamentals for the Field

✓ Chapter 7 shows you how to formulate estimates and evaluate bid opportunities.

✓ Chapter 8 takes you through the key elements of contracts and what is needed to make them enforceable.

✓ Chapter 9 covers scheduling techniques and the fundamental skills needed to effectively manage construction projects.

✓ Chapter 10 explains the importance of understanding customer expectations and handling change orders effectively. The basics of successful negotiation are also addressed.

✓ Chapter 11 is your resource for employment law, hiring and retaining of good employees, and discipline and termination of employees if unfortunate employment circumstances arise.

✓ Chapter 12 gives you the fundamentals for understanding OSHA laws and setting up a safety program for your company. Environmental considerations and possible permitting situations are covered in the event you are creating or working with environmental hazards.

✓ Chapter 13 covers the basics of finding and hiring good subcontractors and establishing good working relationships with them.

## Part 3: Office Administration

✓ Chapter 14 takes you through the accounting cycle, the preparation and analysis of financial statements and payroll procedures.

✓ Chapter 15 gives you federal and state tax basics and helps you understand the forms you need to file.

✓ Chapter 16 covers lien law regulations and the process for filing a lien.

Supplemental forms and links are available at **NASCLAforms.org** using access code **LA129354**.

Whether you are studying for the contractors' licensing exam or need an ongoing reference manual for managing your business, the NASCLA Contractors Guide to Business, Law and Project Management will serve as a valuable resource. We hope you find this reference useful in your daily operations and that the concepts discussed give you the tools for running a successful business.

# TABLE OF CONTENTS

## PART I
## Getting Your Business Off the Ground

**CHAPTER 1: THE PLAN**

Being an Entrepreneur ........................................................................................... 1-1
The Benefits of a Business Plan ............................................................................. 1-2
Elements of a Business Plan .................................................................................. 1-2
Business Plan Pitfalls ............................................................................................. 1-3

**CHAPTER 2: CHOOSING YOUR BUSINESS STRUCTURE**

Sole Proprietorships .............................................................................................. 2-1
Partnerships ........................................................................................................... 2-2
C Corporations ....................................................................................................... 2-3
S Corporations ....................................................................................................... 2-4
Limited Liability Company (LLC) ........................................................................... 2-4
Summary of Business Legal Structures ................................................................. 2-6
Joint Ventures ........................................................................................................ 2-7
Naming Your Business ........................................................................................... 2-7
Reserving Your Name in Louisiana ....................................................................... 2-7
Contacting the Louisiana Secretary of State ........................................................ 2-8

**CHAPTER 3: BECOMING A LICENSED CONTRACTOR**

Purpose of Licensing ............................................................................................. 3-1
Louisiana State Licensing Board for Contractors ................................................. 3-1
License Requirements ............................................................................................ 3-2
Commercial and Residential License Classifications ............................................ 3-2
Commercial Contractors ........................................................................................ 3-2
Residential Building Contractors .......................................................................... 3-4
Licensing Process for Commercial and Residential Contractors .......................... 3-4
Summary of Licensing Process .............................................................................. 3-5
Mold Remediation Contractors ............................................................................. 3-5
Home Improvement Contractors .......................................................................... 3-5
Reciprocity ............................................................................................................. 3-6
License Renewals ................................................................................................... 3-7
Disciplinary Action ................................................................................................ 3-7
Bid Requirements .................................................................................................. 3-8

**CHAPTER 4: MANAGING RISK**

Risk Management Benefits .................................................................................... 4-1
Insurance ............................................................................................................... 4-1

Property Insurance ........................................................................................................ 4-2

*All-Risk Builders' Risk Insurance* ........................................................................... 4-2

*Named Peril Builders' Risk Insurance* ................................................................... 4-3

*Inland Marine/Equipment Theft Insurance* .......................................................... 4-3

*Equipment Floater Policy* ....................................................................................... 4-3

*Transportation Floater and Motor Truck Cargo Insurance* .................................. 4-3

Liability Insurance ........................................................................................................ 4-4

*Commercial General Liability (CGL)* ...................................................................... 4-4

*Umbrella Liability Insurance* .................................................................................. 4-4

*Director's and Officer's Liability Insurance (D and O)* ........................................... 4-4

*Other Types of Liability Insurance* ......................................................................... 4-4

Business Owner's Policies (BOPs) ............................................................................... 4-4

Automobile Insurance .................................................................................................. 4-4

Burglary and Theft Insurance ...................................................................................... 4-5

Key Man Life Insurance ................................................................................................ 4-5

Coverage Gaps and Overlaps ...................................................................................... 4-5

Employment-Related Insurance .................................................................................. 4-5

*Workers' Compensation Insurance* ........................................................................ 4-5

Unemployment Insurance ............................................................................................ 4-6

Social Security Insurance ............................................................................................. 4-6

Insurance Coverage for Subcontractors ..................................................................... 4-7

What is a Bond? ............................................................................................................ 4-7

Bond Language ............................................................................................................. 4-7

Types of Bonds ............................................................................................................. 4-7

Qualifying for a Bond ................................................................................................... 4-8

Bond Claims .................................................................................................................. 4-8

Laws Governing Bonding of Federal Construction Projects ....................................... 4-9

# CHAPTER 5: YOUR BUSINESS TOOLBOX

Time Management ........................................................................................................ 5-1

Delegation .................................................................................................................... 5-1

Business Ethics ............................................................................................................. 5-2

Technology .................................................................................................................... 5-2

Small Business Assistance and Loans .......................................................................... 5-3

*State of Louisiana, Secretary of State, GeauxBiz* ................................................... 5-3

*Local Community Colleges & Universities* .............................................................. 5-4

*Louisiana Small Business Development Center (LSBDC)* ........................................ 5-4

*Small Business Administration (SBA)* ..................................................................... 5-4

*Service Corps of Retired Executives (SCORE)* ........................................................ 5-4

*Louisiana Economic Development Department* ...................................................... 5-4

Small Business Certifications ....................................................................................... 5-5

# CHAPTER 6: MARKETING AND SALES

Executing Your Marketing Plan ................................................................................... 6-1

Logos, Stationery, and Business Cards ........................................................................ 6-1

Promotional Materials ................................................................................................. 6-2

Public Relations ............................................................................................................ 6-2

Effective Selling Skills ............................................................................................... 6-2

Organizing the Sales Process ..................................................................................... 6-3

Your Sales Presentation .............................................................................................. 6-3

# PART II
# Fundamentals for the Field

## CHAPTER 7: BIDDING AND ESTIMATING

Bid Documents .......................................................................................................... 7-1

Ethics in Bidding ....................................................................................................... 7-2

Estimate Planning ...................................................................................................... 7-2

*Project Documents* ............................................................................................... 7-2

*Site Visit* ............................................................................................................... 7-3

Estimating Framework ............................................................................................... 7-3

*Define the Phases* ................................................................................................. 7-3

*List Each Task and Materials Needed* .................................................................. 7-3

*Estimating Checklist* ............................................................................................ 7-3

Determining Estimated Costs .................................................................................... 7-4

*Quantity Take-off Method* .................................................................................... 7-4

*Step 1: Determine Labor Cost for Each Task* ...................................................... 7-4

*Step 2: Add Labor Burden* ................................................................................... 7-4

*Step 3: Determine Materials Cost* ....................................................................... 7-4

*Step 4: Determine Project Equipment Cost* ........................................................ 7-5

*Step 5: Add Subcontractor Fees* .......................................................................... 7-6

*Step 6: Add Allowances* ....................................................................................... 7-6

*Step 7: Add Contingencies* ................................................................................... 7-6

*Step 8: Add Project Overhead* ............................................................................. 7-6

*Step 9: Add Company Overhead* .......................................................................... 7-6

*Calculating an Overhead Percentage* ................................................................... 7-6

*Step 10: Add Markup and Determine Profit Margin* ........................................... 7-7

Other Methods of Estimating ..................................................................................... 7-7

Estimating Pitfalls ...................................................................................................... 7-8

*Preliminary Estimates* .......................................................................................... 7-8

*Inaccurate Estimates* ............................................................................................ 7-8

Using an Estimator ..................................................................................................... 7-8

Submitting Your Bid ................................................................................................... 7-8

Job Cost Recording System ........................................................................................ 7-9

Technology Tools for Estimating ................................................................................ 7-9

## CHAPTER 8: CONTRACT MANAGEMENT

Required Contract Elements ...................................................................................... 8-1

*Offer and Acceptance* ........................................................................................... 8-1

*Consideration* ...................................................................................................... 8-2

*Competent Parties* ............................................................................................... 8-2

*Legal Purpose* ...................................................................................................... 8-2

Contract Provisions..................................................................................................8-2

    *Contract Price and Payment Terms*..........................................................8-2

    *Obligations of the Parties*........................................................................8-3

    *Supplemental Conditions*.........................................................................8-4

Breach of Contract.................................................................................................8-4

Boilerplate Provisions............................................................................................8-4

Provisions to Limit Risk.........................................................................................8-5

What Are Recitals?.................................................................................................8-5

Types of Construction Contracts...........................................................................8-5

    *Lump-Sum Contract*.................................................................................8-5

    *Unit-Price Contract*..................................................................................8-6

    *Cost-Plus Contract*...................................................................................8-6

Contracting Methods.............................................................................................8-6

    *Single Prime*.............................................................................................8-6

    *Design/Build*............................................................................................8-6

    *Construction Management*.......................................................................8-6

    *Turnkey*....................................................................................................8-6

    *Fast-Track Construction*...........................................................................8-6

    *Multiple Prime Contracts*.........................................................................8-6

    *Partnering*................................................................................................8-6

Sources of Contracts..............................................................................................8-7

Making Changes to the Contract...........................................................................8-7

Resolving Claims....................................................................................................8-7

Alternative Dispute Resolution..............................................................................8-7

Making Substitutions.............................................................................................8-8

Contract Documents and Project Manual..............................................................8-9

Are Oral Agreements Legally Binding?..................................................................8-9

Legal Interpretation...............................................................................................8-9

Subcontracting.....................................................................................................8-10

# CHAPTER 9: SCHEDULING AND PROJECT MANAGEMENT

Scheduling Process................................................................................................9-1

Scheduling Methods..............................................................................................9-2

    *Calendar Scheduling*...............................................................................9-3

    *Bar Chart Scheduling*...............................................................................9-4

    *Critical Path Method*................................................................................9-5

Scheduling and Cash Management........................................................................9-6

What is Project Management?................................................................................9-6

Who is the Project Manager?.................................................................................9-6

Project Supervisory Team.......................................................................................9-7

Project Life Cycle...................................................................................................9-8

    *Contract Award*.......................................................................................9-8

    *Pre-Construction Phase*...........................................................................9-8

    *Construction Phase*.................................................................................9-8

    *Job Completion and Closeout*.................................................................9-8

Tracking the Progress of the Project.....................................................................9-8

    *Daily Reports*...........................................................................................9-8

*Status Reports* .................................................................................................................... 9-9

*Tracking the Schedule* .......................................................................................................... 9-9

Budget and Cost Controls ............................................................................................................ 9-9

*Materials* .............................................................................................................................. 9-9

*Budget Tracking* ................................................................................................................... 9-9

Quality Assurance .................................................................................................................... 9-10

*Accurate and Detailed Specifications and Plans* ................................................................... 9-10

*Detailed Shop Drawings* ..................................................................................................... 9-10

*Quality Assurance Program* ............................................................................................... 9-10

*Customer Satisfaction Surveys* ........................................................................................... 9-10

Value Engineering ................................................................................................................... 9-10

## CHAPTER 10: CUSTOMER RELATIONS

Communication with Customers ................................................................................................. 10-1

Handling Customer Change Orders ............................................................................................ 10-1

Negotiation Basics .................................................................................................................... 10-2

## CHAPTER 11: EMPLOYEE MANAGEMENT

Interviewing and Hiring Employees ............................................................................................ 11-1

New Hire Reporting .................................................................................................................. 11-2

Hiring Minors for Construction Work ......................................................................................... 11-2

Employee Documentation .......................................................................................................... 11-3

Key Employment Laws .............................................................................................................. 11-4

Fair Labor Standards Act (FLSA) ................................................................................................ 11-4

*Recordkeeping under the FLSA* ............................................................................................ 11-5

*Penalties* ............................................................................................................................ 11-5

Immigration and Nationality Act ............................................................................................... 11-5

*Completing the I-9 Form for New Hires* ................................................................................ 11-6

Americans with Disabilities Act (ADA) ....................................................................................... 11-7

Other Labor Laws ..................................................................................................................... 11-8

Louisiana Wage and Hour Laws ................................................................................................. 11-8

Required Postings ..................................................................................................................... 11-9

Employee Handbook and Policies ............................................................................................. 11-10

*Writing Your Employee Handbook* ...................................................................................... 11-10

Employee Satisfaction ............................................................................................................. 11-11

*The Value of Job Descriptions* ............................................................................................ 11-11

Providing Benefits ................................................................................................................... 11-12

Disciplining Employees ............................................................................................................ 11-14

Terminating Employees ............................................................................................................ 11-14

*Contractual Employees* ...................................................................................................... 11-14

*At-Will Employees* ............................................................................................................. 11-14

Sample I-9 Form ..................................................................................................................... 11-17

## CHAPTER 12: JOBSITE SAFETY AND ENVIRONMENTAL FACTORS

Safety Standards ...................................................................................................................... 12-1

Written Safety Plan Requirements ............................................................................................. 12-2

Safe Hiring and Training ........................................................................................................... 12-3

Substance Abuse Policies .......................................................................................................... 12-3

Safety Equipment...................................................................................................................12-4
Emergency Action Plan.........................................................................................................12-4
OSHA Recordkeeping............................................................................................................12-4
OSHA Injury Decision Tree...................................................................................................12-6
Material Safety Data Sheets (MSDS)....................................................................................12-7
Overhead Power Line Safety................................................................................................12-7
Benefits of Providing a Safe and Healthy Workplace.........................................................12-7
Employee Rights...................................................................................................................12-8
Penalties...............................................................................................................................12-8
Environmental Considerations............................................................................................12-9
U.S. Environmental Protection Agency................................................................................12-9
Louisiana Department of Environmental Quality..............................................................12-10
Environmental Law............................................................................................................12-10
Air Quality..........................................................................................................................12-11
Asbestos.............................................................................................................................12-11
Clean Water Act.................................................................................................................12-12
Sedimentation and Erosion Control Measures.................................................................12-14
Excavation Safety...............................................................................................................12-14
Hazardous and Non-Hazardous Solid Waste....................................................................12-14
Hazardous Substances.......................................................................................................12-15
Lead....................................................................................................................................12-16
Remodeling or Renovating a Home with Lead-Based Paint (Lead PRE)...........................12-16
Sample OSHA Forms 300, 300A and 301..........................................................................12-20

**CHAPTER 13: WORKING WITH SUBCONTRACTORS**
Sources for Finding the Right Subcontractor......................................................................13-1
Creating a Winning Partnership..........................................................................................13-1
Site Rules for Contractors...................................................................................................13-2
Employee or Independent Contractor: IRS Guidelines.......................................................13-2
  *Behavioral Control* .........................................................................................................13-2
  *Financial Control*............................................................................................................13-2
  *Type of Relationship* ......................................................................................................13-3

# PART III
## Office Administration

**CHAPTER 14: FINANCIAL MANAGEMENT**
Bookkeeping........................................................................................................................14-1
The Accounting Cycle..........................................................................................................14-1
  *Step 1: Classify and Record Transactions*......................................................................14-2
  *Step 2: Post Transactions*..............................................................................................14-2
  *Step 3: Prepare Trial Balance*........................................................................................14-2
  *Step 4: Prepare Adjusted Trial Balance* ........................................................................14-3
  *Step 5: Prepare Financial Statements* ..........................................................................14-3
  *Balance Sheet* ...............................................................................................................14-3
  *Income Statement*.........................................................................................................14-5

*Statement of Cash Flows* .................................................................................................14-7

*Step 6: Analyze Financial Statements Using Financial Ratios* ..................................14-7

Methods of Accounting .......................................................................................................14-8

*Cash Method* ......................................................................................................................14-8

*Accrual Method* .................................................................................................................14-8

*Changing Your Method of Accounting* ..........................................................................14-8

Contract Accounting...........................................................................................................14-8

*Completed Contract Method*...........................................................................................14-8

*Percentage of Completion Method*................................................................................14-8

*Cost Comparison Method* ...............................................................................................14-9

Cash Management...............................................................................................................14-9

*Cash Flow* ..........................................................................................................................14-9

*Payments*........................................................................................................................14-10

*Petty Cash Fund* .............................................................................................................14-11

Equipment Records and Accounting ..............................................................................14-11

Depreciation Methods ......................................................................................................14-11

Accounting Process for Materials ...................................................................................14-12

Payroll Accounting ............................................................................................................14-12

*Calculate Gross Pay*.......................................................................................................14-13

*Calculate and Deduct Applicable Taxes and Deductions*........................................14-14

*Calculate Net Pay and Issue Checks*...........................................................................14-15

*Update Payroll Journal* ..................................................................................................14-16

Technology Solutions for Accounting.............................................................................14-16

## CHAPTER 15: TAX BASICS

Employer Identification Number ......................................................................................15-1

Federal Business Taxes.......................................................................................................15-1

Income Tax ...........................................................................................................................15-3

*Estimated Tax* ...................................................................................................................15-3

Self-Employment Tax..........................................................................................................15-3

Federal Employment Taxes ...............................................................................................15-3

*Circular E* ...........................................................................................................................15-3

*Social Security and Medicare Taxes (FICA)* .................................................................15-4

*Federal Income Tax Withholding* ..................................................................................15-4

*Deposit Schedule* .............................................................................................................15-4

*Federal Unemployment Tax (FUTA)* ..............................................................................15-4

Penalties................................................................................................................................15-5

Information Returns – 1099-MISC ....................................................................................15-5

Tax Calendar ........................................................................................................................15-6

Louisiana State Tax Specifics.............................................................................................15-7

*Corporate Tax* ...................................................................................................................15-7

*Corporation Franchise Tax*.............................................................................................15-7

*Estimated Tax* ...................................................................................................................15-8

*Contractor Fee and Bond for Nonresidents* ................................................................15-8

*State Withholding Tax*......................................................................................................15-9

*Local Occupational License Tax* ....................................................................................15-9

*Sales and Use Tax*..........................................................................................................15-10

**CHAPTER 16: LOUISIANA MECHANICS' LIEN LAW**

What is a Lien?..................................................................................................................................16-1

Who is Entitled to a Lien?................................................................................................................16-1

Notice of Contract............................................................................................................................16-2

Priority ..............................................................................................................................................16-2

Notice of Termination of the Work ................................................................................................16-2

Statement of Claim or Privilege ......................................................................................................16-3

Time in which to Foreclose on a Lien.............................................................................................16-3

Residential Truth in Construction Act ...........................................................................................16-3

**APPENDIX A: GLOSSARY**

**APPENDIX B: BUSINESS PLAN TEMPLATE**

**APPENDIX C: USEFUL LINKS**

**APPENDIX D: NEW BUSINESS CHECKLIST**

**APPENDIX E: LOUISIANA CONTRACTORS LICENSING LAW**

**APPENDIX F: RULES AND REGULATIONS OF THE LOUISIANA LICENSING BOARD FOR CONTRACTORS**

**APPENDIX G: LOUISIANA UNDERGROUND UTILITIES AND FACILITIES DAMAGE PREVENTION LAW**

# PART 1
# Getting Your Business Off the Ground

# Chapter 1
# THE PLAN

## Chapter Survey...
⇨ Being an Entrepreneur
⇨ The Benefits of a Business Plan
⇨ Elements of a Business Plan
⇨ Business Plan Pitfalls

Just as you need trade tools to successfully complete contracting jobs, you need organization tools to successfully manage your business. As a business owner you go from being an expert in your trade to requiring expertise in project management, marketing, employee management, financial management, contract management and much more.

**Success Factors:** It takes an organized, consistent approach to achieve success in today's market. Businesses fail every day. The top reasons businesses fail are

- ✓ poor sales,
- ✓ competitive weakness,
- ✓ high operating expenses,
- ✓ difficulty collecting on invoices,
- ✓ inventory problems,
- ✓ too many fixed assets,
- ✓ poor location, and
- ✓ fraud.

> **To Sum It Up...**
> Poor planning and inadequate management are overriding factors in business failure.

From this point forward, we will build your business management expertise so you can identify and understand these obstacles, thereby, increasing your chances of building and operating a successful business.

## Being an Entrepreneur

**Understanding Entrepreneurship:** As a business owner, you may be referred to as an entrepreneur. There are many definitions of "entrepreneur." For our purposes, an entrepreneur is a person engaged in strategic activities that involve the initiation and development of a new business, created to build long-term value and steady cash flow streams.

**Risk Taking:** Entrepreneurs are often regarded as risk takers. There is risk associated with any venture, but entrepreneurs understand the importance of taking calculated risks. A calculated risk is a risk that is well-thought through where all outcomes are considered. This chapter will introduce the business planning process and help you understand the risks and opportunities associated with business ownership and how to manage them.

> **Something to Consider...**
> Entrepreneurship has its rewards as well as its drawbacks. Before embarking on any business venture, an entrepreneur must weigh all of these factors carefully.

**Rewards and Challenges:** Rewards of owning your own business include

- ✓ being your own boss;
- ✓ having flexibility of time;
- ✓ having more freedom and independence;
- ✓ making your own decisions; and
- ✓ receiving personal satisfaction from completing a job.

Entrepreneurship also has many frustrations and challenges, including

- ✓ long working hours;
- ✓ managing cash flow and payroll;

- ✓ high potential for overwhelming responsibility;
- ✓ finding and keeping qualified employees;
- ✓ paying taxes; and
- ✓ knowing and following government regulations.

*Entrepreneurs need to decide if the rewards of entrepreneurship outweigh the challenges.*

# The Benefits of a Business Plan

Preparing a business plan that outlines strategies and goals for your business is useful for a newly-formed or early-stage business. It can also be a helpful tool for a company that is making major strategic changes (i.e., providing additional product or service offerings). A business plan should be a living document that changes as your business and the market change.

Think of the business plan as a blueprint for your business. Just as you would not perform your trade without a blueprint or plan from the customer, you should not operate your company without a business plan.

*Key Functions:* A business plan serves three key functions:

- ✓ **Planning Tool:** Your business plan is a road map for the growth of the business. Putting together the plan helps you think through all possible scenarios for growth in the market.
- ✓ **Loan or Investor Document:** If you are planning to seek loan financing or approach an investor, you will need a business plan. Investors or loan officers will review this document to evaluate the qualifications of your management team, your projected growth, and your competitive advantage.
- ✓ **Benchmarking Tool:** Your business plan should also serve as a base against which to measure and monitor the company's performance. If your company exceeds or falls short of your projections, you can investigate the reasons for the difference.

A business plan will allow you to think through all aspects of your business, thus providing you with a competitive edge.

# Elements of a Business Plan

The following are the typical elements found in a business plan:

- ✓ **Cover Page:** Contact information and a confidentiality statement are stated on the cover page.
- ✓ **Executive Summary:** Placed after the cover page at the beginning of the business plan, the executive summary includes highlights of the plan and gains the interest of the reader. It is usually written last.
- ✓ **Company Summary:** The company vision and mission, legal structure, management personnel, business location, and facilities are outlined in the company summary section.
- ✓ **Products and Services:** Your specific products and services, primary subcontractors and suppliers, the effect of technology on your business, and expansion opportunities are all covered in the products and services section.
- ✓ **Market Analysis:** Your target market, market trends, and major competitors are defined under market analysis.
- ✓ **Marketing Strategy:** The uniqueness of your product or service as well as your pricing, advertising, and promotional strategies are outlined in the marketing strategy.
- ✓ **Financial Plan:** If you already have financial statements, you should include a balance sheet, an income statement, and a cash flow statement as part of your business plan. New and existing businesses can put together financial projections as additional documentation.

A business plan template that can be customized for your company is located in Appendix B. The template provides specific guidance for completing each section.

*Samples:* The websites listed below offer sample business plans:

- ✓ www.allbusiness.com
- ✓ www.bplans.com
- ✓ www.inc.com
- ✓ www.sba.gov

# Chapter 1: The Plan

- ✓ www.americanexpress.us/small-business/openforum
- ✓ www.bizmove.com/small-business/business-plan.htm

Business planning software packages that provide a step-by-step guide to creating a business plan are also available for purchase.

*Your business plan is the blueprint for your business.*

## Business Plan Pitfalls

As you start creating your business plan, there are guidelines you should follow to make sure you are giving investors an accurate and honest picture of your business.

- ✓ Make sure your assumptions are realistic.
- ✓ Keep the language simple. Don't use technical terminology or jargon.
- ✓ Cover the risks as well as the opportunities.
- ✓ Analyze your competition thoroughly.

By applying these simple guidelines, your business plan will have a solid foundation.

## Final Inspection...

**Being an Entrepreneur:** Entrepreneurs should take calculated risks and weigh all factors when making business decisions.

**The Benefits of a Business Plan:** A business plan is sometimes required by bank loan officers or by investors. It can also be used as a planning and benchmarking tool.

**Elements of a Business Plan:** A business plan typically contains a cover page, an executive summary, a company summary, a listing of products and/or services, a market analysis, an explanation of the marketing strategy, and a financial plan.

**Business Plan Pitfalls:** It is important to portray an accurate picture of your business when formulating your business plan.

## Supplemental Forms

Supplemental forms and links are available at **NASCLAforms.org** using access code **LA129354**.

| | |
|---|---|
| **Business Plan Template** | This template gives an outline for the business plan, including questions that help create detailed assumptions for each section of the plan. |
| **Profit and Loss Pro Forma** | This spreadsheet automatically calculates totals when you enter profit and loss numbers. You can adjust the numbers to determine your revenue and expense break-even point. |

# Chapter 2
# CHOOSING YOUR BUSINESS STRUCTURE

## Chapter Survey...
⇨ Sole Proprietorships
⇨ Partnerships
⇨ C Corporations
⇨ S Corporations
⇨ Limited Liability Company (LLC)
⇨ Summary of Business Legal Structures
⇨ Joint Ventures
⇨ Naming Your Business
⇨ Reserving Your Name in Louisiana
⇨ Contacting the Louisiana Secretary of State

When starting a business, one of the first things you need to decide is the legal structure your business will take. Each form of business has its advantages and disadvantages. The right choice depends on the nature of your business, plus various tax and liability issues. To ensure you are making the appropriate choice, it is best to consult with an attorney and an accountant.

## Sole Proprietorships

**Getting Started:** Many businesses begin as sole proprietorships because it is the simplest ownership form to set up. In a sole proprietorship, you are the sole owner of the company. If the sole proprietorship does business under a name different than your own, typically, a fictitious name certificate needs to be filed at a local or state government office.

If you are doing significant business, a sole proprietorship may be a risky legal business structure, because it exposes you to unlimited liability for the business' debt.

**Key Characteristics of Sole Proprietorships:**

✓ **Existence:** You own the assets of the company. If you decide to sell your sole proprietorship business, you are actually selling the assets of the business. You would have to close out your business license and the new buyer would have to obtain all appropriate licenses and accounts in his or her name. A sole proprietorship is terminated upon the owner's death.

✓ **Financial Management:** Business and personal expenses must be separated and careful records must be kept, because the IRS may question the handling of these funds and you may be asked to provide supporting documentation.

✓ **Liability:** You bear personal liability for all actions undertaken in the name of the business.

✓ **Taxes:** Your net income from the business is reported as ordinary income. Sole proprietors do not pay corporate income taxes.

**Advantages of a Sole Proprietorship:**

✓ Minimal legal restrictions
✓ Simple ownership form
✓ Low startup costs
✓ Sole ownership of profits
✓ Freedom in decision-making process

**Disadvantages of a Sole Proprietorship:**

✓ Unlimited personal liability
✓ Less available capital
✓ Possible difficulty obtaining long-term financing
✓ Dissolution of the business in the event of the owner's death

*Sole proprietorships are easy to form but are risky because the owner has unlimited personal liability.*

# Partnerships

***Partnering Up:*** A partnership is a relationship between two or more persons who join to carry on a trade or business. Each person contributes money, property, labor, or skill, and each partner expects to share in the profits and losses of the business. A partnership may be considered when neither partner can operate the business alone. Each partner should bring specific advantages to the business. There are two types of partnerships—general and limited. The differences are outlined in the following key characteristics.

***Key Characteristics of Partnerships:***

- ✓ **Existence:** A general partnership can be formed through an oral agreement, but it is recommended that a written partnership agreement be made. General partners own the assets of the company, just as an individual owns assets in a sole proprietorship. A limited partnership consists of one or more general partners and one or more limited partners. Limited partners have limited liability in the company. A partnership exists as long as the partners agree it will and as long as all of the general partners remain in the partnership. If a general partner leaves the partnership or dies, the partnership dissolves and the assets of the partnership must be sold or distributed to first pay the creditors and then the partners.

- ✓ **Financial Management:** The partnership should keep separate bank accounts and financial records for the business so that partners know whether there are profits and losses and the distribution of these amounts. The use of an outside accountant for record-keeping is recommended to prevent suspicion or doubt among partners.

- ✓ **Liability:** All owners in a general partnership have personal and unlimited liability for all actions undertaken in the name of the business, including all debts. Each partner is responsible for the acts of other partners when they act in the name of the business. Limited partners have no personal liability for the business of the partnership. Limited partners are liable only for the previously agreed-upon contribution to or investment in the business.

- ✓ **Taxes:** Business, income, and sales taxes are the responsibility of every partner. For federal income taxes, partners must file returns on IRS Form 1065.

***Advantages of a General Partnership:***

- ✓ Ease of formation
- ✓ Direct profit rewards
- ✓ Larger management base than that of a sole proprietorship

***Disadvantages of a General Partnership:***

- ✓ Unlimited personal liability of general partners
- ✓ Multiple decision makers
- ✓ Limited life of the business
- ✓ Changes of partners or partnership agreement may be difficult
- ✓ Partnership dissolves in the event of the death of a general partner

***Use Caution:*** Partnerships should be entered into carefully. Potential partners should discuss their expectations of the business before deciding to go into business together.

Questions to ask include these:

- ✓ Do the partners want to grow and operate a company long-term?
- ✓ Do the partners want to grow a short-term company to sell?
- ✓ How will profits be distributed: 100 percent to partners, or a part to the business, the rest to partners? What are the profit distribution percentages?
- ✓ Do the partners agree on the nature of the business, including the types of jobs the business will accept?

Also, be sure to define each partner's individual responsibilities as well as the group responsibilities.

- ✓ Who can sign debt instruments, such as notes, bonds, and leases for the partnership?
- ✓ Who determines the amount and frequency of compensation, salaries, draws, or profit-sharing for the partners?
- ✓ Who will handle record-keeping?
- ✓ If required, who oversees recruitment of additional partners or dissolution of the partnership?

Chapter 2: Choosing Your Business Structure

✓ Who can make amendments to the partnership agreement?

***Louisiana General and Limited Partnerships:*** To register a Louisiana-based general or limited partnership, file the Louisiana Partnership Registration Form (#342) with the Louisiana Secretary of State, Commercial Division.

***Louisiana Limited Liability Partnership:*** To register a Louisiana-based limited liability partnership, file the Application of a Registered Limited Liability Partnership Form (#975) with the Louisiana Secretary of State, Commercial Division.

***Foreign Partnerships:*** To conduct business in Louisiana, foreign partnerships (formed outside of Louisiana) must file a Statement and Affidavit of Registration of Foreign Partnership (#344) with the Secretary of State, Commercial Division.

*Carefully examine business expectations and responsibilities before entering into a partnership.*

# C Corporations

***Your Corporate Identity:*** If you decide to do business under a corporate identity, you will have to comply with the formal requirements of state law to create the corporation. A business assumes a corporate identity in Louisiana when it files as a corporation with the Louisiana Secretary of State, Corporations Division.

***Key Characteristics of Corporations:***

✓ ***Existence:*** Incorporation gives your business a legal existence. That is, the business can own assets and conduct business in its own name. A corporation lasts as long as the stockholders determine it should. A corporation continues to exist even if one or more of the shareholders die.

✓ ***Financial Management:*** The corporation needs separate bank accounts and separate business records. The corporation, not the shareholders, owns the money that the shareholders pay to buy the corporation's stock, all the assets, and the money earned by the corporation.

✓ ***Liability:*** The owners of the corporation, known as stockholders, are not personally liable for the losses of the business. Generally speaking, the corporate entity is responsible for business debts.

✓ ***Taxes:*** The corporation must file income tax returns and pay taxes on the profits. Dividends paid to shareholders by the corporation are also taxed to each shareholder individually. That is why there is said to be a "double tax" on corporations.

Other requirements for a corporation include

✓ a board of directors and corporate officers;

✓ stockholders as owners of the company;

✓ periodic board meetings, maintenance of board minutes, and approval of corporate resolutions; and

✓ a board empowered to authorize certain actions such as borrowing money, entering into contracts, and allocating corporate resources beyond routine business transactions.

***Advantages of a C Corporation:***

✓ Separate legal entity

✓ Limited liability for stockholders

✓ Unlimited life of the business

✓ Availability of capital resources

✓ Transfer of ownership through sale of stock

***Disadvantages of a C Corporation:***

✓ Complex and expensive organization

✓ Limitations on corporate activities and decisions by the corporate charter

✓ Extensive regulation and record-keeping requirements

✓ Double taxation (one on corporate profits and again on dividends)

***Filing for Incorporation in Louisiana:*** To begin the filing process, contact the Secretary of State, Corporations Division to obtain the proper forms.

*Louisiana Secretary of State*
*Corporations Division*

*Mailing Address:*
*P.O. Box 94125*
*Baton Rouge, Louisiana 70804-9125*

*Office Location:*
*8585 Archives Avenue*
*Baton Rouge, Louisiana 70809*

Telephone: (225) 925-4704
Fax: (225) 932-5314

Email: commercial@sos.la.gov

Website: www.sos.la.gov

Complete the forms with appropriate signatures and submit with the appropriate fees.

The Corporations Section staff can answer questions about the type of business entities that are available. The staff cannot give legal or tax advice. If you are not sure what type of business entity is best for your company, seek legal counsel.

The Corporations Section also works with the Secretary of State, Office of Trade Names because the laws pertaining to corporate names are similar to those governing trade names. The name of the corporation must include "Corporation," "Incorporated," or "Limited," or the abbreviation of the word, or may instead contain the word "Company" or the abbreviation "Co." if not immediately proceeded by the word "and" or the symbol "&".

**Louisiana Businesses:** To incorporate a business in Louisiana, Articles of Incorporation (#399) must be filed with the Secretary of State, Corporations Division.

**Foreign Corporations:** Foreign corporations (formed outside of Louisiana) must file an Application of Foreign Corporation for Certificate of Authority (#326) with the Secretary of State, Corporations Division to conduct business in Louisiana.

Any significant changes to the Articles of Incorporation in the form of amendments, mergers, consolidations, dissolutions, or withdrawals are also filed with the division. All filings are public record and available for inspection.

**Annual Report:** Annual reports for domestic and foreign corporations are due on or before the anniversary date of incorporation. Forms are prepared by the Corporations Division and mailed thirty days before the anniversary date. Failure of corporations to file annual reports can result in revocation of registration and the inability to conduct business in Louisiana. If an annual report has not been received by the anniversary date, the Secretary of State's office should be contacted at (225) 925-4704 so a form can be sent.

> *Corporations are more complex to form and operate but reduce personal liability of the owners.*

# S Corporations

If your business is an eligible domestic corporation, you can avoid double federal taxation (corporate and shareholder taxes on the same earnings as in a C corporation) by electing to be treated as an S corporation under the rules of Subchapter S of the Internal Revenue Code. In this way, the S corporation passes its items of income, loss, deduction, and credits through to its shareholders to be included on their separate returns.

**Requirements for an S Corporation:**

✓ Domestic corporation with one class of stock

✓ No more than 75 shareholders who are citizens or legal residents of the U.S.

✓ All shareholders must consent to S corporation status

✓ Use of a permitted tax year

✓ Filing of IRS Form 2553

> *S corporations have special tax considerations. Consult with the appropriate financial and legal professionals to find out if this option is right for you.*

# Limited Liability Company (LLC)

**A Hybrid Structure:** This legal arrangement shares characteristics of both sole proprietorships and corporate identities. LLCs must consist of at least one member. Ownership in the LLC is invested in memberships rather than shares of stock.

Limited liability companies offer some protection from liability for actions taken by your company or by other members of your company. It does not protect from liability for personal actions. In this way, it resembles a sole proprietorship rather than a corporation.

# Chapter 2: Choosing Your Business Structure

Like an S corporation, federal income taxes are paid only on income distributed to members as ordinary income. A limited liability company can be expensive to organize and requires more administrative work. This form of organization is useful to professionals and general partnerships.

**Advantages of a Limited Liability Company:**

✓ Limited disclosure of owners

✓ Limited documentation

✓ No advance IRS filings

✓ No public disclosure of finances

✓ Limited liability for managers and members

✓ Ability to delegate management to a non-member

**Tax Implications:** LLCs are not taxed at an entity level. Depending on the number of business owners, the LLC is taxed differently.

✓ An LLC with one owner is taxed as a sole proprietorship.

✓ An LLC with more than one owner may elect to be taxed as a partnership or as a corporate entity.

**Louisiana Limited Liability Company Registration:** Limited liability companies are created by filing Articles of Organization (#365) with the Secretary of State, Corporations Division. The name of the limited liability company must include "Limited Liability Company," "L.L.C.," or "L.C."

**Foreign Limited Liability Companies:** Foreign limited liability companies (formed outside of Louisiana) file an Application of Foreign Limited Liability Company (#972) with the Secretary of State, Corporations Division to conduct business in Louisiana.

Any significant changes to the Articles of Organization for limited liability companies in the form of amendments, mergers, consolidations, dissolutions, or withdrawals are also filed with the division. All filings are public record and available for inspection.

**Annual Report:** Annual reports for domestic and foreign limited liability companies are due on or before the anniversary date of organization or registration. Forms are prepared by the division and mailed thirty days before the anniversary date. Failure of limited liability companies to file annual reports can result in revocation of registration and the inability to conduct business in Louisiana. If an annual report has not been received by the anniversary date, the Secretary of State's office should be contacted at (225) 925-4704 so a form can be sent.

# Summary of Business Legal Structures

| | Ownership | Liability | Formation Documents | Taxation | Management |
|---|---|---|---|---|---|
| **Sole Proprietorship** | One Owner | Unlimited personal liability | Doing Business As (DBA) Filing | Entity not taxed; profits and losses claimed on personal taxes | Owner |
| **General Partnership** | Unlimited number of general partners | Unlimited personal liability | General Partnership Agreement | Entity not taxed; profits and losses claimed on personal taxes of general partners | General partners |
| **Limited Partnership** | Unlimited number of general and limited partners | Unlimited personal liability of the general partners; limited partners generally have no personal liability | Limited Partnership Certificate<br><br>Limited Partnership Agreement | Entity not taxed; profits and losses claimed on personal taxes of general and limited partners | General partners |
| **Limited Liability Company (LLC)** | Unlimited number of members | Generally no personal liability of the members for obligations of the business | Articles of Organization<br><br>Operating Agreement | Entity not taxed (unless chosen to be taxed); profits and losses are passed through to the members | Manager or members designated in Operating Agreement |
| **C Corporation** | Unlimited number of shareholders | Generally no personal liability of the shareholders | Articles of Incorporation<br><br>Bylaws<br><br>Organizational Board Resolutions<br><br>Stock Certificates<br><br>Stock Ledger | Corporation taxed on its earnings at the corporate level and the shareholders may have a further tax on any dividends distributed ("double taxation") | Board of Directors |
| **S Corporation** | Up to 75 shareholders allowed | Generally no personal liability of the shareholders | Articles of Incorporation<br><br>Bylaws<br><br>Organizational Board Resolutions<br><br>Stock Certificates<br><br>Stock Ledger<br><br>IRS and State S Corporation Election | Entity generally not taxed, as profits and losses are passed through to the shareholders ("pass-through" taxation) | Board of Directors |

## Joint Ventures

**Complement Your Strengths:** A joint venture is a special business arrangement that exists when two or more companies join to undertake a specific project. The management of a joint venture is often assigned to one individual or company. This arrangement brings together companies with complementary resources and strengths. When forming this type of venture, it is important to consult an attorney to ensure that all aspects of risk are covered.

*Joint Venture Licensing Requirements:*
At the time a bid is submitted for work in the amount of $50,000 or more ($1 or more for hazardous), all parties in a joint venture are required to be licensed. Each party in the joint venture may perform only within the applicable classifications of the work (found in Section 1103 of the Rules and Regulations of the Board) according to the limitations of the license. Further information on licensing is located in Chapter 3, Becoming a Licensed Contractor.

## Naming Your Business

**Choose Wisely:** Selecting a name is an important part of forming your business. The name you choose affects your customers' impression of your company. The individuality of the name affects future trademarks and service marks. It is important to select a name that is distinctive.

Do your homework before you decide on a business name for your company. A search can be conducted using the following sources:

- ✓ U.S. Patent and Trademark Office (800) 786-9199 or at www.uspto.gov
- ✓ Secretary of State Office in the state where you intend to do business
- ✓ Internet search engines such as www.yahoo.com or www.google.com

## Reserving Your Name in Louisiana

A corporate or limited liability company name may be reserved for 60 days prior to incorporation or organization by completing the Reservation of Corporate/Limited Liability Company Name (#398) form and submitting it to the Secretary of State with your fee.

A corporate or limited liability company name must be distinguishable from other corporate or limited liability company names previously registered with the Louisiana Secretary of State. A preliminary check for name availability should take into consideration the various spellings of words (i.e., Cajun vs. Kajun, K-Jun) as well as words that are spelled differently but are phonetically similar (i.e., caret, carat, carrot). Do not rely on a preliminary check. Formally reserve the name or wait for confirmation of your filing prior to obtaining stationery, business cards, phone listings, bank accounts, etc.

Most companies, including sole proprietorships, select a business name other than the owner's name and often design a logo to be used on advertising, stationery, and other materials. Registration for companies that are not incorporated or organized through the Secretary of State are filed with the Clerk Court's Office, Recording Department in the parish in which business is being conducted. Filing fees vary between parishes. The Secretary of State maintains the State Registry for trade name filings.

A business may choose to file for a trademark or service mark. A trademark can be a word, name, symbol, sound, or color used to represent and distinguish a company's products. A service mark can be a word, name, symbol, sound, or color used to represent and distinguish a company's services. A trademark or service mark is not the same as a trade name. Although, a business can trademark a trade name. Trademarks and service marks can be filed on the state and federal level. State information is available through the Louisiana Secretary of State. Federal information is available through the U.S. Patent and Trademark Office.

## Contacting the Louisiana Secretary of State

The Louisiana Secretary of State, Corporations Division is the agency to contact to file Articles of Incorporation and Organization, to determine name availability for corporate and limited liability companies (LLCs), to file applications by foreign corporations seeking authority to transact business in Louisiana, and to file annual reports. The Corporations Division also maintains and certifies copies of any and all corporate and LLC documents on file.

> Louisiana Secretary of State
> Corporations Division
>
> Mailing Address:
> P.O. Box 94125
> Baton Rouge, Louisiana 70804-9125
>
> Office Location:
> 8585 Archives Avenue
> Baton Rouge, Louisiana 70809
>
> Telephone: (225) 925-4704
> Fax: (225) 932-5314
>
> Email: commercial@sos.la.gov
>
> Website: www.sos.la.gov

## Final Inspection...

**Sole Proprietorships:** This business structure offers easy formation and operation. However, unlimited personal liability is a concern because the business and owner are considered the same legal entity.

**Partnerships:** Partnerships can bring together two or more people with strengths and resources in different areas but also allow for unlimited personal liability of general partners. To reduce conflicts among partners, responsibilities and business goals must be clearly outlined at the beginning of the business arrangement.

**C Corporations:** C corporations offer liability protection to the owners and easy ownership transfer through stock sales. This business structure is more complex to operate and shareholders may be "double-taxed" on their earnings.

**S Corporations:** S corporations are similar to C corporations but offer special tax considerations. S corporation status can be filed with the IRS, if companies meet the specified criteria.

**Limited Liability Company (LLC):** LLCs have characteristics of both sole proprietorships and corporations.

**Summary of Business Legal Structures:** Each type of business entity has unique ownership, liability, taxation, and management characteristics. Required formation documents differ for each business structure.

**Joint Ventures:** Joint ventures are generally formed on a project basis in order to integrate positive attributes and resources of two or more companies.

**Naming Your Business:** An appropriate business name is important and defines how your customers perceive you.

**Reserving Your Name in Louisiana:** A corporate or limited liability company name may be reserved 60 days prior to incorporation or organization. Names must be distinguishable from existing registered names.

**Contacting the Louisiana Secretary of State:** The Secretary of State, Corporations Division can be contacted about registering your business in Louisiana, obtaining various business forms, and filing guidelines for businesses.

## Supplemental Forms

Supplemental forms and links are available at **NASCLAforms.org** using access code **LA129354**.

| | |
|---|---|
| Summary of Business Legal Structures | Table showing the primary features of each type of business entity (featured earlier in the chapter). |
| IRS Form 2553 | IRS form to elect S corporation status |

# Chapter 3
# BECOMING A LICENSED CONTRACTOR

## Chapter Survey...
⇨ Purpose of Licensing
⇨ Louisiana State Licensing Board for Contractors
⇨ License Requirements
⇨ Commercial and Residential License Classifications
⇨ Commercial Contractors
⇨ Residential Building Contractors
⇨ Licensing Process for Commercial and Residential Contractors
⇨ Mold Remediation Contractors
⇨ Home Improvement Contractors
⇨ Reciprocity
⇨ License Renewals
⇨ Disciplinary Action
⇨ Bid Requirements

## Purpose of Licensing

A major purpose of contractor licensing is to protect the health, safety, and welfare of the public. Licensing also defines the work that a contractor is allowed to do under a particular license.

Licensing establishes entrance requirements, standards of practice, and disciplinary authority to protect the public from unqualified, incompetent, and unethical contractors.

✓ **Entrance Requirements:** Licensing ensures that those practicing a trade or occupation have met a minimum set of qualifications, such as experience, training, and required examination.

✓ **Standards of Practice:** Contractors are required to adhere to standards of practice established by law. The standards ensure an appropriate level of quality workmanship is given to the public. Continuing education may be required for certain trades.

✓ **Disciplinary Authority:** Statutes and regulations define illegal and prohibited activities. The law provides licensing authorities with a mechanism to conduct investigations and to administer discipline to problem contractors. Violations can result in penalties, including fines and loss of license.

## Louisiana State Licensing Board for Contractors

The Louisiana State Licensing Board for Contractors regulates commercial, residential, home improvement, mold remediation, and hazardous material contractors.

**Board Membership:** The board is appointed by the Governor and composed of fifteen members representing each voting district in Louisiana. The board directs administrative policy for the agency's operations. Membership includes

✓ four members with experience in highway, street, and bridge construction;
✓ four members with experience in building or industrial construction;
✓ one member with experience in mechanical construction;
✓ one member with experience in electrical construction;
✓ one member with experience in oilfield construction;
✓ two members with experience as a subcontractor in a field other than electrical or mechanical construction; and
✓ two members of the public who are not employed in a construction-related industry.

A five-member residential committee conducts business regarding residential matters in a manner similar to the commercial board.

**Agency Staff:** Staff members receive and process applications for new contractor licenses, additional classifications, changes of license records, and annual license renewals. The board staff administers the trade and business and law examinations for contractor applicants and qualifying parties.

**Agency Investigators:** Enforcement of the contractor licensing law is done through agency investigators. Construction project investigations are conducted to determine compliance. Public records are kept on these matters.

**Board Contact Information:** All Board meetings and administrative hearings are conducted at the Board's Baton Rouge headquarters.

> *Louisiana State Licensing Board for Contractors*
> *2525 Quail Drive*
> *Baton Rouge, Louisiana 70808*
>
> *Main Phone: (225) 765-2301*
> *Administration Fax: (225) 765-2431*
> *Applications Fax:(225) 765-2690*
> *Examinations Fax: (888) 510-0130*
> *Compliance Fax: (888) 510-0129*
> *Reciprocity Fax: (888) 510-0132*
>
> *Commercial Applications:*
> *capplications@lslbc.louisiana.gov*
>
> *Residential Applications:*
> *rapplications@lslbc.louisiana.gov*
>
> *Administration:*
> *administration@lslbc.louisiana.gov*
>
> *Contractor Testing and Scheduling:*
> *testing@lslbc.louisiana.gov*
>
> *Website: www.lslbc.louisiana.gov*

# License Requirements

A contractor's license is required to bid, contract, or perform work in the following amounts in Louisiana:

✓ Commercial projects of $50,000 or more

✓ Electrical work of $10,000 or more

✓ Mechanical work of $10,000 or more

✓ Plumbing work of $10,000 or more

✓ Residential projects of more than $75,000

✓ Home improvement projects of $7,500 or more (Home improvement projects exceeding $75,000 are considered residential projects. The person performing these projects must be licensed accordingly.)

✓ Mold remediation projects of $1 or more

✓ Hazardous materials projects (including asbestos, lead removal and abatement, underground storage tank installation and removal, and hazardous waste treatment or removal) of $1 or more

# Commercial and Residential License Classifications

The board issues licenses in the following major classifications:

✓ Building Construction

✓ Highway, Street, and Bridge Construction

✓ Heavy Construction

✓ Municipal and Public Works Construction

✓ Electrical Work

✓ Mechanical Work

✓ Plumbing Work

✓ Hazardous Materials

✓ Residential Building Contractor

Many subclassifications fall under these major classifications (outlined in §2156.2 of the Licensing Law printed in Appendix E).

A specialty classification may be obtained under 2156.2.

Contractors can bid and perform work only in the classifications for which their license is issued. To obtain changes in classifications, a contractor must submit a written request, pay the required fees, and pass the written exam.

# Commercial Contractors

**Definition:** A commercial project is any construction undertaking other than residential homes consisting of four or fewer units. A construction project for which the contractor has a single contract for the construction of more than two residential homes within the same subdivision is considered a commercial contract.

A commercial license is required for commercial contracts and subcontracts valued at $50,000 or more. To determine whether the job is $50,000 or

# Chapter 3: Becoming a Licensed Contractor

3-3

above, the total cost of the job must be counted, which includes all materials, labor, rentals, and all direct and indirect project expenses. If the owner buys all of the materials separately, the costs of the materials must still be included when determining whether the job cost is $50,000 or above.

**Exemptions:** The Louisiana commercial licensing requirements have several exemptions. These include the following categories:

✓ Public utilities regulated by the Louisiana Public Service Commission or the Council of the City of New Orleans (this applies to public utilities doing work for themselves, but not to contractors performing work for public utilities)

✓ Property owners who construct or manage the construction of a project for their own use and which will be controlled by the owner so that only employees and nonpublic invitees will be allowed access

✓ Donated labor for the construction, maintenance, or repair of churches

✓ Rail or pipeline construction activities owned or leased by the rail or pipeline industries (this applies to rail or pipeline companies doing work for themselves but not to contractors performing work for such companies)

✓ Projects completely owned by the federal government

✓ Farmers doing construction for agricultural purposes on leased or owned land

✓ Donated labor for projects funded by the Louisiana Community Development Block Grant, Louisiana Small Towns Environment Program

✓ Assembly, maintenance, or repair of patented and proprietary environmental equipment supplied to and used solely by the contractor for construction projects

✓ The manufactured housing industry for residential dwellings mounted on chassis and wheels

**Penalties:** The following actions by commercial contractors are subject to a misdemeanor conviction and fines as high as $500 per day of violation, three months in prison, or both.

✓ Engaging in contracting without holding an active license.

✓ Advertising as a licensed contractor without specifying the type of license.

**Additional Requirements:** In addition to the requirements for a commercial contractors license, there are other state agencies from which contractors must obtain additional licenses or permits for certain types of work.

Some examples include:

✓ The Louisiana Department of Transportation and Development, for truck permits.

✓ The Louisiana State Plumbing Board, for plumbing work.

✓ The Louisiana Department of Public Safety, licensing or permits for construction work on casinos and for work involving explosives.

✓ The Office of State Fire Marshal, licensing for burglar alarms, fire alarms, fire suppression systems, fire sprinkler systems, closed circuit television monitoring systems, locks and locking systems, and other related type work. Contractors holding the Electrical Work (Statewide) classification or the Mechanical Work (Statewide) classification with the Louisiana State Licensing Board for Contractors are exempted from some of the State Fire Marshal's licensing requirements.

✓ The Louisiana Department of Agriculture and Forestry, Horticulture Commission, licensing for landscaping, irrigation, and tree cutting.

✓ The Louisiana Department of Agriculture and Forestry, Pesticides Commission for licensing for spraying pesticides and for purchasing certain types of chemicals.

✓ The Louisiana Department of Environmental Quality, for certification and/or permits to conduct Asbestos Removal and Abatement, Hazardous Waste Treatment or Removal, Lead Based Paint Removal and Abatement, Underground Storage Tanks, Refrigerants, and certain septic system installations.

✓ The Louisiana Department of Natural Resources, for licensing of water well drillers.

✓ The Louisiana Manufactured Housing Commission, for certain modular homes and for mobile homes.

✓ The Department of Health and Hospitals, Office of Public Health, Center for Environmental Health, Sanitarian Services, for licensing of onsite wastewater treatment plant installers and constructors.

# Residential Building Contractors

A residential building project is the construction or management of construction of a fixed building or structure, not more than three floors in height, for use by another as a residence or for sale by another to be used as a residence.

It does not include manufactured housing or residential structures that are mounted on metal chassis and wheels, such as mobile homes and recreational vehicles. It does include modular homes that are manufactured in one or more sections to install onto a permanent foundation, when all costs (excluding the cost of those manufactured components at the time they leave the factory) exceed $37,500.

A home improvement project exceeding $75,000 is also considered a residential project.

Not all house construction falls under a Residential Building Contractor License. Construction projects in which the contractor has a single contract for the construction of more than two homes within the same subdivision is considered a commercial undertaking. Also, construction projects of more than one duplex, triplex or fourplex are considered commercial projects.

**Building Permit Issuance:** Before a building permit is issued, the local building permit official must obtain proof that the contractor holds an active and applicable contractor's license, or that the activity falls under the licensing law exemptions. If the building permit applicant claims that the project falls under an exemption for residential activities, an affidavit verifying the claimed exemption must be executed. This affidavit is required before the building permit is issued.

Nonresident commercial, residential, or home improvement contractor applicants are required to provide to the local building permit official a federal taxpayer identification number and proof of registration to do business in the state of Louisiana.

# Licensing Process for Commercial and Residential Contractors

You must complete the licensing process to obtain a contractor's license. The following is a summary of this process.

1. Complete the contractor's license application and include the proper documentation.

    ✓ Corporations must include a Certificate of Good Standing and a copy of the Articles of Incorporation.

    ✓ LLCs must include a copy of the Certificate of Existence and Articles of Organization.

    ✓ A current (within 12 months of filing) notarized financial statement is required in the format found in the application. It must be prepared by an independent auditor (certified public accountant). Commercial and residential contractors must show a minimum net worth of $10,000. If net worth requirements are not met, a bond, letter of credit, or other acceptable security in the amount of the shortfall may be presented to the board.

    ✓ For asbestos abatement and removal, underground storage tanks, or lead-based paint abatement and removal classifications, proper certifications and approvals from the Louisiana Department of Environmental Quality are required.

    ✓ For plumbing classifications, a copy of the master plumber license is required.

    ✓ For residential contractors, a certificate of workers' compensation coverage and minimum liability coverage or protection of $100,000 is required.

    ✓ Applications are available at the board office or online at www.lslbc.louisiana.gov.

2. Designate a qualifying party and complete qualifying party application.

    Note: If the qualifying party terminates employment, the board must receive notification within 30 days. Another qualifying party must qualify within 60 days of termination.

3. Submit application and pay appropriate fees. Out-of-state contractors must submit an additional $400 surcharge in addition to the regular licensing fee.

4. Take examination(s).

5. Review of application by the board to determine eligibility for licensure. Outstanding tax liens, judgments, etc. must be addressed before the applicant is considered eligible.

6. Issuance of license by the board. Out-of-state applications have a waiting period of 60 days between the time the application is submitted and the license is issued.

## Summary of Licensing Process

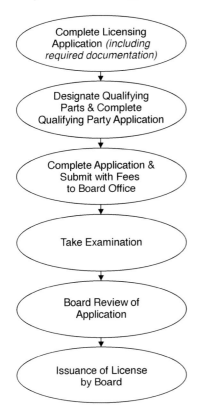

## Mold Remediation Contractors

A mold remediation project is defined as the removal, cleaning, sanitizing, demolition, or other treatment, including preventive activities, of mold or mold-contaminated matter that was not purposely grown at that location.

A mold remediation license is required for mold remediation projects valued at $1 or more.

**Exemptions:** Exemptions to holding a mold remediation license include

- ✓ routine cleaning that is not for the purpose of mold remediation;
- ✓ residential property owners performing mold remediation on their own property;
- ✓ nonresidential property owners, or the employees of such owners, who perform mold remediation on an apartment building with more than four dwelling units owned by that person;
- ✓ an owner or tenant, or a managing agent or employee of an owner or tenant, who performs mold remediation on property owned or leased by the owner or tenant. This exemption does not apply if the managing agent or employee engages in the business of performing mold remediation for the public;
- ✓ employees of a licensee who perform mold remediation while supervised by the licensee; and
- ✓ licensed residential building contractors who perform mold assessment or mold remediation services for no more than twenty square feet when acting within the scope of the license.

**Licensing:** Application for a mold remediation license must be made to the board. A financial statement showing a minimum net worth of $10,000 is required to be submitted with the application. Additionally, applicants must meet the following criteria:

- ✓ be at least 18 years of age with a high school diploma or its equivalent;
- ✓ be able to document 24 hours of training in mold remediation and basic mold assessment;
- ✓ complete four hours of instruction in Louisiana's "Unfair Trade Practices and Consumer Protection Law";
- ✓ pay the appropriate fees; and
- ✓ provide insurance certificates showing evidence of workers' compensation coverage and liability insurance of at least $50,000.

## Home Improvement Contractors

A home improvement project is defined as the reconstruction, alteration, renovation, repair, modernization, conversion, improvement, removal, or demolition of a pre-existing owner-occupied residence, or the construction of an addition to any pre-existing owner occupied residential building or dwelling unit, or to structures adjacent to such a residence or building.

A home improvement registration or other contractor's license is required for home improvement projects valued at $7,500 or more. Home improvement projects exceeding $75,000 require a residential builder's license.

**Written Contract Requirements:** Under Louisiana licensing law, a written contract is required before beginning work on home improvement contracts of $1,500 or more. To be considered valid, the contract must contain the following elements:

✓ Complete agreement between the owner and the contractor and a clear description of any other documents that are or shall be incorporated into the agreement

✓ Full names and addresses of all parties and the registration number of the home improvement contractor

✓ Detailed description of the work to be done and the materials to be used in the performance of the contract

✓ Total amount agreed to be paid for the work contract including all change orders and work orders

✓ Approximation of the cost expected to be borne by the owner under a cost-plus contract or a time-and-materials contract

✓ Signatures of all parties

✓ If the contract is for goods or services in connection with the repair or replacement of a roof system to be paid from the proceeds of a property or casualty insurance policy, a statement must be included in boldface type of a minimum size of ten points, in substantially the following form:

"You may cancel this contract in connection with the repair or replacement of a roof system at any time within seventy-two hours after you have been notified that your insurer has denied all or any part of your claim to pay for the goods and services to be provided under this contract. See attached notice of cancellation form for an explanation of this right."

If the contract is for goods or services in connection with the repair or replacement of a roof system to be paid from the proceeds of a property or casualty insurance policy, a fully completed form in duplicate, captioned "NOTICE OF CANCELLATION", must be attached to the contract but easily detachable. It must contain, in boldface type of a minimum size of ten points, the following statement:

NOTICE OF CANCELLATION

If your insurer denies all or any part of your claim to pay for goods and services in connection with the repair or replacement of a roof system to be provided under this contract, you may cancel the contract by mailing or delivering a signed and dated copy of this cancellation notice or any other written notice to (name of home improvement contractor) at (address of contractor's place of business) at any time within seventy-two hours after you have been notified that your claim has been denied. If you cancel, any payments made by you under the contract, except for certain emergency work already performed by the contractor, shall be returned to you within ten business days following receipt by the contractor of your cancellation notice.

I HEREBY CANCEL THIS TRANSACTION

_____

(Date)


_____

(Insured's Signature)

**Registration Process:** Home improvement contractors must complete the Home Improvement Registration Application. A certificate of workers' compensation and proof of general liability insurance in a minimum amount of one hundred thousand dollars must be submitted with the application along with the proper application fee.

# Reciprocity

The Board has reciprocity agreements with the following state boards:

✓ Alabama Licensing Board for General Contractors;

✓ Alabama Board of Heating & Air Conditioning Contractors;

# Chapter 3: Becoming a Licensed Contractor

- ✓ Alabama Electrical Contractors Board;
- ✓ Alabama Home Builders Licensure Board;
- ✓ Arkansas Contractors Licensing Board;
- ✓ General Contractors Division of the Georgia State Licensing Board for Residential and General Contractors;
- ✓ Georgia Construction Industry Board;
- ✓ Kentucky Department of Housing, Buildings and Construction;
- ✓ Mississippi Board of Contractors;
- ✓ North Carolina Board of Examiners of Electrical Contractors;
- ✓ Ohio Construction Industry Licensing Board;
- ✓ South Carolina Contractor's Licensing Board;
- ✓ South Carolina Residential Builders Commission;
- ✓ Tennessee Board for Licensing General Contractors;
- ✓ Texas Department of Licensing and Regulation;
- ✓ Utah Construction Trades Bureau Division of Occupational & Professional Licensing; and
- ✓ Virginia Board of Contractors.

Any applicant holding a comparable license for three consecutive years with one of these boards, free of official disciplinary action, may have the sixty day waiting period waived and be given credit for the examination(s) upon approval of the Board. Applicants must comply with all other Louisiana licensing requirements.

## License Renewals

Licenses and renewals expire on the anniversary of the date on which the license was originally issued. Licenses may be renewed for a one, two, or three year term. Unless renewed, a license becomes invalid on the last day of the term for which it was issued. After a license has expired, the license holder has fifteen days to file an application for the renewal without late fees or further examination. After the fifteen days, renewals are granted at the discretion of the board and require a late fee of up to $50.

If licenses are not renewed within one year of expiration, the license holder must submit a new application and follow the entire license application process.

Residential contractors must maintain workers' compensation and general liability coverage and attend four hours of continuing education.

## Disciplinary Action

The board may revoke any license it issues, suspend the right of the licensee to use the license, refuse to renew the license, issue cease-and-desist orders to stop work, or prohibit any person or licensee from working for any of the following causes:

1. Any dishonest or fraudulent act as a contractor which has caused substantial damage to another;

2. Willful misrepresentation of material fact by an applicant in obtaining a license;

3. Willful failure to comply with licensing law or the licensing rules and regulations;

4. Entering into a contract with an unlicensed contractor involving work or activity for the performance of which a license is required;

5. Permitting the contractor's license to be used by another when the other contractor does not hold a license for the classification of work for which the contract is entered;

6. Failure to maintain a qualifying party to represent the licensee;

7. Insolvency or involuntary cessation of business operation;

8. Failure to continue to fulfill any of the requirements for original licensure;

9. Problems relating to the ability of the contractor, its qualifying party, or any of its principal owners or principal shareholders to engage in the business of contracting, as demonstrated by their prior contracting business experience;

10. Disqualification or debarment by any public entity; and

11. Failing to possess any insurance required by law.

If the Board issues a cease-and-desist order, the contractor must stop all actions constituting the violation. Work may not resume until the contractor is in compliance with Louisiana licensing law and pays a civil penalty to the Board of not more than 10 percent of the total contract amount.

If a licensed contractor fails to follow a cease-and-desist order, the board may issue an injunction. In addition, the contractor will be ineligible to apply for a contractor's license for up to one year.

Licensed contractors committing violations are also subject to fines up to $1,000 plus costs and attorney's fees for each offense. Fines and penalties levied against violators of the contractor licensing law are sent annually to the Contractor's Educational Trust Fund (CETF), whose mission is to promote programs used for contractor educational purposes.

Administrative and disciplinary hearings are conducted monthly for alleged violations by both commercial and residential contractors.

Contractors performing work who are not properly licensed are subject to a misdemeanor, fines of up to $500 per day of violation, and three months in prison.

If an unlicensed contractor performs work causing damage or harm to another in excess of three hundred dollars, upon conviction, shall be fined not less than five hundred dollars nor more than five thousand dollars, or imprisoned, with or without hard labor, for not less than six months nor more than five years, or both.

## Bid Requirements

Contracts may be awarded only to contractors with an active license. All architects, engineers, and awarding authorities must state in the bid specifications the requirement that a contractor hold an active license and show the license number on the bid envelope.

If the bid does not require an active license the exception shall be stated on the bid envelope.

If the bid does not contain the contractor's certification and show the contractor's license number on the bid envelope, the bid is automatically rejected.

## Final Inspection...

**Purpose of Licensing:** A major purpose of licensing is to protect the health, safety, and welfare of the public.

**Louisiana State Licensing Board for Contractors:** The Louisiana State Licensing Board for Contractors regulates contracting activities through examination, licensure, and disciplinary action.

**Commercial and Residential License Classifications:** Contractors are permitted to perform work only within the classification on the issued license.

**Commercial Contractors:** A commercial license is required for commercial contracts valued at $50,000 or more. A license for electrical work, mechanical work, or plumbing is required for work of that nature of $10,000 or more. A license with the proper classification is required for hazardous materials contracts of one dollar or more.

**Residential Building Contractors:** A residential license is required for residential projects valued at more than $75,000.

**Licensing Process for Commercial and Residential Contractors:** To obtain a contractor license or certificate, you must complete the licensing process.

**Mold Remediation Contractors:** A mold remediation license is required for mold remediation projects valued at $1 or more.

**Home Improvement Contractors:** A home improvement license is required for home improvement contracts valued at $7,500 or more, and less than $75,000, for those contractors who do not already hold a current contractor's license.

**Reciprocity:** Louisiana has reciprocal agreements with Alabama, Arkansas, Georgia, Kentucky, Mississippi, the North Carolina Electrical Examiners Board, Ohio, South Carolina, Tennessee, Texas, Utah, and Virginia.

**License Renewals:** To maintain a valid contractor's license, the renewal process must be completed in a timely manner.

**Disciplinary Action:** The board handles disciplinary action against a licensee, which can result in refusal to grant, renew or reinstate a license, suspension or revocation of a license, criminal penalties, and administrative penalties.

**Bid Requirements:** Only contractors with an active license can bid on projects that meet the monetary requirement for licensure.

# Chapter 4
# MANAGING RISK

## Chapter Survey...
- Risk Management Benefits
- Insurance
- Property Insurance
- Liability Insurance
- Business Owner's Policies (BOPs)
- Automobile Insurance
- Burglary and Theft Insurance
- Key Man Life Insurance
- Coverage Gaps and Overlaps
- Employment-Related Insurance
- Insurance Coverage for Subcontractors
- What is a Bond?
- Bond Language
- Types of Bonds
- Qualifying for a Bond
- Bond Claims
- Laws Governing Bonding of Federal Construction Projects

Managing risk can be one of the biggest challenges you'll face in the construction industry. The weather, site conditions, customer changes, and employees can be just a few of the unpredictable factors in a job. Some of the risks that you face are preventable and others can be minimized.

Risk assessment is one of the most important steps in the risk management process. You must determine the probability of loss occurring and the consequences if the loss occurs. Your approach to a risk with the potential for a large loss and a low probability of occurring is handled differently from a risk with a potential for minimum loss but a high likelihood of occurring.

Potential risk must be examined on both a project and overall business basis. Future chapters will focus on the skills you need to assess, manage, and ultimately protect yourself against risks for certain situations, such as environmental and safety risks.

## Risk Management Benefits

Unmanaged risk can harm your business, resulting in financial loss, lower profit margins, and unnecessary liabilities. Risk management involves assessing all areas of your business from operations to administrative functions. Good risk management provides several benefits that can affect your reputation and bottom line:

- ✓ Lower business and liability insurance premiums
- ✓ Reduce chances of being sued
- ✓ Improve chances of prevailing in a lawsuit

Risk is managed in several ways. There may be provisions added to a contract to reduce your risk (discussed in Chapter 8), or safety programs or operating procedures can be put in place.

Other risks can be minimized through insurance coverage and bonding, which will be discussed in this chapter.

## Insurance

While some risks can be minimized, others are uncontrollable. Insurance is a way to supplement your risk management program to protect your business against unforeseen events, such as accidents and theft. Without it, you could lose your business in a lawsuit as a result of one bad accident. The less coverage your business has, the more risk you assume. As you increase coverage, you reduce your risk.

***Insurance Defined:*** Insurance is a protective measure in which coverage is obtained for a specific risk (or set of risks) through a contract. In this contract or policy, one party indemnifies another against specified loss in return for premiums paid. Indemnity is a way to transfer risk and exemption from loss incurred by any course of action. Sometimes an insurance payout is called an indemnity.

An insurance policy outlines the specifics of the contract between your business and the insurance company. At a minimum, the policy lists the policy term, coverage, premiums, and deductibles.

**Finding the Right Insurance Company and Agent:** Large companies often employ full-time risk managers. Most small business owners do not have this benefit, and this makes finding the right insurance company and agent important to the risk management process. There are two types of agents: those who work with only one insurance company and independent agents who can shop around for policies with competing companies. Regardless of which type of agent you choose, it is important to find a professional you can trust. Your agent will provide you with a wealth of knowledge on insurance and risk management topics and help you assess your insurance needs.

**Required Coverage:** The law may require you to carry a certain level of coverage, such as workers' compensation, unemployment, and vehicle insurance.

Many construction contracts require a contractor to maintain certain types of insurance and coverage levels. The following chart gives an example of how insurance coverage requirements might be outlined in a contract.

| Type of Insurance | Minimum Insurance Coverage (Combined Single Limit Per Occurrence / Aggregate) |
|---|---|
| Commercial General Liability including: Premises - Operations Products / Completed Operations Contractual Insurance Property Damage Independent Contractors Bodily Injury | $3,000,000 / $3,000,000 |
| Automobile Liability Owned, Non-owned, or Rented | $3,000,000 / $3,000,000 |
| Workers' Compensation and Occupational Diseases | As Required by Applicable Laws |
| Employer's Liability | $3,000,000 |

It is important to conduct a site survey to assess any special conditions that may cause added risk to a project. You should also consider the nature of each project to be sure you have adequate coverage for the work you are performing. You may want to talk this over with your insurance agent and add supplemental coverage when necessary.

In this chapter, we will focus on policies that apply to the construction industry, but you should consult with your insurance carrier for a plan that is right for you and provides your business with the best protection.

# Property Insurance

Property insurance typically covers your business and personal property when damage, theft, or loss occurs. You can buy property insurance to cover specific risks such as fire or theft or you can purchase a broad-based policy to cover a variety of risks (including fire, theft, vandalism, and "acts of God" such as lightning strikes). In considering property insurance, evaluate your physical location and the region in which you do business to determine which risks are likely to occur, such as hurricanes or floods.

***Types of Property You May Want to Cover:***

- ✓ Buildings and other structures (owned or leased)
- ✓ Furniture, equipment, and supplies
- ✓ Inventory
- ✓ Machinery
- ✓ Computers
- ✓ Intellectual property (i.e., books and documents)
- ✓ Automobiles, trucks, and construction equipment
- ✓ Intangible property (i.e., good will, trademarks, etc.)
- ✓ Leased equipment

## All-Risk Builders' Risk Insurance

All-risk builders' risk insurance is a form of property insurance that covers property owners and builders for buildings under construction. This type of insurance typically covers machinery, equipment, materials, supplies, and fixtures that are part of the structure or will become part of the structure. Additional coverage can be added for items, such as temporary structures

# Chapter 4: Managing Risk

and scaffolding, used during construction. In general, major construction defects such as poor workmanship and faulty design are not covered. Your tools also may not be covered under this type of policy. You should talk to your insurance agent about getting separate coverage for these items.

All-risk coverage provides for direct loss by those perils that are not specifically excluded by the policy. It generally provides coverage for almost all risks, including theft, vandalism, accidental losses, and damage or destruction. Construction must be in progress for coverage to exist.

The American Institute of Architects (AIA) and the Associated General Contractors of America (AGC) publish contract documents useful for owners and contractors (for AIA documents, check the AIA website at www.aia.org/docs_default; for AGC documents, see the organization's website at www.agc.org). These standard documents require the purchase of all-risk coverage. An owner has the option of giving the responsibility of purchasing all-risk coverage to the general contractor. If this is the case, the owner is required to notify the general contractor in writing. General contractors may prefer to purchase the insurance because they have a deeper understanding of the project and the potential risk. The cost of the insurance is then passed on to the owner.

The standard AIA and AGC documents require replacement cost coverage for losses that occur. Replacement cost coverage replaces damaged property without any allowances or deductions, such as depreciation.

If you use documents other than the AIA and AGC standard forms, carefully examine the insurance obligations for both you and the owner and discuss any concerns with your insurance agent.

A subrogation clause is generally included in the builders' risk insurance policy. Subrogation typically occurs when the insurance company pays the insured for damage or loss and then sues the negligent third party to pay for the loss. This can lead to a situation where the contractor is sued by the owner's insurance company for a loss that occurred.

To avoid this situation between the owner, contractor, and subcontractors, the contract may contain a clause waiving the parties' right to sue one another.

## Named Peril Builders' Risk Insurance

Named peril builders' risk insurance policies have narrower coverage than all-risk insurance and specify what perils are covered. Typical named peril policies are written for fire and lightning but can also include events such as wind damage, explosion, water damage, terrorism, or earthquake.

## Inland Marine/Equipment Theft Insurance

Inland marine insurance is a type of property insurance that you can purchase for your tools and equipment. It provides coverage for goods in transit and projects under construction. The cost of the insurance may be more than the cost of putting preventive measures in place to deter theft. It is important to secure your equipment by using the proper locks, creating limited access through fencing and locked storage areas, and removing keys from the ignition of all vehicles. Equipment theft increases the cost of insurance premiums, and if it happens often, you might find it difficult to obtain coverage.

## Equipment Floater Policy

An equipment floater policy is a type of inland marine insurance. Coverage for equipment is available on an all-risk or specified-peril basis. The coverage provided is for direct physical loss to the equipment and is designed to cover mobile equipment while it is stored on premises, in transit, or at temporary locations or jobsites. An endorsement can be added for rented or leased equipment. Normal wear and tear is generally not covered by the equipment floater policy.

## Transportation Floater and Motor Truck Cargo Insurance

Both transportation floater and motor truck cargo insurance are types of inland marine insurance. A transportation floater policy protects the transporter against damage that occurs to freight during transport. Motor truck cargo insurance protects the transporter in the event of damaged or lost freight. This protection also applies to contractors who transport equipment or materials to and from the jobsite.

# Liability Insurance

Liability insurance is designed to protect against third-party claims that arise from alleged negligence resulting in bodily injury or property damage. Payment is not typically made to the insured but rather to someone suffering loss who is not a party to the insurance contract.

## Commercial General Liability (CGL)

Commercial general liability (CGL) insurance offers basic liability coverage. CGL covers four types of injuries, including

✓ bodily injury that results in actual physical damage or loss for individuals who are not employees;

✓ damage or loss to property not belonging to the business;

✓ personal injury, including slander or damage to reputation; and

✓ advertising injury, including charges of negligence that result from promotion of goods or services.

Most businesses in the construction industry will need to supplement their CGL policy with other types of insurance, such as a vehicle insurance policy.

## Umbrella Liability Insurance

An umbrella liability insurance policy can supplement your CGL policy. The umbrella policy provides additional coverage in the areas that are not covered in the CGL policy. This type of insurance takes effect once a certain deductible or self-insured retention level is met. Umbrella insurance coverage can be customized to meet the needs of your business.

## Director's and Officer's Liability Insurance (D and O)

Director's and officer's liability insurance protects directors and officers from liability due to actions connected with their corporate positions. These actions include such things as misstatement of financial reports, misuse of company funds, and failure to honor an employment contract. This insurance does not cover intentional or illegal acts.

## Other Types of Liability Insurance

Other types of liability insurance may be purchased in order to cover exclusions that exist in your CGL policy. Examples of additional liability coverage include:

✓ **Contractual liability insurance** provides contractors with protection for damages that result from their negligence while under written contract.

✓ **Completed operations liability insurance** provides coverage for loss arising out of completed projects. Contractor's protective public and property damage liability insurance protects contractors who supervise and subsequently are held liable for actions of subcontractors from claims for personal injury and property damage.

✓ **Professional liability insurance** (sometimes called errors and omissions insurance) protects contractors from negligence resulting from errors or omissions of designers and architects.

✓ **Construction wrap-up liability insurance** bundles liability and workers' compensation insurance for general contractors and subcontractors on large construction projects. This type of insurance helps eliminate gaps in coverage. To qualify for this type of insurance, certain contract cost requirements must be met. These requirements vary by state.

# Business Owner's Policies (BOPs)

Business owner's policies (BOPs) bundle property and liability coverage together. This type of coverage can eliminate gaps or overlaps between separate property and liability policies. Small and mid-sized companies usually qualify for this type of policy. A business selects the amount of liability coverage it needs based on its assets. Additional coverage can be purchased depending on the particular risks of the company.

# Automobile Insurance

If you have a company vehicle or a fleet of vehicles, auto insurance provides coverage for liability and physical damage associated with vehicles owned by your company. All states require vehicle owners to carry some level of liability insurance covering bodily injury and property damage incurred in a vehicle accident. Physical damage coverage pays for the damage to the insured vehicle. Different types of automobile insurance are available. Various options include coverage for only vehicles owned; vehicles

Chapter 4: Managing Risk                                                                          4-5

owned, leased or hired; and for all automobiles, including those not owned, leased, or hired.

# Burglary and Theft Insurance

Burglary and theft insurance covers loss or damage by burglary, theft, larceny, robbery, forgery, fraud, and vandalism. However, this type of insurance generally does not cover employee acts.

A fidelity bond or employee theft insurance is used to cover criminal acts of burglary and theft by employees.

# Key Man Life Insurance

This type of coverage is beneficial if your company depends on specific individuals for continuing success of your business. For example, if your legal structure is a partnership, the success or ongoing existence of the company would not continue if one of the partners died or became incapacitated. Key man insurance is available as life insurance, disability insurance, or both.

# Coverage Gaps and Overlaps

It is important to understand the coverage that each of your policies provides. You must be aware of gaps and overlaps that may exist between policies. Differences in coverage can cause difficulties in claim settlement, particularly when a claim falls in the gray area between coverages. For example, if a claim involves both an automobile and property, there may be a conflict between which policy covers the damage. To minimize these conflicts, you may want one insurer for all policies. If you have overlapping coverage, make sure that each policy has fairly equal reimbursement levels. This will ensure that you receive equal coverage if more than one policy covers a claim.

. . . . . . . . . . . . . . . . . . . . . . . . . . . . .
*Carefully evaluate your risk management program and supplement it with the appropriate insurance coverage.*
. . . . . . . . . . . . . . . . . . . . . . . . . . . . .

# Employment-Related Insurance

## Workers' Compensation Insurance

Workers' compensation insurance provides coverage for employees who are injured on the job. The insurance is purchased by the employer; no part of it should be paid for by employees or deducted from their pay.

***Louisiana Coverage Requirements:*** The Louisiana program is administered through the Department of Labor, Office of Workers' Compensation.

> *Office of Workers' Compensation Administration*
>
> *Office Location:*
> *1001 North 23rd Street*
> *Baton Rouge, Louisiana 70802*
>
> *Mailing Address:*
> *P.O. Box 94040*
> *Baton Rouge, Louisiana 70804-9040*
>
> *Telephone: (225) 342-7555*
> *Fax: (225) 342-5665*
>
> *Email: owca@lwc.la.gov*
>
> *Website: www.laworks.net*

Workers' compensation insurance can be provided in one of the following ways:

✓ workers' compensation insurer,

✓ self-insurance, or

✓ group self-insurance.

If an employee is hurt at work or becomes ill due to something that is work-related,

✓ the employee must submit to a medical examination paid for by the employer,

✓ the employee must keep the employer informed of any change in his/her condition, and

✓ the employer must report the injury or illness to its insurance provider and the Office of Workers' Compensation Administration (OWCA) within 10 days.

Employees are not eligible for workers' compensation if the employee

✓ intentionally injured him- or herself or was injured while intentionally injuring another employee; or

✓ was intoxicated at the time of the injury.

Upon receipt of the notice of injury, OWCA will mail the employer and the injured employee a brochure which sets forth a summary of rights, benefits, and obligations.

To determine benefit amounts, every employer is required to maintain the following information for one year from the date of the record:

✓ name, address, and occupation of employees;

✓ daily and weekly hours worked;

✓ wages paid; and

✓ if the employee is a minor, the employer must procure and keep on file an employment certificate or work permit.

**Required Posting:** Employers are required to display the Workers' Compensation Compliance Poster in a convenient and conspicuous location at the place of business. A copy of the poster is available online at www.laworks.net.

Employer's liability insurance can be purchased to supplement your workers' compensation insurance in the event you are sued for negligence as a result of an employee injury or death.

Chapter 11, Employee Management, covers workers' compensation insurance in more detail.

> **Follow the Law...**
>
> Workers' compensation insurance coverage may be required by law for your business. It is 100 percent employer-paid and premiums cannot be deducted from the employee's pay.

# Unemployment Insurance

Unemployment insurance (UI) programs provide unemployment benefits to eligible workers who become unemployed through no fault of their own and meet certain other eligibility requirements. This program is jointly financed through federal and state employer payroll taxes (federal/state UI tax).

Generally, employers must pay both state and federal unemployment taxes if

✓ they pay wages to employees totaling $1,500 or more in any quarter of a calendar year; or

✓ they had at least one employee during any day of a week during 20 weeks in a calendar year, regardless of whether or not the weeks were consecutive.

**Louisiana Requirements:** The contribution you pay under state law may be taken as a credit against the federal tax. The credit is limited to 5.4 percent, and all employers in the state receive that much credit against the federal tax regardless of the amount they pay to the state.

The tax is payable quarterly. Tax wage base and tax rate may vary from year to year. For the most current information, refer to your local unemployment office. Current tax rates are available online at www.laworks.net. Rates are calculated annually based on the employer's taxable wages, taxes paid (contributions), and benefit charges through June 30th preceding the calendar rate year.All employers doing business in Louisiana are required to complete and file Status Report LDOL-ES 1 to determine their liability for unemployment insurance.

**SUTA Dumping:** SUTA dumping is a transfer of employees between businesses for the purpose of obtaining a lower unemployment compensation tax rate. SUTA dumping is prohibited and subject to hefty civil and criminal penalties. The Department of Labor investigates suspicious activity in the transfer or acquisition of a business or shifting of employees to identify SUTA dumping.

**Additional Information:** Specific information about the Louisiana Employment Security Law can be obtained from the Louisiana Department of Labor.

> *Louisiana Department of Labor*
> *UI Tax Liability and Adjudication*
>
> *Office Location:*
> *1001 North 23rd Street*
> *Baton Rouge, Louisiana 70802*
>
> *P.O. Box 94186*
> *Baton Rouge, Louisiana 70804-9186*
>
> *Phone: (225) 342-2944*
> *Toll-free: (866) 783-5567*
>
> *Website: http://www.laworks.net*

# Social Security Insurance

The Social Security Administration (SSA) is a federal agency responsible for paying retirement, disability, and survivors benefits to workers and their families. The SSA is also responsible for administering the Supplemental Security Income program. The SSA issues Social Security numbers, which are required for employees to legally work in the United States. Chapter 15, Tax Basics, explains how to submit Social Security tax for employees.

# Insurance Coverage for Subcontractors

When hiring subcontractors, you should verify their insurance coverage to ensure it is adequate enough to cover any liability arising from their work.

There are a few simple questions you can ask to assess proper coverage.

✓ **Does the subcontractor carry the appropriate insurance?** Determine what type of insurance is needed. For example, you may require the subcontractor to carry commercial general liability (CGL) insurance.

✓ **Is the coverage adequate for the type of work being performed?** You can be held responsible for damages not covered by the subcontractor's insurance. Make sure their coverage limits are large enough to cover your project.

✓ **Is the insurance coverage current?** You can check with the insurance company listed on the insurance certificate to verify that the subcontractor's insurance coverage is current and that it will cover your project.

If insurance coverage is required, it is prudent to write the requirements into the contract. Chapter 8, Contract Management, talks about indemnification clauses as a contract provision to limit risk. This provision can also be included in your contract with the subcontractor. Indemnification absolves your company or holds your company free from liability from any losses or damages incurred by the subcontractor.

# What is a Bond?

A surety bond is a risk transfer mechanism between a surety bonding company, the contractor, and the project owner. The agreement binds the contractor to comply with the terms and conditions of a contract. If the contractor cannot perform the contract, the surety bonding company assumes the contractor's responsibilities and ensures that the project is completed.

*Statutory and Common-Law Bonds:* The federal government uses surety bonds on construction projects as a way to pre-qualify prospective construction firms. A surety bond is often required by law for public projects. It is referred to as a statutory bond. The owner of a private construction project may also opt to require a bond as an added guarantee that a project will be completed on-time, on budget, and within specified requirements. These private construction bonds are sometimes referred to as common-law bonds.

*Surety Bonding Companies:* When selecting a surety bonding company, check with the U.S. Department of the Treasury or a similar state agency (i.e., Department of Insurance) to ensure that the company is licensed for bonding. The surety company is the primary risk-taker in a bonding agreement, so it is important that it complies with all applicable laws and regulations.

# Bond Language

Bonds generally contain four basic requirements:

✓ **Total dollar amount required for the bond**
The bond amount is generally set as a percentage of the estimated cost. This number can vary and can be up to 100 percent of the estimated cost of construction. Maintenance bonds often use a figure of 10 percent of construction cost as the required amount.

✓ **Length of the bond**
Bond lengths are typically required for a fixed rate of time following a project milestone, after which the bond is released. For construction performance bonds, this is usually after completion and final approval of the project.

✓ **Requirements for notice of defect or lack of maintenance**
A period for completion of corrections is generally outlined after a notice of defect. The bond also establishes a time period for response from the bonding company, if the contractor fails to meet the obligations of the contract.

✓ **Bond enforcement**
If the contractor does not successfully complete all required work or violates any requirement of the bond, enforcement measures are outlined to ensure project completion and proper maintenance.

# Types of Bonds

A **bid bond** guarantees that the contractor, if awarded the job, will do work at the submitted bid price, enter into a contract with the owner, and furnish the required performance and payment bonds. Bid bonds serve as a deterrent against frivolous or unqualified bidders. If the contractor defaults on the bid agreement, the bid bond can be used to make up the pricing difference with the next lowest bidder.

A **performance bond** guarantees that the contractor will complete a contract within its time frame and conditions.

A **payment bond** guarantees subcontractors and suppliers that they will be paid for work if they perform properly under the contract.

A **maintenance bond** guarantees that for a stated period, typically for one year, no defective workmanship or material will appear in the completed project.

A **completion bond** provides assurance to the financial backers of a construction project that it will be completed on time.

A **fidelity bond** covers business owners for losses due to dishonest acts by their employees.

A **lien bond** guarantees that liens cannot be placed against the owner's property by contractors for payment of services. This type of bond allows someone to "bond around" a labor or materialmen's lien.

Just as the owner may require the general contractor to obtain a performance bond, a payment bond, or both, the general contractor may require the same of the subcontractor. The **subcontractor's bond** protects the general contractor in the event that the subcontractor does not fully perform the contract and/or pay for labor and materials.

A **bank letter of credit** is not a bond but is a cash guarantee to the owner. It is not a guarantee of performance but can be converted to a payment to the owner by a bank or lending institution. The letter of credit typically does not cover 100 percent of the contract but customarily 5 percent to 10 percent of the contract.

*Various types of bonds are issued as a protective measure in the event that contractual obligations are not met.*

## Qualifying for a Bond

Before issuing a bond, a surety company will examine your business thoroughly to make sure it is established, profitable, and well-managed. Some of the items the surety company will evaluate to make this determination include

- ✓ good references;
- ✓ ability to meet current and future obligations;
- ✓ experience matching contract requirements;
- ✓ necessary equipment to complete the work;
- ✓ financial stability;
- ✓ good credit; and
- ✓ established bank relationship and line of credit.

A surety's underwriting process consists of an extensive prequalification process in order to guarantee to the project owner that the contractor will fulfill the terms of the contract.

Bonds are priced on the basis of a percentage of the contract amount. Market conditions and prevailing industry practices set the percentage. Bond premiums vary among surety companies, but typically range from a half percent to two percent of the contract amount.

## Bond Claims

***Filing Process:*** Construction law and contractual relationships govern the bond claims process. The filing process is outlined in the bond language for common-law bonds. Government statutes outline the filing process for statutory bonds.

***Project Changes:*** Unless specifically outlined in the bond agreement, the surety company will not cover changes to the original contract. In most cases, a request for additional coverage must be made and the bonding company must be notified of the contract changes.

***Payment in the Event of Default:*** In the event of contractor default, the surety has several options. The surety may

- ✓ provide additional financing for the contractor to finish the project; arrange for a new contractor or hire subcontractors to complete the work; or
- ✓ pay out the amount of the bond.

# Laws Governing Bonding of Federal Construction Projects

**Miller Act:** As a result of the high failure rate for completion of public construction projects, the Heard Act was enacted in 1894, allowing the use of surety bonds for federally funded projects. In 1935, the Miller Act replaced the Heard Act. The Miller Act is the current law requiring performance and payment bonds on all federal construction projects valued at greater than $100,000.

The surety amounts are defined as follows:

✓ A performance bond is required in an amount that the contracting officer regards as adequate. The bond is normally 100 percent of the contracted price.

✓ A separate payment bond is required for the protection of the suppliers of labor and materials. The sum of the payment bond varies, based on the size of the contract. These amounts include:

- Fifty percent of the contract amount for projects less than $1 million

- Forty percent of the contract amount for projects between $1 million and $5 million

- $2.5 million payment bond for contracts in excess of $5 million

**Little Miller Acts:** Most states and local governments also have similar surety laws on public works projects that are referred to as "Little Miller Acts."

**Construction Industry Payment Protection Act of 1999:** The Construction Industry Payment Protection Act of 1999 makes several amendments to the Miller Act of 1935. Its purpose is to improve payment bond protections for persons who furnish labor or material for use on federal construction projects. This law was passed because the bonding amounts specified in the Miller Act may not provide subcontractors with adequate protection.

The Construction Industry Payment Protection Act of 1999 outlines three specific requirements: The general contractor of a project generally must obtain a payment bond in an amount that is equal to the total value of the federal contract, unless a lesser amount is specified by the contracting officer. The payment bond cannot be less than the performance bond.

✓ Subcontractors are permitted to notify contractors of intent to sue by any means which provides written, third-party verification of delivery.

✓ Waivers of Miller Act payment bond protections are void before the work begins. Any waiver of a subcontractor's right to sue on a payment bond must be in writing, signed, and executed after the subcontractor has first furnished labor or materials for use in the project.

# Final Inspection...

**Risk Management Benefits:** Managing risk is challenging but is important to your reputation and bottom line.

**Insurance:** Insurance should supplement your risk management program. It provides protection against unforeseen events and is sometimes required by law. Several different types of insurance coverage are available to fit the needs of your business.

**Property Insurance:** Property insurance typically covers your business and personal property when damage, theft, or loss occurs. All-risk builders' risk, named peril builders' risk, inland marine/equipment theft, equipment floater, transportation floater, and motor truck cargo policies are types of property insurance that may benefit your business.

**Liability Insurance:** Liability insurance is designed to protect against third-party claims that arise from alleged negligence resulting in bodily injury or property damage. Several types of liability insurance policies are available, such as commercial general, umbrella, and director's and officer's liability insurance.

**Business Owner's Policies (BOPs):** Property and liability coverage are bundled under business owner's policies.

**Automobile Insurance:** Liability and physical damage associated with vehicles owned or leased by your company are covered under automobile insurance. Several types of coverage are available.

**Burglary and Theft Insurance:** Loss or damage by burglary, theft, larceny, robbery, forgery, fraud, and vandalism is covered under burglary and theft insurance.

**Key Man Life Insurance:** This type of insurance is available as life insurance or disability insurance, or both, to protect the continuing success of the business.

**Coverage Gaps and Overlaps:** It is important to evaluate all of your insurance coverage. Using one insurer may minimize gaps and overlaps in coverage.

**Employment-Related Insurance:** Workers' compensation, unemployment, and social security are employment-related insurance regulated by state and/or federal government.

**Insurance Coverage for Subcontractors:** When hiring subcontractors, ensure that they carry proper insurance coverage. These requirements should be outlined in the construction contract.

**What is a Bond?** Bonds provide protection in the event that contractual obligations are not met.

**Bond Language:** At a minimum, bonds should contain the total dollar amount, length of the bond, requirements for notice of defect or lack of maintenance, and bond enforcement.

**Types of Bonds:** Several types of bonds are available depending on the desired coverage.

**Qualifying for a Bond:** Before issuing a bond, the surety company will review your business to ensure it is established, profitable, and well-managed.

**Bond Claims:** The bond claim filing process is outlined in the bond language for common-law bonds and in the government statutes for statutory bonds.

**Laws Governing Bonding of Federal Construction Projects:** The Miller Act and Construction Industry Payment Protection Act of 1999 outline bonding requirements for federal construction projects.

# Chapter 5
# YOUR BUSINESS TOOLBOX

## Chapter Survey...
⇨ Time Management
⇨ Delegation
⇨ Business Ethics
⇨ Technology
⇨ Small Business Assistance and Loans
⇨ Small Business Certifications

Just as you need a toolbox filled with tools to accomplish jobs in your trade, you need a toolbox of resources and skills to help you run your business. This chapter will introduce a few of these tools and will lay a foundation for tools covered in subsequent chapters.

## Time Management

**Time Is Money:** This familiar phrase holds special meaning for business owners. Your ability to manage time effectively can make the difference between completing a job successfully and failing to meet customer expectations. Time is one of your most important tools. Use it wisely.

**Setting Goals:** Effective goal setting is a key cornerstone to time management success. Once goals are set, they should be documented. This gives you a visual reminder and ensures proper communication to the whole work team. A methodical approach should be used to move forward towards achieving your goals. Your management team and employees should understand your goals and can help put together the plan tactics.

**Four Time Management Tips:** These habits will help you organize and manage your time.
- ✓ Prioritize tasks daily
- ✓ Delegate effectively when possible
- ✓ Use checklists and calendars (find a time management system that works for you)
- ✓ Do not procrastinate

**Advantage of Technology:** Learning about new technology and using it in your operations can save you time. Research ways to automate your operations without taking away from the quality of your products and services. Putting a new technology or process in place can give you more time to focus on strategic activities.

**Competitive Edge:** Although multitasking is an important skill, effective time management requires that you focus on the necessary task at hand to move forward towards achievement of the set goals. It gives you a competitive edge and helps you anticipate problems before they occur. Planning your time puts you in control, gives you the ability to be proactive and helps reduce anxieties caused by "putting out fires". Your professionalism will be appreciated by your customers, subcontractors, and suppliers.

*Time is money.*
*Use it wisely.*

## Delegation

**You Can't Do It All:** When you become a business owner, you go from a tradesperson to a manager of many jobs and a business administrator. Delegation is a key tool that will ensure that you get all tasks accomplished. You simply cannot do it all and be efficient.

**Preparing to Delegate:** Learning to delegate is often difficult because you are giving up control of certain tasks. You may feel that a task won't be done correctly or that it takes longer to explain a task than just doing it yourself.

Delegation is a way of developing your employees and building a solid team. Giving your employees increased responsibility builds their self-confidence, provides motivation, and makes them more productive and loyal. Delegation gives you the chance to concentrate strategically on running your business.

***How to Delegate:*** Here are simple steps on how to delegate:

1. Identify a person for the task.
2. Explain the task clearly and make sure you are understood. You may want to ask the person to repeat their understanding of the task back to you.
3. Follow up with the person throughout the process.
4. Give positive feedback and provide guidance on how the task can be improved, if necessary.

*Effective delegation increases your efficiency.*

## Business Ethics

***Your Reputation:*** Good business ethics are a must if you want to safeguard your reputation in the industry. Practicing good business ethics, when dealing with customers, employees, subcontractors, and suppliers, is not only the right thing to do, it is the best way to avoid litigation.

***Defining Ethics:*** You may ask, "What are ethics?" In general, the term as it applies to business means behaving in a trustworthy, fair, honest, and respectful manner toward everyone with whom you interact. Your core values serve as your moral compass and guide this standard.

> ***Studies Say...***
> Top management has the strongest influence on employees' ethical behavior. If top managers demonstrate unethical behavior, employees are likely to do the same.

Establishing a code of conduct is the first step to ensuring that good ethics are practiced throughout your company. A code of conduct is a documented way that an organization should operate.

This document can include

- guidelines for employees, management, subcontractors, and suppliers;
- standards for doing business; and
- a statement of commitment to the community.

You may want to provide your customers with your code of conduct. It will reinforce your commitment to good ethics and demonstrate professionalism.

*Make the right ethical choices to protect your reputation and avoid litigation.*

## Technology

***Technology as an Essential Tool:*** Technology is an essential tool for communicating and keeping your business competitive. Purchasing technology is becoming increasingly cost-effective. There are many technological tools specifically designed for the construction industry. These tools increase efficiency and aid in various tasks, such as

- ✓ estimating and bidding,
- ✓ accounting,
- ✓ job costing,
- ✓ scheduling, and
- ✓ construction management.

If you have not jumped into the technology age, here are a few basics to start with:

***Computer:*** For a business owner, a computer has many uses which will help in streamlining administrative functions. This is the basic tool you will need to operate programs for applications such as writing, accounting, scheduling, estimating, and e-mail. Some builders opt to have laptop computers to perform these functions on the jobsite.

***Phone:*** Cell phone technology has advanced in the area of two-way radio communications (sometimes referred to as a push-to-talk feature), use of e-mail, photography, and calendar management. Regardless of the features you choose for your business cell phone, it is important that you are always accessible to your customers and employees.

***Fax Machine:*** Although e-mail has become a prevalent means for communication, it is still important for businesses to have a fax machine so that copies of important documents can be transmitted quickly and efficiently.

# Chapter 5: Your Business Toolbox

**Printer:** A printer allows you to produce hard copies of the files you have on your computer. A printer will come in handy when creating customer correspondence and contracts. Portable printers small enough to bring to the jobsite are also available.

**Scanner:** Documents and small objects can be copied or scanned in a form that can be stored on a computer and then these files can be manipulated and printed for use.

**Multifunction Hardware:** You can purchase a single machine that works as a photocopier, fax, printer, and scanner. This type of hardware can be convenient and cost-effective if your business uses such functions frequently. However, bear in mind that if the unit breaks, you may lose several or all of the functions until it is repaired or replaced.

**Digital Camera:** A digital camera is a great way to store your photos on the computer. It is important for you to document your work every step of the way, and digital pictures are a cost effective way to organize that information. Your pictures can be stored on a disk with the project files and e-mailed as necessary.

**Internet:** The Internet is a powerful tool. It can be used for research, communication, or marketing your company.

**Word Processing Software:** Word processing can save you a lot of time because the information you need is stored in the computer. Handwritten documents need to be rewritten each time, while documents entered in the computer can be modified and reused. Many word processing programs have templates of commonly used business documents which can be used, modified, and reused at any time.

**Spreadsheet Program:** This type of software gives you the flexibility to create financial worksheets on the computer. You can set up the worksheet to automatically calculate figures, reducing mathematical errors.

**A Warning about Software:** Although software is designed to streamline your processes, you must still understand the basics. For example, if you purchase accounting software but do not understand the fundamentals of accounting, the software is useless to you. In future chapters, we will cover basic skills that will help you utilize software packages.

Once you become comfortable with technology, you may want to purchase other advanced tools and software.

*Using technology can increase your efficiency and keep you competitive.*

# Small Business Assistance and Loans

Various federal, state and local resources can help you with small business services or education you might need. Many of these services may be free or available at a minimal cost to business owners. Below are some of the resources available to you.

### State of Louisiana Secretary of State GeauxBiz

This division of the Louisiana state government has business development resources. The website has several links to topics such as business planning, licensing, regulations, and small business development.

*State of Louisiana*
*Secretary of State*
*GeauxBiz*

*Mailing Address:*
*P.O. Box 94125*
*Baton Rouge, Louisiana 70804-9125*

*Office Location:*
*8585 Archives Avenue*
*Baton Rouge, Louisiana 70809*

*Telephone: (225) 925-4704*
*Fax: (225) 932-5314*

*Website: geauxbiz.sos.la.gov*

## Local Community Colleges & Universities

Business education opportunities are available through local community colleges and universities. Seminars, workshops, and courses are offered on business skills and small business management.

America's Small Business Development Center Network utilizes universities, colleges and state economic development agencies to provide service centers are available to provide no-cost business consulting and low-cost training throughout the United States. To find a location near you, visit the website at www.asbdc.org.

## Louisiana Small Business Development Center (LSBDC)

The Louisiana Small Business Development Center is a partnership between Louisiana Universities, the U.S. Small Business Administration, and Louisiana Economic Development. LSBDCs provide assistance to entrepreneurs starting a business and business owners looking to expand and manage their current operations.

There are several centers located throughout Louisiana. A location nearest to you can be found on the website.

*Lead Center:*
*Louisiana Small Business Development Center*
*State Office*
*Stubbs Hall, Room 217*
*700 University Avenue*
*Monroe, Louisiana 71209-6435*

*Telephone: (318) 342-1224*

*Website: www.lsbdc.org*

## Small Business Administration (SBA)

The Small Business Administration's mission is to counsel, assist, and protect the interests of small business. The SBA provides training and online help for small businesses.

The SBA website at www.sba.gov has several online resources to Federal, state, and local information for business owners. Resources include:

✓ Starting a Business

✓ Registrations, Licenses, and Permits

✓ Finance and Taxes

✓ Expanding Your Business

✓ Legal Compliance

✓ Industry Specifics

✓ State and Local Resources

A partnership program through the SBA links business owners from across the nation to create a social network and provide access to experts.

The SBA Headquarters is located in Washington, D.C., but you can check the website at www.sba.gov or call 1-800-U-ASK-SBA to find an office near you.

*New Orleans District Office*
*365 Canal Street, Suite 2820*
*New Orleans, Louisiana 70130*

*Telephone: (504) 589-6685*

*Website: www.sba.gov/la*

## Service Corps of Retired Executives (SCORE)

SCORE is a national volunteer organization of retired executives who can provide counseling and training to you if you are an entrepreneur and/or business owner. There are several SCORE offices located throughout the state. You can find the SCORE office nearest to you on the website.

*SCORE Association*
*409 3rd Street, SW*
*6th Floor*
*Washington, D.C. 20024*

*Telephone: (800) 634-0245*

*Website: www.score.org*

Appendix C contains additional references and website links on topics covered in this book.

## Louisiana Economic Development Department

The Louisiana Economic Development Department provides assistance with starting, maintaining, and expanding businesses located in Louisiana. This department has valuable information on various incentive and community resource programs and an online business resource guide.

Chapter 5: Your Business Toolbox

*Louisiana Economic Development*
*1051 North Third Street*
*Baton Rouge, Louisiana 70802-5239*

*Telephone: (225) 342-3000*
*Toll-free: (800) 450-8115*

*Website: www.louisianaeconomicdevelopment.com*

# Small Business Certifications

Federal and state governments often have opportunities for businesses to bid on contracts. These contracts are highly sought after for a number of reasons. To level the playing field, the government has established certifications for small, minority-owned, and women-owned businesses. If your company fits the criteria, you can obtain one or more certifications, which can provide additional opportunities for you to bid on government contracts.

The U.S. Small Business Administration has several different certification and assistance programs for small businesses. These programs include the following:

✓ Historically Underutilized Business Zone (HUBZone) Certification

✓ 8(a) Business Development Program

✓ Small Business Certification

✓ Women-Owned Small Business Federal Contract Program

✓ Veteran and Service-Disabled Veteran Owned Business Assistance Program

✓ Native American Owned Business Certification

✓ Alaskan Owned Business Assistance Program

✓ Native Hawaiian Owned Business Assistance Program

Information on these certifications is found on the SBA website at www.sba.gov or by calling 1-800-U ASK SBA. In addition to certification information, the SBA website contains helpful links about government contracting and business development.

The Louisiana Minority Supplier Development Council offers a Minority Business Certification. Information is available on their website at www.lamsdc.org or by calling (504) 293-0400.

# Final Inspection...

**Time Management:** Effective time management gives you a competitive edge and helps you anticipate problems before they occur.

**Delegation:** Effective delegation increases your efficiency and helps develop your employees.

**Business Ethics:** The right ethical choices help protect your reputation and avoid litigation.

**Technology:** Technology is an essential tool for communicating and keeping your business competitive.

**Small Business Assistance and Loans:** Several organizations are available to help small businesses with a variety of functions.

**Small Business Certifications:** Certifications for small, minority, and women-owned businesses are available through the government. If your company qualifies, certifications can provide additional opportunities for you to bid on government contracts.

# Chapter 6
# MARKETING AND SALES

## Chapter Survey...
⇨ Executing Your Marketing Plan
⇨ Logos, Stationery, and Business Cards
⇨ Promotional Materials
⇨ Public Relations
⇨ Effective Selling Skills
⇨ Organizing the Sales Process
⇨ Your Sales Presentation

**Start Off on the Right Foot:** First impressions can tell your potential customers a lot about your business. Customers may judge your professionalism or reputation on this initial contact. Marketing, in some cases, may be the first impression of your business, and you want to make sure customers feel comfortable with you and your company from this point on.

The purpose of marketing is to bring in new customers and retain current customers. A good marketing program helps ensure a steady flow of leads and customers and, more important, a steady flow of incoming cash.

*First impressions are lasting ones.
Make your company's first impression a positive one.*

## Executing Your Marketing Plan

**Maximize Your Marketing Potential:** When developing your market analysis and marketing strategy (featured in the business plan template in Appendix B), you should answer questions such as these:

✓ What is the vision for my business?
✓ Who are my customers?
✓ What is the best way to reach these customers?
✓ What is my competitive advantage?
✓ What is the best way to promote my products and services (e.g. advertising, public relations, online marketing, direct sales, etc.)?
✓ What will my marketing efforts cost?
✓ How much revenue do I expect to gain as a result of marketing efforts?
✓ Who will manage the marketing program? Will I need to hire outside help to execute the program?
✓ What growth opportunities exist in my industry?
✓ What challenges for growth exist in my industry?

Now it is time to put these thoughts into action. Developing a promotion plan will help you bring these ideas to life.

## Logos, Stationery, and Business Cards

**Create Your Identity:** A simple start to developing your promotion plan is to create a logo. Not only will your name distinguish you in the market but a logo will set you apart from your competitors. Logos become part of your company identity and convey a professional look, which is important for that first impression.

A good logo design should be

✓ simple and easy to remember;
✓ attractive in color and black and white;
✓ limited to one or two colors;
✓ representative of your company identity; and
✓ scalable up or down and attractive in any size.

Once your logo is created, you should include it on your business cards and stationery.

> **Money Saving Tip...**
> A local print shop or graphic designer can design a logo for your company. You may also be able to approach a graphic arts class at a local community college to develop your logo. One of the students may be able to use this as a class project and save you a few dollars.

## Promotional Materials

You may also apply your logo to several different promotional items. These items include

- ✓ brochures,
- ✓ direct mailings,
- ✓ jobsite signs,
- ✓ truck signs,
- ✓ yellow pages, and
- ✓ websites.

Using promotional materials will give you name recognition. When potential customers have an upcoming job, they may be more likely to approach your company to put in a bid because your name is out in the market.

Business promotion through social media has become a prevalent means of marketing. You can create a business account on social media websites, such as Facebook, Twitter, and LinkedIn, to advertise your services, post updates on your business, and gain name recognition. Participation in social media can be an inexpensive way to market and increase traffic to your business website. In addition to creating a business page on social media sites for promotion, these sites have areas where you can buy advertising space.

A good marketing program is an investment that can help you gain customers and strengthen your reputation.

## Public Relations

**Benefits of Networking:** Public relations are an inexpensive but effective marketing tool. It is important to build name recognition; good public relations constantly keeps your business in the eye of the public—your potential customers. The downside to public relations is its labor-intensive nature, but the time invested will give you great rewards. You may use this approach to not only get potential customers but as a way to get referrals to good subcontractors, suppliers, or employees.

**In the Public Eye:** Here are some ideas to get you started.

- ✓ **Join local trade associations**
  This is a good opportunity to meet new people in your industry. You can also volunteer to speak at meetings and conferences to showcase your knowledge and expertise.
- ✓ **Participate in a local non-profit initiative (for example, be a volunteer Habitat for Humanity worker)**
  High-profile projects will put you in a positive light in the public eye and may get some press coverage.
- ✓ **Volunteer for local leadership opportunities**
  Leadership positions in organizations such as schools or the local Chamber of Commerce may give you time with other influential people in the community who can make good referrals about you and your business.
- ✓ **Sponsor community events**
  When you sponsor community events, your business name is often featured in event brochures, signage, and media promotions such as newspapers and radio advertisements.
- ✓ **Send press releases to the local media**
  This public relations technique offers exposure to a broad audience and gives you credibility because it is communicated through a third-party. Press releases can report your involvement in the local community, new construction trends, or any ideas that might be interesting to the public and will promote your company.
- ✓ **Hold an open house**
  You can hold an open house at your office or at a job where you can showcase your work. An open house gives you a chance to reinforce current business relationships and make new ones.

## Effective Selling Skills

**Don't Underestimate Your Selling Skills:** Selling is often perceived as a salesperson pitching a product or service and the customer saying yes or no. Many

# Chapter 6: Marketing and Sales

people don't feel comfortable with the process of selling, because it makes them feel pushy and overbearing. Selling should be the simple process of matching your company's skills and expertise with what the customer needs.

**Listen Up:** Active listening is the golden rule to effective selling. Without listening, you cannot clearly understand what your customer needs. You may ask yourself, "What exactly is active listening?" Here are a few simple rules:

✓ Maintain good eye contact.

✓ Be attentive.

✓ Keep an open mind.

✓ Don't interrupt.

✓ Ask clarifying questions.

✓ Put yourself in the "shoes" of the other person.

✓ Pay attention to body language (i.e., facial expressions).

Using these simple guidelines, you will gain a more thorough understanding of your potential customers and be able to target your response to their needs.

### A Word of Caution...

Be careful not to make unrealistic or inaccurate statements just to make a sale. You will hurt your business in the long run and potentially leave yourself open to a lawsuit. All advertising and marketing claims must be truthful and not deceptive. Individual state contractor licensing boards may have specific guidelines regarding licensed contractor advertising such as including a licensing number and specific verbiage required by law.

## Organizing the Sales Process

**Track and Prioritize:** Selling is a process. Generally speaking, higher-value sales have a longer selling process than a lower-value sale. To manage the selling process and provide the best service possible, you must be organized. Tracking potential customers is made simple by developing a sales tracking sheet for each contact you make. Your tracking sheet should contain the contact information for the potential customer, the type of work the customer wants, a

summary of communication, the source of referral for that customer, and any other information you feel is necessary.

The next step is to prioritize your sales leads. Prioritizing leads is a way to manage your time in the sales process and can give you key insights into the effectiveness of your marketing program. You want to concentrate most of your time on the strongest leads.

*Tracking and prioritizing leads makes the sales process most effective.*

## Your Sales Presentation

**Present Your Best Side:** Once you have determined your strongest sales leads, you should schedule time to make a sales presentation. This is your opportunity to show customers how your company can meet their needs; in the sales presentation you try to gain a commitment to perform the work.

Presentation materials are important visuals and give the customer something concrete to take away and read after the meeting. These materials can include

✓ a company information sheet,

✓ brochures,

✓ business cards,

✓ past customer testimonials,

✓ warranty information, and

✓ photographs of past projects.

To avoid awkward stumbling in the presentation, have materials prepared ahead of time. This demonstrates your professionalism and ensures that you have thought through the presentation.

**Overcoming "No":** Handling objections is one of the more difficult parts of the sales process. This is the time to use your active listening skills and overcome the objection.

✓ Repeat the objection to ensure that you completely understand the potential customer's reservation.

✓ No question is a stupid question. The person with the objection may just not understand the process.

✓ Give an example of a customer with the same question and how you effectively fulfilled his/her needs.

**Communication Is Key:** Closing the sale is a very important part of the process. Try to gain a commitment from the potential customer, whether it is hiring your company to do the work or just scheduling a follow-up appointment.

Follow up on all sales presentations. This may be as simple as making a phone call or sending a card or small gift. Consistent follow-up ensures that you are at the top of your potential customer's mind and gives you an advantage over competitors.

*Clearly understanding your potential customer's needs is imperative.*

# Final Inspection...

**Executing Your Marketing Plan:** Once you develop your marketing plan, the next step is implementing it.

**Logos, Stationery, and Business Cards:** These simple marketing tools can help establish your company's identity.

**Promotional Materials:** You can extend your marketing program by using various promotional materials.

**Public Relations:** This is an inexpensive but effective way to market your company.

**Effective Selling Skills:** Effective selling involves carefully listening to your potential customer's needs.

**Organizing the Sales Process:** Tracking potential sales leads can help you organize the process of selling.

**Your Sales Presentation:** Preparation and follow-up are important when presenting to potential customers.

# PART 2
# Fundamentals for the Field

# Chapter 7
# BIDDING AND ESTIMATING

## Chapter Survey...
⇨ Bid Documents
⇨ Ethics in Bidding
⇨ Estimate Planning
⇨ Estimating Framework
⇨ Determining Estimated Costs
⇨ Other Methods of Estimating
⇨ Estimating Pitfalls
⇨ Using an Estimator
⇨ Submitting Your Bid
⇨ Job Cost Recording System
⇨ Technology Tools for Estimating

Accurate estimating is important to the profitability of a construction company. If a job is estimated correctly, the contractor has a good chance at getting the job and making money. If the job is poorly estimated, the contractor may lose the bid or win the bid and lose money on the project.

The estimator must ask these questions when assessing whether to bid on a project.

✓ **Company Resources and Type of Work:** Does our company have the resources to perform this work? Is this project consistent with the type of work we do?

✓ **Site Considerations:** Are there any special site considerations that we need to consider? Do the site conditions create any additional costs for our company?

✓ **Location and Cost Effectiveness:** How can we do the work efficiently and in the most cost effective manner? Does the location present special considerations and added cost through travel time and limited accessibility?

✓ **Risk Assessment:** What are the risks and how will we manage them?

✓ **Profitability of Project:** What is our profit margin on this work?

If you know you cannot complete the job on time or there is a chance you could lose money on the project, we recommend that you not bid the job. The jobs you choose should contribute to your long-term goals and the reputation you want your company to have in the market.

## Bid Documents

In a competitive bid situation, a bid package is often put together that includes

✓ **an invitation to bid** that gives a brief overview of the project, deadlines, and general requirements;

✓ **bid instructions** that contain specifics of how the bid should be completed and submitted;

✓ **bid forms**, including but not limited to items such as a bid sheet, bid schedule, bidder's questionnaire on experience, financial responsibility and capability, and a copy of the contract; and

✓ **supplements**, including items important to the overall bid process such as a property survey and soil analysis.

It is important to follow all the instructions in the bid package carefully and submit all documents according to the required specifications. The bidder can be found unresponsive if information is incorrectly submitted or omitted altogether.

Pre-bid meetings may also be scheduled, especially for larger projects. In a pre-bid meeting, the project specifications and any changes to the bid package are discussed.

> **Bidding Guidelines Under Louisiana Law**
>
> In the State of Louisiana, a contractor's license is required prior to bidding on commercial projects of $50,000 or more; electrical, mechanical, or plumbing projects exceeding $10,000; residential projects of more than $75,000; home improvement projects exceeding $7,500 (home improvement projects exceeding $75,000 are considered residential projects); mold remediation projects of $1 or more; and hazardous materials projects (including asbestos, lead removal and abatement, underground storage tank installation and removal, and hazardous waste treatment or removal) of $1 or more.
>
> All architects, engineers, and awarding authorities must state in the bid specifications the requirement that a contractor hold an active license and show the license number on the bid envelope.
>
> If the bid does not contain the contractor's certification and show the contractor's license number on the bid envelope, the bid is automatically rejected.

If changes are made to a bid package before it is due, an addendum is issued. The addendum becomes part of the bid documents and, ultimately, part of the contract when awarded. It is important to carefully review all addenda to evaluate the impact on your bid. Changes in plans and specifications may affect your bid pricing or even your decision to bid at all.

> Carefully evaluate whether bidding on a project is the right decision for your company.

## Ethics in Bidding

Good ethical conduct is necessary to maintain the integrity of the bidding process. The situations listed below are not only a poor way to do business, but some state statutes forbid these practices on public projects.

✓ **Bid Shopping**
Bid shopping occurs when the general contractor approaches subcontractors other than those who have submitted bids to seek a lower offer than what was quoted in original bids. In this situation, the general contractor reveals the original bids submitted and tries to reduce the price.

✓ **Bid Peddling**
Bid peddling occurs when the subcontractor approaches the general contractor after the project was awarded with the intent of lowering the original price submitted on bid day.

✓ **Bid Rigging**
Bid rigging is a form of collusion where contractors coordinate their bids to fix the award outcome of a project.

## Estimate Planning

Once you have determined that you want to submit a bid, you must prepare your estimate. An estimate is the sum of the costs to complete the project, plus your added overhead and profit margin. Before you start putting numbers down on paper, you should understand all the factors that impact the cost of the job. A good estimate will fall within 1 percent to 2 percent of actual construction costs.

### Project Documents

A complete set of project documents is required to prepare an accurate cost estimate. These documents include the following:

✓ **Construction or architectural drawings** that show a schematic diagram of the job. The drawings may illustrate many different views or elevations of the job.

✓ **Specifications** are details that determine the type of materials or methods to be used in construction. If there is a conflict between the specifications and applicable codes, you must follow the stricter of the two. The codes are the minimum requirements by law. You must always meet or exceed the applicable codes.

✓ The **contract** is the agreement between you and your customer to complete the specified work. The conditions outlining the obligations of each party, such as the owner and contractor, are included in the contract. If your bid is accepted, the construction drawings and specifications become part of the contract package. Contracts are covered in more detail in Chapter 8.

Chapter 7: Bidding and Estimating

✓ **Bonds** may be required as part of the bid submittal (discussed in Chapter 4). Bonds commonly required are bid and performance bonds.

You should carefully review these documents to understand the project and the expectations of the customer.

## Site Visit

There may be specifics about the site that influence the cost estimate. These details cannot always be determined from the construction documents. It is important that you go to the actual site and look at any factors that may impact the project. Soil type, grading, vehicle access, and availability to electricity and water are some of the variables that could affect the cost of the project. You want to anticipate as many of these problems as you can before beginning work.

During this time, you should consider the environmental aspects of the project. If you need to obtain environmental permits, this process will affect your estimated costs.

*Louisiana Pollutant Discharge Elimination System (LPDES) Permits*

It is important to note that Louisiana Pollutant Discharge Elimination System (LPDES) permit requirements may have a significant impact on your project. Projects that involve the discharge of pollutants from any point source into waters of the State of Louisiana require an LPDES discharge permit. As defined under LAC 33:IX.2313, a point source is any discernible, confined, and discrete conveyance, including but not limited to any pipe, ditch, channel, tunnel, conduit, well, discrete fissure, container, rolling stock, concentrated animal feeding operation, landfill leachate collection system, vessel, or other floating craft from which pollutants are or may be discharged. Additional information on LPDES permits is covered in Chapter 12, Jobsite Safety and Environmental Factors.

Your project may also require special equipment and processes that should be factored into your estimate. Chapter 12, Jobsite Safety and Environmental Factors, discusses environmental impacts in more depth.

# Estimating Framework

Estimating should be a systematic process. Approaching the estimate in an organized way will help you avoid errors or omissions. Taking the extra time to construct a framework for the estimate will increase your accuracy.

Your estimating framework essentially lists the process for completing the job. This can be accomplished by

✓ defining the phases of the project; and

✓ listing each task and materials needed for each phase.

Once your framework is established, you can enter the time and cost for each task. If you are awarded the job, you can easily convert your estimating framework into your job schedule.

## Define the Phases

The first thing you need to consider when you build your estimate is the phases of the project that you are working on. For example, you might list the phases as preconstruction, construction, and post-construction. The order of tasks will drive your scheduling process.

## List Each Task and Materials Needed

Once you list the phases of the project, you need to develop a list of tasks and materials for each phase. Be very specific in this step. If you omit an item or add an unnecessary item, your estimate will be inaccurate. The task and material list should also include labor time needed and material amounts. By identifying these items early in the process, you may determine the need for items such as overtime to meet certain project deadlines and temporary storage. All of these items play a part in the cost estimate.

## Estimating Checklist

The Construction Specifications Institute publishes a classification system called MasterFormat. This system includes numbers and job tasks grouped by major construction activities. This is a helpful tool when setting up your estimating framework to ensure that you have accounted for all aspects of materials and labor. After you become familiar with the estimating process, you may develop your own estimating checklist customized for your needs.

# Determining Estimated Costs

## Quantity Take-off Method

One accurate method of estimating is the quantity take-off method. Using this method, you individually estimate units of materials and labor for each task you listed in your estimating framework.

After estimating materials and labor, the following items are added:

- ✓ subcontractor fees,
- ✓ labor burden,
- ✓ project overhead costs,
- ✓ project equipment,
- ✓ contingencies,
- ✓ allowances,
- ✓ company overhead, and
- ✓ profit.

By going through the items individually, you can adjust your estimate to accommodate the unique aspects of the project you may have uncovered when reviewing the construction documents or during your site survey.

### STEP 1: Determine Labor Cost for Each Task

Using your estimating framework, you can begin to enter your labor cost. Information from previous jobs can help you determine accurate job costs. There are also published costs available through books such as the RSMeans cost data series, but this is no substitute for your knowledge of the industry. Your experience with your local labor market and wages should be factored into your estimated costs.

For each labor item on your estimating framework list, use the following formula to determine the labor cost.

**Required Labor Hours per Task x Labor Rate = Labor Cost per Task**

The required labor hours can vary based on several different factors, such as employee skill level, size of crew, and weather conditions. These factors must be taken into account when determining the required labor hours. Hours spent planning and scheduling must also be figured into the labor cost equation.

Another helpful tool when determining labor cost is your historical cost data. Determining your final labor cost from past projects will help you put together more accurate estimates for future jobs. Developing a cost-tracking system is discussed later in this chapter.

### STEP 2: Add Labor Burden

As an employer, you incur costs such as employment taxes and insurance. These obligations add approximately 30 percent to your labor cost. This additional amount is referred to as labor burden.

Labor burden includes items such as

- ✓ Medicare and social security (discussed in Chapter 15),
- ✓ federal unemployment insurance (discussed in Chapter 15),
- ✓ workers' compensation,
- ✓ liability insurance,
- ✓ state unemployment insurance, and
- ✓ company benefits (such as medical insurance, vacations, etc.).

Labor burden must be factored into your total labor cost.

### STEP 3: Determine Materials Cost

Just as you plugged labor cost into your estimating framework, you can do the same with materials cost. For each material item listed on your estimating framework, you need to obtain a cost.

Your suppliers can provide you with the materials price per unit or a lump sum. The cost of materials can fluctuate according to the availability of raw materials and demand, so it is important to keep current cost data. In addition to tracking wage, earnings, employment, and benefit statistics, the Bureau of Labor Statistics (www.bls.gov) tracks the prices of major groups of construction materials as part of its Producer Price Index (PPI) program. Periodically reviewing this resource can help you understand potential increases and decreases in materials cost.

You may receive the materials cost as a unit cost. If necessary, use the following formula to determine the total material cost per unit for each of the materials categories on your take-off sheet.

**Price per Unit x Number of Units Needed = Total Material Unit Cost**

To make sure you receive the best price, obtain at least three bids from suppliers. You should also add a small contingency for waste. Depending on the type of material and the job specifications, your waste contingency will vary.

## Determine Project Equipment Cost

Equipment needed to complete the job is figured as a direct cost of the project and added to your estimate.

For example, if you need a crane to set an air handling unit on top of a building as part of a HVAC project, it is considered a direct cost.

Small tools and pickup trucks are considered an indirect cost and not part of project equipment. These indirect costs are figured into project overhead.

Figuring the direct cost of equipment differs depending if you rent or own the equipment.

***Owned Equipment:*** To estimate owned equipment, you must arrive at a unit cost for the equipment. To calculate unit cost, consider the following factors:

- ✓ actual value of equipment factoring in its age and amount of depreciation from the original purchase price;
- ✓ maintenance and operating costs;
- ✓ taxes and fees;
- ✓ labor to operate equipment, including any training or licensing costs; and
- ✓ insurance.

Unit cost is calculated by estimating the number of hours you will use the equipment per year and dividing this number by the total yearly cost of the equipment calculated by considering the operational factors.

For example, if you figure the total cost of the equipment for the year is $30,000 and you plan to use the equipment for a total of 1,000 hours, your unit cost to operate the equipment is $30 an hour.

If you estimate using the equipment for 40 hours on a project, your estimated project equipment cost for that project is $1,200.

***Rental Equipment:*** The following items are considered when figuring the cost of rental equipment:

- ✓ equipment rental rate;
- ✓ labor cost to pick up and return equipment or delivery fees;
- ✓ labor cost to operate equipment; and
- ✓ other costs associated with operating the equipment (e.g., cost of fuel).

***Subcontracting:*** You may decide that neither option is cost effective or feasible and subcontract the work. In this case, this line item would appear under subcontractor fees.

***Rent, Lease, or Buy?*** Construction equipment is vital to the completion of construction projects. Equipment can range from cranes to computers. The decision to rent, lease, or purchase this equipment is a challenging one, and there are many considerations to each option.

Leasing is a long-term rental agreement that provides the benefits of using the equipment without purchasing. Lease payments are made to the owner of the equipment in exchange for the use of the equipment. At the end of the lease term, the owner takes possession of the equipment.

Leasing equipment has many advantages. One of the biggest is the ability to use the equipment with a limited capital expenditure. Other advantages compared to purchasing include

- ✓ no down payment;
- ✓ duration of payments over a longer period making them lower;
- ✓ lease payments (as defined by the IRS) are deductible as operating expenses; and
- ✓ obsolete equipment is returned to the owner at end of the lease.

Equipment ownership allows you to take advantage of certain tax benefits and in the long run usually costs are less than leasing. Leases are long-term contractual agreements that generally cannot be cancelled. If you no longer need the equipment, you must still make payments for the full term of the lease.

Purchasing equipment is advantageous when the equipment has a long and useful life and will not become obsolete in the short-term. You gain ownership of the equipment after the purchase is made but you should consider how the equipment will hold value over a long-term period. For this reason, salvage value is a benefit to purchasing equipment.

Renting equipment may be an alternative to purchasing or leasing. Although renting equipment is usually the costliest, it is the best option in certain circumstances. These include

- ✓ short-term, specialized projects;
- ✓ replacement for equipment being repaired;
- ✓ equipment with high maintenance costs; and
- ✓ jobs that require transportation and storage to distant locations.

The decision to rent, purchase, or lease is one that should be analyzed carefully to provide the most cost-effective solution for your company.

### Add Subcontractor Fees

Subcontractors will be a consideration if you need to outsource work that your company does not have the resources to complete. Chapter 13 covers hiring and working with subcontractors. You should get at least three bids from subcontractors, so you have a good measure of comparison. Carefully evaluate subcontractors to determine that they have the proper qualifications, licensure, and insurance coverage. Subcontractor fees must be added to the estimate that you give your customer.

### Add Allowances

There may be items that are not specified in the project plans, such as finish materials (carpeting, fixtures, lighting, etc.). For these items, you can specify an allowance in your estimate. This is the owner's budget for these items. If the owner's choices exceed or fall short of the allowance amount, the contract should clearly address who is responsible for the difference. Typically, a change order is created stating the amount under or over what is stated in the contract. Change orders are discussed in Chapter 8.

### Add Contingencies

A contingency percentage is sometimes added to an estimate to protect the contractor if an unanticipated problem or condition arises during the course of the project. Contingency markups are generally based on the risk level of the project.

For example, a low risk project might have a 2 percent contingency markup, but a project that has more unknown factors would have a higher markup.

### Add Project Overhead

Project overhead costs are items that are necessary to complete the project but are not directly associated with labor and materials. These costs typically account for 5 percent to 10 percent of the total bid, but these costs should be itemized as much as possible to achieve the most accurate result.

Examples of project overhead costs include

- ✓ bonds,
- ✓ temporary storage,
- ✓ temporary office,
- ✓ security guard,
- ✓ utilities,
- ✓ dumpsters, and
- ✓ portable toilets.

Project overhead differs from company overhead. Company overhead cannot be directly linked with a project.

### Add Company Overhead

Company overhead is the cost of doing business. These expenses are necessary to keeping the operation running. Examples of these expenses are

- ✓ office rent,
- ✓ accounting fees,
- ✓ taxes,
- ✓ telephone,
- ✓ legal fees, and
- ✓ administrative labor.

### Calculating an Overhead Percentage

Using historical information from the past year is the best way to predict overhead for the following year. Overhead percentages generally average between 5 percent and 20 percent, so it is best to calculate the overhead rates specific to your company.

**Company Overhead:** To arrive at a company overhead percentage, you can make the following calculations.

## Chapter 7: Bidding and Estimating

- Add up all of your overhead costs from the previous year. These numbers may be found on your income statement as part of your administrative expenses.
- Divide your overhead costs by your revenues (found on your income statement) to arrive at your overhead percentage.

**Project Overhead:** Project overhead is a similar calculation.

- Add up all of your project overhead costs from the previous year.
- Divide your project overhead costs by your revenues (found on your income statement) to arrive at your overhead percentage.

**Adding Overhead to the Bid:** You must add these overhead percentages to your estimate to cover overhead costs.

For example, let's say you calculated the direct costs for your bid at $100,000, your project overhead at 9 percent, and company overhead percentage at 11 percent. Your direct costs are then 80 percent of your total bid price. Since overhead is a percentage of revenue, you should divide the direct costs of your bid by 80 percent (.80).

Here is what the calculation should look like:

$$\$100,000 \div .80 = \$125,000$$

After adding in overhead, the bid price with direct costs and overhead is $125,000.

### Add Markup and Determine Profit Margin

Considerations for properly pricing a job include

- cost estimate,
- customer needs and expectations,
- local market and competition, and
- expected profit margin.

Determining the right pricing based on these factors is important to maximizing your profit and satisfying your customers.

Cost-based pricing is one of the most common ways to price a bid. Essentially, the cost of the project is determined through the cost estimate and an overhead percentage, plus a markup percentage. The markup percentage is divided into the direct costs of the project, just like the overhead costs in the previous example. If you estimated correctly, you will achieve your internal profit margin goals.

The standard industry markup is 15 percent, but you should consider the market and competition. You must be careful to keep your estimate in line with your competition and understand how much your customers are willing to pay for your work.

In your estimate, markup is applied to the direct costs of the project, such as labor, material, project equipment, project overhead, and subcontractors.

If your markup is too low, you may not cover your project costs, causing you to break even, or lose money on the job. To get the work, you may decide to bid low by lowering your profit markup and make it up on future projects, but this should not be a common practice. You will eventually go out of business if an insufficient amount of profit is achieved over time.

On the flip side, if your markup is too high, you may bid yourself out of jobs. Typically, the higher the markup, the fewer jobs you receive. The lower the markup, the more jobs you receive. You must estimate and choose your markup carefully to ensure a steady flow of jobs and profits for your company.

*Attention to detail is important to preparing an accurate estimate.*

## Other Methods of Estimating

Quantity take-off is generally the most accurate way to estimate, but there are other estimating methods you can use.

- A conceptual estimate is generally prepared by the architect using cost models from previous projects. The contractor may arrive at a much different cost because of the project's unique characteristics.
- Using the square-foot method of estimating, the project cost is a calculation of the square footage of the project multiplied by a unit cost. This is a quick way to arrive at an estimated cost, but this method does not account for project specifics that affect cost. Another variation of this method is putting together an estimate using cubic feet of the project multiplied by a unit cost.

- ✓ The unit price method of estimating bundles all cost factors such as labor, materials, equipment, and subcontractors to come up with a unit price for the entire task. For example, let's say you are placing and finishing a 2,000-square-foot concrete slab and you determined that your unit price is $2.00 per square foot for this task. The total unit price is $4,000.

# Estimating Pitfalls

Accurate estimating is a vital function for construction businesses and can make the difference between getting the right jobs and making a profit on a job. There are pitfalls that are detrimental to the estimating function that you want to avoid.

## Preliminary Estimates

Your customers may be eager to determine what their project will cost and will ask for an estimate on the spot. Quoting a price before you have a chance to make accurate calculations is a risky practice. If you quote a price too high, it is possible that you could lose the bid. If you quote a price too low, the potential customer may be disappointed and feel you were dishonest in your initial contact.

## Inaccurate Estimates

Inaccuracies occur when you make errors and omissions in your estimate. To avoid inaccuracies, you should always check your estimates. Errors to look for:

- ✓ **Mathematical errors:** Always check your work and if possible, have someone else check the mathematical accuracy of the estimate.

- ✓ **Omissions in labor or materials:** Be as thorough as possible when setting up the framework for your estimate. The use of a standard format, such as MasterFormat, will help you avoid this mistake.

- ✓ **Non-standard abbreviations:** Non-standard abbreviations may be interpreted as a different measurement or material. Spell out the actual word rather than inventing an abbreviation that is unclear or vague.

- ✓ **Units of measure:** Define linear, square, and cubic measure accurately. The difference between these measures can make a drastic difference in cost.

The more accurately you prepare your estimates, the better chance you have to make your projected profit.

*Accurate estimates help you get the right jobs and make a profit.*

# Using an Estimator

Estimators develop the cost information business owners or managers need to bid for a contract. Small business owners or managers may perform this function without the use of a professional estimator. Large companies or a large project may need to use an estimator.

Estimators follow the same estimating process: performing the quantity take-off, analyzing subcontractor bids, determining equipment needs and sequence of operations, analyzing physical constraints at the site and contingencies, and determining allowances and overhead costs. The estimator may also have a say in setting the profit for the project and the terms and conditions of the contract. The estimator's job is solely to perform the estimating function and, if used, the estimator is an important member of the project team.

# Submitting Your Bid

Once your estimate is complete and you are ready to submit your bid, you must make sure to follow all of the instructions in the bid package. These instructions include submitting all of the required documents and the exact information requested by the bid submission deadline. Even though you may have a template put together for the estimating process, you may need to customize your bid so as to respond to the bid specifications. Once your bid is submitted, it is reviewed by the owner. Bid review is generally a 30- to 90-day process. You are notified of the acceptance or rejection of your bid after this review process is complete.

## Job Cost Recording System

A job cost recording system provides many benefits to the estimating and project management process.

- ✓ Current projects are monitored more closely with a cost tracking system. Cost overruns are identified and corrective action is taken sooner.
- ✓ Information from a job cost recording system helps with future estimates by creating more accurate unit costs.
- ✓ Many analytical reports can be generated from cost data to review performance by project, activity, year, etc. Using this data can help you make more strategic decisions.

There are many ways to set up a job cost recording system, but to ensure accuracy, it must remain consistent for all projects.

The first step is to develop a cost code system. A cost code system includes the following components.

- ✓ **Project Number:** A project numbering system could be as simple as starting with the number one (1) and consecutively numbering subsequent projects. A more complex project numbering system might also include a code for the type of project and the year it was started. For example, let's say you are working on a remodel project (R) that started in 2006 (06) and was the first (01) project of the year. Your project number could be R-06-01.
- ✓ **Activity Classification Code:** You may want to develop your own system or use a classification system such as the CSI MasterFormat. For example, for a finish carpentry job you could use MasterFormat number 06200. If you use the same classifications on your estimate, it will be easier to compare estimated to actual costs.
- ✓ **Distribution Code:** These are items such as material, labor, equipment, and project overhead. For example, coding might be as simple as one-letter abbreviations:

    Material = M
    Labor = L
    Equipment = E
    Project Overhead = P

    This code can be placed behind the activity classification code. For example, the labor for finish carpentry could be classified as 06200L and materials as 06200M.

Once your system is set up, you can begin entering the cost data. Materials, equipment, and project overhead costs can be gathered from purchase orders, receipts, and invoices. Labor costs can be taken from timecards. It is important that employees fill out timecards completely and with enough detail so you can accurately record labor costs. A sample time card is located in Chapter 14.

## Technology Tools for Estimating

Many computer tools are available to help streamline the estimating process. This technology provides many benefits:

- ✓ shorter time to prepare the estimate;
- ✓ improved accuracy; and
- ✓ professional presentation to the customer.

Estimating software ranges from a basic spreadsheet format to complex databases. However, the programs share some common features:

- ✓ databases for unit cost items, such as material and labor;
- ✓ multiple estimate report formats to present to the customer (hard copy and electronic);
- ✓ tracking method for historical information;
- ✓ ability to recall and modify past projects; and
- ✓ job costing capabilities.

As with any software, you must understand the fundamentals. If you do not know how to estimate, the software available will provide limited benefits to the process.

## Final Inspection...

**Bid Documents:** All bid documents should be completed according to the specific requirements of the bid.

**Ethics in Bidding:** Good ethical practices are important to maintaining the integrity of the bid process.

**Estimate Planning:** Careful review of construction documents and a site visit are important first steps to creating an accurate estimate.

**Estimating Framework:** An estimating framework includes the project phases and the labor and materials needed for each phase.

**Determining Estimated Costs:** The quantity take-off method is one of the more accurate estimating methods. All direct and indirect costs must be added to ensure the estimate is complete.

**Other Methods of Estimating:** Estimates can be prepared using different methods with varying degrees of accuracy.

**Estimating Pitfalls:** It is important to be accurate and detailed when estimating a job. You may not make your expected profit if you make mistakes in your estimate.

**Using an Estimator:** An estimator is used to perform the estimating function on a project. The estimator may also make recommendations on the project profit margin and terms of the contract.

**Submitting Your Bid:** All instructions in a bid package must be followed or the bid may be rejected. There is typically a 30- to 90-day bid review process.

**Job Cost Recording System:** Monitoring current projects, creating more accurate future estimates, and providing reports for analysis are benefits of implementing a job cost recording system.

**Technology Tools for Estimating:** There are several computer tools to help you create your estimate, but it is still important to fully understand the process.

# Chapter 8
# CONTRACT MANAGEMENT

## Chapter Survey...
- Required Contract Elements
- Contract Provisions
- Breach of Contract
- Boilerplate Provisions
- Provisions to Limit Risk
- What Are Recitals?
- Types of Construction Contracts
- Contracting Methods
- Sources of Contracts
- Making Changes to the Contract
- Resolving Claims
- Alternative Dispute Resolution
- Making Substitutions
- Contract Documents and Project Manual
- Are Oral Agreements Legally Binding?
- Legal Interpretation
- Subcontracting

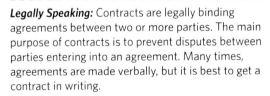

**Legally Speaking:** Contracts are legally binding agreements between two or more parties. The main purpose of contracts is to prevent disputes between parties entering into an agreement. Many times, agreements are made verbally, but it is best to get a contract in writing.

Contracts serve many purposes including
- defining the obligations of the agreement;
- outlining payment terms; and
- limiting the liability of the parties involved.

Contracts need to be worded carefully to protect your company. It is recommended you consult with an attorney experienced in construction law to ensure you have a legally enforceable contract.

## Required Contract Elements

**Make it Binding:** You may have reached an agreement to do work for a customer, but that does not mean that you have a contract. There are four key elements that must be in effect to make a contract binding.
- ✓ Offer and Acceptance
- ✓ Consideration
- ✓ Competent Parties
- ✓ Legal Purpose

### Offer and Acceptance

**The Offer is on the Table:** An offer specifically outlines the obligations of the contract, including the work to be done and compensation for this work. When you submit an estimate or bid for work, this is considered an offer. All parties must be clear on the essential details and obligations of the contract to have a valid offer. Once an offer is made, you are bound to what you have agreed to do.

An offer generally has a specific amount of time in which an acceptance needs to be made. This time frame is typically 30 days, but it should be stated in the offer. If a deadline for acceptance is not outlined in the offer, it expires in a "reasonable time." Reasonable time is up to court interpretation and is considered on an individual case basis.

**Negotiation:** Negotiation is the process where the owner and contractor come to an agreement on the price and terms of the contract. Chapter 10 discusses techniques that help guide you through the negotiation process. An offer is usually the outcome of a negotiation, but parties are not bound to the contract terms until an offer is made and acceptance is achieved. It is important to be clear when a communication is for negotiation purposes so it is not misconstrued as an offer.

**Acceptance:** The next step of the process is acceptance. Acceptance is agreeing to the offer made and generally is done by signing the offer. In some cases, a counteroffer is made. A counteroffer is not considered acceptance. It is only when both parties agree to the contract terms that you obtain acceptance.

**Offer Checklist:** Your offer should contain certain components because, if accepted, you are contractually bound to it:

✓ Date of offer

✓ Names and contact information of contracting parties

✓ Name and location of project

✓ Description of the work to be performed

✓ Contract time or start and completion date

✓ Payment terms, including progress payment schedule and final payment

✓ Conditions for schedule delays

✓ List of contract documents, including general conditions, drawings, and specifications

✓ Contract sum, including contract type such as lump sum, unit price, or cost plus (discussed later in this chapter)

✓ Expiration date of offer

Once accepted, this agreement becomes part of the contract's Standard Form of Agreement.

## Consideration

**An Exchange:** Both parties must give up something of value to have consideration. Most likely this will be money, but it could be anything of value. Payment terms should be clearly outlined in the contract. Typically, the contractor provides services and in exchange, the owner provides monetary compensation.

## Competent Parties

**Legal Capacity:** The parties in agreement should have the legal capacity to enter into a contract. Simply put, the parties must both be of sound mind in order for the contract to be valid. A situation where parties may not have legal capacity might be if you contracted with

someone who is heavily under the influence of drugs or alcohol. The courts may rule someone incompetent if they are mentally disabled. Minors are prohibited from entering into contracts without parental consent.

## Legal Purpose

Contracts must be possible to perform, not intended to harm anyone, and cannot require any illegal activity. For example, a contract that requires the contractor to build a house that does not comply with building codes does not have a legal purpose and is invalid.

- - - - - - - - - - - - - - - - - - - - - - - - - - - - - -

*Consult with an attorney to ensure your contracts are legally enforceable.*

- - - - - - - - - - - - - - - - - - - - - - - - - - - - - -

# Contract Provisions

**Make it Clear:** Contracts should be clear and concise. It is important that both parties understand the terms of the contract. There are provisions that you need to include in your contracts to ensure that all details are clearly outlined. Provisions are simply clauses that outline the stipulations of the contract.

**Key Contract Provisions:** Contracts are full of provisions, but a few key ones you will want to include:

✓ Contract Price and Payment Terms

✓ Obligation of the Parties

✓ Supplemental Conditions

✓ Breach of Contract

## Contract Price and Payment Terms

**Getting Paid:** The contract should specify how the contract price is calculated. Whether you choose to use a lump-sum, unit-price or cost-plus method, include all fees the customer is expected to pay.

Payment terms should be very specific and include

✓ who is issuing payment,

✓ amount of the payment,

✓ form of payment, and

✓ when the payment will be issued.

**Progress Payments:** Progress payments are partial payments made after specified phases of construction are complete. Payments are generally calculated by taking the difference between the completed work and

# Chapter 8: Bidding and Estimating

materials delivered and a predetermined schedule of unit costs.

Requirements for the schedule of progress payments should be clearly outlined in the construction contract including

✓ number of payments,

✓ amount of each payment,

✓ stage of progress between payments, and

✓ date or stage when each one is due.

It is important to monitor the progress payment schedule to ensure timeliness. You may be required to submit a partial payment estimate to the project architect or engineer prior to the payment due date. The partial payment estimate outlines the work performed and proof of materials and equipment delivery required for the next stage of construction. The architect or engineer certifies each progress payment by confirming the information in the partial payment estimate.

Progress payments have two functions: one, to protect the owner by holding the contractor responsible for following the planned schedule and two, to allow the contractor to pay for labor and material expenditures as they occur. This method of payment also protects both parties in the event of a contract breach on either side.

**Retainage:** Retainage is used by the owner to ensure completion of the construction project and provide protection against liens, claims, and defaults. It is calculated as a percentage (generally 10 percent) withheld from each progress payment. The retainage amount may be reduced further after substantial completion of the project (for example, retainage amounts may drop to 5 percent after 75 percent completion of the project). Retainage amounts must be clearly stated in the construction contract. Prime contractors generally hold the same percentage of retainage for their subcontractors.

The architect or engineer certifies when the project is complete and the work meets the conditions of the contract documents.

The retained amounts are generally due to the contractor upon completion and acceptance of the work.

**Final Payment:** Once the structure can be used for its intended purpose, the architect issues a certificate of substantial completion. A certificate of occupancy, issued by a building inspector, deems the structure meets all applicable codes and is safe for occupancy.

Final payment is generally due when all punch list items are complete as agreed between the owner and contractor, proper approvals are obtained, and all paperwork is complete.

To receive a final payment, the following documentation should be prepared and delivered to the owner upon completion of the project:

✓ Completion certificates issued by the architect

✓ Inspection certificates

✓ Guaranties and warranties

✓ Affidavits that all subcontractors and project bills have been paid

✓ Equipment operation manuals

✓ Final lien waivers for those who submitted preliminary notices

✓ Final project drawings

✓ Any other documents as required by contract

It is important to organize paperwork throughout the construction process. A delay in putting the final paperwork together can consequently delay the final payment.

## Obligations of the Parties

**Contract Conditions:** The obligations of the parties should be specifically outlined in the contract and include both the contractor's obligations and the owner's obligations. The obligations of the parties are the contract conditions.

Contractor's obligations include but are not limited to

✓ having proper licensure;

✓ securing building permits;

✓ ordering all materials and supplies and arranging for site delivery;

✓ furnishing all labor, including obtaining required subcontractors to complete the job;

✓ completing all work in compliance with all applicable codes and scheduling inspections on a timely basis;

✓ completing all work according to plans and specifications; and

- keeping the construction site clean and removing all debris during and upon completion of construction.

Owner's obligations include but are not limited to

- ensuring prompt approval of all plans and specifications;
- ensuring project meets zoning specifications;
- issuing payments according to the specified progress payment schedule;
- paying for all required permits, assessments, and charges required by public agencies and utilities;
- furnishing all surveys and recording plats and a legal description of the property; and
- providing access to the construction site in a timely manner.

Each list of obligations must be customized according to the agreement reached and the individual job being performed. Most contracts require agreement by both parties if obligations are assigned to another party.

## Supplemental Conditions

The supplemental conditions modify the general conditions of the contract and are often prepared in a separate document. Supplemental conditions are tailored specifically to each project. They may outline items such as specific insurance requirements, project procedures, and local law requirements.

*Be very specific when outlining the obligations of both parties.*

## Breach of Contract

A breach of contract occurs when one of the parties involved fails to perform in accordance with any of the terms and conditions of the contract.

A breach may occur when a party

- refuses to perform the contract;
- performs an act prohibited by the contract; or
- prevents the other party from performing its obligations.

There are two types of breaches: **material** and **immaterial**.

A **material breach** is a serious violation of the contract. For example, if a contractor refuses to perform or complete a job or if an owner refuses to pay for completed or partial jobs, this is considered a breach of contract. This type of breach may void the contract and will most likely end up in litigation.

The injured party can seek monetary damages for the loss suffered as a result of the breach. Sometimes the damages are written into the contract. These are called liquidated or stated damages.

Breach of contract can occur if contracts are not completed within the time frame specified in the contract. If a time is not specified in the contract, the project must be completed in a "reasonable time." If the project has an unexcused delay, the owner may be entitled to liquidated damages for the "loss of use." Some contracts specify a per-day rate for liquidated damages. For example, if a contract specifies a $400 per day assessment and the contractor finishes 30 days late, $12,000 in liquidated damages is assessed to the contractor. An owner who sues for liquidated damages cannot sue for actual damages.

If you sue for breach of contract, you must do so within the statute of limitations. Statutes of limitations are laws that set a maximum period of time within which a lawsuit or claim may be filed. The deadlines vary depending on the circumstances of the case and the type of claim. If a claim is not filed before the statutory deadline, you may lose the right to file a claim.

An **immaterial or partial breach** is a less serious violation and usually does not result in termination of the contract. The injured party may only sue for the value of the damages.

## Boilerplate Provisions

*Standard Language:* The term "boilerplate" refers to standard language or clauses used in a legal contract. Sometimes they are referred to as "miscellaneous" clauses. They generally appear at the end of the contract and their purpose is to protect the business in the event of a lawsuit. Attorney's fees, arbitration, and consent to jurisdiction (meaning where the disputes will be settled) are a few examples of boilerplate provisions. When dealing with contracts, make sure to draft and read the boilerplate provisions carefully. These provisions affect your legal rights just as much as the other parts of the contract.

# Chapter 8: Bidding and Estimating

## Provisions to Limit Risk

*Allocating Risk:* As mentioned at the beginning of the chapter, one of the purposes of a contract is to limit the liabilities of the parties involved. Your contract should address the allocation of risk among parties. Examples of risk allocation provisions are listed below:

✓ **Force majeure** addresses "acts of God" and other external events such as war or labor strikes. This provision is written to either absolve the owner or contractor of costs associated with these occurrences.

✓ **Indemnification** absolves the indemnified party from any payment for losses and damages incurred by a third party. Simply put, it is a way to shift payment or liability for any loss or damage that has occurred. Indemnification clauses must be examined carefully to ensure the proper liability is distributed between the contractor and owner.

✓ **Differing site conditions** provision allocates the responsibility for extra costs due to unexpected site conditions. As discussed in Chapter 7, the site conditions must be investigated and taken into consideration when putting together the bid. The owner is responsible for disclosing all site information during the bid process. If errors or omissions occur, the owner may be responsible for incurring the extra construction cost.

✓ **Warranties or guarantees** define the contractor's responsibility for the repair of defects to the construction project after the completion of work. Warranties are often set forth for a defined time period.

✓ **Delays and extensions of time** provide a contingency in case the completion deadline is not met. Delays at no fault of the contractor, such as changes by the owner or architect and environmental or severe weather delays, are generally not considered breach of contract. These types of delays are considered excusable and are granted time extensions. This contingency needs to be clearly outlined in the contract.

✓ **Schedule acceleration** provides assignment of costs incurred to complete a project ahead of schedule. In general, if the owner requires the contractor to accelerate the schedule, the owner is responsible for all associated costs. If the owner requests the schedule be accelerated due to project delays caused by the contractor, the contractor is generally liable for additional costs incurred.

✓ **Artistic changes** clause addresses changes made by the architect or design professional during the course of the project for artistic or creative purposes. The drawings and specifications outline the technical aspects of the project, but may not show the artistic objectives of the project. Including an artistic changes clause will put a limit on the number of changes that can occur as a result of artistic decisions.

Standard legal language must be used when specifying risk assignments to make the contract enforceable. Since legal language is often difficult to understand, it is recommended that you consult with legal counsel when drafting and/or interpreting these provisions.

## What Are Recitals?

*Background Information:* Recitals are language at the beginning of the contract that provide background to the contract, such as the parties entering into the contract, the contract contents, and reasons for the parties' entering into the contract. Recitals cannot always be enforced by law, so it is important to provide specific terms throughout the contract.

## Types of Construction Contracts

The differences in the types of contracts are primarily

✓ who takes the risk that the work will be performed for the estimated cost;

✓ who pays for cost overruns; and

✓ who keeps the cost savings if the project performed is less than the estimate.

Contracts between the owner and primary contractor may differ from contracts between the primary contractor and subcontractors.

### Lump-Sum Contract

In a lump-sum contract, the contractor agrees to complete the project for a predetermined, specified price. The contractor essentially assumes all of the risk under this contract agreement because the contractor is responsible for additional costs associated with unforeseen circumstances. For example, if extra cost is incurred due to inclement weather, the contractor must absorb these costs. Conversely, the contractor gets to keep any cost savings achieved.

If you use this type of contract, you may be required to formally submit a specific schedule and your quality assurance program so your customer knows you are completing the project to the highest standards. You should avoid this type of contract unless plans and specifications are detailed enough that a final cost can be determined in advance.

## Unit-Price Contract

A unit-price contract may be used for jobs where the extent of work cannot be fully determined, or the actual quantities of required items cannot be accurately calculated in advance. A price per unit is calculated for each item and the contractor is paid according to the actual quantities used.

## Cost-Plus Contract

Using the cost-plus contract method, the contractor is reimbursed for the actual cost of labor and materials and is paid a markup fee for overhead and profit. The cost-plus contract can be calculated different ways. The owner may pay the actual costs, plus a percentage markup or a fixed fee markup.

# Contracting Methods

## Single Prime

The single prime method is the traditional form of contracting. The project owner typically hires an architectural firm to design the project. The contractor then performs the work according to the specifications of the project and is responsible for the costs of all materials and labor to obtain project completion.

## Design/Build

Using the design/build method of construction, the owner contracts with one company to complete the process from start to finish. The company awarded the design/build contract puts together a team of construction professionals, which may include designers, architects, engineers, and contractors that take a project from design through completed construction. The team works closely to satisfy the owner's needs within a predetermined budget.

## Construction Management

Under the construction management method, the project owner contracts with a professional construction manager to coordinate and manage the project. The construction manager generally receives a fee to manage, coordinate, and supervise the construction process from the conceptual development stage through final construction. Work must be performed in a timely manner and on an economical basis.

## Turnkey

Turnkey construction is similar to the design/build construction model. In addition to managing the construction and design team, the contractor also obtains financing and land. Under the turnkey model, the construction firm is obligated to complete a project according to pre-specified criteria but with expanded responsibilities and liability. A price is generally fixed at the time the contract is signed.

## Fast-Track Construction

Under fast-track construction management, the construction process begins before completion of the contract documents. Fast-track construction involves a phased approach to the project. A contract may be drawn up for each phase. Generally, the cost is not fixed until after construction documents are complete and some construction commitments have already been made.

## Multiple Prime Contracts

Large construction projects may involve multiple prime contracts. The owner may contract with two or more prime contractors to complete the same project. This contracting method may integrate elements of the construction management and fast-track construction models. The owner takes on a more active role in managing the different prime contractors. Contractor and owner obligations must be clearly defined in the contract.

## Partnering

Partnering starts with setting common objectives and goals for a construction project. All parties involved, such as the owner, design professionals, engineers, and contractors, work together to achieve these objectives and goals. Several meetings are held throughout the bid and construction process to evaluate the decisions made by all parties and adjustments occur when necessary. Partnering increases communication and trust, consequently reducing potential litigation and claims.

## Sources of Contracts

Standard forms for contracts are readily available through many sources. There are numerous books available that provide sample contracts and forms. Associations such as the American Institute of Architects (AIA) or the Associated General Contractors (AGC) also have standard forms for contracts.

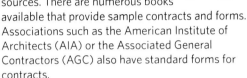

In situations where the form of the contract is not written by you, it is important to

- ✓ read the contract very carefully;
- ✓ highlight anything that is vaguely worded for further clarification;
- ✓ make necessary additions;
- ✓ review changes with the other party;
- ✓ make sure any requested changes have been added prior to signing; and
- ✓ review the contract again, prior to signing.

Always make sure you keep a signed copy of every contract you sign, in case you need to refer to it in the future.

## Making Changes to the Contract

A **change order** is a written agreement between the owner and contractor to change the contract. Change orders add to, delete from, or otherwise alter the work set forth in the construction documents. Change orders are standard in the construction industry as a legal means for making changes to the contract.

Common reasons for generating a change order include

- ✓ change in scope (for example, owner requests a design change or owner exceeds allowance amount);
- ✓ unforeseen conditions when site conditions differ from the expected; and
- ✓ errors or omissions in construction plans or specifications.

The AIA and AGC have standardized forms that you can use to execute change orders. Change orders are legally binding and it is important that all of the provisions are clear to both parties. Change orders should include

- ✓ date of change order;
- ✓ description of the change in work;
- ✓ reason for change;
- ✓ change in contract price;
- ✓ change, if any, in contracted time; and
- ✓ signatures from both parties.

Chapter 10 also discusses how to handle change orders from a customer relations perspective.

Changes prior to the contract award are called **addenda**. Changes made after the contract is signed and executed are called **modifications**.

## Resolving Claims

The claims resolution process provides a way for the owner and contractor to resolve disputes about additional amounts owed as a result of contract changes. As discussed in the previous section, the purpose of written change orders is to avoid disputes. If a change is made to the contract without a change order, claims may arise.

*Claims Procedure:* The contract may stipulate specific procedures for handling claims. Many times, the contract defers to the architect to initially resolve claims. If claims cannot be resolved by the architect, the contractor and owner may proceed to mediation. If mediation fails, the next step is arbitration. The contract should specify the time allowed to request arbitration. A typical deadline for an arbitration request is 30 days from the time the architect makes a decision on the claim.

*Project Schedule:* During the claims resolution process, the project cannot be delayed. All schedules and deadlines must be followed. The only exception is disputes involving safety. Work must cease on disputed activities until all safety issues are resolved.

## Alternative Dispute Resolution

Alternative dispute resolution (ADR) involves settling legal disputes by avoiding the often costly and time intensive process of a government judicial trial.

The most common forms of ADR are: negotiation, mediation, collaborative law, and arbitration.

**Negotiation:** Negotiation is a dialogue entered into for the purpose of resolving disputes or producing an agreed upon course or courses of action. Negotiation is inexpensive and generally the first step in ADR. Negotiation allows for an unstructured discussion between both parties and generally does not involve anyone other than the affected parties. If an agreement is not reached, more formal methods of dispute resolution are required.

**Mediation:** In mediation, the parties themselves set forth the conditions of any agreement with dialogue facilitated by an independent, third party mediator. The mediator is not a judge or arbitrator who sets forth the terms of an agreement, rather a mediator is a trained professional in negotiations and the process of mediation. The goal of mediation is to find areas of agreement between the parties involved by using strategies and techniques designed to allow the parties to work towards a mutual and fair agreement. If a settlement is not reached, the dispute may go through mediation again or sent to arbitration. The option to take legal disputes to mediation is desirable from a cost perspective because it is generally less expensive and allows for a quicker resolution than going to trial.

**Collaborative Law:** Collaborative law is a facilitative process wherein all parties agree at the onset to work to identify a solution that is beneficial to all parties involved. In collaborative law, the parties use their advocates, most often their lawyers, to facilitate a mutually beneficial result through the process of negotiation. There is no neutral mediator or arbitrator involved and the parties are expected to reach a settlement without using further methods of ADR or litigation.

**Arbitration:** Arbitration uses a third-party arbitrator or arbitrators to act as a judge or judges to render a decision by which all parties are legally bound. Arbitration is held in a format less formal than a trial. The arbitrator(s), unlike a mediator, is not involved in the negotiation discussion towards a settlement. Arbitrators may be attorneys or retired judges who serve individually or as a panel. They are either chosen by the parties involved in the dispute or appointed by the court according to the terms of the contract. Arbitrators with industry-specific experience (such as construction litigation experience) may be appointed to certain types of disputes. The decision or arbitral award made by the arbitrator(s) is legally binding unlike in mediation. Many times, contracts call for disputes to be resolved through arbitration over taking matters to a costly trial. Arbitration may be required by law for certain types of disputes. Nearly all states have adopted the federal Uniform Arbitration Act making arbitral awards binding by both state and federal law.

# Making Substitutions

When bidding on a project, many contractors bid from their normal manufacturers and suppliers and not the manufacturer that appears on the plans. When bidding, you need to make sure you can pay for the cost of all items and products as specified. Failure to do so could cost you a lot of money.

**Substitution Approval Process:** The best way to ensure a specific substitution is by the "prior approval" process. A "prior approval" occurs during the bid stage only. If a particular product or item is desired other than the specified item, you must submit a request while the project is being bid. If approved, all bidders will be allowed to use that item or product in their bids. That is why the "prior approval" is done in the bidding stage. It keeps the playing field level for all competitors.

**Substitutions After the Bid Process:** A substitution may be made after the bid has been accepted. Nevertheless, any substitution must meet certain criteria to even be considered. The specifications should describe the conditions for such substitutions. Usually there are only four reasons that a substitution would be entertained:

✓ the specific item or product is no longer available;

✓ a cost savings;

✓ a time savings; or

✓ combination of cost and time savings.

**Discontinued Products:** A product no longer available is generally the only event that will not require a change order reducing cost and/or time, unless it was approved under the "prior approval" process. Do not forget to note those reductions in the substitution request. The reason a reduction of cost and/or time is required is due to the fact that it is understood that the bid was based on the specific item or product. To make a change, the result must benefit the owner; otherwise, there is no reason to make the substitution.

# Chapter 8: Bidding and Estimating

*Substitution Specifications:* If there is a basis for the substitution, the next requirement is that the item or product must be equal to that which was specified. Just as the reference of a 2 x 4 to contractors is not measured as 2" x 4", its nomenclature is referred to as "nominal." Many other products are referred to as "nominal" sizing. HVAC systems are especially that way. Just because one manufacturer references a unit as five-tons, it does not mean that it produces the same capacity as a five-ton unit from another manufacturer under the same conditions.

The specifications must be analyzed carefully before submitting the substitution request. Be sure to cover the cost of the specified item, as a substitution may not be granted, not even in the "prior approval" process.

## Contract Documents and Project Manual

The project manual is a central location for bid documents, contract provisions, technical specifications, and addenda. This bound manual is a useful tool easily referenced on the jobsite. It can be reproduced and distributed to contractors, subcontractors, and suppliers. The following is a detailed summary of the documents contained in a typical project manual.

**Bid Documents:**
- ✓ Invitation to bid
- ✓ Bid instructions
- ✓ Bid forms
- ✓ Supplements
- ✓ Addenda

**Contract Provisions:**
- ✓ Form of agreement
- ✓ General conditions or obligation of parties
- ✓ Supplemental conditions
- ✓ Change orders
- ✓ Index of drawings

**Supplemental Forms:**
- ✓ Required bonds
- ✓ Certificate of insurance

**Technical Specifications** are generally organized by a classification system, such as the CSI MasterFormat.

The **construction drawings** are also part of the contract documents. For larger projects, the drawings are divided by design discipline and trades. Drawings may include but are not limited to:

- ✓ architectural,
- ✓ structural,
- ✓ plumbing,
- ✓ electrical,
- ✓ mechanical,
- ✓ landscape, and
- ✓ civil.

The drawings are kept separate but can be indexed in the project manual.

## Are Oral Agreements Legally Binding?

Under most circumstances, oral agreements are just as binding as written agreements with a few exceptions. Exceptions include contracts which have a high risk of fraud such as the sale or purchase of land. Oral agreements present a challenge because it is difficult to prove what terms were agreed upon if a dispute arises. Needless to say, it is a risky way to do business and it is best to get everything in writing.

Sometimes parties enter into agreements that are partially oral and partially written. For example, you may have carefully put together a written contract to do work. The customer then verbally gives you a change order. Now you are in a situation where you have an oral agreement for the change. To protect yourself, it is best to follow up with a written change order. In a legal judgment, written agreements always take precedence over oral agreements.

*Oral agreements are not a good way to do business. Get it in writing!*

## Legal Interpretation

Clarity of language and meaning is one of the most important aspects of interpreting contracts and avoiding disputes. It is strongly recommended that you use an attorney when drafting contracts to ensure that the contract will stand up in a dispute. There are also necessary provisions that should be included in a contract. A contract lawyer can advise you on this matter.

The use of plain language is important when establishing intent in a contract. If a dispute arises, the contract will be interpreted using the plain meaning of the words in the contract. If your contract goes to litigation, the judge may not have a background in the construction industry. This is why it is important to clearly state the terms in the contract using plain language.

Technical terminology in contracts between parties who understand their technical meaning may be used. However, many customers may not understand technical jargon so you may want to use caution putting these terms in a contract. Rather, you should express your intentions in layman terms. Disputes may arise when parties do not understand undefined technical language and contract interpretation may not end up in your favor.

If the provision being disputed is vague, the actions of the parties will be examined first. If the parties conducted themselves consistently with what they thought the provision meant at that time, the provision would likely take that meaning. If the contract cannot be clarified based on this method, the interpretation will go against the party who wrote it.

# Subcontracting

Subcontractors contract with the general contractor or other subcontractors to complete a portion of a larger project. The same principles that apply to owner/contractor contracts also apply to subcontracts.

Subcontracts should include similar content as owner/contractor contracts, such as

✓ Date

✓ Names and contact information of contracting parties

✓ Name and location of project

✓ Description of the work to be performed

✓ Subcontract time or start and completion date

✓ Payment terms, including progress payment schedule and final payment

✓ Conditions for schedule delays

✓ Drawings and specifications

✓ Contract sum

✓ Any general and supplemental conditions that apply

✓ Signatures from both parties

Depending on the stipulations in the owner/contractor agreement, the owner may need to approve subcontractors.

It is also important to get subcontracts in writing to avoid disputes. In providing a written contract, both parties have a clear understanding of the agreement. Oral contracts can lead to ambiguity and one party may interpret the agreement differently than the other.

*Clarity is very important to an enforceable contract.*

# Final Inspection...

**Required Contract Elements:** Required contract elements include offer and acceptance, consideration, competent parties, and legal purpose.

**Contract Provisions:** Your contract should contain provisions that clearly outline the terms of the contract. A few key provisions you want to include are contract price and payment terms, obligation of the parties, and breach of contract.

**Breach of Contract:** A breach of contract occurs when one of the parties involved fails to perform in accordance with any of the terms and conditions of the contract.

**Boilerplate Provisions:** These provisions contain standard language designed to protect you in the event of a lawsuit.

**Provisions to Limit Risk:** These provisions limit the liability of the contracting parties by addressing allocation of risk.

**What Are Recitals?** This language appears at the beginning of the contract and is intended to give background information.

**Types of Construction Contracts:** Different types of contracts address who is responsible for cost savings and overruns for estimated work.

# Chapter 8: Bidding and Estimating

**Contracting Methods:** Depending on the level of involvement in a construction project, different types of contracting methods are used.

**Sources of Contracts:** Contracts are available through several different sources, including associations such as the American Institute of Architects (AIA) or the Associated General Contractors (AGC).

**Making Changes to the Contract:** To change the contract, a change order is written and agreed to by the owner and contractor.

**Resolving Claims:** The claims resolution process provides a way for the owner and contractor to resolve disputes about additional amounts owed as a result of contract changes.

**Making Substitutions:** Specifications must be analyzed carefully before submitting the substitution request. Substitutions may be granted if products are discontinued or to provide a cost or time savings.

**Contract Documents and Project Manual:** The project manual is a central location for bid documents, contract provisions, technical specifications, and addenda.

**Are Oral Agreements Legally Binding?** Oral agreements can be binding, but it makes good business sense to get a contract in writing.

**Legal Interpretation:** Clarity of language and meaning in contracts is important to avoid disputes and ensure proper legal interpretation in the event of a lawsuit.

**Subcontracting:** The same principles that apply to owner/contractor contracts also apply to subcontracts. Similar language is used to ensure that each party is clear on terms and conditions of the contract.

# Chapter 9
# SCHEDULING AND PROJECT MANAGEMENT

## Chapter Survey...
⇨ Scheduling Process
⇨ Scheduling Methods
⇨ Scheduling and Cash Management
⇨ What is Project Management?
⇨ Who is the Project Manager?
⇨ Project Supervisory Team
⇨ Project Life Cycle
⇨ Tracking the Progress of the Project
⇨ Budget and Cost Controls
⇨ Quality Assurance
⇨ Value Engineering

Many construction jobs are performed every day without using a formal scheduling method. Knowing how to schedule and organize tasks helps you complete projects on time, which increases customer satisfaction and ultimately your competitive edge.

Using the quantity take-off method, as explained in Chapter 7, you developed the basis for your project schedule. Each task was assigned the number of labor hours for completion to determine labor cost. Scheduling takes the list of tasks and labor hours and assigns an order of completion.

## Scheduling Process

Planning is a key element to formulating an accurate schedule and effectively managing the project. Planning allows you to visualize the project and anticipate potential conflicts and challenges. The project start and completion dates are outlined in the contract. It is the job of the scheduler to fit in all necessary tasks within this time frame in the most efficient manner.

**Sequence of Tasks:** Understanding the correct sequence of tasks is critical to completing your project on time. As you created your estimate (discussed in Chapter 7), you probably listed your tasks in the order of completion. This determination is particularly important when scheduling subcontractors. Be sure to review the tasks outlined in the estimate and make any necessary corrections to the sequence of tasks.

Some tasks may be completed at the same time while other tasks must come before starting the next task. For example, interior and exterior paint may be applied at the same time but drywall must be completed before paint is applied.

**Activity Duration:** When creating your estimate, you determined the number of labor hours it takes to complete each task on the project. Using this estimate, you need to determine the duration of the task. The duration of each task depends on a few factors:

✓ size of the project;
✓ labor hours estimated; and
✓ length of time dedicated to the task each day. For example, if a task is estimated at four hours but your crew only has two hours per day to work on the task, the activity duration is two working days.

When determining activity duration, it is important to get input from your subcontractors and the experienced members of your crew.

Once the duration is determined for each activity, you can compare the total time against the project completion time outlined in the contract. If the total time exceeds the project completion time, adjustments must be made. Consideration must be given to increasing labor resources, requiring overtime, or extending the project completion date. These options must be weighed carefully due to added costs and possible timeline conflicts with the owner.

**Contingency Time:** Contingency time is used as a buffer between tasks to protect against unforeseen task delays. To determine contingency time, the task is analyzed to determine the likelihood of a delay occurring. A few general rules apply to determining contingency time.

✓ Tasks subject to weather delays require more contingency time.

✓ Standard work requires less contingency time than custom work.

✓ Tasks performed in areas with limited access require more contingency time.

With contingency time in place, the likelihood of a delayed task impacting the entire schedule is reduced.

**Task Time Ranges:** After completing the sequence of tasks, activity duration, and contingency time, the earliest and latest start date and earliest and latest end date are calculated. If the task completion falls outside these dates during the construction process, the project manager has an accurate calculation of the amount of time the project is ahead or behind.

**Float Time:** Float time is the remaining time after a task is complete and before the next task begins.

✓ The amount of time an activity can be delayed without impacting the early start of the next activity is called free float time.

✓ Total float time refers to the amount of leeway allowed in starting or completing an activity without delaying the project completion date.

✓ Activities with "zero float" are considered critical activities.

# Scheduling Methods

A schedule is your blueprint to finishing the project on time. There are three main types of scheduling methods used in the construction industry:

✓ **Calendar Scheduling**

✓ **Bar Chart Scheduling**

✓ **Critical Path Method**

The type of schedule you use depends on factors such as project size, complexity, and location.

# Chapter 9: Scheduling and Project Management

## Calendar Scheduling

Calendar scheduling is a simple method and can be done on a regular desk calendar. The primary advantage to this method is that you can link project tasks to specific dates, such as

- ✓ dates of other projects,
- ✓ delivery dates of materials,
- ✓ payment schedules, and
- ✓ employee vacations and holidays.

To create a calendar schedule, you need to know the sequence of tasks and activity duration. After these factors are determined, you can plug the activities into the calendar.

The following is a sample calendar schedule. Calendar scheduling works for smaller, less complex projects but is not recommended for large ones.

### SAMPLE CALENDAR SCHEDULE

Project Name: _____  Start Date: _____  End Date: _____

| Sunday | Monday | Tuesday | Wednesday | Thursday | Friday | Saturday |
|---|---|---|---|---|---|---|
| 1 Off | 2 Excavation— | 3 | 4 Layout Slab Foundation Forms | 5 Under-ground Plumbing | 6 Pour Concrete | 7 Concrete Cure Time |
| 8 Concrete Cure Time | 9 | 10 | 11 Frame Exterior Walls | 12 | 13 | 14 Off |
| 15 Off | 16 Frame Roof— | 17 Install Doors & Windows | 18 | 19 Lay Roofing Materials | 20 | 21 |
| 22 Off | 23 Electrical Rough-In  Plumbing Rough-In | 24 | 25 HVAC | 26 Siding— | 27 Off | 28 Off |
| 29 Off | 30 Siding  Insulation | 31 | 1 Install Drywall  Paint Exterior | 2 | 3 Off | 4 |
| 5 Off | 6 Install Wood/Tile Flooring | 7 | 8 | 9 Install Trim | 10 | 11 Off |
| 12 Off | 13 Paint Interior | 14 | 15 Finish Electrical  Finish Plumbing | 16 | 17 Install Carpeting | 18 Site Clean-up |

## Bar Chart Scheduling

Similar to the calendar scheduling method, the bar chart schedule shows the activity duration and sequence of tasks to be completed. It is an easy-to-read visual showing a graphical depiction of the schedule in its entirety.

One of the main weaknesses of the bar chart and calendar scheduling methods is that they do not show the interdependencies of activities.

For example, if there is a delay in a task, the bar chart does not show the impact it has on other tasks. The following is a sample bar chart schedule.

### SCHEDULE BAR CHART FOR RETAIL STORE CONSTRUCTION

| Description of Tasks | March | | | | April | | | | May | | | | June | | | |
|---|---|---|---|---|---|---|---|---|---|---|---|---|---|---|---|---|
| | W1 | W2 | W3 | W4 | W1 | W2 | W3 | W4 | W1 | W2 | W3 | W4 | W1 | W2 | W3 | W4 |
| Contract Award | ■ | | | | | | | | | | | | | | | |
| Field Survey | | ■ | | | | | | | | | | | | | | |
| Documents Reviewed | | ■ | | | | | | | | | | | | | | |
| Building Permit | | | ■ | | | | | | | | | | | | | |
| Pre-Meeting | | | | ■ | | | | | | | | | | | | |
| Demolition | | | | ■ | | | | | | | | | | | | |
| Door & Windows | | | | | ■ | | | | | | | | | | | |
| Electrical Rough In | | | | | ■ | | | | | | | | | | | |
| Plumbing Rough In | | | | | | ■ | | | | | | | | | | |
| Lighting | | | | | | ■ | | | | | | | | | | |
| HVAC | | | | | | ■ | | | | | | | | | | |
| Fire Protection | | | | | | ■ | | | | | | | | | | |
| Ceiling | | | | | ■ | | | | | | | | | | | |
| Drywall | | | | | | ■ | | | | | | | | | | |
| Plumbing Fixtures | | | | | | | ■ | | | | | | | | | |
| Caulking & Sealants | | | | | | | ■ | | | | | | | | | |
| Flooring | | | | | | | | ■ | | | | | | | | |
| Cash Wrap | | | | | | | | | | ■ | | | | | | |
| Product Racks | | | | | | | | | | ■ | ■ | | | | | |
| Electrical Fixtures | | | | | | | | | | | ■ | | | | | |
| Painting | | | | | | | | | | | ■ | | | | | |
| Signage | | | | | | | | | | | | | ■ | | | |
| Construction Cleaning | | | | | | | | | | | | | | | ■ | |
| Project Closeout | | | | | | | | | | | | | | | ■ | |

## Critical Path Method

The critical path method (CPM) of scheduling illustrates the interdependent relationship of tasks. To develop a CPM schedule, you start by determining the sequence of tasks and activity duration as you would with bar chart or calendar scheduling. In addition, you need to outline the following:

- ✓ Relationship between tasks
- ✓ Simultaneous events
- ✓ Critical path

***Relationship between Tasks:*** Most construction tasks are interrelated. For example, you can't start framing until you pour the foundation. A CPM schedule graphically shows which tasks are related and which ones are not. When you create your CPM schedule, you need to determine how each task impacts another.

***Simultaneous Events:*** If you know which tasks can be performed simultaneously, you can shorten project completion time. When creating the CPM schedule, you must show when simultaneous tasks are possible.

***Critical Path:*** The critical path is the sequence of tasks that determines the duration of the project. If a task on the critical path is delayed by one week, the project is delayed by one week. You must know which subsequent tasks cannot begin until a critical path item is completed.

The following diagram illustrates a simple critical path example.

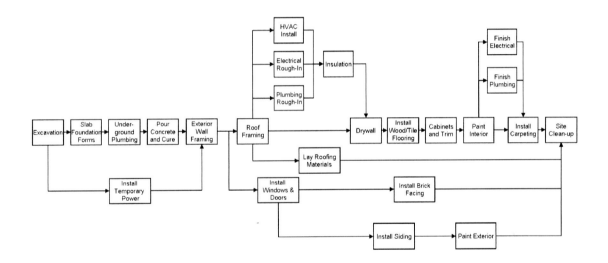

*Adding Activity Duration to the CPM Schedule:* The CPM schedule can be placed against a timeline. An example of this is illustrated in the bar chart schedule earlier in the chapter. Another alternative is to place the activity duration with each task. You can also put a code with the activity to correlate it to your estimate. If you use your estimating format, you could use the CSI MasterFormat to code the tasks in your schedule. For example, let's say the task of painting the interior has a three-day duration and you use MasterFormat code 09900. Your task might look like this on the CPM chart.

| Paint Interior | |
|---|---|
| 09900 | 3 |

Many different types of software are available to help you create schedules. You want to choose a program that is right for your needs whether it is simple or more complex. Some programs allow you to adjust the timelines if, for example, you experience a delay in the project. Scheduling software also facilitates the tracking function of a project schedule, which is a key project management tool.

# Scheduling and Cash Management

It is important to track incoming cash and expenditures during the construction project to ensure you have enough working capital to complete the job. "Working capital" refers to the amount of cash available after the liabilities or debts are paid. Balancing incoming progress payments and outgoing expenditures is important to manage the project effectively and should be a consideration when preparing your schedule.

If you have more expenditures than incoming cash in any stage of construction, you may not have enough money to proceed to the next stage of construction or pay your debts.

A preliminary cash flow budget, outlining stages of construction with anticipated revenues and expenditures, should be completed during the scheduling phase to anticipate any cash shortages. Cash flow should be tracked through the duration of the project.

# What is Project Management?

Effective project management is a challenging task on a construction project. It requires a carefully balanced combination of management skills with an understanding of the design and construction process. Project managers may manage several projects at the same time with projects at different stages of the process. A project manager not only has to manage time through the scheduling process but must also consider many other factors:

✓ Budget constraints

✓ Quality standards

✓ Project plans and specifications

✓ Resource management such as labor, materials, etc.

Project management has applications that are unique in nearly every industry, including construction.

*The ability to effectively manage significantly contributes to the success or failure of the project.*

# Who is the Project Manager?

Construction project managers plan and coordinate construction projects to meet the overall goals of the project and serve as the main contact with the owner. Responsibilities generally include but are not limited to

✓ preparing budgets;

✓ reviewing shop drawings to determine appropriate construction methods;

✓ determining labor requirements and preparing schedules;

✓ monitoring overall progress of the project and preparing job records;

✓ monitoring compliance with building and safety codes;

✓ ensuring proper handling of change orders; and

✓ regularly meeting with owners, trade contractors, architects, and other design professionals on project progress.

Construction project managers work closely with the project superintendent who manages daily site operations.

Chapter 9: Scheduling and Project Management

Construction managers may be owners or salaried employees of a construction management or contracting firm, or they may work under contract or as a salaried employee of the owner, developer, contractor, or management firm overseeing the construction project. They may plan and direct a whole project or just a part of a larger project.

### What Qualities Does a Good Manager Need?

A good manager must possess several qualities to effectively lead a team.

✓ Good communication skills

✓ Honesty and integrity

✓ Positive attitude

✓ Effective delegation skills

✓ Team and morale building skills

# Project Supervisory Team

While the project manager has a high level understanding of the project, supervisors coordinate and monitor the daily aspects of the project. Depending on the size of the project, the number of supervisory team members may vary.

**Superintendent:** The superintendent is the onsite supervisor responsible for daily operations. Depending on the size of the project and amount of responsibility the project manager wants to delegate, the superintendent's duties may include

✓ coordinating project activities and serving as a liaison with subcontractors, architects, utilities, and others;

✓ participating in project construction development and planning;

✓ processing utility requests for construction projects;

✓ representing the company regarding onsite construction quality control reviews;

✓ making recommendations and processing change order requests;

✓ reviewing punch lists;

✓ assuring construction specifications are met;

✓ tracking deviations from project schedules and costs; and

✓ maintaining project records and reports.

Communication between the project manager and superintendent is important to keeping the project on-time and within budget and providing a quality product.

**Foreman:** The foreman assists the superintendent with daily project operations. The superintendent generally oversees all of the daily operations, but the foreman usually supervises specific areas by trade. For example, a carpentry foreman may supervise rough and finish carpentry while the masonry foreman supervises formwork and concrete installation.

The foreman assists the supervisor by

✓ reviewing project plans and blueprints;

✓ providing input on estimated time, material, equipment and supplies needed;

✓ developing schedules and crew assignments;

✓ inspecting work areas;

✓ evaluating employee and subcontractor performance;

✓ completing time sheets, accident reports, and work orders; and

✓ training employees.

**Materials Expediter:** Timely delivery of materials is important to keeping a project schedule on track.

A materials expediter supervises the materials procurement process to ensure accurate and timely delivery of materials.

Later in the chapter, we will discuss the importance of effective materials management.

**Architect and Owner's Representative:** The owner will sometimes defer to an appointed representative to oversee a project. In this case, the owner's representative and/or architect will deal with the project manager. The owner's representative and architect usually do not have supervisory authority over the employees and subcontractors but they may communicate with the project manager in order to express any concerns with the project work.

In general, the owner's representative and architect have access to the jobsite and work records and can contribute to quality control on the project. The architect (or sometimes the engineer) must certify each progress payment, so it is in the best interest of the project manager to work closely with the architect and owner's representative.

## Project Life Cycle

Each project has a start point, project life cycle, and end point. Through each phase of the project life cycle, you must manage each aspect of the project such as customer relations, materials, budget, and subcontractors. Using the customer relations category as an example, the following illustrates various management aspects in the project life cycle.

### Contract Award

After you are successfully offered the job, you should get a contract signed as soon as possible. A few weeks before the job starts, schedule a pre-construction meeting with your customer and any other relevant parties (i.e., architect, subcontractors, etc.).

### Pre-Construction Phase

During the pre-construction meeting, you should go over customer expectations. Chapter 10 discusses creating realistic expectations for your customer to avoid disappointment. At this time, you should have a preliminary schedule prepared, so potential scheduling conflicts can be discussed. Be sure to follow up with written meeting notes and distribute to those in attendance as well as those who could not attend.

### Construction Phase

As the project progresses, you should carefully monitor the budget, schedule, and project quality. Regularly meet with your customer to discuss the progress of the project and any issues or questions that arise. If you are billing in progress payments, make sure you are invoicing regularly and collecting payments within the defined terms.

### Job Completion and Closeout

After the job is complete, you must do a walkthrough and develop a punch list of follow-up items. Discuss any warranties contained in your contract and how the customer can request warranty repairs. Send a customer satisfaction survey to gather feedback for future improvements.

---

*Key Elements for a Successful Project Outcome*

Many elements go into a successful project outcome:

- ✓ Project manager who understands the total project as a big picture
- ✓ Early preparation and planning
- ✓ Good management and front-line supervision
- ✓ Effective responses to problems and changes
- ✓ Active customer involvement
- ✓ Good communication skills

## Tracking the Progress of the Project

### Daily Reports

Many contractors find that keeping a daily log is a useful project tool. You can use a log to track the progress of a project and as legal back up in case any disputes arise.

The daily log can list:

- ✓ Project name and location
- ✓ Date
- ✓ Weather conditions
- ✓ Personnel on the job
- ✓ Description of work
- ✓ Hours worked on each task
- ✓ Change orders
- ✓ Progress of the job
- ✓ Other relevant information

Personal comments should not be made in the daily report. It should just contain factual information.

There are specific guidelines you should follow to increase the credibility of the daily report, if a legal dispute arises.

- ✓ The report should be completed daily. If there was no work completed, note that fact and the reason for it.
- ✓ Writing should be in ink and not altered.
- ✓ Pages should be in consecutive order and in a bound book.

Photos are a good way to document the progress of a project and can serve as a supplement to the daily log. Photos should be taken of the site prior to starting work and at critical points during the project to document any problem areas. Digital cameras make photo-taking easy with instant results. You also have the flexibility to store photos on your computer and send them through e-mail.

## Status Reports

Status reports summarize project highlights, addressing items completed, in progress, and outstanding. This report is a helpful tool to communicate with the customer, managers, subcontractors, and suppliers periodically throughout the project.

To support your status reports, you should have work records easily accessible for review. These work records include

- ✓ daily reports,
- ✓ project photographs,
- ✓ previous status reports,
- ✓ safety and accident reports,
- ✓ change orders,
- ✓ shop drawings,
- ✓ purchase orders,
- ✓ receiving documentation, and
- ✓ relevant written correspondence.

You should solicit feedback on any anticipated problems or concerns and encourage two-way communication throughout the project. Status reports are a good way to initiate this communication.

## Tracking the Schedule

A good project manager makes sure that deadlines are met on time. As discussed earlier, the first step is to develop the schedule. Next, you want to make sure you communicate the schedule to anyone who is impacted by it, such as your crew, subcontractors, and suppliers. You need to make sure they understand the deadlines and their assignments. You may want to present the schedule in a graphical format so team members can get a visual snapshot of the timeline.

## Budget and Cost Controls

Project management involves working with budget constraints. A good project manager will control costs and make sure that the project comes in on budget.

If the budget is not monitored carefully, a job that was estimated correctly can turn into a loss for the company.

## Materials

***Just-In-Time (JIT):*** Just-in-time deliveries will keep your inventory cost low. This process allows you to time deliveries to arrive as you need the materials in the construction process. Using your schedule, you can closely predict when you need materials according to the work being completed and then coordinate timing with your suppliers. Less inventory onsite will also cut down the risk of theft or vandalism.

***Purchase Orders:*** Using a purchase order system can help you organize and document your materials purchases. If you prepare your purchase orders in advance, you can review these with your customers. This process can potentially reduce change orders by allowing customers to make decisions and sign off on them in advance. Your purchase orders can also serve as delivery date documentation so you can organize just-in-time deliveries.

***Receiving:*** You can control material costs through proper receiving. When materials are delivered, someone should check the materials against the purchase order to confirm the correct quantity and items ordered were received. If there are discrepancies, follow up with the supplier as soon as possible to ensure you receive the proper credits or replacements.

To the best of your ability, you want to estimate and order the correct amount of materials. If you have excess materials, check with your supplier for a return policy. Excess materials should be stored correctly to preserve their condition. Some suppliers charge a restocking fee, but it is generally nominal and worth your time to receive a materials credit.

## Budget Tracking

The easiest way to track your budget is to use the cost estimate and a job cost system to determine if you have any cost overruns.

Cost overruns occur when you exceed budgeted amounts in your estimate. These overruns can happen in many areas of the project such as exceeding the amount of labor through improper scheduling and excessive materials waste. Chapter 7, Contract Management, summarizes types of contracts that address who is responsible for cost overruns.

It is important to track costs as the project progresses because cost overruns can indicate a possible problem. The sooner these problems are identified, the easier it will be to take corrective action.

Cost overruns may occur because you have a bad estimate. Tracking your budget will help you or your estimator prepare more accurate estimates in the future.

Cost overruns reduce the amount of profit you make on the job. If you are not making a profit or you are losing money on your projects, you will eventually go out of business.

# Quality Assurance

Ensuring the customer receives a quality built product is one of the most important aspects of project management. You may find ways to cut corners, but neglecting quality can cost you in the long run. You may also run into ethical considerations when neglecting quality. Concealing defective work and design flaws can leave you open to a lawsuit and ruin your reputation.

## Accurate and Detailed Specifications and Plans

Accurate and detailed specifications and plans are important to setting the quality standards of the project. These items will help you put together a more accurate estimate and should be part of the contract documents. If details are vague, your decisions on material quality and construction methods may differ from the owner's. This misunderstanding can cause conflict and disappoint your customer. It is best to set expectations and obtain agreement from the customer early in the project.

## Detailed Shop Drawings

In addition to specifications and plans, shop drawings are often required to detail specific aspects of a project. Shop drawings outline specific details, materials, dimensions, and installation for specific items. Product data and samples may accompany shop drawings to provide additional information. Shop drawings are produced by the material supplier, contractor, subcontractor, or manufacturer. As part of the quality control process, the architect and contractor must review and approve shop drawings.

## Quality Assurance Program

Setting up a quality assurance program is a good way to let your employees and customers know the importance of producing a high quality product. Internal inspections should take place at different stages of the construction process to review the completed work and confirm that it meets your quality standards.

Your company philosophy should stress quality. You want your employees to take pride in their work. As an employer, you can create a positive work atmosphere and provide the tools employees need to be successful. Providing ongoing training for employees so they can expand their knowledge base helps improve the quality of their work. Employees should know the standards they are expected to follow. Documenting work standards and conducting regular performance reviews are good ways to create a mutual understanding of the level of quality you expect.

## Customer Satisfaction Surveys

Customer satisfaction surveys are also a good tool to receive feedback about the quality of your work. Customer surveys are good for asking about the professionalism of your employees, quality of work, and overall service. Potential customers may be interested that you have a continuous improvement program. Positive feedback from your current or former customers can serve as a good marketing tool to gain new business.

# Value Engineering

Value engineering is a project management approach. The objective is to understand the owner's cost, quality, and time priorities to deliver a product of the highest value. Many owners will provide incentives to contractors to meet these objectives. For example, an

Chapter 9: Scheduling and Project Management

owner may provide a bonus for a contractor who can cut costs without sacrificing quality while meeting all deadlines. If value engineering bonuses exist, it is important that they are included in the construction contract.

The Society of American Value Engineering International (SAVE) publishes a methodology for the construction industry. The purpose of this methodology is to reduce costs, improve productivity, and develop innovative ways to solve problems.

# Final Inspection...

**Scheduling Process:** During the project scheduling process, the sequence of tasks, activity duration, contingency time, task time ranges, and float time are determined.

**Scheduling Methods:** The three main types of scheduling are calendar scheduling, bar chart scheduling, and critical path method (CPM).

**Scheduling and Cash Management:** Effective cash management helps ensure you have enough working capital to complete your project.

**What is Project Management?** Project management involves managing several different factors including budgets, quality controls, project plans and specifications, and resource management.

**Who is the Project Manager?** Construction project managers plan and coordinate construction projects to meet the overall goals of the project and serve as the main contact with the owner. The ability to manage effectively contributes significantly to the success or failure of a project.

**Project Supervisory Team:** Depending on the size of the project, the supervisory team may consist of a superintendent, foreman, materials expediter, architect, and owner's representative.

**Project Life Cycle:** Through each phase of the project life cycle, you must manage each aspect of the project such as customer relations, materials, budget, and subcontractors.

**Tracking the Progress of the Project:** A good project manager makes sure that deadlines are met on time. Daily reports and status reports are tools you can use to track your progress.

**Budget and Cost Controls:** A good project manager will control costs and make sure the project comes in on budget.

**Quality Assurance:** Ensuring that the customer receives a quality built product is one of the most important aspects of project management.

**Value Engineering:** Balancing the owner's cost, quality, and time priorities while delivering the highest value product are objectives of the value engineering approach.

# Chapter 10
# CUSTOMER RELATIONS

## Chapter Survey...
⇨ *Communication with Customers*
⇨ *Handling Customer Change Orders*
⇨ *Negotiation Basics*

**Understanding Expectations:** You will find customers have specific expectations of the outcome of your work. If those expectations are not satisfied, your customers will be disappointed, which will reflect poorly on your company. Instead of promising your customers an unrealistic outcome, it is easier to be honest and bring expectations to a realistic level. If customers have a realistic picture of the project, you can avoid disappointing them. The best way to accomplish this is through consistent and effective communication with your customers.

## Communication with Customers

It is important for customers to understand the status of their project and have all the information needed to make informed decisions. This communication will not only keep the customer's expectations realistic but also build a trusting relationship with you and your company.

**Communication Opportunities:** You have several opportunities to communicate with your customers and keep their expectations at a realistic level, including

- ✓ contract negotiations,
- ✓ contract acceptance,
- ✓ weekly meetings,
- ✓ punch list and final walkthrough, and
- ✓ post-job follow-up.

Establishing communication at these times will ensure that your customer is aware of your progress and of issues that arise during any step of the process.

**Communication Basics:** Now that we have established when to communicate with customers, let's go over a few basics on how to communicate.

- ✓ Understand that your customer may not have the same level of technical knowledge as you. Avoid using technical terminology and clarify when necessary.
- ✓ Give your customer a chance to ask questions and express any concerns. Use active listening skills, and remember that all questions are important to the customer.
- ✓ When dealing with difficult customers, always remain professional.
- ✓ Use e-mail or written communication as a follow-up to verbal conversations to document key items discussed and any changes agreed to.
- ✓ Don't forget the personal touch. E-mail and fax are great tools, but schedule time to talk to the customer in person.
- ✓ Return phone calls promptly.

Good communication can build customer trust and help you understand customer expectations.

## Handling Customer Change Orders

Proper handling of customer change orders is very important. This is a critical point in the customer-contractor relationship that can result in a positive or negative outcome. If you do not follow through with the change order as the customer expects, it will result in disappointment and mistrust. If you follow through to the customer's specifications, you will reinforce that you are responsive and understand the importance of customer service.

You should always apply a few general rules when change orders arise:

- ✓ Always obtain a signed change order for significant amounts of change work.
- ✓ Small changes done with verbal approval should be followed up with a written and signed change order.
- ✓ Invoice for change order work promptly.
- ✓ Include any complimentary work done without charge on the invoice.
- ✓ Show labor and quantity details when pricing change orders as you would when creating your initial estimate.

# Negotiation Basics

Good negotiation skills can benefit you personally and in all areas of your business. When a successful negotiation occurs, both parties are satisfied with the outcome.

*Preparing to Negotiate:* Negotiation is a process and it is important to prepare ahead of time to get the most out of the negotiation. Considering these questions will help:

- ✓ What are you negotiating (i.e., money, time, conditions, etc.)?
- ✓ What is the ideal outcome?
- ✓ How much are you willing to compromise?
- ✓ What is the other person trying to achieve?

A negotiation may not always involve price. Consider what is valuable to your business. For example, if time is a critical factor to completing your current projects, you may want to negotiate on project timelines. It is important not to compromise your reputation in a negotiation. You don't want to lose your best customer or future referrals.

*Confident Negotiations:* Now that you are prepared, you can come to the negotiation confident in knowing what you want. Aim high in your negotiation and you will get more. If you ask for more than you want, people will tend to meet you in the middle. It is important to be flexible during the negotiation. Even though you have prepared ahead of time, the other party may change the direction of the negotiation to different terms. For example, you may have prepared to negotiate on price, but your counterpart may want to deal on the timeline of the work.

When possible, it is important to get the final outcome of your negotiation in writing. Once it is in writing, both parties can sign off on what they agreed to, which will help avoid any disappointment or confusion.

# Final Inspection...

*Communication with Customers:* Good communication helps you build trust and understand customer expectations.

*Handling Customer Change Orders:* Change orders should be handled carefully and accurately documented.

*Negotiation Basics:* Come to a negotiation prepared, and, when possible, make sure you get any agreement in writing.

# Chapter 11
# EMPLOYEE MANAGEMENT

## Chapter Survey...
⇨ *Interviewing and Hiring Employees*
⇨ *New Hire Reporting*
⇨ *Hiring Minors for Construction Work*
⇨ *Employee Documentation*
⇨ *Key Employment Laws*
⇨ *Fair Labor Standards Act (FLSA)*
⇨ *Immigration and Nationality Act*
⇨ *Americans with Disabilities Act (ADA)*
⇨ *Other Labor Laws*
⇨ *Louisiana Wage and Hour Laws*
⇨ *Required Postings*
⇨ *Employee Handbook and Policies*
⇨ *Employee Satisfaction*
⇨ *Providing Benefits*
⇨ *Disciplining Employees*
⇨ *Terminating Employees*
⇨ *Sample I-9 Form*

Finding good, hardworking employees can sometimes mean the difference between success and failure in business. It is easier to delegate to good employees and produce high-quality work from employees who care about their job. Poor employees can cost a company wasted time and ultimately money. The first step to finding good employees is taking the extra time to hire the right people for the job.

Employees should start off with a few fundamental qualities. They should be

✓ qualified for the position;
✓ motivated to do the job and show initiative;
✓ responsible for their work and actions;
✓ dependable to show up on time and keep work commitments; and
✓ open to learning new skills.

These basic qualities will result in an employee who is capable of performing their present job responsibilities and taking on more tasks in the future.

## Interviewing and Hiring Employees

***Asking Questions:*** Asking the right interview questions is key to finding the right employee. The wrong interview questions can get you into trouble. You must convey that you are a fair and non-discriminatory employer. If you ask questions implying otherwise, you will open yourself to a lawsuit. Some questions could lead to legal action and are strictly off-limits, especially the following:

✓ How old are you?
✓ Do you have any disabilities?
✓ Are you pregnant?
✓ Are you married?
✓ Do you have children?
✓ What is your religious affiliation?
✓ What is your sexual orientation?
✓ What ethnic background are you?

Now that you know what questions not to ask, here are some areas to cover during the job interview that will be helpful in determining if an employee is the right fit for your company.

Questions should be asked to elicit information about the candidate's

✓ ability to work with other members of a construction team;
✓ ability to handle conflict;
✓ expectations of the job (e.g. salary, benefits, working hours, etc.);

- ✓ past work history and reasons for leaving previous jobs;
- ✓ level of skill or expertise;
- ✓ training and education;
- ✓ safety record;
- ✓ ability to solve problems;
- ✓ knowledge of your company; and
- ✓ questions about the job.

Appendix C contains links to websites that provide sample job interview questions for the construction industry that you can customize for your business.

*Hiring the right people for the job is the first step to finding good employees.*

## New Hire Reporting

**Reporting Requirements:** You are required to report all new hires and rehired employees to the Louisiana **New Hire Reporting Program** no later than 20 days from the worker's first day on the job. There are several reporting methods you can use.

- ✓ **Internet:** Use the online data entry form or secure file upload at www.la-newhire.com
- ✓ **Diskette:** Download the new hire information onto a diskette and mail it to
  **Louisiana Directory of New Hires**
  **P.O. Box 142513**
  **Austin, Texas 78714-2513**
  **Telephone: (888) 223-1461**
- ✓ **Mail:** Mail W-4 forms, state reporting form, or other approved paper report
- ✓ **Magnetic Tape or Cartridge:** Download the new hire information onto a magnetic tape or cartridge and mail it to the address above
- ✓ **Fax:** Fax W-4 forms, state reporting form, or other approved paper report to (888) 223-1462
- ✓ **Payroll Service:** If you use a payroll service, ask if it can report new hires for you.

Failure to report a new hire or rehire may result in a $25.00 fine per incident, or, if conspiracy to avoid reporting is determined, a fine of up to a $500.00.

**Required Information:** The following data must be included for each new hire:
- ✓ Employer Name
- ✓ Employer Address
- ✓ Employer Federal Identification Number (If you have more than one FEIN, use the same FEIN you use to report your quarterly wage information when reporting new hires)
- ✓ Employer State Identification Number (required if available)
- ✓ Employee Name
- ✓ Employee Address
- ✓ Employee Social Security Number
- ✓ Employee Occupation (required if available)
- ✓ Employee Date of Hire (required)

**Purpose of New Hire Reporting:** New hire information submitted by employers is used to establish and enforce child support orders, detect unemployment benefits fraud, detect workers' compensation fraud, and detect fraud in other government programs, such as welfare and food stamps.

## Hiring Minors for Construction Work

The State of Louisiana and U.S. Department of Labor have strict rules for the hiring of minors. Minors under the age of 14 are not permitted to work.

**Employment Certificate:** By law, minors under the age of 18 must have on file an employment certificate or work permit issued by the superintendent of the city or parish schools.

To begin the process of obtaining an employment certificate, an Intent to Employ form can be downloaded from the Department of Labor website at www.laworks.net. Employers must complete the form and return it to the minor for a parent or legal guardian signature. The minor must submit the signed form to the school or school board office. The school or school board office must apply for an employment certificate. Employers must obtain the original employment certificate before the minor can begin work.

The employment certificate must be accessible at the worksite and is valid only for the employer for whom it was issued. The employer must return the

# Chapter 11: Employee Management

certificate to the issuing officer within three days after termination of the employment.

**Working Hours:** Minors under the age of 16 cannot work more than 8 hours in a day or more than 40 hours per week.

They may not be employed

- between the hours of 7:00 p.m. and 7:00 a.m. before the start of any school day, or
- between the hours of 9:00 p.m. and 7:00 a.m. on any day,
- more than six consecutive days, and
- more than three hours a day or more than 18 hours per week when school is in session.

Minors 16 years of age who have not graduated from high school may not be employed between the hours of 11:00 p.m. and 5:00 a.m. before the start of any school day.

Minors under 17 who have not graduated from high school may not be employed between the hours of 12:00 a.m. and 5:00 a.m. before the start of any school day.

Minors under 18 years of age must have a 30 minute break for every five hours worked.

**Prohibited Tasks:** Minors are prohibited from working in hazardous or detrimental jobs. Except for office or sales work, most construction jobs fall into the category of hazardous. Specific tasks categorized as hazardous or detrimental that apply to the construction industry (with the exception of apprentices as defined by law) include but are not limited to

- operating power-driven woodworking machines or off-bearing from circular saws;
- oiling, cleaning, wiping machinery or shafting or applying belts to pulleys;
- operation of machinery used in the cold rolling of heavy metals or operation of power-driven machinery for punching, shearing, stamping, bending or planing metals;
- operation of passenger or freight elevators or hoisting machines;
- driving any motor vehicle on a public road (prohibited by minors 16 and under; minor 17 and older can drive under certain restrictions);
- any occupation involving exposure to lead or its compounds; and
- any occupation that is considered hazardous.

## Employee Documentation

Once you hire an employee, you should make sure you set up an employee file.

These items should be included in your employee files:

- **Form I-9:** The United States Customs and Immigration Service requires this form. It shows that the worker has legal immigration status in the United States. (For more information on I-9s, see the following section on the Immigration and Nationality Act.)
- **IRS Form W-4:** This form is required to determine the appropriate level of federal tax withholding. Employees can change the amount of federal tax withholding at any time by completing a new W-4 form.
- **IRS Form W-5:** To receive earned income credit (EIC) in advance, employees can complete a W-5 form. Advance EIC is a special tax benefit for working people who earn low or moderate incomes. If the employee wants to continue to receive advance EIC, he or she must complete a new W-5 form each year.
- **State Tax Form:** This form is required to determine the appropriate level of state tax withholding, if applicable. Employees must complete the L-4 Employee Withholding Exemption Certificate to designate the amount of state tax withholding.
- **Employment Application:** All employees should complete an application before being hired. It should contain basic information such as the employee's name, address, and phone number. The application should also be signed, giving your company authorization to check references on the employment history section.
- **Policy Signoffs:** If you have written policies or an employee handbook, have your employees sign a receipt that the employee has received and reviewed it.
- **Emergency Notification Form:** It is important that you know who to contact in the event of an

emergency. Make sure to update this information periodically.

The employee file should be maintained throughout employment and other relevant documentation can be added, such as disciplinary action forms or insurance enrollment forms.

*Setting up employee files will help keep you organized.*

## Key Employment Laws

There are several key laws governing equal employment opportunities and prohibiting discrimination in employment. It is important to understand and abide by these laws, not only to protect your company from a lawsuit but also to safeguard your reputation as a good employer.

## Fair Labor Standards Act (FLSA)

The Fair Labor Standards Act, which prescribes standards for the basic minimum wage and overtime pay, affects most private and public employment. It applies to employers who have one or more employees. Individual states may also have additional minimum wage requirements.

- ✓ Effective July 24, 2009, federal minimum wage increased to $7.25 per hour. If the state minimum wage rate differs from the federal rate, the employer must pay the higher of the two rates. Minors under 20 years of age may be paid a minimum wage of not less than $4.25 per hour during the first 90 consecutive calendar days of employment. Employers may not displace any employee to hire someone at the youth minimum wage.
- ✓ Employers must pay overtime compensation of one-and-one-half-times the regular rate after 40 hours of work in a workweek.
- ✓ Wages must be paid on the regular payday for the pay period covered.
- ✓ The act restricts the hours that children under age 16 can work and forbids the employment of children under age 18 in certain jobs deemed too dangerous.

FLSA is administered by the Employment Standards Administration's Wage and Hour Division within the U.S. Department of Labor.

**Determining Exemption Status:** Some employees are exempt from the overtime pay provisions or both the minimum wage and overtime pay provisions as defined under the Fair Labor Standards Act (FLSA). This rule would apply to the following examples of employees who might be employed in the construction industry:

- ✓ Executives
- ✓ Administrative personnel
- ✓ Professional employees
- ✓ Outside sales employees
- ✓ Employees in certain computer-related occupations as defined in the Department of Labor regulations

**Workweek Defined under FLSA:** A workweek is a period of 168 hours during seven consecutive 24-hour periods. It may begin on any day of the week and at any hour of the day established by the employer. Generally, for purposes of minimum wage and overtime payment, each workweek stands alone; you may not average two or more workweeks. Employee coverage, compliance with wage payment requirements, and the application of most exemptions are determined on a workweek basis.

**Work Hours Defined Under FLSA:** Work hours ordinarily include all time during which an employee is required to be on the employer's premises, on duty, or at a prescribed work place.

Bona fide meal periods (typically 30 minutes or more) generally need not be compensated as work time. The employee must be completely relieved from duty for the purpose of eating regular meals. The employee is not relieved if he or she is required to perform any duties, whether active or inactive, while eating.

**Employment Practices Not Covered:** While FLSA does set basic minimum wage and overtime pay standards and regulates the employment of minors, there are a number of employment practices that FLSA does not regulate.

FLSA does not require

- ✓ vacation, holiday, severance, or sick pay;
- ✓ meal or rest periods, holidays off, or vacations;
- ✓ premium pay for weekend or holiday work;
- ✓ pay raises or fringe benefits; or

Chapter 11: Employee Management

11-5

✓ reason for discharge, immediate payment of final wages to a terminated employee, or discharge notices.

Also, FLSA does not limit the number of hours in a day or days in a week an employee may be required or scheduled to work, including overtime hours, if the employee is at least 16 years old.

These matters not covered by FLSA are left for agreement between the employer and the employees or their authorized representatives. Individual state labor departments may have specific regulations separate from FLSA regarding these requirements.

*State of Louisiana*
*Department of Labor*
*1001 North 23rd Street*
*Baton Rouge, Louisiana 70802*

*Phone: (225) 342-3111*

*Website: www.laworks.net*

## Recordkeeping under the FLSA

The FLSA requires employers to keep records on wages, hours, and other items as specified in Department of Labor recordkeeping regulations. Most of this information is maintained by employers in ordinary business practice and in compliance with other laws and regulations. The records do not have to be kept in any particular form and time clocks need not be used.

*Required Information:* For employees subject to the minimum wage provisions or both the minimum wage and overtime pay provisions, the following records must be kept:

✓ personal information, including employee's name, home address, occupation, sex, and birth date (if under 19 years of age);

✓ basis on which employee wages are paid;

✓ hour and day when workweek begins;

✓ total hours worked each workday and each workweek;

✓ total daily or weekly straight-time earnings;

✓ regular hourly pay rate;

✓ weekly overtime earnings;

✓ total overtime pay for the workweek;

✓ deductions from or additions to wages;

✓ total wages paid each pay period; and

✓ date of payment and pay period covered.

Special information is required for home workers, for employees working under uncommon pay arrangements, for employees to whom lodging or other facilities are furnished, and for employees receiving remedial education.

Chapter 14, Financial Management, covers the basics of payroll accounting and how to process the listed information.

## Penalties

Enforcement of FLSA is carried out by investigators stationed across the U.S. They conduct investigations and gather data on wages, hours, and other employment conditions or practices in order to determine compliance with the law. Where violations are found, they may recommend changes in employment practices to bring an employer into compliance.

Retaliation against an employee for filing a complaint or for participating in a legal proceeding under FLSA is against the law.

Willful violations of employment under FLSA may be prosecuted criminally and the violator fined up to $10,000. A second conviction may result in imprisonment.

Employers who willfully or repeatedly violate the minimum wage or overtime pay requirements are subject to a civil money penalty of up to $1,100 for each violation.

# Immigration and Nationality Act

The employment eligibility provisions of the Immigration and Nationality Act require employers to verify the employment eligibility of all individuals hired. Immigration and Naturalization Service forms (I-9) must be kept on file for at least three years after the date of hire or for one year after the date employment ends, whichever is later.

I-9 forms must be completed with required documentation within three days of hire. A sample I-9 form is located at the end of this chapter.

The law does not require businesses to obtain I-9 documentation for independent contractors and their employees.

*Unlawful Discrimination:* Discrimination based on national origin or citizenship status is prohibited. If an Office of Special Counsel for Unfair Employment-Related Discrimination (OSC) or Equal Employment Opportunity Commission (EEOC) investigation reveals employment discrimination covered by the Immigration and Nationality Act, the employer will be ordered to cease the prohibited practice and may be ordered to take one or more of the following steps:

✓ hire or reinstate, with or without back pay, individuals directly injured by the discrimination;

✓ lift any restrictions on an employee's assignments, work shifts, or movements;

✓ post notices to employees about their rights and about employers' obligations;

✓ educate all personnel involved in hiring and in complying with employer sanctions and anti-discrimination laws; and

✓ remove a false performance review or false warning from an employee's personnel file.

Employers may also be ordered to pay civil monetary penalties of $375 to $3,200 per individual discriminated against for the first offense, $3,200 to $6,500 per individual discriminated against for the second offense, and $4,300 to $16,000 per individual discriminated against for subsequent offenses.

## Completing the I-9 Form for New Hires

Form I-9 is available for download on the U.S. Citizenship and Immigration Services website at www.uscis.gov or by calling (800) 870-3676. The National Customer Service Center at (800) 375-5283 can answer questions on USCIS forms and information on immigration laws, regulations and procedures.

A sample of the I-9 form is located at the end of this chapter. The following gives step-by-step instructions on how to complete the form properly.

### Section One

The employee completes section one of the I-9 form at the start of employment. The employee's name, address, date of birth, and social security number (optional unless the employer participates in the USCIS E-Verify Program), certification of legal status, and expiration date for temporary work authorization are required. Permanent aliens and authorized aliens must fill in either their alien number or authorization number. The employee must sign and date the form. If a preparer or translator is used, the appropriate signature block must be completed.

### Section Two

An authorized employer representative completes section two by examining one document from list A or by examining one document from list B and one document from list C. A summary of approved documents is listed in the following section and a complete list is on the back of the I-9 form. The representative must view original documentation and keep copies of the front and back of this documentation on file.

*Acceptable Documentation:* The purpose of providing documentation is to establish identity and employment eligibility. Listed below are common forms of identification used when completing the I-9 form. A complete list is included on the back of the I-9 form located at the end of this chapter. If employers participate in the USCIS E-Verify Program, only documents from List B on the I-9 form that bear a photograph are acceptable. I-9 forms must be updated when identity and employment eligibility documents are changed or renewed.

Employees can provide one of the following documents that establishes both identity and employment eligibility:

✓ U.S. passport

✓ Certificate of U.S. citizenship

✓ Certificate of naturalization

✓ Unexpired foreign passport with I-551 stamp or attached I-94 form indicating current employment authorization

✓ Permanent resident card or alien registration receipt with photograph

Employees also have the option of providing two documents—one to establish identity and the other to establish employment eligibility.

Documents that establish identity include

✓ state-issued driver's license with photo;

✓ ID card with photo issued by federal, state or local government agencies;

✓ voter's registration card; and

✓ U.S. military card.

Documents that establish employment eligibility include

✓ U.S. Social Security card issued by the Social Security Administration;

✓ original or certified birth certificate;

# Chapter 11: Employee Management

✓ U.S. citizen ID card (form I-197);

✓ resident ID card; and

✓ Native American tribal document.

## Certification

The date to be used in the certification section must correspond with the current employment date. The authorized employer representative must sign and date this section.

***Additional Information:*** U.S. Citizen and Immigration Services publishes a Handbook for Employers, which is a helpful resource for completing the I-9 form. This publication is available online at www.uscis.gov.

# Americans with Disabilities Act (ADA)

This law prohibits discrimination against persons with disabilities and applies to employers with 15 or more employees. In general, the employment provisions of the ADA require

✓ equal opportunity in selecting, testing, and hiring qualified applicants with disabilities;

✓ job accommodation for applicants and workers with disabilities when such accommodations would not impose "undue hardship;" and

✓ equal opportunity in promotion and benefits.

***Employment Discrimination:*** ADA prohibits discrimination in all employment practices, including job application procedures, hiring, firing, advancement, compensation, training, and other terms, conditions, and privileges of employment. It applies to recruitment, advertising, tenure, layoff, leave, fringe benefits, and all other employment-related activities.

***Qualified Individuals with Disabilities:*** Employment discrimination is prohibited against "qualified individuals with disabilities" including applicants for employment and employees. An individual is considered to have a "disability" if that individual has a physical or mental impairment that substantially limits one or more major life activities or has a record of such an impairment, or is regarded as having such an impairment.

***Conditions Covered:*** The ADA applies to persons who have impairments that substantially limit major life activities such as seeing, hearing, speaking, walking, breathing, performing manual tasks, learning, caring for oneself, and working.

Examples include an individual with

✓ epilepsy,

✓ paralysis,

✓ HIV infection,

✓ AIDS,

✓ substantial hearing or visual impairment,

✓ mental retardation, or

✓ specific learning disability.

An individual with a minor, non-chronic condition of short duration, such as a sprain, broken limb, or the flu, generally would not be covered by the ADA.

***Reasonable Accommodations:*** An employer is required to accommodate a "known" disability of a qualified applicant or employee unless it imposes an "undue hardship" on the operation of the employer's business. A reasonable accommodation is any modification or adjustment to a job or the work environment that will enable a qualified applicant or employee with a disability to participate in the application process or to perform essential job functions. Reasonable accommodations also include adjustments to assure that a qualified individual with a disability has rights and privileges in employment equal to those of employees without disabilities.

***Additional Resources:*** The Equal Employment Opportunity Commission has developed several resources to help employers and people with disabilities understand and comply with the employment provisions of the ADA. Resources include

✓ a technical assistance manual that provides "how-to" guidance on the employment provisions of the ADA as well as a resource directory to help individuals find specific information; and

✓ a variety of brochures, booklets, and fact sheets.

For more information about the ADA, contact:

*U.S. Equal Employment Opportunity Commission*
*131 M Street, NE*
*Fourth Floor, Suite 4NWO2F*
*Washington, D.C. 20507*

*Telephone: (202) 669-4000*
*TTY: (202) 669-6820*

*Website: www.eeoc.gov*

# Other Labor Laws

Many other labor laws protect the rights of employees.

- ✓ The **Davis-Bacon Act** requires payment of prevailing wage rates and fringe benefits on federally-financed or assisted construction.
- ✓ The **Walsh-Healey Public Contracts Act** requires payment of minimum wage rates and overtime pay on contracts that provide goods to the federal government.
- ✓ The **Service Contract Act** requires payment of prevailing wage rates and fringe benefits on contracts to provide services to the federal government.
- ✓ The **Contract Work Hours and Safety Standards Act** sets overtime standards for service and construction contracts on federal projects.
- ✓ The **Wage Garnishment Law** limits the amount of an individual's income that may be legally garnished and prohibits firing an employee whose pay is garnished for payment of a single debt.
- ✓ The **Employee Polygraph Protection Act** prohibits most private employers from using any type of lie detector test, either for pre-employment screening of job applicants or for testing current employees during the course of employment.
- ✓ The **Family and Medical Leave Act** entitles eligible employees of covered employers to take up to 12 weeks of unpaid job-protected leave each year, with the maintenance of group health insurance, for the birth and care of a child, for the placement of a child for adoption or foster care, for the care of a child, spouse, or parent with a serious health condition, or for the employee's serious health condition.
- ✓ **Title VII of the Civil Rights Act of 1964** prohibits discrimination on the basis of race, color, religion, national origin, and sex. Sexual harassment is considered a form of sex discrimination and is a violation of Title VII. An amendment to Title VII provides protection against sex discrimination on the basis of pregnancy, childbirth, and related medical conditions.
- ✓ The **Equal Pay Act of 1963** prohibits employers from paying different wages to men and women who perform essentially the same work under similar working conditions.
- ✓ The **Age Discrimination in Employment Act (ADEA)** prohibits discrimination against individuals who are age 40 or older. It applies to employers with 20 or more employees.
- ✓ The **Worker Adjustment and Retraining Notification Act (WARN)** offers protection to workers, their families, and communities by requiring employers to provide notice 60 days in advance of covered plant closings and covered mass layoffs.
- ✓ **Title III of the Consumer Credit Protection Act (CCPA)** protects employees from being discharged by their employers because their wages have been garnished for any one debt and limits the amount of employees' earnings that may be garnished in any one week.
- ✓ The **Uniformed Services Employment and Reemployment Rights Act (USERRA)** protects service members' reemployment rights when returning from a period of service in the uniformed services, including those called up from the reserves or National Guard, and prohibits employer discrimination based on military service or obligation.
- ✓ **Numerous labor organizing, collective bargaining and dispute resolution acts** give employees the right to organize, join labor unions, bargain collectively, and strike.
- ✓ **Right-to-work laws** secure the right of employees to decide for themselves whether or not to join or financially support a union. Louisiana is a right-to-work state.

*Be aware of the labor laws that apply to your business.*

## Louisiana Wage and Hour Laws

Louisiana has no wage laws pertaining to overtime, minimum wage, or regulation of salaried employees. Louisiana employers fall under the U.S. Department of Labor rules with regard to these matters.

***Laws Concerning Payroll:***
Louisiana does have laws on specific payroll issues.

Chapter 11: Employee Management                                                                11-9

Below is a summary of the payroll laws that may apply to your business.

✓ **Payment of Wages:** Under Louisiana law, employees must be informed of what wages they will be paid, frequency of payment, and method of payment. If payment dates are not designated, employees must be paid on the 1st and 16th of each month. This law does not apply to executive, administrative, supervisory, or professional personnel as defined under the FLSA.

✓ **Payment on Termination:** Louisiana employees who are laid off, fired, or who quit must be paid their wages in full, including vacation time, at the next regular payday, not to exceed 15 days from the date of their discharge or termination. If wages are not received, an employee should send a written demand for payment of their final wages to their employer. After receipt of a written demand, the employer must pay all wages owed to the employee on a timely basis or be subject to a penalty that may be imposed by a civil court. Claims against an employer for late payment may be filed by way of a private lawsuit. The Louisiana Department of Labor has no authority to enforce this law (Louisiana Rev. Stat. 23:631-632).

✓ **Withholding of Wages:** No employer may withhold or divert any portion of an employee's wages unless required or empowered by state or federal law or unless the employer has written authorization from the employee. Even with written permission, employers cannot deduct a sum of money as a penalty or fine. The only exception is when the employee damages property belonging to the employer or property in the possession of the employer. The deduction cannot exceed the actual damage done.

*Minimum Wage:* Louisiana has no minimum wage law and falls under the U.S. Department of Labor regulations. Certain exemptions exist for workers under the age of 20, full-time students, and student learners.

# Required Postings

Some of the statutes and regulations enforced by agencies within the U.S. Department of Labor require that posters or notices be posted in the workplace. A complete list of postings can be found at www.dol.gov.

A summary of postings that may apply to you as listed on U.S. Department of Labor website is as follows:

| Poster | Description of Employers Required to Post Notice |
| --- | --- |
| Safety and Health Protection on the Job | Employers located in states with OSHA-approved state plans should obtain and post the state's equivalent poster. |
| Equal Opportunity is the Law | Businesses holding federal contracts or subcontracts or federally assisted construction contracts of $10,000 or more. |
| Employee Rights for Workers with Disabilities/Special Minimum Wage Poster | All employers having workers employed under special minimum wage certificates must post this notice. |
| National Labor Relations Act (NLRA) Poster (effective January 31, 2012) | All private-sector employers (excluding agricultural, railroad and airline employers) must post this notice. |
| Your Rights Under the Family and Medical Leave Act | Public agencies (including state, local, and federal employers), public and private elementary and secondary schools, as well as private sector employers who employ 50 or more employees in 20 or more work weeks and who are engaged in commerce or in any industry or activity affecting commerce, including joint employers and successors of covered employers |
| Fair Labor Standards Act (FLSA): Minimum Wage Poster | All private, federal, state and local government employers subject to the FLSA |
| Uniformed Services Employment and Reemployment Rights Act | The full text of the notice must be provided by each employer to persons entitled to rights and benefits under USERRA. |
| Notice to All Employees Working on Federal or Federally Financed Construction Projects | Any contractor/subcontractor engaged in contracts in excess of $2,000 for the actual construction, alteration/repair of a public building or public work or building or work financed in whole or in part from federal funds, federal guarantee, or federal pledge |

| Poster | Description of Employers Required to Post Notice |
|---|---|
| Notice to Employees Working on Government Contracts | Every contractor or subcontractor engaged in a contract with the United States or the District of Columbia in excess of $2,500 the principal purpose of which is to furnish services in the U.S. through the use of service employees. |
| Notice: Employee Polygraph Protection Act | Any employer engaged in or affecting commerce or in the production of goods for commerce. Does not apply to federal, state and local governments, or to circumstances covered by the national defense and security exemption. |
| Notification of Employee Rights Under Federal Labor Laws | Federal contractors and subcontractors are required to post the prescribed employee notice conspicuously in plants and offices where employees covered by the National Labor Relations Act (NLRA) perform contract-related activity, including all places where notices to employees are customarily posted both physically and electronically. |

Additional postings may be required for federal contractors.

Louisiana state law requires posting of the following notices.
- ✓ Louisiana Minor Labor Law Placard
- ✓ Age Discrimination
- ✓ Sickle Cell Trait Discrimination
- ✓ Genetic Discrimination
- ✓ Rights of Military Personnel Under State Law
- ✓ Timely Payment of Wages
- ✓ Workers' Compensation
- ✓ Earned Income Credit
- ✓ Unemployment Insurance
- ✓ Out of State Motor Vehicles
- ✓ Equal Opportunity for All (if distributing federal funds)
- ✓ Whistleblower Protection (for public employees)

Posters are available online for download at www.laworks.net or by contacting a local Louisiana Workforce Commission, Business and Career Solutions Center.

Other state agencies may also require display of specific documents in the workplace. Please contact the appropriate agencies directly to verify any posting requirements.

Posters are periodically updated. Ensure you post the most current version, if required.

# Employee Handbook and Policies

Having clear and well-documented policies helps employees understand the rules of the workplace and protects you if a disgruntled employee files a lawsuit or complaint against you.

**Enforcing Policies and Procedures:** An employee handbook is a document you put together that lists company policies and employee benefits and rights. It is important for employees to sign a receipt that they have read and understood the contents of the handbook. This documentation is helpful in enforcing the policies and procedures of your company.

**Changing Your Handbook:** An employee handbook is not a static document. You can add items to the handbook but make sure you distribute amendments to employees and have them sign off on the changes.

## Writing Your Employee Handbook

It may be difficult to determine where to start when writing your employee handbook and policies. Consider the following sections when putting your handbook together:
- ✓ Company history
- ✓ Compensation guidelines (i.e., introductory period, full-time status requirements, etc.)
- ✓ Payroll distribution dates and times
- ✓ Benefits
- ✓ Normal working hours
- ✓ Overtime pay
- ✓ Vacation time
- ✓ Sick days
- ✓ Policy on sexual harassment
- ✓ Policy on the use of illegal drugs or alcohol
- ✓ Non-discrimination policy

# Chapter 11: Employee Management

- ✓ Rules of conduct (i.e., disciplinary action for insubordination, fighting, etc.)
- ✓ Safety policies
- ✓ Equipment and tool policies
- ✓ Disciplinary action procedures

You may want to have an attorney review your employee handbook. In many states, the employee handbook is considered an employment contract. There may be certain wording and disclaimers that should be contained in your employee handbook to protect you against legal action.

# Employee Satisfaction

*Benefits of Employee Satisfaction:* Keeping your employees happy and motivated can have a tremendous effect on the performance of your work teams. Your company can benefit from satisfied employees in several ways:

- ✓ Stronger company loyalty and corporate culture
- ✓ Higher quality work and customer satisfaction
- ✓ Lower employee turnover
- ✓ Increased productivity

Maintaining employee satisfaction is not as easy as it sounds. Even though employers may have good intentions, when faced with tight deadlines and day-to-day operations, employee satisfaction sometimes drops to the bottom of the priority list.

*Motivating Employees:* The following checklist includes simple ways you can motivate your employees and give them a feeling of achievement:

- ✓ Provide informal and formal training opportunities for employees to learn new skills.
- ✓ Empower employees to make decisions and give positive and constructive feedback.
- ✓ Provide clear expectations for your employees.
- ✓ Conduct performance reviews on a regular basis.
- ✓ Mentor your employees and tell them about advancement opportunities in your company and the industry.
- ✓ Recognize and reward employees for good work.

## The Value of Job Descriptions

Job descriptions give employees a guideline for the responsibilities of their job. Job descriptions benefit the employee because employees understand your expectation for their performance. It also makes it easier for you to monitor their performance, give reviews, and conduct disciplinary action if necessary.

Job descriptions should contain a few basic elements:

- ✓ Job title
- ✓ Job description, including who the position reports to and summary of job purpose
- ✓ Key responsibilities
- ✓ Required licenses and/or certifications
- ✓ Skills and knowledge needed

*Sample Job Description:* Listed below is a sample job description for a construction superintendent position using the above categories. All job descriptions must be carefully reviewed and modified to fit the individual company's requirements.

**Job Title: Construction Superintendent**

**Description:** Under general direction of the company owner, the construction superintendent serves as a member of the construction management team with broad authority over assigned projects, participating in all phases of construction from project planning to completion. Emphasis is on quality control, evaluation of change order requests, and timely completion of construction schedules.

**Key Responsibilities:** The duties listed below are intended only as illustrations of the various types of work that may be performed by the construction superintendent:

- ✓ Coordinates activities associated with the company's construction projects.
- ✓ Serves as liaison with subcontractors, architects, utilities, and others.
- ✓ Participates in project construction development and planning.
- ✓ Processes utility requests for construction projects.
- ✓ Represents the company regarding onsite construction quality control reviews.
- ✓ Makes recommendations and processes change order requests.
- ✓ Reviews punch lists.
- ✓ Assures construction specifications are met.
- ✓ Notes deviations from project schedules and costs.
- ✓ Maintains records and prepares reports.

The omission of specific statements of duties does not exclude them from the position if the work is similar, related, or a logical assignment to this class.

**Required Licenses or Certifications:** Requires a valid driver's license.

Skills and Knowledge Needed:

✓ **Principles and practices of construction** management, building operation and maintenance, quality assurance programs and systems, budget administration, construction specifications, and bidding processes.

✓ Ability to plan, organize, and manage time to track progress and elements of assigned construction projects effectively.

✓ Establish and maintain effective working relationships with coworkers, employees of subcontractors, and outside entities.

✓ Prepare or participate in the development of construction and other budgets and monitor performance against the approved budget.

✓ Communicate effectively, both orally and in writing.

✓ Ability to lift up to 50 pounds.

# Providing Benefits

Offering benefit plans can be an effective means of attracting and retaining good employees, keeping up with the competition, and boosting employee morale. Traditional employee plans include

✓ health insurance,
✓ dental insurance,
✓ vision insurance,
✓ long-term disability,
✓ life insurance, and
✓ 401(k) or other retirement plan.

Some employers also opt to offer more creative benefit options, such as tuition reimbursement, gym subsidies, and child care referral services.

However you decide to package your benefits plan, a few key laws are important.

**Workers' Compensation Laws** provide monetary compensation to employees who are injured or disabled on the job. These laws also provide benefits for dependents of those workers who are killed because of work-related accidents or illnesses. Some laws protect employers by limiting the amount an injured employee can recover from an employer and by eliminating the liability of coworkers in most accidents. Workers' compensation laws and programs are established at the state level for most employment.

Workers' compensation fraud is committed when an individual willfully intends to provide false or inaccurate information to receive workers' compensation benefits. Examples of fraud include

✓ reporting an injury as work-related when it was not;

✓ continuing to work and receive benefits at the same time; and

✓ misrepresenting an injury.

Employers are in the best position to identify workers' compensation fraud. Workers' compensation fraud is illegal. Your workers' compensation administrator should be notified if you suspect fraud.

Workers' compensation insurance is purchased by the employer; no part of it should be paid for by employees or deducted from their pay.

***Louisiana Coverage Requirements:*** The Louisiana program is administered through the Department of Labor, Office of Workers' Compensation.

> *Office of Workers' Compensation Administration*
>
> *Office Location:*
> *1001 North 23rd Street*
> *Baton Rouge, Louisiana 70802*
>
> *Mailing Address:*
> *P.O. Box 94040*
> *Baton Rouge, Louisiana 70804-9040*
>
> *Telephone: (225) 342-7555*
> *Fax: (225) 342-5665*
>
> *Email: OWCA@ldol.state.la.us*
>
> *Website: www.laworks.net*

All employers must provide workers' compensation insurance for their employees at no cost to the employee. Workers' compensation insurance can be provided in one of the following ways.

✓ Workers' Compensation Insurer
✓ Self-Insurance
✓ Group Self-Insurance

## Chapter 11: Employee Management

If an employee is hurt at work or becomes ill due to something that is work-related:

✓ The employee must notify the employer within 30 days to be eligible for benefits.

✓ The employee must submit to a medical examination paid for by the employer.

✓ The employee must keep the employer informed of any change in his or her condition.

✓ The employer must report the injury or illness to its insurance provider and the Office of Workers' Compensation Administration (OWCA) within 10 days.

Employees are not eligible for workers' compensation if the employee intentionally injured him- or herself, was injured while intentionally injuring another employee, or was intoxicated at the time of the injury.

Upon receipt of the notice of injury, OWCA will mail the employer and the injured employee a brochure that provides a summary of rights, benefits, and obligations.

To determine benefit amounts, every employer must maintain the following information for one year from the date of the record:

✓ name, address, and occupation of employees;

✓ daily and weekly hours worked;

✓ wages paid; and

✓ if the employee is a minor, the employer must procure and keep on file an employment certificate or work permit.

**Required Postings:** Employers are required to display the Workers' Compensation Compliance Poster in a convenient and conspicuous location at the place of business. A copy of the poster is available online at www.laworks.net.

**Safety Plan:** Employers with 15 or more employees are required to have a written safety plan. Specific safety plan information is available in Chapter 12, Jobsite Safety and Environmental Factors.

Unemployment Compensation programs provide unemployment benefits to eligible workers who become unemployed through no fault of their own and meet certain other eligibility requirements. This program is jointly financed through federal and state employer payroll taxes through the federal/state unemployment insurance tax.

Generally, employers must pay both state and federal unemployment taxes if

✓ they pay wages to employees totaling $1,500 or more in any quarter of a calendar year; or

✓ they had at least one employee during any day of a week during 20 weeks in a calendar year, regardless of whether or not the weeks were consecutive.

***Louisiana State Unemployment Program:*** The contribution you pay under state law may be taken as a credit against the federal tax. The credit is limited to 5.4 percent and all employers in the state receive that much credit against the federal tax regardless of the amount they pay to the state.

***Taxable Wage Base and Tax Rate:*** Tax wage base and tax rate may vary from year to year. For the most current information, refer to your local unemployment office. Current tax rates are available online at www.laworks.net. Rates are calculated annually based on the employer's taxable wages, taxes paid (contributions), and benefit charges through June 30th preceding the calendar rate year.

***Liability Determination:*** All employers doing business in Louisiana are required to complete and file Status Report LDOL-ES 1 to determine their liability for unemployment insurance.

***Quarterly Filings and Payment of Tax:*** To report unemployment taxes, you must file form LDOL-ES 4, Quarterly Report of Wages Paid. This form is mailed to all employers. Form LDOL-ES 4 is due no later than the last day of the month following the close of the calendar quarter.

You can pay unemployment tax electronically through the Department of Labor's Electronic Funds Transfer (EFT) system. There is no cost to use EFT. You can enroll by calling (225) 342-2951 or (800) 408-9762 or online at www.laworks.net.

***SUTA Dumping:*** SUTA dumping is a transfer of employees between businesses for the purpose of obtaining a lower unemployment compensation tax rate. SUTA dumping is prohibited and subject to hefty civil and criminal penalties. Penalties include a fine of up to $10,000 for each incident and/or imprisonment for up to six months. The Department of Labor investigates suspicious activity in the transfer or acquisition of a business or shifting of employees to identify SUTA dumping.

***Further Information:*** Specific information about the Louisiana Employment Security Law can be obtained from the Louisiana Department of Labor.

>  Louisiana Department of Labor
>  UI Tax Liability and Adjudication
>
>  Office Location:
>  1001 North 23rd Street
>  Baton Rouge, Louisiana 70802
>
>  P.O. Box 94186
>  Baton Rouge, Louisiana 70804-9186
>
>  Phone: (225) 342-2944
>  Toll-free: (866) 783-5567
>
>  Website: www.laworks.net

The Consolidated Omnibus Budget Act of 1985 (COBRA) includes provisions for continuing health care coverage. These provisions apply to group health plans of employers with 20 or more employees on 50 percent of the typical working days in the previous calendar year. COBRA gives "qualified beneficiaries" (a covered employee's spouse and dependent children) the right to maintain, at their own expense, coverage under their health plan that would be lost due to a "qualifying event," such as termination of employment, at a cost comparable to what it would be if they were still members of the employer's group.

Health Insurance Portability and Accountability Act of 1996 (HIPAA) provides for improved portability and continuity of health insurance coverage connected with employment. These provisions include rules relating to exclusions of preexisting conditions, special enrollment rights, and prohibition of discrimination against individuals based on health status-related factors. HIPAA also addresses an employee's right to privacy concerning their health information. As an employer, you need to be aware of this act and keep records concerning any employee's medical conditions in a confidential file.

## Disciplining Employees

Corrective action may be necessary from time to time for employees who are not following employment policies and procedures properly. Employers need to administer discipline fairly to promote a respectful work environment and to avoid trouble later.

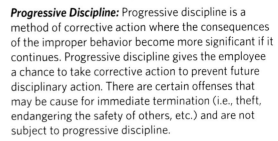

***Progressive Discipline:*** Progressive discipline is a method of corrective action where the consequences of the improper behavior become more significant if it continues. Progressive discipline gives the employee a chance to take corrective action to prevent future disciplinary action. There are certain offenses that may be cause for immediate termination (i.e., theft, endangering the safety of others, etc.) and are not subject to progressive discipline.

The employee manual is a good place to have written disciplinary policies and a comprehensive list of offenses that lead to immediate dismissal.

## Terminating Employees

At one time or another, most employers run into circumstances where they need to terminate employees. It is not a fun or rewarding task but sometimes a necessary one. When terminating an employee, you want to make sure you have followed the proper procedures to minimize your risk of a wrongful termination lawsuit.

Employment relationships are either contractual or at-will; the definition of the relationship influences the procedures for termination.

### Contractual Employees

Union employees and some executives have employment contracts. When terminating a contractual employee, it is important to comply with the terms of the contract. If the contract is breached, you may be subject to a lawsuit.

### At-Will Employees

"At-will employment" means that either the employer or the employee may terminate employment at any time without notice or cause. It is not exactly that easy, and there are restrictions that you should be aware of as an employer. These restrictions include:

- ✓ An employer may not terminate an employee for discriminatory reasons (i.e., race, gender, etc.).
- ✓ An employer cannot terminate an employee for taking time off to serve on a jury.
- ✓ Reporting health and safety violations and abuses of power cannot lead to termination. There are "whistle-blower laws" that protect employees if this circumstance does occur.

Chapter 11: Employee Management

✓ All employers should use good faith and fair dealing throughout employment. This is why documenting poor performance is strongly recommended. Without documentation, the termination may be perceived as a breach of good faith.

These are general guidelines and it is recommended you consult with an expert in Human Resources or an attorney regarding specific situations.

*Louisiana Law:* Louisiana is known as an employment-at-will state. However, exceptions exist to Louisiana's employment-at-will doctrine. Louisiana employees may not be disciplined or discharged at-will for

✓ being called to military service;

✓ political opinions or voting;

✓ exercising right of association;

✓ wage garnishment;

✓ filing a workers' compensation claim; or

✓ being called to jury duty (employer must also pay the employee one day's wages during the jury service).

Louisiana's "whistle-blower's law" is found in the Louisiana Revised Statutes 23:967 and 30:2027. It specifically prohibits employers from taking any reprisal against an employee who advises the employer that the business is in violation of a law; who discloses, threatens to disclose, or testifies about the violation of law; or who objects to or refuses to participate in an employment act in violation of law.

Employees who are fired may apply for unemployment insurance benefits. The Louisiana Department of Labor's Office of Regulatory Services determines eligibility for benefits.

*Proper documentation is important when disciplining and terminating employees.*

# Final Inspection...

*Interviewing and Hiring Employees:* Your interviews should focus on skills, experience, and qualities. There are certain questions you should avoid because they are not legal to ask.

*New Hire Reporting:* Louisiana has mandatory new hire reporting requirements.

*Hiring Minors for Construction Work:* The State of Louisiana and U.S. Department of Labor have strict rules for the hiring of minors, including restricted work hours and prohibited job tasks.

*Employee Documentation:* Employee files should be maintained throughout employment with relevant documents such as tax forms and disciplinary forms.

*Key Employment Laws:* There are several employment laws that you must comply with, such as the Fair Labor Standards Act (FLSA), Immigration and Nationality Act, and the Americans with Disabilities Act (ADA).

*Fair Labor Standards Act (FLSA):* Standards for basic minimum wage and overtime pay are outlined in the Fair Labor Standards Act. The Act applies to most private and public employers who have one or more employees.

*Immigration and Nationality Act:* Employers are required to verify the employment eligibility of all individuals hired through I-9 forms. These forms must be kept on file for at least three years after the date of hire or for one year after the date employment ends, whichever is later.

*Americans with Disabilities Act (ADA):* This law prohibits discrimination against persons with disabilities. It applies to employers with 15 or more employees.

*Other Labor Laws:* Several other labor laws protect the rights of employees. Specific laws exist that set guidelines for federal contractors, wage garnishment, and an employee's right to join a union. Other laws provide protection against the discriminatory actions of employers.

**Required Postings:** Employers must post certain notices for employees under federal and state law.

**Louisiana Wage and Hour Laws:** Louisiana has specific laws pertaining to employment, such as payment of wages, payment on termination, and withholding of wages.

**Employee Handbook and Policies:** An employee handbook is a useful document for communicating your policies and procedures.

**Employee Satisfaction:** Your company can benefit in several ways from putting employee satisfaction programs in place.

**Providing Benefits:** There are some mandatory benefits you must provide employees. Other benefits, such as health insurance, may also be offered to attract and retain employees.

**Disciplining Employees:** Discipline should be administered in a fair manner and documented appropriately.

**Terminating Employees:** Using proper termination procedures will help minimize your risk of a wrongful termination lawsuit.

## Supplemental Forms

Supplemental forms and links are available at **NASCLAforms.org** using access code **LA129354**.

| | |
|---|---|
| IRS Form W-4 | IRS form to determine federal income tax withholding |
| IRS Form W-5 | IRS form for employees to elect advance earned income credit |
| Form I-9 | Required form to confirm legal immigration status |
| Fair Labor Standards Act (FLSA) | Copy of the FLSA law from the U.S. Department of Labor |
| Americans with Disabilities Act (ADA) | ADA guide for small businesses published by the U.S. Department of Justice |
| Job Description Template | Form featured earlier in the chapter that shows a sample job description |
| Employer's Tax Guide (Circular E) | Publication used to determine federal income tax withholding for employees |

# Instructions for Employment Eligibility Verification

**Department of Homeland Security**
U.S. Citizenship and Immigration Services

USCIS
Form I-9
OMB No. 1615-0047
Expires 03/31/2016

**Read all instructions carefully before completing this form.**

**Anti-Discrimination Notice.** It is illegal to discriminate against any work-authorized individual in hiring, discharge, recruitment or referral for a fee, or in the employment eligibility verification (Form I-9 and E-Verify) process based on that individual's citizenship status, immigration status or national origin. Employers **CANNOT** specify which document(s) they will accept from an employee. The refusal to hire an individual because the documentation presented has a future expiration date may also constitute illegal discrimination. For more information, call the Office of Special Counsel for Immigration-Related Unfair Employment Practices (OSC) at 1-800-255-7688 (employees), 1-800-255-8155 (employers), or 1-800-237-2515 (TDD), or visit www.justice.gov/crt/about/osc.

## What Is the Purpose of This Form?

Employers must complete Form I-9 to document verification of the identity and employment authorization of each new employee (both citizen and noncitizen) hired after November 6, 1986, to work in the United States. In the Commonwealth of the Northern Mariana Islands (CNMI), employers must complete Form I-9 to document verification of the identity and employment authorization of each new employee (both citizen and noncitizen) hired after November 27, 2011. Employers should have used Form I-9 CNMI between November 28, 2009 and November 27, 2011.

## General Instructions

Employers are responsible for completing and retaining Form I-9. For the purpose of completing this form, the term "employer" means all employers, including those recruiters and referrers for a fee who are agricultural associations, agricultural employers, or farm labor contractors.

Form I-9 is made up of three sections. Employers may be fined if the form is not complete. Employers are responsible for retaining completed forms. Do not mail completed forms to U.S. Citizenship and Immigration Services (USCIS) or Immigration and Customs Enforcement (ICE).

## Section 1. Employee Information and Attestation

Newly hired employees must complete and sign Section 1 of Form I-9 **no later than the first day of employment**. Section 1 should never be completed before the employee has accepted a job offer.

Provide the following information to complete Section 1:

**Name:** Provide your full legal last name, first name, and middle initial. Your last name is your family name or surname. If you have two last names or a hyphenated last name, include both names in the last name field. Your first name is your given name. Your middle initial is the first letter of your second given name, or the first letter of your middle name, if any.

**Other names used:** Provide all other names used, if any (including maiden name). If you have had no other legal names, write "N/A."

**Address:** Provide the address where you currently live, including Street Number and Name, Apartment Number (if applicable), City, State, and Zip Code. Do not provide a post office box address (P.O. Box). Only border commuters from Canada or Mexico may use an international address in this field.

**Date of Birth:** Provide your date of birth in the mm/dd/yyyy format. For example, January 23, 1950, should be written as 01/23/1950.

**U.S. Social Security Number:** Provide your 9-digit Social Security number. Providing your Social Security number is voluntary. However, if your employer participates in E-Verify, you must provide your Social Security number.

**E-mail Address and Telephone Number (Optional):** You may provide your e-mail address and telephone number. Department of Homeland Security (DHS) may contact you if DHS learns of a potential mismatch between the information provided and the information in DHS or Social Security Administration (SSA) records. You may write "N/A" if you choose not to provide this information.

**EMPLOYERS MUST RETAIN COMPLETED FORM I-9**
**DO NOT MAIL COMPLETED FORM I-9 TO ICE OR USCIS**

Form I-9 Instructions 03/08/13 N

All employees must attest in Section 1, under penalty of perjury, to their citizenship or immigration status by checking one of the following four boxes provided on the form:

1. **A citizen of the United States**

2. **A noncitizen national of the United States:** Noncitizen nationals of the United States are persons born in American Samoa, certain former citizens of the former Trust Territory of the Pacific Islands, and certain children of noncitizen nationals born abroad.

3. **A lawful permanent resident:** A lawful permanent resident is any person who is not a U.S. citizen and who resides in the United States under legally recognized and lawfully recorded permanent residence as an immigrant. The term "lawful permanent resident" includes conditional residents. If you check this box, write either your Alien Registration Number (A-Number) or USCIS Number in the field next to your selection. At this time, the USCIS Number is the same as the A-Number without the "A" prefix.

4. **An alien authorized to work:** If you are not a citizen or national of the United States or a lawful permanent resident, but are authorized to work in the United States, check this box.

   If you check this box:

   a. Record the date that your employment authorization expires, if any. Aliens whose employment authorization does not expire, such as refugees, asylees, and certain citizens of the Federated States of Micronesia, the Republic of the Marshall Islands, or Palau, may write "N/A" on this line.

   b. Next, enter your Alien Registration Number (A-Number)/USCIS Number. At this time, the USCIS Number is the same as your A-Number without the "A" prefix. If you have not received an A-Number/USCIS Number, record your Admission Number. You can find your Admission Number on Form I-94, "Arrival-Departure Record," or as directed by USCIS or U.S. Customs and Border Protection (CBP).

      **(1)** If you obtained your admission number from CBP in connection with your arrival in the United States, then also record information about the foreign passport you used to enter the United States (number and country of issuance).

      **(2)** If you obtained your admission number from USCIS *within the United States*, or you entered the United States without a foreign passport, you must write "N/A" in the Foreign Passport Number and Country of Issuance fields.

Sign your name in the "Signature of Employee" block and record the date you completed and signed Section 1. By signing and dating this form, you attest that the citizenship or immigration status you selected is correct and that you are aware that you may be imprisoned and/or fined for making false statements or using false documentation when completing this form. To fully complete this form, you must present to your employer documentation that establishes your identity and employment authorization. Choose which documents to present from the Lists of Acceptable Documents, found on the last page of this form. You must present this documentation no later than the third day after beginning employment, although you may present the required documentation before this date.

### Preparer and/or Translator Certification

The Preparer and/or Translator Certification must be completed if the employee requires assistance to complete Section 1 (e.g., the employee needs the instructions or responses translated, someone other than the employee fills out the information blocks, or someone with disabilities needs additional assistance). The employee must still sign Section 1.

### Minors and Certain Employees with Disabilities (Special Placement)

Parents or legal guardians assisting minors (individuals under 18) and certain employees with disabilities should review the guidelines in the *Handbook for Employers: Instructions for Completing Form I-9 (M-274)* on **www.uscis.gov/ I-9Central** before completing Section 1. These individuals have special procedures for establishing identity if they cannot present an identity document for Form I-9. The special procedures include **(1)** the parent or legal guardian filling out Section 1 and writing "minor under age 18" or "special placement," whichever applies, in the employee signature block; and **(2)** the employer writing "minor under age 18" or "special placement" under List B in Section 2.

## Section 2. Employer or Authorized Representative Review and Verification

Before completing Section 2, employers must ensure that Section 1 is completed properly and on time. Employers may not ask an individual to complete Section 1 before he or she has accepted a job offer.

Employers or their authorized representative must complete Section 2 by examining evidence of identity and employment authorization within 3 business days of the employee's first day of employment. For example, if an employee begins employment on Monday, the employer must complete Section 2 by Thursday of that week. However, if an employer hires an individual for less than 3 business days, Section 2 must be completed no later than the first day of employment. An employer may complete Form I-9 before the first day of employment if the employer has offered the individual a job and the individual has accepted.

Employers cannot specify which document(s) employees may present from the Lists of Acceptable Documents, found on the last page of Form I-9, to establish identity and employment authorization. Employees must present one selection from List A **OR** a combination of one selection from List B and one selection from List C. List A contains documents that show both identity and employment authorization. Some List A documents are combination documents. The employee must present combination documents together to be considered a List A document. For example, a foreign passport and a Form I-94 containing an endorsement of the alien's nonimmigrant status must be presented together to be considered a List A document. List B contains documents that show identity only, and List C contains documents that show employment authorization only. If an employee presents a List A document, he or she should **not** present a List B and List C document, and vice versa. If an employer participates in E-Verify, the List B document must include a photograph.

In the field below the Section 2 introduction, employers must enter the last name, first name and middle initial, if any, that the employee entered in Section 1. This will help to identify the pages of the form should they get separated.

Employers or their authorized representative must:

1. Physically examine each original document the employee presents to determine if it reasonably appears to be genuine and to relate to the person presenting it. The person who examines the documents must be the same person who signs Section 2. The examiner of the documents and the employee must both be physically present during the examination of the employee's documents.

2. Record the document title shown on the Lists of Acceptable Documents, issuing authority, document number and expiration date (if any) from the original document(s) the employee presents. You may write "N/A" in any unused fields.

   If the employee is a student or exchange visitor who presented a foreign passport with a Form I-94, the employer should also enter in Section 2:

   a. The student's Form I-20 or DS-2019 number (Student and Exchange Visitor Information System-SEVIS Number); **and** the program end date from Form I-20 or DS-2019.

3. Under Certification, enter the employee's first day of employment. Temporary staffing agencies may enter the first day the employee was placed in a job pool. Recruiters and recruiters for a fee do not enter the employee's first day of employment.

4. Provide the name and title of the person completing Section 2 in the Signature of Employer or Authorized Representative field.

5. Sign and date the attestation on the date Section 2 is completed.

6. Record the employer's business name and address.

7. Return the employee's documentation.

Employers may, but are not required to, photocopy the document(s) presented. If photocopies are made, they should be made for **ALL** new hires or reverifications. Photocopies must be retained and presented with Form I-9 in case of an inspection by DHS or other federal government agency. Employers must always complete Section 2 even if they photocopy an employee's document(s). Making photocopies of an employee's document(s) cannot take the place of completing Form I-9. Employers are still responsible for completing and retaining Form I-9.

**Unexpired Documents**

Generally, only unexpired, original documentation is acceptable. The only exception is that an employee may present a certified copy of a birth certificate. Additionally, in some instances, a document that appears to be expired may be acceptable if the expiration date shown on the face of the document has been extended, such as for individuals with temporary protected status. Refer to the *Handbook for Employers: Instructions for Completing Form I-9 (M-274)* or I-9 Central (www.uscis.gov/I-9Central) for examples.

**Receipts**

If an employee is unable to present a required document (or documents), the employee can present an acceptable receipt in lieu of a document from the Lists of Acceptable Documents on the last page of this form. Receipts showing that a person has applied for an initial grant of employment authorization, or for renewal of employment authorization, are not acceptable. Employers cannot accept receipts if employment will last less than 3 days. Receipts are acceptable when completing Form I-9 for a new hire or when reverification is required.

Employees must present receipts within 3 business days of their first day of employment, or in the case of reverification, by the date that reverification is required, and must present valid replacement documents within the time frames described below.

There are three types of acceptable receipts:

1. A receipt showing that the employee has applied to replace a document that was lost, stolen or damaged. The employee must present the actual document within 90 days from the date of hire.

2. The arrival portion of Form I-94/I-94A with a temporary I-551 stamp and a photograph of the individual. The employee must present the actual Permanent Resident Card (Form I-551) by the expiration date of the temporary I-551 stamp, or, if there is no expiration date, within 1 year from the date of issue.

3. The departure portion of Form I-94/I-94A with a refugee admission stamp. The employee must present an unexpired Employment Authorization Document (Form I-766) or a combination of a List B document and an unrestricted Social Security card within 90 days.

When the employee provides an acceptable receipt, the employer should:

1. Record the document title in Section 2 under the sections titled List A, List B, or List C, as applicable.

2. Write the word "receipt" and its document number in the "Document Number" field. Record the last day that the receipt is valid in the "Expiration Date" field.

By the end of the receipt validity period, the employer should:

1. Cross out the word "receipt" and any accompanying document number and expiration date.

2. Record the number and other required document information from the actual document presented.

3. Initial and date the change.

See the *Handbook for Employers: Instructions for Completing Form I-9 (M-274)* at **www.uscis.gov/I-9Central** for more information on receipts.

## Section 3. Reverification and Rehires

Employers or their authorized representatives should complete Section 3 when reverifying that an employee is authorized to work. When rehiring an employee within 3 years of the date Form I-9 was originally completed, employers have the option to complete a new Form I-9 or complete Section 3. When completing Section 3 in either a reverification or rehire situation, if the employee's name has changed, record the name change in Block A.

For employees who provide an employment authorization expiration date in Section 1, employers must reverify employment authorization on or before the date provided.

Some employees may write "N/A" in the space provided for the expiration date in Section 1 if they are aliens whose employment authorization does not expire (e.g., asylees, refugees, certain citizens of the Federated States of Micronesia, the Republic of the Marshall Islands, or Palau). Reverification does not apply for such employees unless they chose to present evidence of employment authorization in Section 2 that contains an expiration date and requires reverification, such as Form I-766, Employment Authorization Document.

Reverification applies if evidence of employment authorization (List A or List C document) presented in Section 2 expires. However, employers should not reverify:

1. U.S. citizens and noncitizen nationals; or

2. Lawful permanent residents who presented a Permanent Resident Card (Form I-551) for Section 2.

Reverification does not apply to List B documents.

If both Section 1 and Section 2 indicate expiration dates triggering the reverification requirement, the employer should reverify by the earlier date.

For reverification, an employee must present unexpired documentation from either List A or List C showing he or she is still authorized to work. Employers CANNOT require the employee to present a particular document from List A or List C. The employee may choose which document to present.

To complete Section 3, employers should follow these instructions:

1. Complete Block A if an employee's name has changed at the time you complete Section 3.

2. Complete Block B with the date of rehire if you rehire an employee within 3 years of the date this form was originally completed, and the employee is still authorized to be employed on the same basis as previously indicated on this form. Also complete the "Signature of Employer or Authorized Representative" block.

3. Complete Block C if:

   a. The employment authorization or employment authorization document of a current employee is about to expire and requires reverification; or

   b. You rehire an employee within 3 years of the date this form was originally completed and his or her employment authorization or employment authorization document has expired. (Complete Block B for this employee as well.)

   To complete Block C:

   a. Examine either a List A or List C document the employee presents that shows that the employee is currently authorized to work in the United States; and

   b. Record the document title, document number, and expiration date (if any).

4. After completing block A, B or C, complete the "Signature of Employer or Authorized Representative" block, including the date.

   For reverification purposes, employers may either complete Section 3 of a new Form I-9 or Section 3 of the previously completed Form I-9. Any new pages of Form I-9 completed during reverification must be attached to the employee's original Form I-9. If you choose to complete Section 3 of a new Form I-9, you may attach just the page containing Section 3, with the employee's name entered at the top of the page, to the employee's original Form I-9. If there is a more current version of Form I-9 at the time of reverification, you must complete Section 3 of that version of the form.

## What Is the Filing Fee?

There is no fee for completing Form I-9. This form is not filed with USCIS or any government agency. Form I-9 must be retained by the employer and made available for inspection by U.S. Government officials as specified in the **"USCIS Privacy Act Statement"** below.

## USCIS Forms and Information

For more detailed information about completing Form I-9, employers and employees should refer to the *Handbook for Employers: Instructions for Completing Form I-9 (M-274)*.

You can also obtain information about Form I-9 from the USCIS Web site at www.uscis.gov/I-9Central, by e-mailing USCIS at **I-9Central@dhs.gov**, or by calling **1-888-464-4218**. For TDD (hearing impaired), call **1-877-875-6028**.

To obtain USCIS forms or the *Handbook for Employers*, you can download them from the USCIS Web site at www.uscis.gov/forms. You may order USCIS forms by calling our toll-free number at **1-800-870-3676**. You may also obtain forms and information by contacting the USCIS National Customer Service Center at **1-800-375-5283**. For TDD (hearing impaired), call **1-800-767-1833**.

Information about E-Verify, a free and voluntary program that allows participating employers to electronically verify the employment eligibility of their newly hired employees, can be obtained from the USCIS Web site at www.dhs.gov/E-Verify, by e-mailing USCIS at **E-Verify@dhs.gov** or by calling **1-888-464-4218**. For TDD (hearing impaired), call **1-877-875-6028**.

Employees with questions about Form I-9 and/or E-Verify can reach the USCIS employee hotline by calling **1-888-897-7781**. For TDD (hearing impaired), call **1-877-875-6028**.

## Photocopying and Retaining Form I-9

A blank Form I-9 may be reproduced, provided all sides are copied. The instructions and Lists of Acceptable Documents must be available to all employees completing this form. Employers must retain each employee's completed Form I-9 for as long as the individual works for the employer. Employers are required to retain the pages of the form on which the employee and employer enter data. If copies of documentation presented by the employee are made, those copies must also be kept with the form. Once the individual's employment ends, the employer must retain this form for either 3 years after the date of hire or 1 year after the date employment ended, whichever is later.

Form I-9 may be signed and retained electronically, in compliance with Department of Homeland Security regulations at 8 CFR 274a.2.

## USCIS Privacy Act Statement

**AUTHORITIES:** The authority for collecting this information is the Immigration Reform and Control Act of 1986, Public Law 99-603 (8 USC 1324a).

**PURPOSE:** This information is collected by employers to comply with the requirements of the Immigration Reform and Control Act of 1986. This law requires that employers verify the identity and employment authorization of individuals they hire for employment to preclude the unlawful hiring, or recruiting or referring for a fee, of aliens who are not authorized to work in the United States.

**DISCLOSURE:** Submission of the information required in this form is voluntary. However, failure of the employer to ensure proper completion of this form for each employee may result in the imposition of civil or criminal penalties. In addition, employing individuals knowing that they are unauthorized to work in the United States may subject the employer to civil and/or criminal penalties.

**ROUTINE USES:** This information will be used by employers as a record of their basis for determining eligibility of an employee to work in the United States. The employer will keep this form and make it available for inspection by authorized officials of the Department of Homeland Security, Department of Labor, and Office of Special Counsel for Immigration-Related Unfair Employment Practices.

## Paperwork Reduction Act

An agency may not conduct or sponsor an information collection and a person is not required to respond to a collection of information unless it displays a currently valid OMB control number. The public reporting burden for this collection of information is estimated at 35 minutes per response, including the time for reviewing instructions and completing and retaining the form. Send comments regarding this burden estimate or any other aspect of this collection of information, including suggestions for reducing this burden, to: U.S. Citizenship and Immigration Services, Regulatory Coordination Division, Office of Policy and Strategy, 20 Massachusetts Avenue NW, Washington, DC 20529-2140; OMB No. 1615-0047. **Do not mail your completed Form I-9 to this address.**

# Employment Eligibility Verification
**Department of Homeland Security**
U.S. Citizenship and Immigration Services

**USCIS Form I-9**
OMB No. 1615-0047
Expires 03/31/2016

▶**START HERE.** Read instructions carefully before completing this form. The instructions must be available during completion of this form.
**ANTI-DISCRIMINATION NOTICE:** It is illegal to discriminate against work-authorized individuals. Employers **CANNOT** specify which document(s) they will accept from an employee. The refusal to hire an individual because the documentation presented has a future expiration date may also constitute illegal discrimination.

## Section 1. Employee Information and Attestation (Employees must complete and sign Section 1 of Form I-9 no later than the **first day of employment**, but not before accepting a job offer.)

| Last Name (Family Name) | First Name (Given Name) | Middle Initial | Other Names Used (if any) |
|---|---|---|---|

| Address (Street Number and Name) | Apt. Number | City or Town | State | Zip Code |
|---|---|---|---|---|

| Date of Birth (mm/dd/yyyy) | U.S. Social Security Number | E-mail Address | Telephone Number |
|---|---|---|---|

I am aware that federal law provides for imprisonment and/or fines for false statements or use of false documents in connection with the completion of this form.

**I attest, under penalty of perjury, that I am (check one of the following):**

☐ A citizen of the United States

☐ A noncitizen national of the United States (See instructions)

☐ A lawful permanent resident (Alien Registration Number/USCIS Number): _____

☐ An alien authorized to work until (expiration date, if applicable, mm/dd/yyyy) _____ . Some aliens may write "N/A" in this field.
(See instructions)

For aliens authorized to work, provide your Alien Registration Number/USCIS Number **OR** Form I-94 Admission Number:

1. Alien Registration Number/USCIS Number: _____

   **OR**

2. Form I-94 Admission Number: _____

   If you obtained your admission number from CBP in connection with your arrival in the United States, include the following:

   Foreign Passport Number: _____

   Country of Issuance: _____

   Some aliens may write "N/A" on the Foreign Passport Number and Country of Issuance fields. (See instructions)

**3-D Barcode**
Do Not Write in This Space

| Signature of Employee: | Date (mm/dd/yyyy): |
|---|---|

## Preparer and/or Translator Certification (To be completed and signed if Section 1 is prepared by a person other than the employee.)

I attest, under penalty of perjury, that I have assisted in the completion of this form and that to the best of my knowledge the information is true and correct.

| Signature of Preparer or Translator: | Date (mm/dd/yyyy): |
|---|---|

| Last Name (Family Name) | First Name (Given Name) |
|---|---|

| Address (Street Number and Name) | City or Town | State | Zip Code |
|---|---|---|---|

🛑 **Employer Completes Next Page** 🛑

Form I-9  03/08/13  N

## Section 2. Employer or Authorized Representative Review and Verification

*(Employers or their authorized representative must complete and sign Section 2 within 3 business days of the employee's first day of employment. You must physically examine one document from List A OR examine a combination of one document from List B and one document from List C as listed on the "Lists of Acceptable Documents" on the next page of this form. For each document you review, record the following information: document title, issuing authority, document number, and expiration date, if any.)*

**Employee Last Name, First Name and Middle Initial from Section 1:**

| List A | OR | List B | AND | List C |
|---|---|---|---|---|
| Identity and Employment Authorization | | Identity | | Employment Authorization |

| List A | List B | List C |
|---|---|---|
| Document Title: | Document Title: | Document Title: |
| Issuing Authority: | Issuing Authority: | Issuing Authority: |
| Document Number: | Document Number: | Document Number: |
| Expiration Date *(if any)(mm/dd/yyyy)*: | Expiration Date *(if any)(mm/dd/yyyy)*: | Expiration Date *(if any)(mm/dd/yyyy)*: |
| Document Title: | | |
| Issuing Authority: | | |
| Document Number: | | |
| Expiration Date *(if any)(mm/dd/yyyy)*: | | **3-D Barcode** **Do Not Write in This Space** |
| Document Title: | | |
| Issuing Authority: | | |
| Document Number: | | |
| Expiration Date *(if any)(mm/dd/yyyy)*: | | |

## Certification

**I attest, under penalty of perjury, that (1) I have examined the document(s) presented by the above-named employee, (2) the above-listed document(s) appear to be genuine and to relate to the employee named, and (3) to the best of my knowledge the employee is authorized to work in the United States.**

The employee's first day of employment *(mm/dd/yyyy)*: _____ (*See instructions for exemptions.*)

| Signature of Employer or Authorized Representative | Date *(mm/dd/yyyy)* | Title of Employer or Authorized Representative | | |
|---|---|---|---|---|
| Last Name *(Family Name)* | First Name *(Given Name)* | Employer's Business or Organization Name | | |
| Employer's Business or Organization Address *(Street Number and Name)* | City or Town | | State | Zip Code |

## Section 3. Reverification and Rehires *(To be completed and signed by employer or authorized representative.)*

| A. New Name *(if applicable)* Last Name *(Family Name)* First Name *(Given Name)* | Middle Initial | B. Date of Rehire *(if applicable) (mm/dd/yyyy)*: |
|---|---|---|

**C.** If employee's previous grant of employment authorization has expired, provide the information for the document from List A or List C the employee presented that establishes current employment authorization in the space provided below.

| Document Title: | Document Number: | Expiration Date *(if any)(mm/dd/yyyy)*: |
|---|---|---|

**I attest, under penalty of perjury, that to the best of my knowledge, this employee is authorized to work in the United States, and if the employee presented document(s), the document(s) I have examined appear to be genuine and to relate to the individual.**

| Signature of Employer or Authorized Representative: | Date *(mm/dd/yyyy)*: | Print Name of Employer or Authorized Representative: |
|---|---|---|

Form I-9  03/08/13 N

# LISTS OF ACCEPTABLE DOCUMENTS
## All documents must be UNEXPIRED

Employees may present one selection from List A
or a combination of one selection from List B and one selection from List C.

| LIST A | | LIST B | | LIST C |
|---|---|---|---|---|
| **Documents that Establish Both Identity and Employment Authorization** | **OR** | **Documents that Establish Identity** | **AND** | **Documents that Establish Employment Authorization** |

| LIST A | LIST B | LIST C |
|---|---|---|
| 1. U.S. Passport or U.S. Passport Card | 1. Driver's license or ID card issued by a State or outlying possession of the United States provided it contains a photograph or information such as name, date of birth, gender, height, eye color, and address | 1. A Social Security Account Number card, unless the card includes one of the following restrictions:<br><br>(1) NOT VALID FOR EMPLOYMENT<br><br>(2) VALID FOR WORK ONLY WITH INS AUTHORIZATION<br><br>(3) VALID FOR WORK ONLY WITH DHS AUTHORIZATION |
| 2. Permanent Resident Card or Alien Registration Receipt Card (Form I-551) | | |
| 3. Foreign passport that contains a temporary I-551 stamp or temporary I-551 printed notation on a machine-readable immigrant visa | 2. ID card issued by federal, state or local government agencies or entities, provided it contains a photograph or information such as name, date of birth, gender, height, eye color, and address | |
| 4. Employment Authorization Document that contains a photograph (Form I-766) | | 2. Certification of Birth Abroad issued by the Department of State (Form FS-545) |
| | 3. School ID card with a photograph | 3. Certification of Report of Birth issued by the Department of State (Form DS-1350) |
| 5. For a nonimmigrant alien authorized to work for a specific employer because of his or her status: | 4. Voter's registration card | |
| a. Foreign passport; and | 5. U.S. Military card or draft record | 4. Original or certified copy of birth certificate issued by a State, county, municipal authority, or territory of the United States bearing an official seal |
| b. Form I-94 or Form I-94A that has the following: | 6. Military dependent's ID card | |
| (1) The same name as the passport; and | 7. U.S. Coast Guard Merchant Mariner Card | |
| (2) An endorsement of the alien's nonimmigrant status as long as that period of endorsement has not yet expired and the proposed employment is not in conflict with any restrictions or limitations identified on the form. | 8. Native American tribal document | 5. Native American tribal document |
| | 9. Driver's license issued by a Canadian government authority | 6. U.S. Citizen ID Card (Form I-197) |
| | **For persons under age 18 who are unable to present a document listed above:** | 7. Identification Card for Use of Resident Citizen in the United States (Form I-179) |
| 6. Passport from the Federated States of Micronesia (FSM) or the Republic of the Marshall Islands (RMI) with Form I-94 or Form I-94A indicating nonimmigrant admission under the Compact of Free Association Between the United States and the FSM or RMI | 10. School record or report card | 8. Employment authorization document issued by the Department of Homeland Security |
| | 11. Clinic, doctor, or hospital record | |
| | 12. Day-care or nursery school record | |

**Illustrations of many of these documents appear in Part 8 of the Handbook for Employers (M-274).**

**Refer to Section 2 of the instructions, titled "Employer or Authorized Representative Review and Verification," for more information about acceptable receipts.**

Form I-9   03/08/13  N

# Chapter 12
# JOBSITE SAFETY AND ENVIRONMENTAL FACTORS

## Chapter Survey...

⇨ *Safety Standards*

⇨ *Written Safety Plan Requirements*

⇨ *Safe Hiring and Training*

⇨ *Substance Abuse Policies*

⇨ *Safety Equipment*

⇨ *Emergency Action Plan*

⇨ *OSHA Recordkeeping*

⇨ *OSHA Injury Decision Tree*

⇨ *Material Safety Data Sheets (MSDS)*

⇨ *Overhead Power Line Safety*

⇨ *Benefits of Providing a Safe and Healthy Workplace*

⇨ *Employee Rights*

⇨ *Penalties*

⇨ *Environmental Considerations*

⇨ *U.S. Environmental Protection Agency*

⇨ *Louisiana Department of Environmental Quality*

⇨ *Environmental Law*

⇨ *Air Quality*

⇨ *Asbestos*

⇨ *Clean Water Act*

⇨ *Sedimentation and Erosion Control Measures*

⇨ *Hazardous and Non-Hazardous Solid Waste*

⇨ *Hazardous Substances*

⇨ *Lead*

⇨ *Remodeling or Renovating a Home with Lead-Based Paint (Lead PRE)*

⇨ *Sample OSHA Forms 300, 300A, and 301*

**Safety First:** Creating a safe working environment is not only a good way to run your business, it is the law. Effective management and implementation of workplace safety and health programs add significant value to individuals and companies by reducing the extent, severity, and consequences of work-related injury and illness. As a whole, businesses spend between $145 billion to $290 billion a year in indirect and direct costs associated with occupational injuries and illnesses.

✓ Workplace injuries and illnesses are reduced by approximately 20 to 40 percent when employers establish safety and health programs.

✓ Workers' compensation premiums, employee retraining costs, and absenteeism are decreased by reducing workplace injuries and illnesses.

✓ Increased workplace safety results in increased productivity and morale and ultimately, profits.

## Safety Standards

**Understanding OSHA:** The Occupational Safety and Health Administration (OSHA) was established by the Occupational Safety and Health Act of 1970 (OSH Act). All employers are subject to federal OSHA requirements and some states have adopted a state plan. State standards are at least as strict as the federal plan. The first step to complying with OSHA is to learn the published standards.

The OSHA standards that apply to the construction industry are

✓ 29 CFR 1926, Safety and Health Regulations for the Construction Industry;

✓ 29 CFR 1910, Occupational Safety and Health Standards; and

✓ 29 CFR 1904, Recording and Reporting Occupational Injuries and Illnesses.

It is the employer's responsibility to understand the OSHA standards and quickly correct any violations. Putting together a safety program with these standards in mind can help maximize employee safety and prevent violations before they occur.

**OSHA Poster:** All employers must post the OSHA poster (or state plan equivalent) in a prominent location in the workplace. In construction, employees are generally dispersed to different sites and the OSHA poster must be posted at the location to which employees report each day.

The OSHA poster is downloadable from the OSHA website (www.osha.gov). This website also has useful links to many safety and environmental topics including compliance assistance and laws and regulations. For more information about OSHA, contact

> Occupational Safety and Health Administration (OSHA)
> Office of Small Business Assistance
> Directorate of Cooperative and State Programs
> 200 Constitution Avenue, NW
> Washington, DC 20210
> Telephone: (800) 321-6742 (OSHA)
> Website: www.osha.gov

**OSHA Construction Safety Act:** The Contract Work Hours and Safety Standards Act, commonly known as the Construction Safety Act, sets safety standards for construction contracts on federal projects.

**Louisiana Safety Program:** Louisiana does not have a state-adopted OSHA plan and falls under the federal OSHA laws. The Louisiana Department of Labor (LDOL) promotes workplace safety. There are several resources on the LDOL website to assist employers in writing and implementing safety management programs.

> Louisiana Department of Labor
> OSHA Consultation
> 1001 North 23rd Street
> Baton Rouge, Louisiana 70802-3338
> Telephone: (225) 342-9601
> Email: workplacesafety@ldol.state.la.us
> Website: www.laworks.net

The Safety and Health Achievement Recognition Program (SHARP) provides a free and effective worksite safety program to smaller businesses. Businesses who satisfy specific SHARP requirements are exempt from federal OSHA compliance inspections for a period of one year.

To qualify, a business must

✓ have fewer than 250 employees at one site (or no more than 500 total employees nationwide);

✓ have been in operation for at least one year; and

✓ have a days away/restricted time (DART) rate and total recordable case rate (TRCR) below the national average for that industry.

All requests to participate in the SHARP program are directed to the Workplace Safety Division.

> SHARP Program
> Telephone: (800) 201-2495
> Website: www.laworks.net

# Written Safety Plan Requirements

Employers with 15 or more employees (full- or part-time) are required to have a written safety plan.

The written safety plan must contain the following components:

1. A management policy statement signed by the top executive. The statement must commit resources, responsibility, and accountability to all levels of management and to each employee for the safety program.

2. A list of safety responsibilities for executive and middle-level operating management, supervisors, safety coordinators, and employees.

3. A statement that a supervisor must conduct inspections at least quarterly. A written report of the inspection identifying safety deficiencies and corrective action must be retained for at least one year.

4. Accident investigation procedures of any job-related injury requiring a visit to a clinic or physician, which must be initiated by the injured employee's supervisor as soon as possible on the shift the accident occurs.

Chapter 12: Jobsite Safety and Environmental Factors

5. A statement that a supervisor must conduct safety meetings at least quarterly for all employees.

6. A list of specific safety rules that are distributed to all employees.

7. A training program providing orientation and training of each new employee, existing employees on a new job, or when new equipment, processes, or job procedures are initiated.

8. Recordkeeping documents required to be retained by the employer, including the OSHA logs (kept for five years) and other safety records for a period of one year from the end of the year for which the records are maintained (state requirement).

9. A first aid program providing for a first aid kit and a person trained in first aid.

10. An emergency preparedness plan that protects all employees, visitors, contractors, and vendors in the facility at the time of emergency situations and training procedures for the plan.

# Safe Hiring and Training

**Hire Safe:** The first step to improving safety in the workplace is to hire employees who have a good safety track record. The majority of accidents are caused by unsafe actions, not unsafe conditions. It is important to do thorough applicant screening and check all employment references. If you find that an applicant had safety accidents with a previous employer, chances for additional accidents while working for you are greater.

**Regular Training:** Training on safety practices and policies should be conducted regularly. New employees should receive a copy of your safety policies and sign off on them. Brief 10-minute training sessions can be conducted at the jobsite with your crew daily. During these training sessions, you can review policies and receive feedback from your employees on potential hazards that occur on the jobsite.

*Conduct regular safety training for your employees.*

# Substance Abuse Policies

**Your Bottom Line:** Substance abuse in the workplace can have a profound effect on your business and significantly impact your bottom line. This problem costs American businesses more than $100 billion every year. This loss occurs in

✓ workers' compensation claims,

✓ medical costs,

✓ absenteeism,

✓ lost productivity, and

✓ employee turnover.

For this reason, you should develop a substance free workplace program and make sure that all employees know that substance abuse is not permitted.

**Employee Program:** Develop your program together with your employees. Talk about the benefits of having a substance free workplace and your concern for them to have a safe and healthy work environment. Eliminating substance abuse increases productivity, reduces accidents, and lowers insurance claim costs. Solicit input from your employees on how to implement the program in the workplace and any other suggestions they have.

*Consider this...*

Ninety percent of large businesses have drug-free workplace programs in place today, while 5 percent to 10 percent of small- and medium-sized businesses have implemented similar programs. The irony here is that 75 percent of employed Americans work for small- and medium-sized businesses.

**Communicate Your Policy:** Once you have developed a program, distribute the policy to all employees and have them sign off on it. Your policies should expressly prohibit the illegal use of drugs and/or abuse of alcohol by any employee and spell out the consequences of policy violations. All new employees should receive your policy as part of their orientation. You should also check with your workers' compensation carrier to see if you can receive a credit for having this policy in place.

*Encourage employee participation in developing company safety programs.*

## Safety Equipment

**Prevent Injuries:** Using the proper safety equipment can lower the occurrence of injuries on the job. This equipment might include

- ✓ hard hats,
- ✓ safety shoes/boots,
- ✓ protective eyewear,
- ✓ gloves,
- ✓ fall protection,
- ✓ hearing protection,
- ✓ respirators,
- ✓ protective coveralls, and
- ✓ face shields.

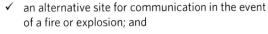

Make sure you consult OSHA safety standards to determine what safety equipment is required by law and assess your jobsite to determine additional equipment you want your employees to have.

## Emergency Action Plan

**Your Plan of Action:** OSHA regulations require you have an emergency action plan. If you have more than 10 employees, your plan must be in writing. If you have fewer than 10 employees, you may communicate the plan orally to employees. The emergency action plan must include procedures for

- ✓ reporting a fire or other emergency;
- ✓ emergency evacuation;
- ✓ employees who remain for critical operations before evacuating;
- ✓ accounting for all employees after evacuation; and
- ✓ employees performing rescue or medical duties.

The plan should also include the name or job title of the plan administrator. You must review the plan with your employees, designate and train employees to assist in a safe evacuation, and have a distinctive signal that serves as an employee alarm system.

Other OSHA recommendations, although not required, for inclusion in the emergency action plan are

- ✓ a description of the employee alarm system defining each of the alarm signals and corresponding employee action;
- ✓ an alternative site for communication in the event of a fire or explosion; and
- ✓ a secure location, either onsite or offsite, where important information, such as accounting documents, legal files, and employee emergency contact numbers, can be stored.

## OSHA Recordkeeping

**For the Record:** Every employer covered by OSHA who has more than 10 employees, except for employers in certain low-hazard industries in the retail, finance, insurance, real estate, and service sectors, must maintain three types of OSHA-specified records of job-related injuries and illnesses.

These forms are located at the end of the chapter.

- ✓ **OSHA Form 300**
- ✓ **OSHA Form 300A**
- ✓ **OSHA Form 301**

The **OSHA Form 300** is an injury/illness log, with a separate line entry for each recordable injury or illness. Such events include work-related deaths, injuries, and illnesses other than minor injuries that require only first aid treatment and that do not involve medical treatment, loss of consciousness, restriction of work, days away from work, or transfer to another job. Construction site operations that last for more than one year must keep a separate OSHA 300 log.

Each year, the employer must conspicuously post in the workplace an OSHA Form 300A, which includes a summary of the previous year's work-related injuries and illnesses. The data from Form 300 is used to complete this form. Form 300A must be posted by February 1 and kept in place until at least April 30 following the year covered by the form.

**OSHA Form 301** is an individual incident report that provides added detail about each specific recordable injury or illness. An alternative form, such as an insurance or workers' compensation form that provides the same details may be substituted for OSHA Form 301.

**Who Needs to Complete the Forms?** Employers with 10 or fewer employees are exempt from maintaining these records. However, such employers must keep these records if they receive an annual illness and injury survey form either from the Bureau of Labor Statistics (BLS) or from OSHA. Employers selected

## Chapter 12: Jobsite Safety and Environmental Factors

for these surveys will be notified before the end of the prior year to begin keeping records during the year covered by the survey.

**Timeframe to Retain Records:** OSHA records must be kept by the employer for five years following the year to which they pertain.

**Exposure Records and Medical Records:** Exposure records (including employee exposure to toxic substances and harmful physical agents) must be maintained for 30 years and medical records for the duration of employment plus 30 years. Analysis using exposure or medical records must be kept for 30 years.

Toxic substances and harmful agents include

✓ any material listed in the National Institute for Occupational Safety and Health (NIOSH) Registry of Toxic Effects of Chemical Hazards (RTECHS);

✓ substances which have evidenced an acute or chronic health hazard in testing conducted by or known to the employer; and

✓ substances in a material safety data sheet kept by or known to the employer, indicating that the material may pose a health hazard.

**Reporting Fatalities and Hospitalizations:** When a work-related fatality or incident that requires hospitalization of three or more employees occurs,

✓ employers must orally report the fatality or incident to the nearest OSHA Area Office within eight hours; and

✓ if a death occurs within 30 days of the incident, employers must report it within eight hours.

Employers do not need to report a death occurring more than 30 days after a work-related incident.

**Recordable Illnesses and Injuries:** Cases that meet the general recording criteria involve a significant injury or illness diagnosed by a physician or other licensed health care professional, even if it does not result in death, days away from work, restricted work or job transfer, medical treatment beyond first aid, or loss of consciousness.

**Medical Treatment Defined:** Medical treatment means the management and care of a patient to combat a disease or disorder. It does not include

✓ visits to a physician or other licensed health care professional solely for observation or counseling;

✓ conduct of diagnostic procedures, such as x-rays and blood tests, including the administration of prescription medications used solely for diagnostic purposes (i.e., eye drops to dilate pupils); or

✓ first aid.

**First Aid Defined:** The following treatments are considered first aid according to 29 CFR 1904:

✓ Using a non-prescription medication at the non-prescription strength

✓ Administering tetanus immunizations (other immunizations, such as the Hepatitis B vaccine or rabies vaccine, are considered medical treatment)

✓ Cleaning, flushing or soaking wounds on the surface of the skin

✓ Using wound coverings such as bandages, Band-Aids™, gauze pads, etc.; or using butterfly bandages or Steri-Strips™; other wound closing devices such as sutures, staples, etc., are considered medical treatment

✓ Using hot or cold therapy

✓ Using any non-rigid means of support, such as elastic bandages, wraps, non-rigid back belts, etc.; devices with rigid stays or other systems designed to immobilize parts of the body are considered medical treatment for recordkeeping purposes

✓ Using temporary immobilization devices while transporting an accident victim (i.e., splints, slings, neck collars, back boards, etc.)

✓ Drilling of a fingernail or toenail to relieve pressure or draining fluid from a blister

✓ Using eye patches

✓ Removing foreign bodies from the eye using only irrigation or a cotton swab

✓ Removing splinters or foreign material from areas other than the eye by irrigation, tweezers, cotton swabs or other simple means

✓ Using finger guards

✓ Using massages; physical therapy or chiropractic treatment are considered medical treatment for recordkeeping purposes

✓ Drinking fluids for relief of heat stress

# OSHA Injury Decision Tree

The OSHA injury decision tree shows the steps involved in making the determination for recording work-related injuries or illnesses.

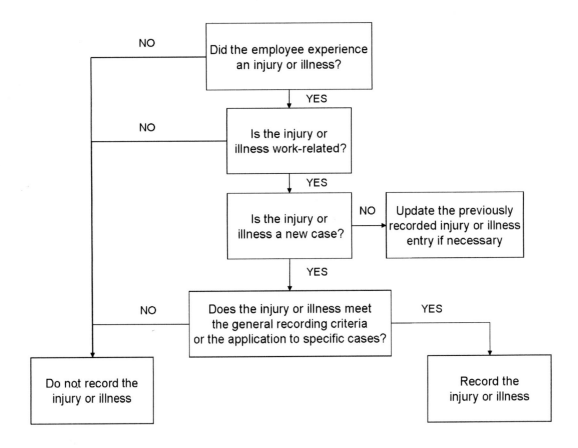

# Material Safety Data Sheets (MSDS)

***Chemical Safety:*** Material safety data sheets (MSDS) are a requirement of OSHA's Hazard Communication Standard (HCS). The purpose of the HCS is to ensure chemical safety in the workplace. Requirements of the MSDS program include:

✓ Manufacturers and importers of hazardous materials are required to conduct hazard evaluations of the products they manufacture or import.

✓ If a product is found to be hazardous under the terms of the standard, the manufacturer or importer must so indicate on containers of the material, and the first shipment of the material to a new customer must include a material safety data sheet (MSDS).

✓ Employers must use these MSDSs to train their employees to recognize and avoid the hazards presented by the materials.

***Emergency Treatment:*** Employers must keep MSDSs on hand for all chemicals used in the workplace. The MSDS provides emergency information in case of contact with the chemical either internally or externally. The MSDS also explains the proper precautions to take when using a chemical. In the event of an OSHA inspection, the compliance officer will confirm that all MSDSs are at the worksite.

***Inspection Guidelines:*** OSHA publishes inspection guidelines for enforcement of the Hazard Communication Standard. A summary of items that are reviewed during an inspection is included below:

✓ Is there a written hazard communication plan?
✓ Who is responsible for obtaining and maintaining MSDSs?
✓ Is there an MSDS for every chemical used?
✓ How are the MSDSs maintained (i.e., in notebooks in the work area(s), in a pickup truck at the jobsite, etc.) and do employees have proper access to them?
✓ Who is responsible for conducting training on chemicals and what are the elements of the training program?

The detailed procedure can be downloaded off the OSHA website (www.osha.gov).

# Overhead Power Line Safety

OSHA has several programs focused on safety for those who work around overhead power lines. Listed below are a few key points from OSHA to consider when formulating a health and safety program and worksite planning.

Considerations include the following:

✓ perform a thorough site survey prior to beginning construction work;

✓ stay at least 10 feet away from overhead power lines;

✓ assume that all power lines are energized unless confirmed by proper authorities;

✓ call the utility company if overhead lines are present to determine voltage and if the lines can be shut off or insulated during construction work;

✓ use non-conductive ladders when working around overhead power lines;

✓ keep conductive objects at least 10 feet away from overhead power lines unless otherwise trained and qualified to use insulated tools specifically designed for high voltage lines; and

✓ perform thorough research on the location and voltage of overhead power lines when using cranes and heavy equipment to determine a minimum safe distance for operation.

Additional information on overhead power line safety is available on the OSHA website at www.osha.gov.

# Benefits of Providing a Safe and Healthy Workplace

Ignoring safety and health regulations in the workplace is detrimental in many ways. Employees are put at risk, company reputation is at stake, and costs are high when accidents happen which effects overall company profits.

The most frequent citations that OSHA issues to the construction industry are for violations pertaining to

✓ scaffolding;
✓ fall protection (scope, application, definitions);
✓ excavations (general requirements and requirements for protective systems);
✓ ladders;
✓ head protection;

- hazard communication;
- fall protection (training requirements);
- construction (general safety and health provisions); and
- electrical (wiring methods, design and protection).

Ensuring workers are healthy and safe provides many direct benefits to employers.

- lower workers' compensation insurance costs;
- reduced medical expenditures;
- smaller expenditures for return-to-work programs;
- fewer faulty products;
- lower costs for job accommodations for injured workers;
- less money spent for overtime benefits.

Following safety and health regulations and proper procedures has indirect benefits as well.

- increased productivity;
- higher quality products;
- increased morale;
- better labor/management relations;
- reduced turnover;
- better use of human resources.

The impact of a safety and health program extends beyond the workplace providing employees and their families the security that their incomes are protected, family life is not hindered by injury, and overall reduced stress.

# Employee Rights

The OSH Act grants employees several important rights. Among them are the rights to

- complain to OSHA about safety and health conditions in their workplace and, to the extent permitted by law, have their identities kept confidential from their employer;
- contest the amount of time OSHA allows for correcting violations of standards; and
- participate in OSHA workplace inspections.

**Retaliation is Prohibited:** Private sector employees who exercise their rights under OSHA can be protected against employer reprisal. Employees must notify OSHA within 30 days of the time they learned of

the alleged discriminatory action. OSHA will then investigate. If it agrees that discrimination has occurred, OSHA will ask the employer to restore any lost benefits to the affected employee. If necessary, OSHA can initiate legal action against the employer. In such cases, the worker pays no legal fees. The OSHA-approved state plans have similar employee rights provisions, including protections against employer reprisal.

# Penalties

**OSHA Enforcement:** Every establishment covered by the OSH Act is subject to inspection by OSHA compliance safety and health officers (CSHOs). These individuals are chosen for their knowledge and experience in occupational safety and health. They are thoroughly trained in OSHA standards and in the recognition of occupational safety and health hazards. In states with their own OSHA-approved state plan, state officials conduct inspections, issue citations for violations, and propose penalties in a manner that is at least as strict as the federal program.

The following table illustrates penalty types, descriptions, and amounts assessed to the employer.

| Penalty Type and Description | Penalty Amount |
|---|---|
| **Other Than Serious Violation** - A violation that has a direct relationship to workplace safety and health, but probably would not cause death or serious physical harm. | Discretionary penalty up to $7,000 for each violation |
| **Serious Violation** - A violation where there is substantial probability that death or serious physical harm could result and that the employer knew, or should have known, of the hazard. | Mandatory penalty up to $7,000 for each violation |

# Chapter 12: Jobsite Safety and Environmental Factors

| Penalty Type and Description | Penalty Amount |
|---|---|
| **Willful Violation** - A violation that the employer knowingly commits or commits with plain indifference to the law. The employer either knows that what he or she is doing constitutes a violation, or is aware that a hazardous condition existed and made no reasonable effort to eliminate it. | Penalties of up to $70,000 with a minimum penalty of $5,000 for each violation. *If an employer is convicted of a willful violation of a standard that has resulted in the death of an employee, the offense is punishable by a court-imposed fine or by imprisonment for up to six months, or both. A fine of up to $250,000 for an individual, or $500,000 for a corporation, may be imposed for a criminal conviction.* |
| **Repeated Violation** - A violation of any standard, regulation, rule, or order where, upon reinspection, a substantially similar violation is found. | Penalties of up to $70,000 |
| **Failure to Abate Prior Violation** - A violation given when a previous violation has not been corrected. | Civil penalty of up to $7,000 for each day the violation continues beyond the prescribed abatement date |
| **De Minimis Violation** – A violation of standards which have no direct or immediate relationship to safety or health. | Violation documented but not cited |

Violations may be adjusted depending on the employer's good faith (demonstrated by efforts to comply with the act), history of previous violations, and size of business.

Additional violations for which citations and proposed penalties may be issued upon conviction include the following:

✓ Falsifying records, reports, or applications can bring a fine of $10,000 or up to six months in jail, or both.

✓ Violations of posting requirements can bring a civil penalty of up to $7,000.

✓ Assaulting a compliance officer, or otherwise resisting, opposing, intimidating, or interfering with a compliance officer while they are engaged in the performance of their duties is a criminal offense, subject to a fine of not more than $5,000 and imprisonment for not more than three years.

Citation and penalty procedures may differ somewhat in states with their own occupational safety and health programs.

*Inspections:* OSHA conducts two general types of inspections: programmed and unprogrammed.

✓ Programmed inspections are performed on establishments with high injury rates.

✓ Unprogrammed inspections are used in response to fatalities, catastrophes, and complaints.

Various OSHA publications and documents detail OSHA's policies and procedures for inspections and the penalties for violations.

# Environmental Considerations

You need to be aware of environmental considerations surrounding construction during all phases of the project.

✓ During the pre-bid phase, you must learn the regulations that pertain to the project and factor the cost of compliance into the estimate.

✓ Obtaining the necessary permits occurs during the pre-construction phase and environmental responsibilities should be assigned to the construction crew.

✓ Self-audits help ensure compliance during the construction phase.

✓ For post-construction, you need to ensure that all the close-down procedures were done properly.

# U.S. Environmental Protection Agency

*Environmental Regulation:* The U.S. Environmental Protection Agency (EPA) leads the nation's environmental science, research, education, and assessment efforts. The EPA works to develop and enforce regulations that implement environmental laws enacted by Congress. The EPA is responsible for researching and setting national standards for a variety of environmental programs and delegates to states the responsibility for issuing permits and for monitoring and enforcing compliance. If national standards are not met, the EPA can issue sanctions and take other steps to assist states in reaching the desired levels of environmental quality.

**Compliance Assistance:** The EPA publishes a guide called Managing Your Responsibilities: A Planning Guide for Construction and Development. This publication is available for download at: http://www.epa.gov.

This guide provides comprehensive information for all types of environmental hazards and compliance requirements. Summarized briefly below are some of the environmental hazards impacting construction projects.

# Louisiana Department of Environmental Quality

The Louisiana Department of Environmental Quality has environmental, compliance, and assessment services.

**Environmental Services:** The Environmental Services Division regulates pollution sources, permits activities consistent with laws and regulations, and provides an interface between the department and businesses. Outreach, educational materials, and environmental assistance related to pollution, manifests, recycling, and litter are available to the public and businesses.

**Environmental Compliance:** The Environmental Compliance Division conducts inspections of permitted facilities and activities, responds to environmental emergencies, and issues sound enforcement actions.

**Environmental Assessment:** The Environmental Assessment Division develops and implements environmental regulations, constructs strategic plans, reports on the performance of the environment, provides technical expertise, and monitors the remediation of environmental contaminants.

> Louisiana Department of Environmental Quality
> 602 N. Fifth Street
> Baton Rouge, Louisiana 70802
>
> Phone: (225) 219-5337 or (866) 896-5337
>
> Website: www.deq.louisiana.gov

Before beginning a project, you should assess the jobsite and determine if you need an environmental permit. The Louisiana Department of Environmental Quality website provides useful links to permitting resources.

# Environmental Law

There are several environmental laws that may impact your construction activities.

✓ The Clean Water Act establishes the basic structure for regulating discharges of pollutants into the waters of the United States. This act gives the EPA authority to implement pollution control programs, such as setting wastewater standards for the industry and water quality standards for all contaminants in surface waters. This act is discussed in more depth later in this chapter.

✓ Through the Clean Air Act, the EPA sets limits on how much of a pollutant is allowed in the air anywhere in the United States.

✓ The Endangered Species Act (ESA) protects threatened or endangered species from further harm. You should consider the impact of your construction activities on these species before you start your project.

✓ The National Environmental Policy Act (NEPA) applies to your construction project only if it is considered a "federal action." This act ensures that federal agencies consider environmental impacts in federal planning and decision making and covers construction and post-construction activities.

✓ The National Historic Preservation Act (NHPA) applies to your construction project if your project might have a potential impact on a property that is eligible for or included on the National Register of Historic Places (NRHP).

A thorough environmental assessment of your construction site is recommended for all projects. This assessment allows you to understand the environmental impacts of your project early, causing fewer delays and problems.

# Air Quality

**Outdoor Air Quality:** Air regulations for construction activities are designed to limit the generation of particulate and ozone depleting substances.

Air quality issues that may impact your business are

- ✓ uncontrolled open burning of debris,
- ✓ dust generation,
- ✓ vehicle emissions,
- ✓ combustion gases from oil-fired equipment, and
- ✓ releases of chlorofluorocarbons (CFCs).

**Indoor Air:** Indoor air quality can be just as important as outdoor air quality. For the safety of those on the construction site, you should give special consideration to materials that contain harmful chemicals including

- ✓ paint/primers,
- ✓ adhesives,
- ✓ floor coatings,
- ✓ carpet, and
- ✓ plywood/particle board.

Properly installed HVAC units and drain pans are important to avoid biological contaminants that breed in stagnant water. Most air permitting requirements for construction activities are at the state and local level.

**Air Permits Division:** The Air Permits Division (APD) of the Louisiana Office of Environmental Services is responsible for preparing the following types of air permits:

- ✓ Part 70 (Title V) Operating permits
- ✓ Part 70 General Operating permits
- ✓ Prevention of Significant Deterioration (PSD) permits
- ✓ Nonattainment New Source Review (NNSR) permits
- ✓ State (minor source) permits
- ✓ State (minor source) General permits
- ✓ Acid Rain (Title IV) permits
- ✓ Clean Air Interstate Rule (CAIR) permits
- ✓ Regulatory

The APD also handles a number of other activities, including requests for administrative amendments, authorizations to construct, changes of tank service, Emission Reduction Credit (ERC) certificates, exemptions to test, small source exemptions, and variances. See the Louisiana Guidance for Air Permitting Actions manual distributed by the Louisiana Department of Environmental Quality for a more thorough description of required permits and the permitting process.

*Air Permits Division*
*P.O. Box 4313*
*Baton Rouge, Louisiana 70821-4313*

*Phone: (225) 219-3181*
*Fax: (225) 219-3309*

*Be aware of both indoor and outdoor pollution.*

# Asbestos

Before beginning any demolition or renovation activities on existing buildings, you should evaluate the potential for releasing asbestos. Exposure to asbestos can cause serious health problems and the EPA and OSHA have published rules regulating its production, use, and disposal.

**Evaluation Guidelines:** When evaluating whether or not asbestos may be present, you want to note possible asbestos-containing material, such as

- ✓ Insulation, including blown, rolled and wrapped
- ✓ Resilient floor coverings (tiles)
- ✓ Asbestos siding shingles
- ✓ Asbestos-cement products
- ✓ Asphalt roofing products
- ✓ Vermiculite insulation

The EPA has a comprehensive list of suspected asbestos-containing materials at: www.epa.gov.

**Inspections:** If you are working with asbestos, you should have your site inspected by a certified asbestos inspector prior to construction. You must submit a written Notice of Intent 10 working days prior to starting construction activities. Written notices should be submitted to your delegated state/local pollution control agency and your EPA Regional Office.

*Asbestos Accreditation and Notification:* The Louisiana Department of Environmental Quality has several resources on their website for working with asbestos. Accreditation and notification forms are available for download. Asbestos abatement and removal contractors must obtain the proper certifications and approvals from the Louisiana Department of Environmental Quality and the proper license classification from the Louisiana Licensing Board for Contractors.

# Clean Water Act

Water pollution can negatively affect the use of water for drinking, household needs, recreation, fishing, transportation and commerce. The EPA enforces federal clean water and safe drinking water laws, provides support for municipal wastewater treatment plants, and takes part in pollution prevention efforts aimed at protecting watersheds and sources of drinking water.

The Clean Water Act establishes the basic structure for regulating discharges of pollutants into the waters of the United States. This includes

✓ giving the EPA the authority to implement pollution control programs such as setting wastewater standards for industry;

✓ continuing requirements to set water quality standards for all contaminants in surface waters; and

✓ making it unlawful for any person to discharge any pollutant from a point source into navigable waters, unless a National Pollutant Discharge Elimination System (NPDES) permit was obtained under its provisions.

*Stormwater Discharges and Construction Site Runoff:* Before beginning any construction project, you must consider runoff and stormwater discharges that may originate from your site. These discharges often contain sediment and pollutants such as phosphorous and nitrogen (fertilizer), pesticides, oil and grease, concrete truck washout, construction chemicals, and solid wastes in quantities that could adversely affect water quality.

*National Pollutant Discharge Elimination System (NPDES):* The EPA has estimated that about 30 percent of known pollution to our nation's waters is

attributable to stormwater runoff. In 1987, Congress directed the EPA to develop a regulatory program to address the stormwater problem. The EPA issued regulations in 1990 authorizing the creation of a NPDES permitting system for stormwater discharges from a select group, including construction activities disturbing five or more acres.

In 1999, the EPA expanded this program (called Phase II). This phase brought about two major new permittees:

✓ Construction sites that disturb one acre but less than five acres with possible exceptions allowing a waiver

✓ Small municipal separate storm sewer systems (MS4)

A "larger common plan of development or sale" is subject to stormwater permitting, even if the land is parceled off or sold, and construction occurs on plots that are less than one acre by separate, independent builders.

*Assessing Stormwater Discharge:* Listed below are questions that you need to consider when determining the need for a stormwater permit for your construction project:

✓ Will your construction project disturb one or more acres of land?

✓ Will your construction project disturb less than one acre of land, but is part of a larger common plan of development or sale that will disturb one or more acres?

✓ Will your construction project disturb less than one acre of land, but is designated by the NPDES (state agency or EPA) permitting authority as a regulated construction activity?

✓ Will stormwater from the construction site flow to a separate municipal storm sewer system or a water of the United States such as a lake, river, or wetland?

*Municipal Technologies Agency:* The EPA's Municipal Technologies Agency provides assistance in the area of municipal wastewater treatment technologies. Available assistance includes

✓ consultation on design, operation, and maintenance of systems;

✓ identification and solution of problems;

## Chapter 12: Jobsite Safety and Environmental Factors

✓ contributions in the development of regulations; and

✓ technical information, guidance, assessments, evaluation, and cost estimates for the design, construction, and operation and maintenance of municipal wastewater treatment facilities.

**Water Permits Division:** The Water Permits Division of the Office of Environmental Services authorizes permits administered under the Water Quality Regulations.

In addition, the Water and Waste Permits Division facilitates Biosolids Management and LDEQ's responsibilities for Water Quality Certifications in conjunction with the U.S. Army Corps of Engineers.

✓ **Water Permits:** LPDES and General Permits are issued through the Water Permits Division (see following section).

✓ **Water Quality Certifications:** A water quality certification is a statement that a proposed activity will not have an unacceptable impact on water quality, and is issued in accordance with Section 401 of the federal Clean Water Act. A Water Quality Certification is not a permit to perform the proposed activity but is often required in order to obtain a permit from another agency.

✓ **Biosolids:** Permit applications for the use or disposal of sewage sludge (biosolids) in Louisiana are available through the Water Permits Division.

Water Permits Division
P.O. Box 4313
Baton Rouge, Louisiana 70821-4313

Phone: (225) 219-9371
Fax: (225) 219-3309

**Louisiana Pollutant Discharge Elimination System (LPDES):** The Louisiana Pollutant Discharge Elimination System (LPDES) program establishes stringent standards to protect Louisiana's water quality. The LPDES program is stricter than the national program. It is important for you to understand your responsibilities to avoid hefty penalties and possible project delays.

Pursuant to Louisiana Administrative Code, Title 33, Chapter IX, permits are required for the discharge of pollutants from any point source into waters of the State of Louisiana. By law, a point source is defined as, "any discernible, confined, and discrete conveyance,

including but not limited to any pipe, ditch, channel, tunnel, conduit, well, discrete fissure, container, rolling stock, concentrated animal feeding operation, landfill leachate collection system, vessel, or other floating craft from which pollutants are or may be discharged."

Several types of LPDES general permits are available and may apply to your construction activities. The following is a list of permits issued under the LPDES General Permits program (not all-inclusive):

✓ Discharges from Construction, Demolition Debris and Woodwaste Landfills

✓ Discharges resulting from Construction Activities greater than 5 acres

✓ Discharges resulting from Construction Activities greater than 1 acre but less than 5 acres

✓ Discharges from Cement, Concrete & Asphalt Facilities

✓ Discharges associated with Dewatering of Petroleum Storage Tanks, Tank Beds, New Tanks and Excavations

✓ Discharges from Potable Water Treatment Plants

✓ Discharges from Light Commercial Facilities

✓ Discharges from Sand and Gravel Extraction Facilities

✓ Sanitary discharges totaling less than 5,000 gpd

✓ Sanitary discharges totaling less than 25,000 gpd

✓ Sanitary discharges totaling less than 50,000 gpd

✓ Sanitary discharges totaling less than 100,000 gpd

✓ Discharges of Hydrostatic Test Wastewater

✓ Discharges of Exterior Vehicle Washwater

✓ Discharges resulting from Implementing Corrective Action Plans for Cleanup of Petroleum UST Systems

✓ Discharges of Treated Groundwater, Potentially Contaminated Stormwater, and/or associated waters

✓ Discharges from Small Municipal Separate Storm Sewer Systems

✓ Multi-Sector General Stormwater Permit

✓ Short-Term and Emergency Discharges

✓ Discharges from Construction, Demolition Debris and Woodwaste Landfills

General permits expire five years after the effective date. Individual permit holders must apply for and obtain a new permit after the expiration date. Unless the appropriate permission is granted, you must reapply for an individual permit at least 180 days prior to expiration of your current permit.

If you are unsure about the type of permit needed, a formal request for assistance can be made through the Water Permits Division. The Request for Preliminary Determination of LPDES Permit Issuance form must be submitted with proper documentation.

Permit noncompliance constitutes a violation of the Clean Water Act (CWA) and the Louisiana Environmental Quality Act. Noncompliance may result in permit termination, revocation and reissuance, modification, or denial of a permit renewal application. In addition, violators are subject to criminal and administrative penalties.

Full text of the LPDES regulations is available at www.deq.louisiana.gov or by contacting the Office of Environmental Assessment, Regulations Development Section at (225) 219-3550.

# Sedimentation and Erosion Control Measures

During a short period of time, construction sites can contribute more sediment to streams than can be deposited naturally during several decades. Excess sediment can quickly fill rivers and lakes, requiring dredging, and destroying aquatic habitats.

Measures can be taken to minimize erosion and sedimentation on construction sites:

✓ Sediment control measures include a silt fence or hay bales placed at the down gradient side of the construction site.

✓ Erosion control measures include placing mulch and vegetation as soon as feasible to permanently stabilize the site soil.

✓ A water misting system can control dust generated on the jobsite and loss of soil.

Erosion and sediment control minimizes pollution and contractor costs to rework eroded areas and replace lost soil. Individual states may have required sedimentation and erosion control measures.

# Excavation Safety

Demolishing, excavating, backfilling, tunneling, mechanical probing, pile driving, etc. can often be a part of a construction project. Any jobsite safety program must include necessary precautions to prevent injury either to employees or to the general public. In addition, the Louisiana Underground Utilities and Facilities Damage Prevention Law requires that the jobsite safety program must include precautions to prevent damage to underground utilities, which may include conduit, wire, cable, valves or any other structure that is below ground to transport electricity, oil, gas, fiber optics, hazardous materials, sewer lines, drainage systems, water, etc.

This law also requires that a "notice of intent to excavate or demolish" must be given to a regional notification center between 48 and 120 hours prior to digging.

Louisiana One Call is one such entity and it may be reached by dialing 811.

After receiving notification, the utility company or service that is affected marks the specific location of the underground utility plus eighteen inches on either side. The marks are then considered valid until they are no longer visible, or until 120 calendar days from the "mark by" time. An excavator must protect the marks by using any reasonable means. If the utilities are damaged, all work must stop until the owner or operator of the utilities has the opportunity to make the necessary repairs before excavation may resume.

In the event of an emergency situation that may cause a danger to the general public or to the workmen on the site, the law provides an exception to the required 48 hour notification. In such cases, the contractor may give an oral notification and the affected utility service must provide protection to its facility.

Those who are in violation of this statute shall be fined according to the nature of the violation. For more information about the law concerning notification, refer to the website www.laonecall.com.

# Hazardous and Non-Hazardous Solid Waste

In general, construction sites generate more non-hazardous waste than hazardous waste. You should be aware of the regulations surrounding both.

***Non-Hazardous Waste:*** Common non-hazardous waste generated at construction sites includes

- ✓ scrap wood,
- ✓ drywall,
- ✓ bricks,
- ✓ concrete,
- ✓ plumbing fixtures and piping,
- ✓ roof coverings,
- ✓ metal scraps, and
- ✓ electrical wiring and components.

Non-hazardous waste is regulated at the state and local level and you should identify any requirements. For more information on state requirements, refer to the Construction Industry Compliance Assistance Center at www.cicacenter.org.

***Hazardous Waste:*** Hazardous waste is regulated at the federal level and your state may have additional requirements.

Examples of hazardous waste are

- ✓ lead-based paint,
- ✓ used oil,
- ✓ hydraulic fluid,
- ✓ gypsum drywall (due to sulfate), and
- ✓ mercury-containing demolition wastes such as batteries and thermostats.

***Proper Notification:*** If you discover hazardous waste on your jobsite, you must notify state and local authorities or the National Response Center Hotline at (800) 424-8802. Criminal charges may be filed if hazardous wastes are present at the site and proper notification does not take place. If hazardous waste is produced through construction activities, the party that generated the waste is generally responsible for cleaning it up. Hazardous waste must be treated and disposed of at a facility permitted or licensed for that purpose by the state or federal government.

***Louisiana Right-to-Know Law:*** If you maintain your own construction yard or store chemicals, you may be subject to the rules provided by the state's Right-to-Know law.

This law covers the following:

- ✓ Facilities that handle, use, store, or manufacture any hazardous material(s) in excess of the threshold inventory quantity;
- ✓ Facilities, transportation-related operations, and transport vehicles from which a reportable release occurs; and
- ✓ All surface and subsurface related modes of hazardous materials transportation including but not limited to all water, air, highway, rail, and pipeline operations.

Inventory reporting is required for hazardous materials that exceed threshold quantities as defined by law. You also have the responsibility of reporting hazardous material spills and incidents to your local emergency planning committee and the Office of the State Police, Transportation and Environmental Safety Section through the Hazardous Materials Hotline at (225) 925-6595 or (877) 925-6595.

In addition to the requirements set forth by the Louisiana Licensing Board for Contractors, all hazardous materials and hazardous wastes emergency response and spill contractors are required to register with the Office of the State Police, Right-to-Know Unit.

Full text of the Right-to-Know law is found in the Louisiana Administrative Code, Title 33, Part V, Chapter 101. The Right-to-Know law is administered by the Louisiana State Police, Transportation and Environmental Safety Section, Right-to-Know Unit. Additional information is available online at www.lsp.org/rtk.html or by calling (225) 925-6113.

## Hazardous Substances

***Site Survey:*** Before beginning any construction or demolition activities at your construction site, you should evaluate the site for hazardous substances.

Hazardous substances referred to in this section are chemicals that most likely induce serious acute reactions from short-term airborne exposure.

***Notification:*** When you do a site survey, you should review historical records to determine previous uses of the site. A review of state and local files will help you identify past environmental concerns. If during construction you uncover hazardous substances, you must stop construction activities immediately and notify the owner and contact the National Response Hotline at (800) 424-8802.

**Underground Storage Tanks (UST):** An underground storage tank system (UST) is defined by the EPA as "a tank and any underground piping connected to the tank that has at least 10 percent of its combined volume underground." The federal UST regulations apply only to underground tanks and piping storing either petroleum or certain hazardous substances. Federal regulations do not apply to the following types of underground storage tanks:

✓ Farm and residential tanks of 1,100 gallons or less capacity holding motor fuel used for noncommercial purposes

✓ Tanks storing heating oil used on the premises where it is stored

✓ Tanks on or above the floor of underground areas, such as basements or tunnels

✓ Septic tanks and systems for collecting storm water and wastewater

✓ Flow-through process tanks

✓ Tanks of 110 gallons or less capacity

✓ Emergency spill and overfill tanks

*Conduct a thorough site survey to anticipate any environmental hazards.*

# Lead

**Exposure Hazards:** Lead is considered a toxic and hazardous substance and can cause a serious risk of lead poisoning if overexposure occurs. OSHA regulates the amount of lead that workers can be exposed to (no more than 50 micrograms of lead per cubic meter of air averaged over an 8-hour day). Traditionally, most over-exposure occurs in trades such as plumbing, welding, and painting.

**Hazard Protection:** The most effective way to protect workers is through good work practices and engineering controls. Respirators are not a substitute for these practices, but should be an additional measure of safety. Employers are required to supply respirators at no cost to employees who will

potentially be exposed to lead and adopt a respirator program, including a written standard operating procedure, training, and regular equipment inspection.

Engineering controls to reduce worker exposure include

✓ exhaust ventilation, such as power tools with dust collection shrouds or other attachments exhausted through a high-efficiency particulate air (HEPA) vacuum system;

✓ enclosure or encapsulation of lead particles (for example, lead-based paint can be made inaccessible by encapsulating it with a material that bonds to the surface such as epoxy coating);

✓ substituting lead-based products or products that create lead exposure with a comparable product;

✓ replacing lead components with non-lead components;

✓ process or equipment modifications that create less lead exposure from dust; and

✓ isolating the lead exposure area so other areas are not contaminated.

**Construction Assistance:** OSHA has downloadable software on its website designed to help small business owners understand the Lead in Construction standard. Users should still refer to OSHA standards for specific details as it represents the most up-to-date source.

**Lead Accreditation and Notification:** The Louisiana Department of Environmental Quality has several resources on their website for working with lead. Accreditation and notification forms are available for download. Lead-based paint abatement and removal contractors must obtain the proper certifications and approvals from the Louisiana Department of Environmental Quality and the proper license classification from the Louisiana Licensing Board for Contractors.

# Remodeling or Renovating a Home with Lead-Based Paint (Lead PRE)

If not conducted properly, certain types of renovations can release lead from paint and dust into the air. The Lead Pre-Renovation Education Rule (Lead PRE)

# Chapter 12: Jobsite Safety and Environmental Factors

is a federal regulation involving those performing renovations for compensation in residential housing that may contain lead paint.

In December 2008 (with amendments in 2010 and 2011), the EPA passed the Lead-Based Paint Renovation, Repair and Painting Program Rule that imposes additional lead-based paint regulations. Under this rule, only certified contractors can perform renovation, repair and painting projects that disturb lead-based paint in homes, child care facilities, and schools built before 1978. The EPA has authorized Alabama, Georgia, Iowa, Kansas, Massachusetts, Mississippi, North Carolina, Oregon, Rhode Island, Utah, Washington, and Wisconsin to administer their own Renovation, Repair and Painting Program. Contractors working in these states must follow the regulations put forth by the state program.

Contractors can become certified renovators by submitting an application and fee to the EPA or state-based program and taking an eight-hour training course from an EPA-accredited training provider. Certified contractors must follow specific work practices to prevent lead contamination. Three simple principles are applied when working with lead which includes:

✓ containing the work area to minimize lead contamination in other work areas;

✓ minimizing dust to prevent harmful airborne particles from being inhaled; and

✓ cleaning up the work area thoroughly.

***Required Notification:*** Under Lead PRE, federal law requires that contractors provide lead information to residents before renovating pre-1978 housing. The EPA publishes a pamphlet titled Protect Your Family from Lead in Your Home which must be distributed to the owner and occupants before starting work. Confirmation of receipt of the lead pamphlet or a certificate of mailing must be kept for 3 years. For work in common areas of multi-family housing, renovation notices must be distributed to all tenants.

For renovations to child-occupied facilities, renovators must distribute the pamphlet titled Renovate Right: Important Lead Hazard Information for Families, Child Care Providers and Schools to owners, administrators, and parents or guardians of children under the age of six that attend these facilities.

***Exemptions:*** This rule applies to nearly all remodeling or renovation work with the exception of the following circumstances:

✓ Housing for the elderly or disabled persons unless children will reside there

✓ Zero-bedroom dwellings

✓ Emergency renovations or repairs

✓ Minor repair and maintenance that disturb two square feet or less of paint per component

✓ Housing or components declared lead-free by a certified inspector or risk assessor

***Lead Abatement:*** Work designed to permanently eliminate lead-based paint hazards is considered lead abatement and is not subject to the guidelines under Lead PRE. This does not include renovation, remodeling, landscaping, or other activities designed to repair, restore, and redesign a given building. The EPA outlines strict regulations for this type of work as discussed in the previous section on lead.

***Renovation:*** Renovations under Lead PRE are modifications of all or part of any existing structure that disturbs a painted surface. This includes

✓ removal/modification of painted surfaces, components or structures;

✓ surface preparation activities (sanding/scraping/other activities that may create paint dust); and

✓ window replacement.

***Penalties:*** Failure to comply with regulations concerning lead is a serious violation. Non-compliance carries substantial fines of up to $37,500 per day for each violation. Criminal penalties of imprisonment for up to one year also apply to willful or intentional violation of the regulation.

***Assistance:*** You can obtain additional information by going online to the EPA website at www.epa.gov/lead or by contacting The National Lead Information Center (NLIC) at (800) 424-LEAD.

# Final Inspection...

***Safety Standards:*** It is important to know the OSHA standards that pertain to the construction industry.

***Written Safety Plan Requirements:*** Louisiana employers with 15 or more employees (full- or part-time) are required to have a written safety plan with the required elements as defined by law.

**Safe Hiring and Training:** Background checks can help you hire workers with good safety records. Regular training contributes to a safe working environment.

**Substance Abuse Policies:** Substance abuse compromises safety in the workplace. Clearly written and communicated policies are useful tools in reducing substance abuse.

**Safety Equipment:** Certain safety equipment may be required according to OSHA regulations, depending on the work being performed.

**Emergency Action Plan:** Either a written or an orally communicated emergency action plan is required by OSHA, depending on the number of employees you have.

**OSHA Recordkeeping:** Your company may be required to complete OSHA forms 300, 300A and 301.

**OSHA Injury Decision Tree:** The OSHA injury decision tree outlines the steps in making the determination for recording work-related injuries and illnesses.

**Material Safety Data Sheets (MSDS):** A material safety data sheet (MSDS) is required for all chemicals used.

**Excavation Safety:** Although laws on marking underground utilities vary from state to state, contractors should identify underground utilities before excavating.

**Overhead Power Line Safety:** Overhead power line safety should be considered when formulating a health and safety program and worksite planning. As a general rule, workers should a minimum distance of 10 feet from overhead power lines.

**Benefits of Providing a Safe and Healthy Workplace:** OSHA can assess citations for failing to provide a safe work environment. Ensuring workers are healthy and safe provides many direct and indirect benefits to employers.

**Employee Rights:** Employees are allowed to report OSHA violations without fear of retaliation.

**Penalties:** Penalties vary depending on the severity of OSHA violations. OSHA may conduct programmed or unprogrammed inspections.

**Environmental Considerations:** Environmental factors should be considered throughout all phases of construction. Obtaining proper permits is important for following environmental regulations.

**U.S. Environmental Protection Agency (EPA):** The EPA works to develop and enforce regulations that implement environmental laws enacted by Congress.

**Louisiana Department of Environmental Quality:** The Louisiana Department of Environmental Quality has several programs and activities that provide environmental and permitting assistance.

**Environmental Law:** Several laws exist to protect the environment. An assessment of environmental impacts should be done early on in the construction project.

**Air Quality:** Indoor and outdoor quality should be monitored throughout the construction project.

**Asbestos:** Before beginning remodeling or demolition of any project, assess whether you may encounter asbestos-releasing materials. Certain permitting and notification requirements may apply.

**Clean Water Act:** The Clean Water Act establishes the basic structure for regulating discharges of pollutants into the waters of the United States.

**Sedimentation and Erosion Control Measures:** Erosion and sediment control measures minimize pollution and contractor costs to rework eroded areas and replace lost soil.

**Hazardous and Non-Hazardous Waste:** Most construction waste is non-hazardous. Both hazardous and non-hazardous waste must be disposed of properly.

**Hazardous Substances:** Early identification of hazardous substances is important and proper notification is required.

**Lead:** Contact with lead can cause lead poisoning and you and your employees must follow specific regulations when working with it.

**Remodeling or Renovating a Home with Lead-Based Paint:** The Lead Pre-Renovation Education Rule (Lead PRE) is a federal regulation involving those performing renovations for compensation in residential housing that may contain lead paint.

# Supplemental Forms

Supplemental forms and links are available at **NASCLAforms.org** using access code **LA129354**.

| | |
|---|---|
| OSHA Forms for Recording Work-Related Injuries and Illnesses | OSHA forms 300, 300A and 301 with instructions |
| OSHA Compliance Assistance Employment Law Guide | OSHA guide summarizing employer responsibilities under the OSH Act |
| Managing Your Environmental Responsibilities: A Planning Guide for Construction and Development | EPA guide customized for the construction industry that outlines specific environmental responsibilities |
| Protect Your Family From Lead in Your Home | Mandatory brochure to distribute to the owner if you are doing renovations on pre-1978 housing |

OSHA's Form 300 (Rev. 01/2004)

# Log of Work-Related Injuries and Illnesses

**Attention:** This form contains information relating to employee health and must be used in a manner that protects the confidentiality of employees to the extent possible while the information is being used for occupational safety and health purposes.

Year 20___

**U.S. Department of Labor**
**Occupational Safety and Health Administration**

Form approved OMB no. 1218-0176

*You must record information about every work-related death and about every work-related injury or illness that involves loss of consciousness, restricted work activity or job transfer, days away from work, or medical treatment beyond first aid. You must also record significant work-related injuries and illnesses that are diagnosed by a physician or licensed health care professional. You must also record work-related injuries and illnesses that meet any of the specific recording criteria listed in 29 CFR Part 1904.8 through 1904.12. Feel free to use two lines for a single case if you need to. You must complete an Injury and Illness Incident Report (OSHA Form 301) or equivalent form for each injury or illness recorded on this form. If you're not sure whether a case is recordable, call your local OSHA office for help.*

Establishment name ____________

City ____________ State ____________

| Identify the person | | | Describe the case | | | Classify the case: CHECK ONLY ONE box for each case based on the most serious outcome for that case: | | | | Enter the number of days the injured or ill worker was: | | Check the "Injury" column or choose one type of illness: (M) | | | | | |
|---|---|---|---|---|---|---|---|---|---|---|---|---|---|---|---|---|---|
| | | | | | | | | Remained at Work | | | | | | | | | |
| (A) Case no. | (B) Employee's name | (C) Job title (*e.g., Welder*) | (D) Date of injury or onset of illness | (E) Where the event occurred (*e.g., Loading dock north end*) | (F) Describe injury or illness, parts of body affected, and object/substance that directly injured or made person ill (*e.g., Second degree burns on right forearm from acetylene torch*) | Death (G) | Days away from work (H) | Job transfer or restriction (I) | Other record-able cases (J) | Away from work (K) | On job transfer or restriction (L) | Injury (1) | Skin disorder (2) | Respiratory condition (3) | Poisoning (4) | Hearing loss (5) | All other illnesses (6) |
| | | | / month/day | | | ☐ | ☐ | ☐ | ☐ | ___ days | ___ days | ☐ | ☐ | ☐ | ☐ | ☐ | ☐ |
| | | | / month/day | | | ☐ | ☐ | ☐ | ☐ | ___ days | ___ days | ☐ | ☐ | ☐ | ☐ | ☐ | ☐ |
| | | | / month/day | | | ☐ | ☐ | ☐ | ☐ | ___ days | ___ days | ☐ | ☐ | ☐ | ☐ | ☐ | ☐ |
| | | | / month/day | | | ☐ | ☐ | ☐ | ☐ | ___ days | ___ days | ☐ | ☐ | ☐ | ☐ | ☐ | ☐ |
| | | | / month/day | | | ☐ | ☐ | ☐ | ☐ | ___ days | ___ days | ☐ | ☐ | ☐ | ☐ | ☐ | ☐ |
| | | | / month/day | | | ☐ | ☐ | ☐ | ☐ | ___ days | ___ days | ☐ | ☐ | ☐ | ☐ | ☐ | ☐ |
| | | | / month/day | | | ☐ | ☐ | ☐ | ☐ | ___ days | ___ days | ☐ | ☐ | ☐ | ☐ | ☐ | ☐ |
| | | | / month/day | | | ☐ | ☐ | ☐ | ☐ | ___ days | ___ days | ☐ | ☐ | ☐ | ☐ | ☐ | ☐ |
| | | | / month/day | | | ☐ | ☐ | ☐ | ☐ | ___ days | ___ days | ☐ | ☐ | ☐ | ☐ | ☐ | ☐ |
| | | | / month/day | | | ☐ | ☐ | ☐ | ☐ | ___ days | ___ days | ☐ | ☐ | ☐ | ☐ | ☐ | ☐ |
| | | | / month/day | | | ☐ | ☐ | ☐ | ☐ | ___ days | ___ days | ☐ | ☐ | ☐ | ☐ | ☐ | ☐ |
| | | | / month/day | | | ☐ | ☐ | ☐ | ☐ | ___ days | ___ days | ☐ | ☐ | ☐ | ☐ | ☐ | ☐ |
| | | | / month/day | | | ☐ | ☐ | ☐ | ☐ | ___ days | ___ days | ☐ | ☐ | ☐ | ☐ | ☐ | ☐ |
| | | | | | **Page totals** ➤ | ___ | ___ | ___ | ___ | ___ | ___ | ___ | ___ | ___ | ___ | ___ | ___ |
| | | | | | | | | | | | | Injury (1) | Skin disorder (2) | Respiratory condition (3) | Poisoning (4) | Hearing loss (5) | All other illnesses (6) |

*Be sure to transfer these totals to the Summary page (Form 300A) before you post it.*

Public reporting burden for this collection of information is estimated to average 14 minutes per response, including time to review the instructions, search and gather the data needed, and complete and review the collection of information. Persons are not required to respond to the collection of information unless it displays a currently valid OMB control number. If you have any comments about these estimates or any other aspects of this data collection, contact: US Department of Labor, OSHA Office of Statistical Analysis, Room N-3644, 200 Constitution Avenue, NW, Washington, DC 20210. Do not send the completed forms to this office.

# OSHA's Form 300A (Rev. 01/2004)
## Summary of Work-Related Injuries and Illnesses

**Year 20\_\_\_**
**U.S. Department of Labor**
Occupational Safety and Health Administration

Form approved OMB no. 1218-0176

All establishments covered by Part 1904 must complete this Summary page, even if no work-related injuries or illnesses occurred during the year. Remember to review the Log to verify that the entries are complete and accurate before completing this summary.

Using the Log, count the individual entries you made for each category. Then write the totals below, making sure you've added the entries from every page of the Log. If you had no cases, write "0."

Employees, former employees, and their representatives have the right to review the OSHA Form 300 in its entirety. They also have limited access to the OSHA Form 301 or its equivalent. See 29 CFR Part 1904.35, in OSHA's recordkeeping rule, for further details on the access provisions for these forms.

### Establishment information

Your establishment name _____

Street _____

City _____ State _____ ZIP _____

Industry description (e.g., Manufacture of motor truck trailers) _____

Standard Industrial Classification (SIC), if known (e.g., 3715) \_\_\_\_ \_\_\_\_ \_\_\_\_ \_\_\_\_

OR

North American Industrial Classification (NAICS), if known (e.g., 336212) _____

### Employment information *(If you don't have these figures, see the Worksheet on the back of this page to estimate.)*

Annual average number of employees _____

Total hours worked by all employees last year _____

### Sign here

Knowingly falsifying this document may result in a fine.

I certify that I have examined this document and that to the best of my knowledge the entries are true, accurate, and complete.

_____  _____
Company executive                                            Title

(  )
_____    _____
Phone                                              Date

### Number of Cases

| Total number of deaths | Total number of cases with days away from work | Total number of cases with job transfer or restriction | Total number of other recordable cases |
|---|---|---|---|
| \_\_\_\_\_ | \_\_\_\_\_ | \_\_\_\_\_ | \_\_\_\_\_ |
| (G) | (H) | (I) | (J) |

### Number of Days

| Total number of days away from work | Total number of days of job transfer or restriction |
|---|---|
| \_\_\_\_\_ | \_\_\_\_\_ |
| (K) | (L) |

### Injury and Illness Types

Total number of...
(M)

(1) Injuries _____    (4) Poisonings _____
(2) Skin disorders _____    (5) Hearing loss _____
(3) Respiratory conditions _____    (6) All other illnesses _____

**Post this Summary page from February 1 to April 30 of the year following the year covered by the form.**

Public reporting burden for this collection of information is estimated to average 50 minutes per response, including time to review the instructions, search and gather the data needed, and complete and review the collection of information. Persons are not required to respond to the collection of information unless it displays a currently valid OMB control number. If you have any comments about these estimates or any other aspects of this data collection, contact: US Department of Labor, OSHA Office of Statistical Analysis, Room N-3644, 200 Constitution Avenue, NW, Washington, DC 20210. Do not send the completed forms to this office.

# OSHA's Form 301
## Injury and Illness Incident Report

**U.S. Department of Labor**
Occupational Safety and Health Administration

Form approved OMB no. 1218-0176

**Attention:** This form contains information relating to employee health and must be used in a manner that protects the confidentiality of employees to the extent possible while the information is being used for occupational safety and health purposes.

This *Injury and Illness Incident Report* is one of the first forms you must fill out when a recordable work-related injury or illness has occurred. Together with the *Log of Work-Related Injuries and Illnesses* and the accompanying *Summary*, these forms help the employer and OSHA develop a picture of the extent and severity of work-related incidents.

Within 7 calendar days after you receive information that a recordable work-related injury or illness has occurred, you must fill out this form or an equivalent. Some state workers' compensation, insurance, or other reports may be acceptable substitutes. To be considered an equivalent form, any substitute must contain all the information asked for on this form.

According to Public Law 91-596 and 29 CFR 1904, OSHA's recordkeeping rule, you must keep this form on file for 5 years following the year to which it pertains.

If you need additional copies of this form, you may photocopy and use as many as you need.

Completed by _____
Title _____
Phone ( ___ ) ___ - ____   Date ___ / ___ / ___

### Information about the employee

1) Full name _____
2) Street _____
   City _____ State ____ ZIP _____
3) Date of birth ___ / ___ / ___
4) Date hired ___ / ___ / ___
5) ☐ Male  ☐ Female

### Information about the physician or other health care professional

6) Name of physician or other health care professional _____
7) If treatment was given away from the worksite, where was it given?
   Facility _____
   Street _____
   City _____ State ____ ZIP _____
8) Was employee treated in an emergency room?
   ☐ Yes  ☐ No
9) Was employee hospitalized overnight as an in-patient?
   ☐ Yes  ☐ No

### Information about the case

10) Case number from the *Log* _____ (Transfer the case number from the Log after you record the case.)
11) Date of injury or illness ___ / ___ / ___
12) Time employee began work _____ AM / PM
13) Time of event _____ AM / PM  ☐ Check if time cannot be determined
14) **What was the employee doing just before the incident occurred?** Describe the activity, as well as the tools, equipment, or material the employee was using. Be specific. *Examples:* "climbing a ladder while carrying roofing materials"; "spraying chlorine from hand sprayer"; "daily computer key-entry."
15) **What happened?** Tell us how the injury occurred. *Examples:* "When ladder slipped on wet floor, worker fell 20 feet"; "Worker was sprayed with chlorine when gasket broke during replacement"; "Worker developed soreness in wrist over time."
16) **What was the injury or illness?** Tell us the part of the body that was affected and how it was affected; be more specific than "hurt," "pain," or sore." *Examples:* "strained back"; "chemical burn, hand"; "carpal tunnel syndrome."
17) **What object or substance directly harmed the employee?** *Examples:* "concrete floor"; "chlorine"; "radial arm saw." *If this question does not apply to the incident, leave it blank.*
18) **If the employee died, when did death occur?** Date of death ___ / ___ / ___

Public reporting burden for this collection of information is estimated to average 22 minutes per response, including time for reviewing instructions, searching existing data sources, gathering and maintaining the data needed, and completing and reviewing the collection of information. Persons are not required to respond to the collection of information unless it displays a current valid OMB control number. If you have any comments about this estimate or any other aspects of this data collection, including suggestions for reducing this burden, contact: US Department of Labor, OSHA Office of Statistical Analysis, Room N-3644, 200 Constitution Avenue, NW, Washington, DC 20210. Do not send the completed forms to this office.

# Chapter 13
# WORKING WITH SUBCONTRACTORS

## Chapter Survey...
⇨ Sources for Finding the Right Subcontractor
⇨ Creating a Winning Partnership
⇨ Site Rules for Contractors
⇨ Employee or Independent Contractor: IRS Guidelines

Subcontractors contract with the general contractor or other subcontractors to complete a portion of a larger project.

It is important to hire the right subcontractors because their work impacts your company's reputation. Just as you want employees who are easy to work with, the same applies to subcontractors.

There are basic criteria you can use to evaluate whether you want to hire a subcontractor:

✓ Do they sell or produce quality products?
✓ Are they reliable? Are they able to complete the project according to the schedule?
✓ Do they have good customer service skills?
✓ Are they able to effectively deal with problems?
✓ Do they give an overall impression of professionalism?
✓ Are they properly licensed and carry appropriate insurance coverage?
✓ Do they remedy situations that involve material defects or failures?
✓ How do they handle change orders?
✓ Are they competitively priced?

Now that you have established your requirements, it is time to find qualified leads.

## Sources for Finding the Right Subcontractor

If you have a good reputation, the word travels fast. This also holds true for good subcontractors and suppliers. Some of your best subcontractors can come from referrals. Sources for these referrals might include:

✓ subcontractors in a different field who have worked with other subcontractors on other jobs;
✓ other contractors in your field;
✓ members of your local trade association;
✓ suppliers (for example, electrical supply firms can give referrals on electricians); and
✓ architects or engineers.

Once you come up with credible referrals, you want to make sure that you take extra steps to organize the process.

✓ Keep a list of qualified subcontractors.
✓ Allow sufficient lead time to line up subcontractors for jobs.
✓ Interview subcontractors for their qualifications, even when you are not scheduling them for a job.
✓ Check references if you have not worked with the subcontractor before.
✓ Ensure all subcontractors you work with have proper insurance coverage; request copies of insurance certificates and follow up to ensure coverage is current (as discussed in Chapter 4).

## Creating a Winning Partnership

Once you have done all your homework and made your subcontractor selections, you'll want to create a relationship that will set both parties up for success.

✓ Provide an orientation on your policies and procedures.

- ✓ Be clear on all instructions and solicit questions.
- ✓ Be open to feedback and suggestions.
- ✓ Reward good work and provide constructive comments on improvements.
- ✓ Schedule trades so the job is ready for them and there are minimal barriers for them to complete their job.
- ✓ Visit the jobsite before the start of your portion of the project to tell other subcontractors your requirements (if it applies).
- ✓ Complete an IRS W-9 form prior to starting work.

## Site Rules for Contractors

As part of an orientation with your subcontractors, you may want to review your site rules. Listed below are some rules to consider:

- ✓ Keep the jobsite clean and free of debris.
- ✓ All safety policies and OSHA regulations must be followed.
- ✓ You must provide your own tools and equipment.
- ✓ Work must be compliant with all applicable codes.
- ✓ Keep radios on the jobsite at a moderate listening level and free of offensive content.
- ✓ Behave professionally and do not use foul language.
- ✓ Salvage of items is prohibited without permission.

Site rules can be posted at the jobsite so they are visible to everyone and serve as a continual reminder.

## Employee or Independent Contractor: IRS Guidelines

The IRS outlines specific guidelines regarding the difference between employees and independent contractors. Make sure you are working within an independent contractor relationship and not an employer-employee basis. If you do have an employer-employee relationship, your company is liable for payroll taxes, workers' compensation and employee benefits for that subcontractor.

To determine whether an individual is an employee or an independent contractor under common law, the relationship of the worker and your company must be examined. In any employee-independent contractor determination, all information that provides evidence of the degree of control and the degree of independence must be considered.

Evidence of the degree of control and independence falls into three categories: behavioral control, financial control and the type of relationship of the parties.

### Behavioral Control

Facts that show whether a business has a right to direct and control how the worker does the task for which the worker is hired include the type and degree of:

- ✓ **Instruction the business gives to the worker:** An employee is generally subject to the business' instructions about when, where, and how to work. In a subcontractor relationship, the business generally gives up the right to control the details of the worker's performance.
- ✓ **Training the business gives to the worker:** An employee may be trained to perform services in a particular manner. Independent contractors ordinarily use their own methods.

### Financial Control

Facts that show whether the business has a right to control the business aspects of the worker's job include:

- ✓ **The extent to which the worker has un-reimbursed business expenses:** Independent contractors are more likely to have un-reimbursed expenses than are employees. Fixed ongoing costs that are incurred regardless of whether work is currently being performed are especially important.
- ✓ **The extent of the worker's investment:** An independent contractor often has a significant investment in the facilities he or she uses in performing services for someone else. However, a significant investment is not necessary for independent contractor status.
- ✓ **The extent to which the worker makes his or her services available to the relevant market:** An employee is generally guaranteed a regular wage amount for an hourly, weekly, or other period of

# Chapter 13: Working with Subcontractors

time for one employer. An independent contractor is usually paid a flat fee by the business with which he or she has contracted. An independent contractor is free to manage multiple contracts.

✓ **The extent to which the worker can realize a profit or loss:** An independent contractor can make a profit or loss.

## Type of Relationship

Facts that show the parties' type of relationship include:

✓ Written contracts describing the relationship the parties intend to create

✓ Whether the business provides the worker with employee-type benefits, such as insurance, a pension plan, vacation pay, or sick pay

✓ **The permanency of the relationship:** If you engage a worker with the expectation that the relationship will continue indefinitely rather than for a specific project or period, this is generally considered an employer-employee relationship.

✓ **The extent to which services performed by the worker are a key aspect of the regular business of the company:** If a worker provides services that are a key aspect of your regular business activity, it is more likely that you will have a right to direct and control his or her activities, indicating an employer-employee relationship.

Now that you know the rules, let's look at a few practical examples to demonstrate how classifications are made.

**Example 1:** Milton Manning, an experienced tile setter, orally agreed with a corporation to perform full-time services at construction sites. He uses his own tools and performs services in the order designated by the corporation and according to its specifications. The corporation supplies all materials, makes frequent inspections of his work, pays him on a piecework basis, and carries workers' compensation insurance on him. He does not have a place of business or hold himself out to perform similar services for others. Either party can end the services at any time. Milton Manning is an employee of the corporation.

**Example 2:** Vera Elm, an electrician, submitted a job estimate to a housing complex for electrical work at $16 per hour for 400 hours. She is to receive $1,280 every two weeks for the next 10 weeks. This is not considered payment by the hour. Even if she works more or less than 400 hours to complete the work, Vera Elm will receive $6,400. She also performs additional electrical installations under contracts with other companies that she obtained through advertisements. Vera is an independent contractor.

*Assistance in Determining Status:* If you are unable to determine whether the working relationship is on an employer-employee or employer-independent contractor basis, the IRS can assist by reviewing the circumstances of the working relationship and officially determining the individual's status. To request this review, a Form SS-8, Determination of Worker Status for Purposes of Federal Employment Taxes and Income Tax Withholding, is submitted to the IRS. This form and other assistance are available online at www.irs.gov.

# Final Inspection...

*Sources for Finding the Right Subcontractor:* Referrals are a good way to find the right subcontractors. As you collect referrals, develop a process to organize and appropriately schedule them.

*Creating a Winning Partnership:* Establishing good communication and having clear policies in place set a solid foundation for positive subcontractor relationships.

*Site Rules for Contractors:* Subcontractors should receive an orientation on your site rules before starting work. Site rules should be posted at the jobsite so they are visible to everyone and serve as a continual reminder.

*Employee or Independent Contractor: IRS Guidelines:* The IRS uses behavioral control, financial control, and the type of relationship of the parties to make a determination whether someone is an employee or independent contractor.

# PART 3
# Office Administration

# Chapter 14
# FINANCIAL MANAGEMENT

## Chapter Survey...
⇨ Bookkeeping
⇨ The Accounting Cycle
⇨ Methods of Accounting
⇨ Contract Accounting
⇨ Cash Management
⇨ Equipment Records and Accounting
⇨ Depreciation Methods
⇨ Accounting Process for Materials
⇨ Payroll Accounting
⇨ Technology Solutions for Accounting

Accounting is important to all businesses because it helps measure the financial fitness of the company. It is a process of collecting, analyzing, and reporting information to develop tools, such as financial statements, that are used to evaluate different financial aspects of the company.

## Bookkeeping

The first step in the accounting process is bookkeeping. Bookkeeping involves the accurate recording of all financial transactions that occur in the business. Financial statements are derived from this information.

Here are a few tips to maintain accurate and timely bookkeeping:

✓ Open a separate business checking account and obtain a business credit card to keep business and personal finances separate.

✓ Keep track of all deductible expenses (discussed later in this chapter).

✓ Keep all receipts and identify the source of all receipts so you can separate business from personal receipts and taxable from non-taxable income.

✓ Update business records daily to have quick access to the daily financial position of your business.

✓ Accurately record all information in the checkbook ledger including date, who the check was written to, the amount, and the reason the check was written.

✓ Record expenses when they occur, so you have an accurate picture of your cash situation.

✓ Avoid paying with cash, so you have a "paper trail" of your expenditures.

✓ Balance your checking account monthly. You may want to request month-end bank statements to coordinate with other month-end records.

✓ Keep all financial records for the required amount of time as designated by the IRS.

Bookkeeping involves the clerical side of accounting and requires only minimal knowledge of the entire accounting cycle. You may want to consult with a professional accountant for the more complex financial decision-making of your business.

## The Accounting Cycle

The accounting cycle is a series of events that is repeated each reporting period. The cycle begins with a transaction and ends with closing the books and preparing financial statements. Steps in the accounting cycle include

1. Classifying and recording transactions,
2. Posting transactions,
3. Preparing a trial balance,
4. Preparing an adjusted trial balance,
5. Preparing financial statements, and
6. Analyzing financial statements.

**Classify and Record Transactions**

The accounting cycle begins with classifying and recording daily transactions. A **transaction** is an event that either increases or decreases an account balance. A **source document** is the proof that a transaction took place. Examples of source documents include

- ✓ cash receipts,
- ✓ credit card receipts,
- ✓ customer invoices,
- ✓ purchase orders,
- ✓ materials invoices,
- ✓ deposit slips, and
- ✓ time cards.

Daily transactions are recorded in a set of books called **journals**. Typical journals that companies keep include:

- ✓ **Cash receipts and sales journal:** This journal is used when cash comes in or a sale is charged to a customer.
- ✓ **Purchases journal:** This journal tracks all purchases made by the company.
- ✓ **Cash disbursements journal:** This journal is used when cash is paid out. Transactions such as loan payments and payments on vendor invoices are recorded here.
- ✓ **Payroll journal:** This journal is used to record a summary of payroll details, such as salaries and wages, deductions, and employer contributions.
- ✓ **General journal:** This journal is used for non-cash transactions.

 **Post Transactions**

**Posting** is the process of transferring the transactions recorded in the journals to the appropriate accounts. An **account** is a register of value. Each account can be totaled to determine the balance. For example, cash is an asset account having a specific balance. Most companies use five basic types of accounts:

- ✓ Asset
- ✓ Liability
- ✓ Equity
- ✓ Income
- ✓ Expense

The **chart of accounts** is a numbering system that organizes these account types. A typical chart of accounts is listed below.

1000-1999: Assets

2000-2999: Liabilities

3000-3999: Equity

4000-4999: Revenue

5000-5999: Cost of Goods Sold

6000-6999: Expenses

7000-7999: Other Revenue (i.e., interest income)

8000-8999: Other Expenses (i.e., income taxes)

The accounts are located in the **general ledger**. When you post transactions, you are transferring them from the journal to the general ledger.

 **Prepare Trial Balance**

When you tally the accounts, you prepare a trial balance. The **trial balance** is a total of all the ledger accounts.

At this point in the accounting cycle, you want to make sure the debits equal the credits.

***Understanding Debits and Credits:*** Every accounting entry in the general ledger contains both a debit and a credit which must equal each other. Depending on what type of account you are dealing with, a debit or credit will either increase or decrease the account balance. The entries that increase or decrease each type of account are listed below.

| Account Type | Debit | Credit |
| --- | --- | --- |
| Assets | Increases | Decreases |
| Liabilities | Decreases | Increases |
| Equity | Decreases | Increases |
| Income | Decreases | Increases |
| Expenses | Increases | Decreases |

For the accounts to balance, there must be a debit in one account and a credit in another. You may hear terms such as the *left side* or *right side* of the balance sheet. Something on the left side is simply a debit and the right side is a credit.

If you have any ledger account column totals that do not balance, look for math, posting, and recording errors.

# Chapter 14: Financial Management

## Prepare Adjusted Trial Balance

There are six general types of adjusting entries:

- ✓ prepaid expense,
- ✓ accrued expense,
- ✓ accrued revenue,
- ✓ unearned revenue,
- ✓ estimated items, and
- ✓ inventory adjustment.

When you make adjusting entries, include an explanation as to why the change was made. Once adjusting entries are made, you must go back and tally the account balances where changes were made.

## Prepare Financial Statements

Now that you have posted transactions to your accounts and made adjusting entries, you can prepare your financial statements.

The three basic types of financial statements companies use are

- ✓ **balance sheet,**
- ✓ **income statement, and**
- ✓ **statement of cash flows.**

Financial statements are tools that give insight into the financial health and activities of the company.

## Balance Sheet

The balance sheet is one of the basic accounting financial statements. It gives the owner good insight into the growth and stability of the company at a particular point in time.

The balance sheet equation is comprised of assets, liabilities, and owners' equity:

### Assets = Liabilities + Owners' Equity

Assets are items of value owned by the business. The cash in your bank account and other assets that can be converted into cash in less than one year are considered current assets. They are important because they are used to fund daily operations and can be liquidated easily.

Property and equipment (sometimes referred to as capital or fixed assets) are assets needed to carry on the business of a company and are not normally consumed in the operation of the business. Land, buildings, equipment, and furniture would all be considered fixed assets.

Other current assets consist of prepaid expenses, such as security deposits, and other miscellaneous assets, such as long-term investments.

Your company may also own intangible assets. Examples of these include patents, franchises, and goodwill from the acquisition of another company. It is not as easy to value these assets. Generally, the value of intangible assets is a value both parties agree to when the assets are created.

Liabilities are all debt and obligations owed by the business. Liabilities that will mature and must be paid within one year are called current liabilities. Trade credit is usually considered a current liability because it is a short-term debt.

Long-term liabilities are debt obligations that extend beyond one year. Examples of this type of liability include bank loans and deferred taxes.

Owners' equity is made up of the initial investment in the business, plus accumulated net profits not paid out to the owners.

Working capital can also be determined by looking at the balance sheet. The following equation is used to determine working capital.

### Current Assets – Current Liabilities = Working Capital

Working capital measures the liquidity of the company's assets. Liquid assets are those that are easily converted to cash. Licensing agencies may look at working capital to determine license limitations.

The balance sheet is usually requested by potential lenders to determine credit limits. The following sample illustrates how the balance sheet equation and accounts are used in the balance sheet.

## Quality Construction Compay
## Balance Sheet
## December 31, 20XX

### ASSETS

| | | |
|---|---|---|
| Current Assets: | | |
| Cash | $ 1,200 | |
| Accounts Receivable | 25,200 | |
| Total Current Assets | | $ 26,400 |
| Property and Equipment: | | |
| Equipment | $ 53,200 | |
| Building | 120,000 | |
| Land | 75,000 | |
| Total Property and Equipment | | 248,200 |
| TOTAL ASSETS | | $ 274,600 |

### LIABILITIES AND OWNERS' EQUITY

| | | |
|---|---|---|
| Current Liabilities: | | |
| Accounts Payable | $ 4,900 | |
| Payroll Taxes Payable | $ 3,300 | |
| Total Current Liabilities | | $ 8,200 |
| Long-term Liabilities | | |
| Notes Payable | $ 6,700 | |
| Mortgage Payable | $ 195,000 | |
| Total Long-term Liabilities | | 201,700 |
| Owners' Equity | | 64,700 |
| TOTAL LIABILITIES AND OWNERS' EQUITY | | $ 274,600 |

# Chapter 14: Financial Management

## Income Statement

The income statement, sometimes called the **profit-and-loss statement**, is a summary of the company's revenues and expenses over a given period of time.

The profit equation provides the basis for the income statement and is comprised of the following:

**Income – Cost of Goods Sold = Gross Profit**

**Gross Profit – Expenses = Net Income**

**Revenues** are the income received from the daily operations of the business. Most companies have only a few revenue accounts, but if you have several lines of business, you may want to create an account for each.

**Expenses** are the monies paid out or owed for goods or services over a given period of time. Most companies have separate accounts for the different types of expenses incurred.

**Direct costs** are those directly linked with a particular project. On a construction project, your direct costs might include materials, subcontractor fees, permit fees, and labor.

**Operating expenses** (sometimes called indirect expenses) are the general items that contribute to the cost of operating the business. These expenses can

be put into two categories, **selling expenses** and **fixed overhead.** Selling expenses are the costs incurred to market the business. Fixed overhead expenses are those that cannot be linked to a specific project but are necessary for the operation of the business. For example, if you rent warehouse space to store your equipment year round, you would include this item in your bookkeeping under fixed overhead.

**Tax provision expenses** are the tax liabilities your company has for federal, state, and local taxes. Depending on your business structure, this section of the income statement will vary.

**Net profit** is the difference between revenues and expenses. Net profit directly contributes to the net worth of the company.

If net profit is on the positive side, those earnings are placed in a retained earnings or equity account.

If net profit is negative, it will reduce the net worth of the company.

**The income statement is used by investors or lenders to determine the profitability of the company.** The following sample illustrates how the income statement equation and accounts are used in the income statement.

Quality Construction Compay
Income Statement
For the Period Ended December 31, 20XX

REVENUES:

| | | |
|---|---|---|
| Construction Sales | $ 545,600 | |
| Less Direct Labor | 120,500 | |
| Less Direct Materials | 257,000 | |
| Gross Profit | | $ 168,100 |

EXPENSES:

Selling Expenses:

| | | |
|---|---|---|
| Advertising | $ 3,400 | |
| Salaries - Sales | 49,500 | |
| Total Selling Expense | $ 52,900 | |

Administrative Expenses:

| | | |
|---|---|---|
| Salaries - Office | $ 34,400 | |
| Telephone | 4,800 | |
| Insurance Expenses | 29,700 | |
| Total Administrative Expenses | $ 68,900 | |
| Total Expenses | | 121,800 |
| NET INCOME | | $ 46,300 |

Quality Construction Compay
Statement of Owners' Equity
For the Period Ended December 31, 20XX

| | |
|---|---|
| Beginning Owners' Equity | $ 92,400 |

# Chapter 14: Financial Management

## Statement of Cash Flows

The statement of cash flows summarizes your current cash position, your cash sources, and use of these funds over a given period of time. This financial statement lists changes in cash based on operating, investing, and financing activities.

The **operating activities** portion of the statement shows the performance of the company to generate a positive or negative cash flow from the operations.

The **investing activities** section lists the cash used or provided to purchase or sell revenue-producing assets.

The **financing activities** section measures the flow of cash between the owners and creditors.

**If you want to finance a major project, the lender will likely want to look at your statement of cash flows.** This financial statement provides good insight into the company's ability to meet its obligations. The company may appear profitable on other statements, but a lack of cash flow may indicate pending financial problems.

### Notes to the Financial Statements

The notes to the financial statements contain important information that is relevant but have no specific place within the financial statement.

✓ **Accounting policies and procedures** important to the company's financial condition and results are disclosed in the notes section.

✓ Detailed information about **current and deferred income taxes** is broken down by federal, state, and local categories. The primary factors that affect the company's tax rate are described.

✓ Specific information about the assets and costs of a **pension plan and other retirement programs** are explained and indicate whether the plans are over- or underfunded.

Anything that affects the financial health of the company that cannot be reflected in the financial statements should be reported in this section.

### STEP 6 — Analyze Financial Statements Using Financial Ratios

By using the basic concepts of the balance sheet and income statement, you can analyze them through financial ratios. Ratios can serve as a benchmark for the company's internal performance and as a comparison against industry averages.

## Liquidity Ratio

The liquidity ratio (sometimes called the **current ratio**) is calculated by dividing the current liabilities into the current assets.

### Current Assets ÷ Current Liabilities = Liquidity (or Current) Ratio

The liquidity ratio determines if the company can pay its current debts. If the ratio is greater than one, the company is in a positive liquidity position. The higher the number, the better liquidity position the company has.

## Quick Ratio

The quick ratio (sometimes called the **acid test ratio**) is similar to the liquidity ratio. It is calculated by dividing the current liabilities into the current assets minus inventory.

### (Current Assets – Inventory) ÷ Current Liabilities = Quick Ratio

A quick ratio of one or more is generally acceptable by most creditors. A higher number indicates a stronger financial position and a lower number a weaker position.

## Activity Ratio

The activity ratio measures how effectively the company manages its credit. The formula for determining the average collection period is as follows:

### Revenue ÷ Days in the Business Year = Sales per Day

### Current Receivables ÷ Sales per Day = Average Collection Period

The company is in a better position when the average collection period is shorter (or the number is lower). This means that the company is converting credit accounts into cash faster.

## Debt Ratio

The debt ratio measures the percent of total funds provided by creditors. The formula is as follows:

### Total Debt ÷ Total Assets = Debt Ratio

Companies want to keep their debt ratio relatively low to avoid overextending debt.

## Profitability Ratio

The profitability ratio is used to calculate the profit margin of the company. The formula is as follows:

**Net Income ÷ Revenues =
Profit Margin**

The higher the profit margin percentage, the more profitably the company is performing.

### Return on Total Assets Ratio

The return on total assets ratio is used to determine if the company's assets are being employed in the best manner. The formula is:

**Net Profit (after taxes) ÷ Total Assets =
Return on Total Assets**

The company is in a favorable position when the percentage return on total assets is high.

# Methods of Accounting

An accounting method is a set of rules used to determine when and how income and expenses are reported. There are two basic methods of accounting used to keep track of the company's income and expenses. These are

- ✓ **Cash method**
- ✓ **Accrual method**

The primary difference between the methods is in when the transactions are recorded to your accounts.

## Cash Method

Using the cash method of accounting, you report income in the year you receive it and deduct expenses in the year you paid them. This is the easier of the two accounting methods. Although it is a simpler method, it holds a significant disadvantage. The cash method does not match revenues with the expenses incurred related to that revenue. This gives an inaccurate picture of the company's overall financial situation.

## Accrual Method

Using the accrual method, you recognize income when the services occur, not when you collect the money. The same principal is applied to expenses, which are recorded when they are incurred, not when you pay for them. Most construction businesses use the accrual method of accounting.

## Changing Your Method of Accounting

Once you have set up your accounting method and file your first tax return, you must get IRS approval before you can change to another method. A change in accounting method not only includes a change in your overall system of accounting, but also a change in the treatment of any material item.

# Contract Accounting

Most construction businesses use two tax accounting methods; one for their long-term contracts and one overall method for everything else. A long-term contract is defined as any contract that is not completed in the same year it was started.

The choice of your contract accounting method depends on

- ✓ the type of contracts you have;
- ✓ your contracts' completion status at the end of your tax year; and
- ✓ your average annual gross receipts.

Each method discussed assumes that you use a calendar tax year from January 1 to December 31.

## Completed Contract Method

Under the completed contract method, income or loss is reported in the year the contract is completed. Direct materials, labor costs, and all indirect costs associated with the contract must be allocated or capitalized to the same account as the income or loss. If the completed contract method is used for long-term contracts (contracts spanning over two calendar years), you may not allocate costs properly and you might overstate deductions.

The advantage of the completed contract method is that it normally achieves maximum deferral of taxes.

The disadvantages of the completed contract method are

- ✓ the books and records do not show clear information on operations;
- ✓ income can be bunched into a year when a lot of jobs are completed; and
- ✓ losses on contracts are not deductible until the contracts are completed.

The completed contract method may be used only by small contractors whose average annual gross receipts do not exceed $10 million for the three tax years preceding the tax year of the contract.

## Percentage of Completion Method

The percentage of completion method recognizes income as it is earned during the construction project.

# Chapter 14: Financial Management

The biggest advantage of using this method for long-term contracts is that it does a better job of matching revenue to the expenses incurred related to that revenue. Accurate matching of revenue to expenses gives you a better picture of your financial position.

The disadvantage of the percentage of completion method is that it relies on estimates. You are estimating the degree of completion on the project and the income and expenses. The true numbers are not realized until the project is complete.

Percentage of completion is calculated individually by project. To determine the percentage of completion, use the following formula:

**Project Costs Incurred ÷ Total Estimated Costs = Percentage of Completion**

Once the percentage of completion is calculated, the cumulative earnings can be figured by using the following formula:

**Percentage of Completion x Contract Amount = Cumulative Earnings**

Adjustments must be made on the balance sheet for billings that are over or under the cumulative earnings. To figure the amount over or under cumulative earnings, use the following formula:

**Cumulative Earnings – Amount Billed to Date = Billing Overage/Deficiency**

Billings in excess of the cumulative earnings are considered a current liability. Billings less than cumulative earnings are considered a current asset.

Using these formulas, a percentage of completion worksheet example is shown below.

| Project Name | Contract Amount | Estimated Cost | Project Cost to Date | Percent Complete | Cumulative Earnings | Amount Billed to Date | Billing Overage/ Deficiency |
|---|---|---|---|---|---|---|---|
| Project #1 | 70,000 | 62,350 | 35,500 | 56.94% | 39,858 | 40,150 | -292 |
| Project #2 | 50,000 | 42,150 | 12,140 | 28.80% | 14,400 | 13,500 | 900 |
| Project #3 | 30,000 | 25,110 | 14,050 | 55.95% | 16,785 | 15,220 | 1,565 |

## Cost Comparison Method

The cost comparison method is an approach that combines the completed contract and percentage of completion methods. A 10 percent deferral election is allowed under the cost comparison method. This election allows you to defer recognized revenue on a contract until the total costs incurred equal 10 percent of the estimated contract costs. The initial project costs are capitalized and deferred until costs to date exceed 10 percent of total costs. After exceeding 10 percent, all costs incurred are treated as period costs. Revenue is also fully recognized in that period based on the level of project completion. From that point forward, revenue is calculated using the percentage of completion method until the project is finished.

# Cash Management

## Cash Flow

As discussed in Chapter 9, it is important to track incoming cash and expenditures during the construction project to ensure you have enough working capital to complete the job. Balancing incoming progress payments and outgoing expenditures is important to managing the project effectively and should be a consideration when preparing your schedule.

Positive cash flow, meaning more cash is coming in than going out to pay expenses, is an important indicator of the health of your business. Without positive cash flow, your business cannot pay bills and employees. The business will eventually be unable to sustain itself and ultimately fail.

Two important aspects of maintaining a positive cash flow are collecting accounts receivable (money that is owed to your business) and billing and collecting for current projects.

**Collecting Accounts Receivable:** Collecting accounts receivable should be a systematic process:

✓ Correspondence should look professional, with the services rendered and amount due clearly displayed on the invoice.

✓ Follow-up invoices should be sent on a regular schedule. This will convey that you are serious about receiving prompt payment.

✓ If the account falls delinquent for more than three months, a stern letter outlining the consequences for non-payment should accompany your follow-up invoices.

✓ If you find you are having problems collecting on accounts receivable, you may want to hire a professional collection agency.

Prompt pay and lien laws may also provide additional payment and collection tools.

**Billing and Collecting for Current Projects:** Prompt billing for current projects is important to receiving timely payments. Once you receive approval for partial or final payment, you should immediately send an invoice requesting payment. The payment should clearly outline payment terms. For example, if your payment terms are "Net 30," this means that full payment of the invoice is due in 30 days. If amounts due for current projects are not collected in a prompt manner, you may run into cash flow problems.

**Bad Debts:** When you extend credit to your customers, this debt is recorded in your accounts receivable. Bad debts are uncollectible accounts receivable. It is important to monitor accounts receivable regularly. If you notice that the amount of accounts receivable is increasing, you may need to adjust collection procedures. Bad debts affect cash flow and must be kept to a minimum.

According to IRS guidelines, a business deducts its bad debts from gross income when figuring taxable income. Bad debts may be deducted in part or in full. For more information on the specific IRS guidelines on business bad debts, refer to IRS Publication 535, Business Expenses. This publication can be downloaded from the IRS website at www.irs.gov.

## Payments

**Progress Payments:** As discussed in Chapter 8, it is important to address the schedule of progress payments in the contract. Progress payments are partial payments made after specified phases of construction are complete.

To ensure adequate cash flow, it is important to monitor the progress payment schedule closely. You may be required to submit a partial payment estimate to the project architect or engineer prior to the payment due date. The partial payment estimate outlines the work performed and proof of materials and equipment delivery required for the next stage of construction. The architect or engineer certifies each progress payment by confirming the information in the partial payment estimate.

A retainage amount (commonly 10 percent) is usually withheld from progress payments. Retainage is released and paid out to the contractor after all final approvals are obtained at the end of a project.

Calculation of progress payments differs slightly, depending on the type of contract.

**Payment for Lump Sum Contracts:** Payments for lump sum contracts are calculated by the percentage of work completed. A schedule of estimated costs (sometimes called a schedule of values) is used as a basis to determine the degree of project completion.

Material and subcontractor invoices are compared against the schedule of values to support the degree of project completion.

**Payment for Unit Price Contracts:** Payments for unit price contracts are based on actual work units completed. The unit price payment request is more detailed and may take longer to complete, but it provides a more accurate picture of the degree of work completion.

**Payment for Cost-Plus Contracts:** Payments for cost-plus contracts are based on actual costs rather than a percentage of completed work. The schedule of payments should be clearly outlined in the contract. Cost-plus contracts generally include a markup in addition to costs. The payment request should include a markup proportionate to the costs. If payment estimates are required, reconciliation must be done once the actual costs occur to adjust for any amounts that fall over or under the estimate.

# Chapter 14: Financial Management

**Final Payment:** Final payment requests should include the final payment amount plus any retainages owed. Final payment is released after final inspection, acceptance by the owner, and submittal of proper documentation.

**Prompt Payment Act:** The Federal Prompt Payment Act ensures that federal contractors are paid in a timely manner. If late payment is made, interest penalties are charged on the amount due. Prime contractors must receive payment within 14 days after submitting a progress payment invoice. Prime contractors must pay subcontractors within seven days after receiving payment, or they must pay interest penalties.

**Prompt Payments to Subcontractors and Suppliers:** Louisiana Revised Statute 9:2784 establishes guidelines for payments to subcontractors and suppliers. It requires that contractors promptly pay subcontractors and suppliers within 14 days after receiving payment from the owner for the portion of the work completed. When subcontractors receive payment from the contractor, prompt payment within 14 days is due to sub-subcontractors and suppliers.

If the contractor does not receive full payment from the owner, the contractor may pay the subcontractors and suppliers on a prorated basis.

Late payments are subject to an interest rate of .5 percent of the amount due per day not to exceed 15 percent of the total balance.

**Prompt Payment on Louisiana Public Projects:** Louisiana Revised Statute 38:2191 establishes payment guidelines for public projects. Louisiana law states that payment, including progress and final payments, for public projects is due as agreed upon in the contract. If final payment is not made after final acceptance and within 45 days after receipt of a clean lien certificate, the public entity is liable for reasonable attorney's fees.

## Petty Cash Fund

Small payments may sometimes be made without writing a check. A petty cash fund is used to make these payments. When you use the petty cash fund, it is important to document your expenditure. A voucher or petty cash disbursement slip should be completed and attached to your receipt as proof of payment.

The petty cash fund should be balanced and replenished monthly.

# Equipment Records and Accounting

Options for owning, renting, and leasing equipment were discussed in Chapter 7. Equipment rates were then used to construct the equipment portion of the estimate. For accounting purposes, information on equipment must be tracked. Important information to record includes:

✓ use rate,
✓ use time,
✓ maintenance costs,
✓ repair costs, and
✓ operating costs (i.e., gas, oil, etc.).

A separate record should be prepared for each piece of equipment.

This information is also useful when analyzing the need for future equipment purchases or upgrades.

# Depreciation Methods

Depreciation is the process of devaluing a fixed asset as a result of aging, wear and tear, or obsolescence. The asset is depreciated over the course of its "useful life." Depreciation is considered a non-cash expense. You can depreciate vehicles, office equipment, buildings, and machinery. Land cannot be depreciated, because it does not "wear out" like depreciable items.

To determine the annual depreciation for an item, you must know the initial cost, how many years it will provide value for your business, and the salvage cost of the item when it is fully depreciated. There are two methods to depreciate fixed assets:

✓ **Straight line depreciation**
✓ **Accelerated depreciation**

Using **straight line depreciation**, you simply take the initial cost of the item and subtract the salvage cost. Then you take that total and divide it by the number of "useful life" years.

The calculation is as follows:

**Initial Asset Cost – Salvage Cost = Depreciation Cost**

**Depreciation Cost ÷ Useful Life Years = Yearly Depreciation Amount**

Using the **accelerated depreciation** method, the asset is depreciated at a higher rate during the early part of its useful life permitting larger tax deductions. This method is typically used for an asset that will probably be replaced before the end of its useful life. Depreciation percentages are based on the type of asset.

The **modified accelerated cost recovery system (MACRS)** is a depreciation method approved by the IRS. It allows for faster depreciation over longer periods. MACRS divides property into several different classes and takes into account the date the equipment was put in service, cost of equipment, cost recovery period, convention, and depreciation method that applies to your property. Given all these factors, a percentage rate is applied.

For further information, you may refer to the IRS website (www.irs.gov) on how to depreciate property, using MACRS and MACRS's percentage tables.

# Accounting Process for Materials

As discussed in Chapter 9, purchase orders are an important project management tool. Purchase orders keep your expenses organized and document exactly what you ordered. They also facilitate the receiving process and the timing of deliveries. Purchase orders help track material inventories and related expenses in the accounting system. Invoices should be matched with purchase orders to ensure that the billing is accurate.

*Shipping and Delivery Expenses:* In addition to the actual material costs, shipping and delivery expenses are factored into the final cost. Shipping and delivery expenses are charged in a few different ways. Two common shipping terms are:

- ✓ **FOB Freight Prepaid** requires the seller to pay for shipping charges.
- ✓ **FOB Freight Allowed** requires the buyer to pay shipping charges. A credit for the shipping amount is often given by the seller on the invoice.

It is important to understand the shipping terms ahead of time and note them on the purchase order.

*Payment Terms:* Payment terms depend on the payment agreement between the buyer and seller. They are generally listed on the seller's invoice. Terms can vary by seller. Listed below are some common terms you may see on your invoices.

- ✓ Net 10: Payment is due 10 days after receiving the invoice.
- ✓ Net 30: Payment is due 30 days after receiving the invoice.
- ✓ Net 60: Payment is due 60 days after receiving the invoice.
- ✓ COD: Cash payment is due on delivery.
- ✓ 1/10 Net 30: A 1 percent discount is given to payments received within 10 days; otherwise, payment is due 30 days after receiving the invoice.
- ✓ EOM: Payment is due at the end of the month.
- ✓ 1/10 EOM: A 1 percent discount is given to payments received by the 10th of the month following the shipment; otherwise, payment is due at the end of the month following the shipment.

Early payment discounts are a good way to cut costs. Depending on the contract arrangements, project cost savings may be given to the contractor or credited to the overall project budget.

# Payroll Accounting

If you have employees, payroll distribution is done on a regular basis. Thorough payroll records are important for several reasons, such as calculating tax liabilities and tracking labor costs. The process for preparing payroll is as follows:

- ✓ **calculate gross pay for each employee;**
- ✓ **calculate and deduct applicable taxes and other deductions;**
- ✓ **calculate net pay and issue checks; and**
- ✓ **update payroll journal.**

# Chapter 14: Financial Management

## Calculate Gross Pay

Gross pay is determined either by a salary that you set for the employee or based on an hourly wage multiplied by the number of hours worked. Salaried employees are generally paid the same amount each pay period, no matter how many hours they work. Hourly employees generally complete timecards that track the number of hours worked.

Time cards are important documentation if an unemployment benefit dispute arises. Many states require employers to keep timecards. If projects are tracked on the timecard, this information can be used for job costing purposes. The following is a sample time card.

| Project Name or Number | Hours Worked | | | | | | | | Work Completed | Supervisor Approval |
|---|---|---|---|---|---|---|---|---|---|---|
| | M | Tu | W | Th | F | Sa | Su | Total | | |
| | | | | | | | | | | |
| | | | | | | | | | | |
| | | | | | | | | | | |
| | | | | | | | | | | |
| | | | | | | | | | | |
| Total | | | | | | | | | | |

## Calculate and Deduct Applicable Taxes and Deductions

Several types of taxes must be deducted from an employee's pay.

✓ **Federal income tax** is based on information the employee provided on the W-4 form. Using IRS Publication: Circular E (sample below), you can determine the appropriate deduction.

### Wage Bracket Method Tables for Income Tax Withholding
**MARRIED** Persons—**WEEKLY** Payroll Period
(For Wages Paid through December 31, 2015)

| And the wages are— | | And the number of withholding allowances claimed is— | | | | | | | | | | |
|---|---|---|---|---|---|---|---|---|---|---|---|---|
| At least | But less than | 0 | 1 | 2 | 3 | 4 | 5 | 6 | 7 | 8 | 9 | 10 |
| | | The amount of income tax to be withheld is— | | | | | | | | | | |
| $800 | $810 | $78 | $67 | $55 | $44 | $33 | $26 | $18 | $10 | $2 | $0 | $0 |
| 810 | 820 | 80 | 68 | 57 | 45 | 34 | 27 | 19 | 11 | 3 | 0 | 0 |
| 820 | 830 | 81 | 70 | 58 | 47 | 35 | 28 | 20 | 12 | 4 | 0 | 0 |
| 830 | 840 | 83 | 71 | 60 | 48 | 37 | 29 | 21 | 13 | 5 | 0 | 0 |
| 840 | 850 | 84 | 73 | 61 | 50 | 38 | 30 | 22 | 14 | 6 | 0 | 0 |
| 850 | 860 | 86 | 74 | 63 | 51 | 40 | 31 | 23 | 15 | 7 | 0 | 0 |
| 860 | 870 | 87 | 76 | 64 | 53 | 41 | 32 | 24 | 16 | 8 | 1 | 0 |
| 870 | 880 | 89 | 77 | 66 | 54 | 43 | 33 | 25 | 17 | 9 | 2 | 0 |
| 880 | 890 | 90 | 79 | 67 | 56 | 44 | 34 | 26 | 18 | 10 | 3 | 0 |
| 890 | 900 | 92 | 80 | 69 | 57 | 46 | 35 | 27 | 19 | 11 | 4 | 0 |
| 900 | 910 | 93 | 82 | 70 | 59 | 47 | 36 | 28 | 20 | 12 | 5 | 0 |
| 910 | 920 | 95 | 83 | 72 | 60 | 49 | 37 | 29 | 21 | 13 | 6 | 0 |
| 920 | 930 | 96 | 85 | 73 | 62 | 50 | 39 | 30 | 22 | 14 | 7 | 0 |
| 930 | 940 | 98 | 86 | 75 | 63 | 52 | 40 | 31 | 23 | 15 | 8 | 0 |
| 940 | 950 | 99 | 88 | 76 | 65 | 53 | 42 | 32 | 24 | 16 | 9 | 1 |
| 950 | 960 | 101 | 89 | 78 | 66 | 55 | 43 | 33 | 25 | 17 | 10 | 2 |
| 960 | 970 | 102 | 91 | 79 | 68 | 56 | 45 | 34 | 26 | 18 | 11 | 3 |
| 970 | 980 | 104 | 92 | 81 | 69 | 58 | 46 | 35 | 27 | 19 | 12 | 4 |
| 980 | 990 | 105 | 94 | 82 | 71 | 59 | 48 | 36 | 28 | 20 | 13 | 5 |
| 990 | 1,000 | 107 | 95 | 84 | 72 | 61 | 49 | 37 | 29 | 21 | 14 | 6 |
| 1,000 | 1,010 | 108 | 97 | 85 | 74 | 62 | 51 | 39 | 30 | 22 | 15 | 7 |
| 1,010 | 1,020 | 110 | 98 | 87 | 75 | 64 | 52 | 40 | 31 | 23 | 16 | 8 |
| 1,020 | 1,030 | 111 | 100 | 88 | 77 | 65 | 54 | 42 | 32 | 24 | 17 | 9 |
| 1,030 | 1,040 | 113 | 101 | 90 | 78 | 67 | 55 | 43 | 33 | 25 | 18 | 10 |
| 1,040 | 1,050 | 114 | 103 | 91 | 80 | 68 | 57 | 45 | 34 | 26 | 19 | 11 |
| 1,050 | 1,060 | 116 | 104 | 93 | 81 | 70 | 58 | 46 | 35 | 27 | 20 | 12 |
| 1,060 | 1,070 | 117 | 106 | 94 | 83 | 71 | 60 | 48 | 36 | 28 | 21 | 13 |
| 1,070 | 1,080 | 119 | 107 | 96 | 84 | 73 | 61 | 49 | 38 | 29 | 22 | 14 |
| 1,080 | 1,090 | 120 | 109 | 97 | 86 | 74 | 63 | 51 | 39 | 30 | 23 | 15 |
| 1,090 | 1,100 | 122 | 110 | 99 | 87 | 76 | 64 | 52 | 41 | 31 | 24 | 16 |
| 1,100 | 1,110 | 123 | 112 | 100 | 89 | 77 | 66 | 54 | 42 | 32 | 25 | 17 |
| 1,110 | 1,120 | 125 | 113 | 102 | 90 | 79 | 67 | 55 | 44 | 33 | 26 | 18 |
| 1,120 | 1,130 | 126 | 115 | 103 | 92 | 80 | 69 | 57 | 45 | 34 | 27 | 19 |
| 1,130 | 1,140 | 128 | 116 | 105 | 93 | 82 | 70 | 58 | 47 | 35 | 28 | 20 |
| 1,140 | 1,150 | 129 | 118 | 106 | 95 | 83 | 72 | 60 | 48 | 37 | 29 | 21 |
| 1,150 | 1,160 | 131 | 119 | 108 | 96 | 85 | 73 | 61 | 50 | 38 | 30 | 22 |
| 1,160 | 1,170 | 132 | 121 | 109 | 98 | 86 | 75 | 63 | 51 | 40 | 31 | 23 |
| 1,170 | 1,180 | 134 | 122 | 111 | 99 | 88 | 76 | 64 | 53 | 41 | 32 | 24 |
| 1,180 | 1,190 | 135 | 124 | 112 | 101 | 89 | 78 | 66 | 54 | 43 | 33 | 25 |
| 1,190 | 1,200 | 137 | 125 | 114 | 102 | 91 | 79 | 67 | 56 | 44 | 34 | 26 |
| 1,200 | 1,210 | 138 | 127 | 115 | 104 | 92 | 81 | 69 | 57 | 46 | 35 | 27 |
| 1,210 | 1,220 | 140 | 128 | 117 | 105 | 94 | 82 | 70 | 59 | 47 | 36 | 28 |
| 1,220 | 1,230 | 141 | 130 | 118 | 107 | 95 | 84 | 72 | 60 | 49 | 37 | 29 |
| 1,230 | 1,240 | 143 | 131 | 120 | 108 | 97 | 85 | 73 | 62 | 50 | 39 | 30 |
| 1,240 | 1,250 | 144 | 133 | 121 | 110 | 98 | 87 | 75 | 63 | 52 | 40 | 31 |
| 1,250 | 1,260 | 146 | 134 | 123 | 111 | 100 | 88 | 76 | 65 | 53 | 42 | 32 |
| 1,260 | 1,270 | 147 | 136 | 124 | 113 | 101 | 90 | 78 | 66 | 55 | 43 | 33 |
| 1,270 | 1,280 | 149 | 137 | 126 | 114 | 103 | 91 | 79 | 68 | 56 | 45 | 34 |
| 1,280 | 1,290 | 150 | 139 | 127 | 116 | 104 | 93 | 81 | 69 | 58 | 46 | 35 |
| 1,290 | 1,300 | 152 | 140 | 129 | 117 | 106 | 94 | 82 | 71 | 59 | 48 | 36 |
| 1,300 | 1,310 | 153 | 142 | 130 | 119 | 107 | 96 | 84 | 72 | 61 | 49 | 38 |
| 1,310 | 1,320 | 155 | 143 | 132 | 120 | 109 | 97 | 85 | 74 | 62 | 51 | 39 |
| 1,320 | 1,330 | 156 | 145 | 133 | 122 | 110 | 99 | 87 | 75 | 64 | 52 | 41 |
| 1,330 | 1,340 | 158 | 146 | 135 | 123 | 112 | 100 | 88 | 77 | 65 | 54 | 42 |
| 1,340 | 1,350 | 159 | 148 | 136 | 125 | 113 | 102 | 90 | 78 | 67 | 55 | 44 |
| 1,350 | 1,360 | 161 | 149 | 138 | 126 | 115 | 103 | 91 | 80 | 68 | 57 | 45 |
| 1,360 | 1,370 | 162 | 151 | 139 | 128 | 116 | 105 | 93 | 81 | 70 | 58 | 47 |
| 1,370 | 1,380 | 164 | 152 | 141 | 129 | 118 | 106 | 94 | 83 | 71 | 60 | 48 |
| 1,380 | 1,390 | 165 | 154 | 142 | 131 | 119 | 108 | 96 | 84 | 73 | 61 | 50 |
| 1,390 | 1,400 | 167 | 155 | 144 | 132 | 121 | 109 | 97 | 86 | 74 | 63 | 51 |
| 1,400 | 1,410 | 168 | 157 | 145 | 134 | 122 | 111 | 99 | 87 | 76 | 64 | 53 |
| 1,410 | 1,420 | 170 | 158 | 147 | 135 | 124 | 112 | 100 | 89 | 77 | 66 | 54 |
| 1,420 | 1,430 | 171 | 160 | 148 | 137 | 125 | 114 | 102 | 90 | 79 | 67 | 56 |
| 1,430 | 1,440 | 173 | 161 | 150 | 138 | 127 | 115 | 103 | 92 | 80 | 69 | 57 |
| 1,440 | 1,450 | 174 | 163 | 151 | 140 | 128 | 117 | 105 | 93 | 82 | 70 | 59 |
| 1,450 | 1,460 | 176 | 164 | 153 | 141 | 130 | 118 | 106 | 95 | 83 | 72 | 60 |
| 1,460 | 1,470 | 177 | 166 | 154 | 143 | 131 | 120 | 108 | 96 | 85 | 73 | 62 |
| 1,470 | 1,480 | 179 | 167 | 156 | 144 | 133 | 121 | 109 | 98 | 86 | 75 | 63 |
| 1,480 | 1,490 | 180 | 169 | 157 | 146 | 134 | 123 | 111 | 99 | 88 | 76 | 65 |

$1,490 and over                Use Table 1(b) for a **MARRIED person** on page 45. Also see the instructions on page 43.

# Chapter 14: Financial Management

✓ **Social Security tax** is calculated at the current prevailing rate. The current tax rate is available online at www.ssa.gov. Employers must pay in an equal amount of Social Security tax but cannot deduct that amount from the employee's payroll.

✓ **Medicare tax** is calculated at the rate of 1.45 percent of gross pay. Employers must pay in an equal amount of Medicare tax but cannot deduct that amount from the employee's payroll.

✓ **Advance earned income credit** needs to be taken, based on the information the employee provided on IRS Form W-5.

✓ **State income tax** should be calculated as it applies to each individual state.

✓ **Other deductions** might include an employee's contribution for medical insurance, 401K, life insurance, etc.

Reporting of payroll taxes is covered in Chapter 15, Tax Basics.

## Calculate Net Pay and Issue Checks

Net pay is the payroll amount the employee receives after deductions are taken. Net pay is calculated as:

**Gross Pay – Taxes & Deductions = Net Pay**

Employees should receive a statement of earnings with their paycheck. The statement of earnings shows how the net pay was calculated. The following is a sample statement of earnings.

| Earnings | | | | Current | Year to Date |
|---|---|---|---|---|---|
| Description | Rate | Hours | Overtime | | |
| | | | | | |
| | | | | | |
| | | | | | |
| | | | Total Earnings | | |
| | | | **Taxes** | | |
| Employee Name: | | | Federal Withholding | | |
| | | | Social Security | | |
| Employee ID: | | | | | |
| | | | Medicare | | |
| Pay Period: | | | | | |
| | | | State Withholding | | |
| Check Date: | | | Insurance Deductions | | |
| | | | Total Deductions | | |
| | | | **Net Pay** | | |

## Update Payroll Journal

Once checks are issued, the payroll journal must be updated to reflect the new account balance. The payroll journal should contain the same information as the employee statement of earnings. This topic is discussed in the previous section. This information is important to calculating your employer tax liabilities. Instructions on how to pay in employer taxes are covered in Chapter 15, Tax Basics.

# Technology Solutions for Accounting

There are many accounting software programs on the market that can help make the accounting process easier.

As with all software, you still need to know the fundamentals, but it will help streamline the process and improve accuracy.

Accounting software can automate the process of posting transactions, creating financial statements, invoicing customers, creating purchase orders, and much more. Think of accounting software as an investment to make you more analytical and help you think strategically about your business.

When choosing the right software, consider what your needs are and how the technology can grow with your company. There are many options. You may want to look at programs that integrate job cost analysis with accounting that have been developed specifically for the construction industry.

---

# Final Inspection...

**Bookkeeping:** The first step of the accounting process is bookkeeping. Bookkeeping is the accurate recording of all financial transactions that occur in the business.

**The Accounting Cycle:** The accounting cycle is a process that happens each reporting period, which starts with recording financial transactions and goes through analyzing financial statements.

**Methods of Accounting:** Cash and accrual are the two main methods of accounting. The primary difference between the two methods is the timing of when you record transactions to your accounts.

**Contract Accounting:** The methods for contract accounting include completed contract, percentage of completion, and cost comparison.

**Cash Management:** Positive cash flow is an important indicator of the health of your business. Collecting on accounts receivable and billing and collecting on current accounts are important to the cash management process.

**Equipment Records and Accounting:** For accounting purposes, information on equipment must be tracked. Important information to record includes use rate, use time, maintenance costs, repair costs, and operating costs.

**Depreciation Methods:** Depreciation is the process of devaluing a fixed asset as a result of aging, wear and tear, or obsolescence. The two primary methods of depreciation are straight line and accelerated.

**Accounting Process for Materials:** Purchase orders help track material inventories and related expenses in the accounting system. Invoices should be matched with purchase orders to ensure that the billing is accurate.

**Payroll Accounting:** Thorough payroll records are important for such reasons as calculating tax liabilities and tracking labor costs.

**Technology Solutions for Accounting:** Accounting software can automate the process of posting transactions, creating financial statements, invoicing customers, creating purchase orders, and much more.

# Supplemental Forms

Supplemental forms and links are available at **NASCLAforms.org** using access code **LA129354**.

| | |
|---|---|
| Balance Sheet | Example featured earlier in the chapter that can be modified in Excel |
| Income Statement | Example featured earlier in the chapter that can be modified in Excel |
| Time Card | Sample featured earlier in the chapter to track employee time |
| Earnings Statement | Sample featured earlier in the chapter as a summary of the employee's earnings |

# Chapter 15
# TAX BASICS

## Chapter Survey...
- Employer Identification Number
- Federal Business Taxes
- Summary of Federal Tax Forms
- Income Tax
- Self-Employment Tax
- Federal Employment Taxes
- Penalties
- Information Returns-1099 MISC
- Tax Calendar
- Louisiana State Tax Specifics

## Employer Identification Number

Before you become an employer and hire employees, you need a Federal Employer Identification Number (EIN) which is also referred to as a taxpayer identification number.

The only entities that do not need an EIN are:

- ✓ Sole proprietorships that have no employees and file no excise or pension tax returns; and
- ✓ LLCs with a single owner (where the owner will file employment tax returns).

In these instances, the owner uses his or her social security number as the taxpayer identification number.

All other types of business entities, including partnerships, are required to obtain an EIN.

The EIN is a 9-digit number that the IRS issues. The digits are arranged as follows: 00-0000000. It is used to identify the tax accounts of employers and certain others who have no employees. Use your EIN on all items you send to the Internal Revenue Service (IRS) and Social Security Administration (SSA).

There are several ways to obtain an EIN through the Internal Revenue Service (IRS).

- ✓ Call the Business and Specialty Tax Line at (800) 829-4933.
- ✓ Fax the completed Form SS-4 application to the fax number designated for your state.
- ✓ Mail the completed Form SS-4 application.
- ✓ Apply online at www.irs.gov.

## Federal Business Taxes

The form of business you operate determines what taxes you must pay and how you pay them. The following are three general types of business taxes that you may be responsible for.

- ✓ **Income tax**
- ✓ **Self-employment tax**
- ✓ **Employment taxes**

The following table lists tax responsibilities by business entity type and the corresponding forms to file with the IRS.

# Summary of Federal Tax Forms

| IF you are a... | Then you may be liable for... | Use Form... |
|---|---|---|
| Sole proprietor | Income tax | 1040 and Schedule C [1] or C–EZ |
| | Self-employment tax | 1040 and Schedule SE |
| | Estimated tax | 1040–ES |
| | Employment taxes: | |
| | • Social security and Medicare taxes and income tax withholding | 941 |
| | • Federal unemployment (FUTA) tax | 940 or 940–EZ |
| | • Depositing employment taxes | 8109 [2] |
| | Excise taxes | See *Excise Taxes* |
| Partnership | Annual return of income | 1065 |
| | Employment taxes | Same as sole proprietor |
| | Excise taxes | See *Excise Taxes* |
| Partner in a partnership (individual) | Income tax | 1040 and Schedule E [3] |
| | Self-employment tax | 1040 and Schedule SE |
| | Estimated tax | 1040–ES |
| Corporation or S corporation | Income tax | 1120 or 1120–A (corporation) [3] 1120S (S corporation) [3] |
| | Estimated tax | 1120–W (corporation only) and 8109 [2] |
| | Employment taxes | Same as sole proprietor |
| | Excise taxes | See *Excise Taxes* |
| S corporation shareholder | Income tax | 1040 and Schedule E [3] |
| | Estimated tax | 1040–ES |

[1] File a separate schedule for each business.

[2] Do not use if you deposit taxes electronically.

[3] Various other schedules may be needed.

# Income Tax

All businesses except partnerships must file an annual income tax return. Partnerships file an information return. The form you use depends on how your business is organized.

## Estimated Tax

The federal income tax is a "pay-as-you-go" tax. You must pay the tax as you earn or receive income during the year. If you do not pay your tax through withholding, or do not pay enough tax that way, you might owe estimated tax. If you are not required to make estimated tax payments, you pay any tax due when you file your return.

**Sole proprietors, partners, and S corporation shareholders** generally have to make estimated tax payments if expected owed tax is $1,000 or more when the income tax return is filed. Form 1040–ES, Estimated Tax for Individuals, is available through the IRS to figure and pay estimated tax.

**Corporations** generally have to make estimated tax payments if expected owed tax is $500 or more when the income tax return is filed. Form 1120–W, Estimated Tax for Corporations, is available through the IRS to figure the estimated tax. You must deposit the payments electronically, through the mail, or delivery with a payment coupon.

# Self-Employment Tax

Self-employment tax (SE tax) is a social security and Medicare tax primarily for individuals who work for themselves. Your payments of SE tax contribute to your coverage under the social security system. Social security coverage provides you with retirement benefits, disability benefits, survivor benefits, and hospital insurance (Medicare) benefits.

You must pay SE tax and file Schedule SE (Form 1040) if your net earnings from self-employment were $400 or more.

You must also pay SE tax on your share of certain partnership income and your guaranteed payments.

---

### *A Word About Deductible Expenses...*

As defined by the IRS, to be deductible, a business expense must be both ordinary and necessary. An ordinary expense is one that is common and accepted in your industry. A necessary expense is one that is helpful and appropriate for your trade or business.

It is important to distinguish a business expense from a personal expense. Personal expenses would include living or family expenses which would not be considered deductible business expenses. A deductible business expense would include:

Expenses used to figure cost of goods sold, such as cost of product, storage, direct labor, and project overhead; and

Capital expenses, such as business assets and improvements (Although you generally cannot take a current deduction for a capital expense, you may be able to recover the amount you spend through depreciation, amortization, or depletion. These recovery methods allow you to deduct part of your cost each year.)

---

# Federal Employment Taxes

When you have employees, you have certain employment tax responsibilities and forms you must file. Most employers must withhold (except FUTA), deposit, report and pay the following taxes:

✓ **Social security and Medicare taxes (FICA)**

✓ **Federal income tax withholding**

✓ **Federal unemployment (FUTA) tax**

Keep all records of employment taxes for at least four years.

## Circular E

The *IRS Publication Circular E: Employer's Tax Guide* is a comprehensive reference providing thorough instructions on calculating, withholding and depositing employee taxes. The Circular E is found on the IRS website at www.irs.gov and at NASCLAforms.org using access code LA129354.

## Social Security and Medicare Taxes (FICA)

Social Security and Medicare taxes pay for benefits that workers and families receive under the Federal Insurance Contributions Act (FICA). Social Security tax pays for benefits under the old-age, survivors, and disability insurance part of FICA. Medicare tax pays for benefits under the hospital insurance part of FICA. Medicare is a part of the Social Security Program that provides hospital and medical insurance coverage to persons age 65 and over and those who have permanent kidney failure, or end stage renal disease, and people with other disabilities.

You withhold part of these taxes from your employee's wages and your company must pay a matching amount. Social Security and Medicare tax is calculated at the current prevailing rate. The current tax rate is available online at www.ssa.gov.

## Federal Income Tax Withholding

You generally must withhold federal income tax from your employees' wages. To figure how much to withhold from each wage payment, use the employee's form W-4, Employee's Withholding Allowance Certificate, and the methods described in the previous chapter. The W-4 deductions do not expire unless the employee gives you a new one or if the employee is claiming a tax exemption. A new W-4 form must be completed by February 15 each year from employees claiming a tax withholding exemption.

**Form W-2:** Form W-2, Wage and Tax Statement summarizes the employee's previous year's wages and withholding amounts. All employees must be furnished copies of the form W-2 by January 31 for the previous year's wages. Employees should receive copies B, C, and 2.

If employment ends before the end of the year, the W-2 form can be given to the employee at any time but no later than January 31. If an employee asks for the W-2 form, you must furnish copies within 30 days of the request or 30 days of the final payment, whichever is later.

Employers must send Copy A of the W-2 form with the entire page of the W-3 form to the Social Security Administration (SSA) by the last day of February (or last day of March if you file electronically). Send the forms to:

*Social Security Administration*
*Data Operations Center*
*Wilkes-Barre, Pennsylvania 18769-0001*

## Deposit Schedule

There are three deposit schedules, monthly, semiweekly and daily, for determining when you deposit Social Security, Medicare and withheld income taxes. Prior to the beginning of the calendar year, you must determine which schedule you are required to use.

You are a monthly schedule depositor if your total payroll tax liability for the previous four quarters (July to June) was $50,000 or less. Payments are due on the fifteenth day of the following month after the payments were made. During your first year of business, you are a monthly schedule depositor.

If your total payroll tax liability from the previous four quarters (July to June) is greater than $50,000, you are a semiweekly schedule depositor. The semiweekly deposit schedule depends on your payroll date.

| If your payday is on... | Then your deposit date is... |
|---|---|
| Wednesday, Thursday and/or Friday | Wednesday |
| Saturday, Sunday, Monday and/or Tuesday | Friday |

If your accumulated tax liability is $100,000 or more on any day during a deposit period, you must deposit it on the next banking day. If you are a monthly schedule depositor and accumulate a $100,000 tax liability on any day, you automatically become a semiweekly depositor.

**Form 941:** If you report less than $2,500 for the quarter, you can use the IRS Form 941, Quarterly Employer's Tax Return to make payments by the due date of the return. If your tax obligation exceeds $2,500 for the quarter, you are subject to payments according to a deposit schedule.

## Federal Unemployment Tax (FUTA)

The federal unemployment tax is part of the federal and state program under the Federal Unemployment Tax Act (FUTA) that pays unemployment compensation to workers who lose their jobs.

You report and pay FUTA tax separately from Social Security and Medicare taxes and withheld income

# Chapter 15: Tax Basics

tax. Employers are responsible for FUTA and cannot withhold this amount from the employees' payroll.

You are generally liable for both state and federal unemployment taxes if

✓ you pay wages to employees totaling $1,500, or more, in any quarter of a calendar year, or

✓ you had at least one employee during any day of a week during 20 weeks in a calendar year, regardless of whether or not the weeks were consecutive.

**Calculating FUTA:** The FUTA tax base and tax rate is calculated at the current prevailing rate. The current tax information is available online at www.irs.gov. Employers who pay the state unemployment tax, on a timely basis, will receive an offset credit to the federal tax. State tax rates are based on requirements of state law.

**Deposit Requirements:** For deposit purposes, figure FUTA tax quarterly. If your FUTA tax liability is less than $500, you are not required to deposit the tax. Instead, carry it forward and add it to the liability figured in the next quarter to see if you must make a deposit. Use the following schedule to determine when to deposit FUTA taxes.

| Quarter | Ending | Due Date |
|---|---|---|
| Jan-Feb-Mar | March 31 | April 30 |
| Apr-May-June | June 30 | July 31 |
| July-Aug-Sept | Sept. 30 | Oct. 31 |
| Oct-Nov-Dec | Dec. 31 | Jan. 31 |

**Form 940:** Report FUTA taxes on Form 940, Employer's Annual Federal Unemployment (FUTA) Tax Return or if you qualify, you can use the simpler Form 940-EZ instead.

## Penalties

Accurate and prompt deposits are required to avoid penalties which can range from 2 percent to 100 percent of your tax liability.

Penalties may apply if

✓ you do not make payroll tax deposits on time;

✓ make deposits for less than the required amount; or

✓ do not use the Electronic Federal Tax Payment System (EFTPS) when required.

These penalties are as follows:

| | |
|---|---|
| 2% | Deposits made 1–5 days late. |
| 5% | Deposits made 6–15 days late. |
| 10% | Deposits made more than 16 days late. Also applies to amounts paid within 10 days of the date of the first notice the IRS sent asking for the tax due. |
| 10% | Deposits made at an unauthorized financial institution, paid directly to the IRS, or paid with your tax return. |
| 10% | Amounts subject to electronic deposit requirements but not deposited using EFTPS. |
| 15% | Amounts still unpaid more than 10 days after the date of the first notice that the IRS sent asking for the tax due or the day on which you received notice and demand for immediate payment, whichever is earlier. |
| 100% | Failure to pay "trust fund" taxes defined as withheld income, Social Security and Medicare taxes. The amount of the penalty is equal to the unpaid balance of the trust fund tax. |

# Information Returns – 1099-MISC

You may be required to file information returns to report certain types of payments made during the year to persons not treated as employees. Form 1099-MISC, Miscellaneous Income may be used to report payments of $600 or more to independent contractors. Form 1099-MISC must be filed by January 31 for the prior year's payments. Form 1096, Annual Summary and Transmittal of U.S. Information Returns, is used to transmit 1099 forms to the IRS. Form 1096 is due by February 28 for the previous year's 1099s.

# Tax Calendar

Listed below are key employment tax deadlines as outlined in the IRS Publication Circular E. IRS Publication 509-Tax Calendar is also a good resource to keep track of other various tax due dates including income and employment taxes.

| | |
|---|---|
| By January 31 | Furnish W-2 Form, Wage and Tax Statement to All Employees |
| | Furnish Form 1099 to Each Other Payee (for example, independent contractors with payments of $600 or more) |
| | File Form 940 or 940-EZ, Employer's Annual Federal Unemployment Tax (FUTA) Return |
| | File Form 945, Annual Return of Withheld Federal Income Tax |
| By February 15 | Request a New W-4 Form from Employees Claiming a Tax Withholding Exemption |
| On February 16 | Exempt W-4 Forms Expire |
| By February 28 | File Copy A of All 1099 Forms with Form 1096, Annual Summary and Transmittal of U.S. Information Returns with the IRS |
| | File Copy A of W-2 Forms, Wage and Tax Statement with W-3 Form, Transmittal of Wage and Tax Statements with the Social Security Administration |
| By March 31 | File Electronic Forms 1099 and 8027 with IRS |
| | File Electronic W-2 Forms with the Social Security Administration |
| By April 30, July 31, October 31, and January 31 | Deposit FUTA Taxes |
| | File Form 941, Employer's Quarterly Federal Tax Return and deposit any undeposited income, social security and Medicare taxes |
| Before December 1 | Remind Employees to Submit New W-4 Forms if withholding allowances have changed |
| On December 31 | W-5 Form, Earned Income Credit Advance Payment Certificate Expires |

# Chapter 15: Tax Basics

# Louisiana State Tax Specifics

The Louisiana Department of Revenue is the regulating agency for the state tax program. The following information, including forms and helpful links, is located on the website at www.revenue.louisiana.gov.

*Headquarters:*
*Louisiana Department of Revenue*
*617 North 3rd Street*
*Baton Rouge, Louisiana 70802*

*Mailing Address:*
*P.O. Box 201*
*Baton Rouge, Louisiana 70821*

*New Business Registration: (225) 219-7462*
*Compliance: (225) 219-7462*
*Contractor Registration: (225) 219-7462*
*General Information: (225) 219-7462*

Effective January 1, 2010, the Louisiana Department of Revenue no longer certifies the residency of contractors. Nonresident contractors are not required to pay a ten-dollar application fee or post a bond and resident contractors are not required to renew their registrations. See the Contractor Fee and Bond for Nonresidents section for jobs performed by nonresident contractors certified prior to January 1, 2010.

In addition to any other applicable taxes, resident and nonresident contractors performing jobs in Louisiana are required to register for the Louisiana general sales tax. Before receiving a permit, proof of registration with the Louisiana Department of Revenue is required by the permitting office. Registration is available online at www.revenue.louisiana.gov.

Louisiana residents who install solar photovoltaic systems, solar thermal systems, or wind energy systems on their homes or on rental property may be eligible for significant tax breaks on their Louisiana income tax, in addition to tax breaks on their federal income tax.

Homeowners who hire a Louisiana state licensed contractor holding the classification of "Solar Energy Equipment" to install the systems are eligible for the state tax breaks, if they follow certain requirements spelled out by law and by regulations of the Louisiana Department of Revenue and Taxation.

To learn more about the requirements to obtain this classification on the license, consult the website for

the Louisiana State Licensing Board for Contractors (www.lslbc.louisiana.gov).

To learn more about the rules for eligibility for the tax breaks, consult the website for the Louisiana Department of Revenue and Taxation (www.revenue.louisiana.gov).

## Corporate Tax

All corporations and entities taxed as corporations for federal income tax purposes deriving income from Louisiana sources, whether or not they have any net income, must file a state income tax return. Exempt corporations, as determined by the Internal Revenue Service, must submit a copy of the IRS ruling to the Louisiana Department of Revenue to obtain an exemption for state income tax.

*Tax Rate:* Corporations pay tax on net income computed at the following rates:

✓ four percent on the first $25,000 of net income

✓ five percent on the next $25,000

✓ six percent on the next $50,000

✓ seven percent on the next $100,000

✓ eight percent on the excess over $200,000

*Due Dates:* Returns and payments are due on or before the 15th day of the fourth month following the close of an accounting period (April 15 for a calendar year).

## Corporation Franchise Tax

Any corporation meeting any of the following provisions, unless specifically exempted, must file a Louisiana corporation franchise tax return:

✓ Organized under the laws of Louisiana.

✓ Qualified to do business in the state or doing business in the state.

✓ Exercising or continuing the corporate charter within the state.

✓ Owning or using any of the corporate capital, plant, or other property in the state in a corporate capacity.

*Rate of Tax:* The initial corporation franchise tax is $10. The subsequent rate of tax is $1.50 for each $1,000 or major fraction thereof up to $300,000 of capital employed in Louisiana. For capital amounts over $300,000, the tax rate is $3 for each $1,000 or major fraction thereof. The minimum corporation franchise tax is $10 per year. For information concerning capital employed in Louisiana and computation of the tax, see the instructions for Forms ICFT-620 and 620A.

**Due Dates:** An initial return for the period beginning with the date the corporation first becomes liable for filing a return and ending with the next close of an accounting period must be filed on or before the 15th day of the third month after the corporation first becomes liable.

Louisiana corporation franchise tax accrues on the first day of each accounting year, and the return for that period must be filed on or before the 15th day of the fourth month of that accounting year.

## Estimated Tax

Any corporation that can reasonably expect its estimated tax for the taxable year to be $1,000 or more must file a declaration of estimated tax and pay installments on the tax according to a schedule shown on the declaration voucher. Underpayment of or failure to pay estimated tax may result in an additional amount due at the rate of 12 percent annually on the amount underpaid.

## Contractor Fee and Bond for Nonresidents

*Effective January 1, 2010, the Louisiana Department of Revenue no longer certifies the residency of contractors. Nonresident contractors are not required to pay a ten-dollar application fee or post a bond.*

Jobs performed by nonresident contractors certified prior to January 1, 2010 should continue to abide by LAC 61:I.4373 relative to nonresident contractors. A summary of this rule is outlined below.

Nonresident contractors and subcontractors who operate in Louisiana and who enter into contracts where the total contract price is $3,000 or more must register each contract with the Department of Revenue.

### Determining Residency

Louisiana Revised Statute §47:9A(2) defines the criteria for contractors to be considered residents. Using these criteria, resident contractors include the following:

✓ individuals who have maintained their permanent domiciles in Louisiana for at least one year before bidding on work;

✓ corporations that have operated permanent business facilities in Louisiana for at least one year before bidding on work;

✓ corporations, at least 50 percent of whose outstanding and issued common shares are owned by individuals, who have maintained their domiciles in Louisiana for at least one year before bidding on work; and

✓ partnerships, associations, and other legal entities in which resident corporations or individuals have at least a 50 percent ownership.

Residents are not subject to the contractor fee and bond for nonresidents. To establish residency, contractors must submit the Resident/Nonresident Status (R-1340) form to the Department of Revenue.

**Fees:** The nonresident contractor fee is $10 for each contract job in excess of $3,000.

**Bond Requirement:** Nonresident contractors who are entering into a contract job in Louisiana in excess of $3,000 are required to file a bond or deposit other sureties with the Department of Revenue. A bond is required for each separate contract. The bond amount shall be as determined by the department, but not less than $1,000.

**Return Requirements:** Within 30 days of contract completion, the contractor must provide the Department of Revenue with a complete and accurate accounting of all state sales and use taxes due on the prescribed forms. Sales and use taxes due the state must be paid. Any overpayments will be refunded within 15 days.

**Local Registration:** Contractors are required to register with the central collection agency of the parish where the work is being performed and obtain a certificate

# Chapter 15: Tax Basics

stating that all requirements for surety bonds in that parish have been met.

**Fee and Bond Due Dates:** The fee and bond are due before any work can begin on the contract. The department will issue a certificate to the contractor documenting that bonding requirements have been met. No building permits, licenses, or certificates will be issued by any state or local authorities until the contractor has shown proof of bonding from the Department of Revenue.

**Withholding Requirement:** Nonresident contractors are authorized and required to withhold payments from their subcontractors to guarantee that all state and local taxes due from the subcontractors will be paid.

This withholding requirement is not intended to change the normal procedure under which subcontractors pay state sales and use taxes to their vendors, or when vendors fail to collect taxes, remit taxes directly to the state. In cases where subcontractors' tax liabilities to the Department of Revenue are uncollectible directly from the nonresident subcontractors or their bonding companies, the provisions place nonresident general contractors and nonresident higher-level subcontractors in positions of contingent liability. Nonresident contractors can minimize the possibility of having to remit the state and local taxes owed by their nonresident subcontractors by reasonably assuring that the state and local taxes owed by the subcontractors have been paid, and that the subcontractors have been bonded, as required by the statute. Nonresident contractor bonds are not released or reduced until a "contract completion form" is submitted for each contract certifying that all taxes due to the State of Louisiana and its political subdivisions have been paid.

**Penalties:** Nonresident contractors failing to execute the required bonds before beginning work are subject to penalties. These penalties include

✓ denial of permits, licenses or certificates by state entities, including the fire marshal, code enforcement, and building officials;

✓ refusal of the right to perform the contract and an injunction stopping the work performed on the contract; and

✓ a penalty of two hundred dollars or two percent of the construction contract, whichever is greater.

## State Withholding Tax

Every employer who has resident or nonresident employees performing services (except employees exempt from income tax withholding) within Louisiana is required to withhold Louisiana state income tax based on the employee's withholding exemption certificate. Wages of Louisiana residents performing services in other states are subject to Louisiana income tax withholding unless the wages are not subject to withholding of net income tax by the state in which the services are performed.

**Filing Requirements:** Every employer who has withheld or was required to withhold income tax from wages must file the employer's return of Louisiana state income tax withheld. Employers who withhold from the combined wages of all employees less than $500 per month are required to file on a quarterly basis. Employers who withhold at least $500 but less than $2,000 per month from the combined wages of all employees are required to file on a monthly basis. Employers who withhold from the combined wages of all employees $2,000 per month or more must file on a semimonthly basis.

**Tax Rates:** Income tax withholding tables are published in the Withholding Tables and Instructions for Employers. This publication may be used for computing the proper amount to be withheld based on the employees' income, filing status, and number of exemptions.

**Tax Due Dates:** Quarterly returns and payments are due on the last day of the month following the close of the quarterly period.

Monthly returns and payments are due on the last day of the month following the close of the monthly period.

Semimonthly returns and payments are due on the 15th day of the month for taxes withheld on wages paid during the period between the 16th day and the last day of the previous month and are due on the last day of the month for taxes withheld on wages paid during the first 15 days of the same month.

## Local Occupational License Tax

An occupational license tax is levied in many cities and parishes. The tax amount varies and is based on the gross receipts or earnings.

✓ For lump-sum contractors, the tax amount ranges from $12.50 on gross annual receipts of less than

$10,000, to $350 on gross annual receipts of $1,000,000 or more.

✓ For cost-plus contractors, the tax ranges from $30 per year on gross annual earnings of less than $5,000 to $4,000 on gross annual earnings of $500,000 or more.

To help you understand your local tax responsibilities, information is available from local taxing authorities.

## Sales and Use Tax

*State Tax:* The state sales and use tax rate is 4 percent on the sale or use of equipment, materials, and specified services obtained within or brought into the state. Tax is paid directly to the seller of the property or services. If the seller is not obligated to collect the tax or otherwise fails to charge this tax, it must be paid directly to the Louisiana Department of Revenue. Tax returns with payment must be filed by the twentieth of the month following the month in which the transaction occurred.

*Activities Subject to State Tax:* The tax is applied to the following types of transactions that are commonly encountered in the construction industry.

✓ Lease or rental of any item or tangible personal property in Louisiana

✓ Services provided to repair tangible personal property (does not apply to structures permanently attached to land)

✓ Sale of tangible personal property at retail

To ensure you are meeting your tax obligations, make sure that the proper tax is being charged at the time items are sold or leased.

*Local Tax:* In addition to state sales tax requirements, local sales taxes are levied throughout most parishes and some municipal authorities. These tax rates range from 1 percent to 6 percent. Local sales tax exemptions may differ from state exemptions. To understand your local tax responsibilities, contact the taxing authority for the area where the project is located for filing requirements.

## Final Inspection...

*Employer Identification Number:* An employer identification number is used to identify the tax accounts of employers and certain others who have no employees.

*Federal Business Taxes:* The form of business you operate determines what taxes you must pay and how you pay them.

*Summary of Federal Tax Forms:* You must file the specific federal tax forms that correspond to your business entity type.

*Income Tax:* All businesses except partnerships must file an annual income tax return. Partnerships file an information return.

*Self-Employment Tax:* Self-employment tax (SE tax) is a Social Security and Medicare tax primarily for individuals who work for themselves.

*Federal Employment Taxes:* Federal employment taxes include Social Security and Medicare (FICA), federal income tax withholding, and federal unemployment tax (FUTA).

*Penalties:* Accurate and prompt deposits are required to avoid penalties which can range from 2 percent to 100 percent of your tax liability.

*Information Returns-1099 MISC:* Form 1099-MISC, Miscellaneous Income may be used to report payments of $600 or more to independent contractors.

*Tax Calendar:* IRS Publication Circular E and Publication 509 provide tax calendars for various taxes that may apply to your business.

*Louisiana State Tax Specifics:* Businesses in Louisiana must register with the Louisiana Department of Revenue to establish residency. Nonresident contractors are subject to the nonresident contractor fee and bond requirements. Corporate income, corporation franchise, sales and use, and withholding are a few state taxes that may apply to your business.

# Supplemental Publications and Forms

Supplemental forms and links are available at **NASCLAforms.org** using access code **LA129354**.

| | |
|---|---|
| IRS Publication 334 | Tax Guide for Small Business |
| IRS Publication 463 | Travel, Entertainment and Gift Expenses |
| IRS Publication 505 | Tax Withholding and Estimated Tax |
| IRS Publication 509 | General Tax Calendar |
| IRS Publication 533 | Self-Employment Tax |
| IRS Publication 535 | Business Expenses |
| IRS Publication 538 | Accounting Periods and Methods |
| IRS Publication 541 | Tax Information on Partnerships |
| IRS Publication 542 | Tax Information on Corporations |
| IRS Publication 583 | Taxpayers Starting a Business |
| IRS Publication 587 | Business Use of Your Home |
| IRS Publication 946 | How to Begin Depreciating Your Property |
| IRS Publication 1544 | Reporting Cash Payments of Over $10,000 |
| IRS Form W-2 | Wage and Tax Statement |
| IRS Form W-3 | Tax Reconciliation |
| IRS Form W-4 | Employee Withholding |
| IRS Form SS-4 | Application for Employer Identification Number |
| IRS Form 940 | Employer Annual Federal Unemployment Tax Return |
| IRS Form 941 | Employer's Quarterly Federal Tax Return |
| IRS Form 1040 | U.S. Individual Income Tax Return |
| IRS Schedule C | Profit or Loss from Business |
| IRS Schedule-EZ | Net Profit from Business |
| IRS Schedule SE | Self-Employment Tax |
| IRS Form 1040-ES | Estimated Tax for Individuals |
| IRS Form 1065 | U.S. Partnership Return of Income Schedule K-1, Partner's Share of Income, Credits, Deductions, etc. |
| IRS Form 1120 | U.S. Corporation Income Tax Return |
| IRS Form 1120S | U.S. Income Tax Return for an S Corporation Schedule K-1 |
| IRS Form 4562 | Depreciation and Amortization |
| IRS Form 8300 | Report of Cash Payments over $10,000 Received in a Trade or Business |
| Employer's Tax Guide (Circular E) | Publication used to determine federal income tax withholding for employees |

# Chapter 16
# LOUISIANA MECHANICS' LIEN LAW

## Chapter Survey...
- What is a Lien?
- Who is Entitled to a Lien?
- Notice of Contract
- Priority
- Notice of Termination of the Work
- Statement of Claim or Privilege
- Time in Which to Foreclose on a Lien
- Residential Truth in Construction Act

## What is a Lien?

Mechanic's and materialmen's liens "cloud" the title to real property but can be an effective method (and sometimes the only method) for securing payment for labor or materials used in the improvement of real property. The lien stops the owner from selling the property with a clear title. The lien may be foreclosed in a lawsuit. The court can order that property be sold and the proceeds used to pay the contractor, subcontractor, laborer, or material supplier. This may be true even if the owner has already paid a general contractor, meaning that the owner may have to pay twice.

This is one of the reasons that a lien can be such a powerful collection tool.

The law governing liens is found in the Louisiana Revised Statutes, Title 9, starting in Section 4801. The state statutes and court opinions establish a strict procedure to perfect and foreclose a lien. It is strongly recommended that a professional be routinely used to record and foreclose on construction liens.

## Who is Entitled to a Lien?

The state statutes give the following persons lien rights against property for which they have provided labor, material, or services (usually at the direct request of the owner):

- ✓ contractors,
- ✓ laborers or employees of the owner,
- ✓ suppliers for items sold to the owner,
- ✓ lessors for items rented to the owner, and
- ✓ registered or certified surveyors or engineers or licensed architects or their professional subconsultants.

The state statutes also give the following persons lien rights against the owner's property and a claim against the owner and contractor. Many of these people have contracts with the contractor, not the owner, but have still provided labor, material or services for the benefit of the owner's property:

- ✓ subcontractors;
- ✓ laborers or employees of the contractor or subcontractor;
- ✓ suppliers for items sold to the contractor or subcontractor;
- ✓ lessors who rent items to the contractor or subcontractor; and
- ✓ registered or certified surveyors or engineers or licensed architects or their professional subconsultants employed by the contractor or subcontractor.
- ✓ These persons must give written notice of the general nature of the work to be performed to the owner within thirty days after being employed.

**Work Eligible for Lien:** Work eligible for lien is defined as a "single continuous project for the improvement, construction, erection, reconstruction, modification, repair, demolition, or other physical change of an immovable or its component parts," such as a building or structure.

Work not eligible for lien includes

- ✓ drilling of any well(s);
- ✓ construction or other work done on the permanent bed and structures of a railroad; and
- ✓ public works.

# Notice of Contract

Before beginning work, the contractor must file a notice of contract.

**Required Information:** The notice of contract should include the following information:

- ✓ Name and address of the persons entering into the contract
- ✓ Name of the project and legal description of the property where the work is being performed
- ✓ Price of the work being performed or method by which the price is to be calculated and estimate
- ✓ Schedule of payments
- ✓ General terms of the contract
- ✓ Signature of the owner and contractor

**Time is of the Essence:** If the notice of contract is not filed in a timely manner and the price of work exceeds $25,000, the contractor may lose lien rights.

**Not a "Cloud" on the Title of the Property:** Filing a notice of contract does not constitute a cloud, lien, or encumbrance on the title of the real property involved. It is a step that preserves the contractor's right to lien the property later if not paid.

**Required Bond:** To protect against liens from the contractor's subcontractors, suppliers, design professionals and laborers, the owner can require that a bond in the following amounts be attached to the notice of contract when it is filed.

| Contract Price | Bond Amount |
|---|---|
| $10,000 or less | 100% of the price |
| More than $10,000 to $100,000 | 50% of the price but not less than $10,000 |
| More than $100,000 to $1,000,000 | 331/3% of the price but not less than $50,000 |
| More than $1,000,000 | 25% of the price but not less than $333,333 |

# Priority

The priority of lien rights is in the order as follows:

1. Taxes and local assessments against the property
2. Laborers and employees of the owner, contractor, or subcontractor
3. Mortgages or vendor's privileges
4. Subcontractors, suppliers for items sold to the owner and contractor, and lessors for items rented to the owner and contractor
5. Contractors and registered or certified surveyors or engineers, and licensed architects or their professional subconsultants
6. All other mortgages and privileges

A person acquiring or intending to acquire a mortgage, privilege, or other right under L.R.S. 9:4820(D) has priority, regardless of whether work has begun or materials were delivered to the jobsite after the effective date and time of the affidavit, but prior to the recordation of the mortgage, privilege, or other right, provided that the document creating the right was filed before or within four business days of the filing of the affidavit.

# Notice of Termination of the Work

A notice of termination of the work must be filed in writing, and it must contain the following elements:

- ✓ Reasonable identification of land upon which the work was done, also identifying the notice of contract, if filed or recorded, with the names of the parties to the contract
- ✓ Certification that the work has been substantially completed, that it has been abandoned by the owner, or that a contractor is in default under the terms of the contract
- ✓ Signature of the owner or his representative
- ✓ Shall be conclusive of the matters certified if it is made in good faith by the owner or his representative

A notice of substantial completion containing this information may also be filed.

# Chapter 16: Louisiana Mechanics' Lien Law

## Statement of Claim or Privilege

***Contracts with the General Contractor, Subcontractors, and Suppliers:*** Thirty days after filing a notice of termination of work, a statement of claim or privilege must be filed by those who contracted with the general contractor, subcontractors or suppliers.

***General Contractor:*** Sixty days after filing a notice of termination of work or substantial completion of work, a statement of claim or privilege must be filed by the general contractor.

***Contracts with the Owner:*** Sixty days after filing a notice of termination of work or substantial completion of work, a statement of claim or privilege must be filed by those who contract with the owner.

***Contents of the Statement of Claim or Privilege:*** A statement of claim or privilege must be in writing and contain the following elements:

✓ Signature of the person asserting the claim

✓ Description of the project and work performed or services rendered

✓ Person for whom the contract was performed

✓ Itemization of the amount claimed including the materials supplied and services rendered

## Time in which to Foreclose on a Lien

A lawsuit to foreclose on the lien must be filed within one year after filing the statement of claim or privilege.

## Residential Truth in Construction Act

Before entering into a contract for residential home improvements, the contractor must deliver to the owner or owner's agent a notice of lien rights. A copy of the signed notice must be given to the owner or owner's agent and all parties entitled to lien rights. The following is an example of an acceptable notice of lien rights.

## NOTICE OF LIEN RIGHTS

Delivered this _____ day of _____, 20___, by _____, Contractor.

I, the undersigned owner of residential property located at        (street address)    in the city of _____, parish of _____, Louisiana, acknowledge that the above named contractor has delivered this notice to me, the receipt of which is accepted, signifying my understanding that said contractor is about to begin improving my residential property according to the terms and conditions of a contract, and that in accordance with the provisions of law in Part I of Chapter 2 of Code Title XXI of Title 9 of the Louisiana Revised Statutes of 1950, R.S. 9:4801, et seq.:

(1)  A right to file a lien against my property and improvements is granted to every contractor, subcontractor, architect, engineer, surveyor, mechanic, cartman, truckman, workman, laborer, or furnisher of material, machinery or fixtures, who performs work or furnishes material for the improvement or repair of my property, for the payment in principal and interest of such work or labor performed, or the materials, machinery or fixtures furnished, and for the cost of recording such privilege.

(2)  That when a contract is unwritten and/or unrecorded, or a bond is not required or is insufficient or unrecorded, or the surety therefore is not proper or solvent, I, as owner, shall be liable to such subcontractors, materialmen, suppliers or laborers for any unpaid amounts due them pursuant to their timely filed claims to the same extent as is the herein above designated contractor.

(3)  That the lien rights granted herein can be enforced against my property even though the contractor has been paid in full if said contractor has not paid the persons who furnished the labor or materials for the improvement.

(4)  That I may require a written contract, to be recorded, and a bond with sufficient surety to be furnished and recorded by the contractor in an amount sufficient to cover the cost of such improvements, thereby relieving me, as owner, and my property, of liability for any unpaid sums remaining due and owing after completion to subcontractors, journeymen, cartmen, workmen, laborers, mechanics, furnishers of material or any other persons furnishing labor, skill, or material on the said work who record and serve their claims in accordance with the requirements of law.

I have read the above statement and fully understand its contents.


_____
Owner or Agent


_____
Date

# Chapter 16: Louisiana Mechanics' Lien Law

## Final Inspection...

**What is a Lien?** A lien is a legal claim against real property for payment of fees owed for the improvement of that property.

**Who is Entitled to a Lien?** State statutes give lien rights to contractors, subcontractors, laborers, employees, suppliers, lessors, surveyors, engineers, and licensed architects.

**Notice of Contract:** To preserve lien rights, contractors must file a notice of contract before commencing work.

**Priority:** State statutes establish an order of priority for liens.

**Notice of Termination of the Work:** A notice of termination of the work or notice of substantial completion must be filed and contain the proper information to be valid.

**Statement of Claim or Privilege:** The statement of claim or privilege is filed after the notice of termination of the work. The timeline to file depends on the relationship of the contracting parties.

**Timeline in Which to Foreclose on a Lien:** After filing the statement of claim, a lawsuit to foreclose on a lien must occur within one year.

**Residential Truth in Construction Act:** The owner or owner's agent must receive a notice of lien rights from the contractor before entering into a residential home improvement contract.

# Appendix A: Glossary

## A

**Accelerated Depreciation:** A method of depreciation where an asset is depreciated at a higher rate during the early part of its useful life permitting larger tax deductions.

**Acceptance (Legal):** An agreement to an offer made and generally is done by signing the offer. In some cases, a counteroffer is made. A counteroffer is not considered acceptance. It is only when both parties agree to the contract terms that you obtain acceptance.

**Accounting Cycle:** A process that happens each financial reporting period which starts with recording financial transactions and goes through analysis of financial statements.

**Accounts Receivable:** Monies that are owed to a business for products and/or services provided.

**Accrual Method of Accounting:** A method of accounting where income is recognized when the services occur, not when the money is collected. Expenses are recorded when they are incurred, not when they are paid.

**Acid Test Ratio:** See Quick Ratio.

**Activity Ratio:** A formula that measures how effectively a company manages its credit. It is calculated by dividing sales per day into current receivables.

**Addenda or Addendum:** Changes made to bid documents after they are issued but before they are due. Addenda ultimately become part of the contract after the bid is accepted.

**ADA:** The abbreviation for the Americans with Disabilities Act. See Americans with Disabilities Act.

**AGC:** The abbreviation for the Associated General Contractors of America.

**Age Discrimination in Employment Act (ADEA):** A federal law that prohibits discrimination against individuals who are age 40 or older.

**AIA:** The abbreviation for the American Institute of Architects.

**All-Risk Builders' Risk Insurance:** A form of property insurance that covers property owners and builders for buildings under construction typically covering machinery, equipment, materials, supplies, and fixtures that are part of the structure or will become part of the structure. Additional coverage can be added for items, such as temporary structures and scaffolding, used during construction. In general, major construction defects such as poor workmanship and faulty design are not covered.

**Allowance:** A specified amount designated in an estimate for items that are not specified in the project plans, such as finish materials (carpeting, fixtures, lighting, etc.).

**Americans with Disabilities Act (ADA):** The Americans with Disabilities Act (ADA) makes it unlawful to discriminate in employment against a qualified individual with a disability.

**Arbitration:** Arbitration uses a third-party arbitrator or arbitrators to act as a judge or judges to render a decision by which all parties are legally bound. Arbitration is held in a format less formal than a trial.

**Asbestos:** These naturally occurring, fibrous materials are woven together to create a product with high tensile strength. This material is commonly found in thermal insulation and fireproofing, roofing, and flooring materials. When these fibers become airborne, they cause a hazard due to their ability to enter the lungs. Diseases associated with asbestos include asbestosis, lung cancer, and mesothelioma.

**Asset:** Items of value owned by a business.

**At-Will Employment:** An employment agreement where either the employer or the employee may terminate employment at any time without notice or cause.

**Automobile Insurance:** A type of insurance providing coverage for liability and physical damage associated with a company vehicle or a fleet of vehicles. All states require vehicle owners to carry some level of liability insurance covering bodily injury and property damage incurred in a vehicle accident.

# B

**Bad Debt:** Uncollectible accounts receivable which is deducted from gross income when figuring taxable income.

**Balance Sheet:** One of the basic accounting financial statements that shows a company's assets, liabilities, and owners' equity.

**Bank Letter of Credit:** A cash guarantee that can be converted to a payment to the owner by a bank or lending institution.

**Bid:** A formal offer to complete a project according to the terms and conditions of the contract for a specified price.

**Bid Bond:** A type of bond that guarantees the contractor, if awarded the job, will do work at the submitted bid price, enter into a contract with the owner, and furnish the required performance and payment bonds.

**Bid Documents:** A bid package put together in a competitive bid situation. It may include an invitation to bid, bid instructions, bid sheet, bid schedule, bidder's questionnaire on experience, financial responsibility and capability, copy of the contract, and supplements.

**Bid Peddling:** An unethical situation where the subcontractor approaches the general contractor after the project is awarded with the intent of lowering the original price submitted on bid day.

**Bid Rigging:** A form of collusion where contractors coordinate their bids to fix the award outcome of a project.

**Bid Shopping:** An unethical situation where the general contractor approaches subcontractors other than those who have submitted bids to seek a lower offer than what was quoted in the original bids.

**Boilerplate Provisions:** Standard language or clauses used in a legal contract that generally appear at the end of the contract. Their purpose is to protect the business in the event of a lawsuit.

**Bond:** A risk transfer mechanism between a surety bonding company, the contractor, and the project owner. The agreement binds the contractor to comply with the terms and conditions of a contract. If the contractor cannot perform the contract, the surety bonding company assumes the contractor's responsibilities and ensures that the project is completed.

**Breach of Contract:** When one of the parties involved fails to perform in accordance with any of the terms and conditions of a contract.

**Burglary and Theft Insurance:** A type of insurance covering loss or damage caused by burglary, theft, larceny, robbery, forgery, fraud, and vandalism.

**Business Owner's Policies (BOPs):** A type of insurance that bundles property and liability coverage together to eliminate policy gaps or overlaps.

Appendix A: Glossary                                                                                              A-3

**Business Plan:** A planning document that outlines business strategies and goals. It is particularly useful for newly-formed or early-stage businesses and companies making major strategic changes. Typical contents are an executive and company summary, products and services description, market analysis, marketing plan, and financial plan.

# C

**Capital Assets:** See Fixed Assets.

**Cash Method of Accounting:** A method of accounting where income is reported in the year it is received and expenses are deducted in the year they are paid.

**Certificate of Occupancy:** A certificate issued by a building inspector that deems a structure meets all applicable codes and is safe for occupancy.

**Certificate of Substantial Completion:** A certificate issued by the architect that deems a structure can be used for its intended purpose.

**CFR:** The abbreviation for Code of Federal Regulations.

**Change Order:** A written agreement between the owner and contractor to change the contract. Change orders add to, delete from, or otherwise alter the work set forth in the construction documents.

**Circular E:** An IRS Publication that provides instructions on calculating, withholding and depositing employee taxes and tax tables.

**Clean Air Act:** A federal law that allows the EPA to set limits on how much of a pollutant is allowed in the air anywhere in the United States.

**Clean Water Act:** A federal law that establishes the basic structure for regulating discharges of pollutants into the waters of the United States. This act gives the EPA authority to implement pollution control programs, such as setting wastewater standards for the industry and water quality standards for all contaminants in surface waters.

**Collaborative Law:** A facilitative process wherein all parties agree at the onset to work to identify a solution that is beneficial to all parties involved. In collaborative law, the parties use their advocates, most often their lawyers, to facilitate a mutually beneficial result through the process of negotiation.

**Commercial General Liability Insurance (CGL):** A basic liability insurance covering bodily injury that results in actual physical damage or loss for individuals who are not employees, damage or loss to property not belonging to the business, personal injury, including slander or damage to reputation, and advertising injury, including charges of negligence that result from promotion of goods or services.

**Company Overhead:** The expenses that are necessary to keep business operations running but not directly associated with a project (e.g. taxes, legal fees, etc.).

**Completed Contract Method:** A method of contract accounting where income or loss is reported in the year the contract is completed.

**Completed Operations Liability Insurance:** A type of liability insurance that provides coverage for loss arising out of completed projects.

**Completion Bond:** A type of bond that provides assurance to the financial backers of a construction project that it will be completed on time.

**Conceptual Estimate:** An estimate prepared by the architect using cost models from previous projects.

**Consideration (Legal):** When both parties give up something of value, typically, services and products in exchange for monetary compensation.

**Consolidated Omnibus Budget Act of 1985 (COBRA):** A federal law that gives "qualified beneficiaries" (a covered employee's spouse and dependent children) the right to maintain, at their own expense, coverage under their health plan that would be lost due to a "qualifying event," such as termination of employment, at a cost comparable to what it would be if they were still members of the employer's group.

**Construction Management (Contracting):** A type of contracting where the project owner contracts with a professional construction manager to coordinate and manage a construction project.

**Construction Safety Act:** See Contract Work Hours and Safety Standards Act.

**Construction Wrap-Up Liability Insurance:** A type of insurance that bundles liability and workers' compensation insurance for general contractors and subcontractors on large construction projects to eliminate gaps in coverage. To qualify for this type of insurance, certain contract cost requirements must be met. These requirements vary by state.

**Contingency:** A specified amount added to an estimate to protect the contractor if an unanticipated problem or condition arises during the course of the project.

**Contract:** Legally binding agreement between two or more parties with the main purpose of preventing disputes between parties entering into the agreement. A legally binding contract must have offer and acceptance, consideration, competent parties, and legal purpose.

**Contract Work Hours and Safety Standards Act:** A federal law that sets overtime standards for service and construction contracts on federal projects. Commonly referred to as the Construction Safety Act.

**Contractor's Protective Public and Property Damage Liability Insurance:** A type of liability insurance that protects contractors who supervise and subsequently are held liable for actions of subcontractors from claims for personal injury and property damage.

**Contractual Liability Insurance:** A type of liability insurance that provides contractors with protection for damages that result from their negligence while under written contract.

**Corporation (sometimes referred to as C Corporation):** A legal business entity that has independent ownership of assets and liabilities from its shareholders. Its existence continues even if one or more shareholders leave.

**Cost Comparison Method:** A method of contract accounting that combines the completed contract and percentage of completion methods.

**Cost-Plus Contract:** A type of contract where the contractor is reimbursed for the actual cost of labor and materials and is paid a markup fee for overhead and profit.

**Critical Path:** The sequence of tasks that determines the duration of the project. Subsequent project tasks cannot begin until a critical path item is complete.

**Current Assets:** Cash and other assets that can be converted into cash in less than one year.

**Current Liabilities:** Liabilities that will mature and must be paid within one year.

**Current Ratio:** See Liquidity Ratio.

# D

**Davis-Bacon Act:** The federal law that requires payment of prevailing wage rates and fringe benefits on federally-financed or assisted construction.

Appendix A: Glossary

**Debt Ratio:** A formula that measures the percent of total funds provided by creditors. It is calculated by dividing total assets into total debt.

**De Minimis Violation:** A violation of standards which have no direct or immediate relationship to safety or health.

**Depreciation:** The process of devaluing a fixed asset as a result of aging, wear and tear, or obsolescence.

**Design/Build:** A type of contracting where the owner contracts with one company to complete a construction project from start to finish. The company awarded the design/build contract puts together a team of construction professionals, which may include designers, architects, engineers, and contractors.

**Direct Costs:** Costs directly linked with a particular project.

# E

**EEOC:** Abbreviation for the Equal Employment Opportunity Commission.

**Employee Polygraph Protection Act:** A federal law that prohibits most private employers from using any type of lie detector test, either for pre-employment screening of job applicants or for testing current employees during the course of employment.

**Endangered Species Act (ESA):** A federal law that protects threatened or endangered species from further harm.

**Entrepreneur:** A person engaged in strategic activities that involve the initiation and development of a new business, created to build long-term value and steady cash flow streams.

**Equal Pay Act of 1963:** A federal law that prohibits employers from paying different wages to men and women who perform essentially the same work under similar working conditions.

**Equipment Floater Policy:** A type of inland marine insurance covering direct physical loss to equipment and mobile equipment while it is stored on premises, in transit, or at temporary locations or jobsites.

**Errors and Omissions Insurance:** See Professional Liability Insurance.

**Expenses**: Monies paid out or owed for goods or services.

# F

**Failure to Abate Prior Violation:** A safety violation given when a previous violation has not been corrected.

**Fair Labor Standards Act (FLSA):** The federal law which prescribes standards for the basic minimum wage and overtime pay and affects most private and public employment. It applies to employers who have one or more employees. FLSA is administered by the Employment Standards Administration's Wage and Hour Division within the U.S. Department of Labor.

**Family and Medical Leave Act (FMLA):** A federal law that entitles eligible employees of covered employers to take up to 12 weeks of unpaid job-protected leave each year, with the maintenance of group health insurance, for the birth and care of a child, for the placement of a child for adoption or foster care, for the care of a child, spouse, or parent with a serious health condition, or for the employee's serious health condition.

**Fast Track Construction:** A phased approach where the construction process begins before completion of the contract documents. Generally, the cost is not fixed until after construction documents are complete and some construction commitments have already been made.

**Federal Employer Identification Number (EIN):** A 9-digit number issued by the IRS, which is used to identify the tax accounts of employers and certain others who have no employees (also referred to as a taxpayer identification number).

**Federal Unemployment Tax Act (FUTA):** The federal unemployment tax that is part of the federal and state program under which unemployment compensation is paid to workers who lose their jobs.

**Fidelity Bond:** A type of bond that covers business owners for losses due to dishonest acts by their employees.

**Fixed Assets:** Assets needed to carry on the business of a company, which are not normally consumed in the operation of the business (sometimes referred to as capital assets).

**Foreign Entity:** A business originally established in another state or another country.

**Foreman:** An individual who assists the superintendent with daily project operations and usually supervises specific areas by trade.

**For Profit Corporation:** A corporation in existence to make a profit for its owners or shareholders. Corporate tax status is determined by the Internal Revenue Service.

**FUTA:** An abbreviation for Federal Unemployment Tax Act.

# H

**Health Insurance Portability and Accountability Act of 1996 (HIPAA):** A federal law that provides for improved portability and continuity of health insurance coverage connected with employment.

# I

**I-9 Form:** The form required for employers to complete to verify employment eligibility under the Immigration and Nationality Act. I-9 forms must be kept on file for at least three years after the date of hire or for one year after the date employment ends, whichever is later.

**Immaterial Breach (Partial Breach):** A less serious violation of a contract that usually does not result in termination of the contract. The injured party may only sue for the value of the damages.

**Immigration and Nationality Act (INA):** A federal law that outlines the conditions for the temporary and permanent employment of aliens in the United States. It includes provisions for all employers that address employment eligibility and employment verification.

**Income Statement:** A financial statement that provides a summary of the company's revenues and expenses over a given period of time (sometimes called the profit-and-loss statement).

**Indemnification:** A way to transfer risk and exemption from loss that absolves the indemnified party from any payment for losses and damages incurred by a third party.

**Indemnity:** A way to transfer risk and exemption from loss incurred by any course of action. Sometimes an insurance payout is called an indemnity.

**Indirect Expenses:** See Operating Expenses.

**Inland Marine Insurance (Equipment Theft Insurance):** A type of property insurance for your tools and equipment that provides coverage for goods in transit and projects under construction.

**Insurance:** A protective measure in which coverage is obtained for a specific risk (or set of risks) through a contract. In this contract or policy, one party indemnifies another against specified loss in return for premiums paid.

# K

**Key Man Insurance:** A type of insurance coverage for a specific individual necessary for the continuing success of a business. Key man insurance is available as life insurance, disability insurance, or both.

# L

**Lead-Based Paint Renovation, Repair and Painting Program:** This federal regulation involves those who perform renovations for compensation in residential housing that may contain lead paint. It requires for additional provisions to the Lead PRE regulations. Under the Lead-Based Paint Renovation, Repair and Painting Program, contractors must be certified to perform renovation work that disturbs lead-based paint in homes, child care facilities, and schools built before 1978.

**Lead PRE:** This federal regulation involves those who perform renovations for compensation in residential housing built before 1978 that may contain lead paint. It requires mandatory notification for owners and occupants of the building being renovated.

**Liabilities:** All debt and obligations owed by a business.

**Liability Insurance:** A type of insurance designed to protect against third-party claims that arise from alleged negligence resulting in bodily injury or property damage.

**Lien Bond:** A type of bond that guarantees liens cannot be placed against the owner's property by contractors for payment of services.

**Liquid Assets:** Assets that are easily converted to cash.

**Limited Liability Company (LLC):** A legal business entity that has characteristics of both sole proprietorships and corporations. Federal income taxes are paid only on income distributed to members as ordinary income. Members have protection from liability for actions taken by the company or by other members of your company but are not protected from liability for personal actions.

**Liquidity Ratio:** A calculation used to determine if a company can pay its current debts. Calculated by dividing current liabilities into the current assets (sometimes called current ratio).

**Little Miller Acts:** Laws enacted by individual states and local governments regarding required bonds to bid and perform public works projects.

**Long-Term Liabilities:** Debt obligations that extend beyond one year.

**Lump Sum Contract:** A contract where the contractor agrees to complete the project for a predetermined, specified price. The contractor essentially assumes all of the risk under this contract agreement because the contractor is responsible for additional costs associated with unforeseen circumstances.

# M

**Maintenance Bond:** A type of bond that guarantees for a stated period, typically for one year, no defective workmanship or material will appear in the completed project.

**Marketing:** Strategies and techniques used to bring in new customers and retain current customers to ensure a steady flow of leads and customers. This process includes advertising and promotion, pricing strategies, timely distribution, and product design and attributes to meet customer needs.

**Marketing Plan:** A formal document focusing on a company's marketing strategy by outlining the company's vision, customer base, methods of promotion (e.g. advertising, public relations, online marketing, direct sales, etc.), marketing budget, individual responsible for executing the plan, and industry opportunities and challenges.

**MasterFormat:** A classification system published by the Construction Specifications Institute that includes numbers and job tasks grouped by major construction activities.

**Material Breach:** A serious violation of a contract that may void the contract and will most likely end up in litigation.

**Material Safety Data Sheet (MSDS):** A form that accompanies chemicals and is important to workplace safety. The MSDS contains information such as first aid when contact occurs, disposal, storage, protective equipment required, and spill handling procedures.

**Materials Expediter:** An individual who supervises the materials procurement process to ensure accurate and timely delivery of materials.

**Mechanics' Lien:** A legal action that "clouds" the title to real property and serves as an effective method (and sometimes the only method) for securing payment for labor or materials used in the improvement of real property. The lien stops the owner from selling the property with a clear title.

**Medicare:** Social Security and Medicare taxes pay for benefits that workers and families receive under the Federal Insurance Contributions Act (FICA). Medicare tax pays for benefits under the hospital insurance part of FICA.

**Miller Act:** The Miller Act requires performance and payment bonds on all federal construction projects valued at greater than $100,000.

**Minimum Wage:** The minimum amount an employer can pay employees. FLSA and individual state laws designate the minimum pay rate.

**Minor:** An individual under 18 years of age.

**Modified Accelerated Cost Recovery System (MACRS):** A depreciation method approved by the IRS that allows for faster depreciation over longer periods.

**Motor Truck Cargo Insurance:** A type of inland marine insurance protecting the transporter in the event of damaged or lost freight.

# N

**Named Peril Builders' Risk Insurance:** An insurance policy with narrower coverage than all-risk insurance that specifies which perils are covered.

**National Environmental Policy Act (NEPA):** A federal law that ensures that federal agencies consider environmental impacts in federal planning and decision making and covers construction and post-construction activities.

**National Historic Preservation Act (NHPA):** A federal law that protects property that is eligible for or included on the National Register of Historic Places (NRHP).

**Negotiation (Alternative Dispute Resolution):** A dialogue entered into for the purpose of resolving disputes or producing an agreed upon course or courses of action.

**Negotiation (Contract):** The process where the owner and contractor come to an agreement on the price and terms of the contract.

**Net Pay:** The payroll amount an employee receives after taxes and deductions are taken out.

# Appendix A: Glossary

**Net Profit:** The difference between revenues and expenses. Net profit directly contributes to the net worth of the company.

**NPDES:** The abbreviation for the National Pollutant Discharge Elimination System.

# O

**Occupational Safety and Health Act (OSHA):** Federal law governing safe and healthy working conditions by developing standards, providing assistance, information and training, and conducting research.

**Offer:** An offer specifically outlines the obligations of the contract, including the work to be done and compensation for this work (e.g. estimate or bid).

**Operating Expenses:** General items that contribute to the cost of operating the business. These expenses can be put into two categories, selling expenses and fixed overhead (sometimes called indirect expenses).

**OSHA:** An abbreviation for Occupational Safety and Health Administration; Occupational Safety and Health Act.

**OSHA Form 300:** An OSHA form that serves as an injury/illness log, with a separate line entry for each recordable injury or illness.

**OSHA Form 300A:** An OSHA form that includes a summary of the previous year's work-related injuries and illnesses.

**OSHA Form 301:** An OSHA form that serves as an individual incident report providing details about each specific recordable injury or illness.

**Other Than Serious Violation:** A safety violation that has a direct relationship to workplace safety and health, but probably would not cause death or serious physical harm.

**Overhead:** See company overhead; project overhead.

**Overtime:** The hours an employee works when it exceeds more than 40 hours in a workweek. FLSA designates that eligible employees are paid one-and-one-half-times the regular rate for overtime hours.

**Owners' Equity:** Consists of the initial investment in a business, plus accumulated net profits not paid out to the owners.

**Owner's Representative (Owner's Agent):** An appointed representative designated to oversee a project and serve as a liaison to the owner. The owner's representative (agent) may have legal authority to make certain legal decisions on behalf of the owner.

# P

**Partnership:** A business relationship between two or more persons who join to carry on a trade or business. Each person contributes money, property, labor, or skill, and each partner expects to share in the profits and losses of the business.

**Payment Bond:** A type of bond that guarantees subcontractors and suppliers will be paid for work if they perform properly under the contract.

**Percentage of Completion Method:** A method of contract accounting that recognizes income as it is earned during the construction project.

**Performance Bond:** A type of bond that guarantees the contractor will complete a contract within its time frame and conditions.

**Petty Cash Fund:** A cash fund used to make small payments instead of writing a check.

**Positive Cash Flow:** A term used to describe when more cash is received than is going out to pay expenses.

**Professional Liability Insurance (sometimes called Errors and Omissions Insurance):** A type of liability insurance that protects contractors from negligence resulting from errors or omissions of designers and architects.

**Profitability Ratio:** A formula used to calculate the profit margin of a company. It is calculated by dividing revenues into net income.

**Profit-and-Loss Statement:** See Income Statement.

**Progressive Discipline:** A method of corrective action where the consequences of the improper behavior become more significant if it continues.

**Progress Payments:** Partial payments made after completion of specified phases of construction. Payments are generally calculated by taking the difference between the completed work and materials delivered and a predetermined schedule of unit costs.

**Project Manager:** An individual who plans and coordinates a construction project to meet the overall goals of the project and serves as the main contact with the owner.

**Project Overhead:** Items necessary to complete the project but not directly associated with labor and materials (e.g. temporary storage, dumpsters, etc.).

**Property Insurance:** An insurance policy covering property when damage, theft, or loss occurs. Specific risk provisions are often available for occurrences such as fire or theft. Broad-based policies cover a variety of risks (including fire, theft, vandalism, and "acts of God" such as lightning strikes).

# Q

**Quick Ratio:** Similar to the liquidity ratio, it is calculated by dividing the current liabilities into the current assets minus inventory (sometimes called the acid test ratio).

# R

**Recitals (Legal):** Language at the beginning of a contract that provides background to the contract.

**Repeated Violation:** A safety violation of any standard, regulation, rule, or order where, upon reinspection, a substantially similar violation is found.

**Retainage:** A specified amount withheld from each progress payment as protection for the owner to ensure completion of the construction project and provide protection against liens, claims, and defaults.

**Return on Total Assets Ratio:** A formula used to determine if the company's assets are being employed in the best manner. It is calculated by dividing total assets into net profit (after taxes).

**Revenues:** The income received from the daily operations of the business.

**Right-to-Work Laws:** Laws passed at the state-level that secure the right of employees to decide for themselves whether or not to join or financially support a union.

**Risk Management:** An assessment of all areas of a business from operations to administrative functions for the risk of financial loss, lower profit margins, and unnecessary liabilities.

# Appendix A: Glossary

# S

**S Corporation:** A legal business entity formed under the rules of Subchapter S of the Internal Revenue Code. It is taxed like a partnership by passing items of income, loss, deduction, and credits through to its shareholders to be included on their separate returns.

**Self-Employment Tax:** A social security and Medicare tax primarily for individuals who work for themselves.

**Serious Violation:** A violation where there is substantial probability that death or serious physical harm could result and that the employer knew, or should have known, of the hazard.

**Service Contract Act:** The federal act that requires payment of prevailing wage rates and fringe benefits on contracts to provide services to the federal government.

**Single Prime Contracting:** Traditional form of contracting where the project owner typically hires an architectural firm to design the project and the contractor then performs the work according to the specifications of the project and is responsible for the costs of all materials and labor to obtain project completion.

**Social Security Tax:** Social Security and Medicare taxes pay for benefits that workers and families receive under the Federal Insurance Contributions Act (FICA). Social Security tax pays for benefits under the old-age, survivors, and disability insurance part of FICA.

**Sole Proprietorship:** A business that has one individual as the owner (proprietor) who is responsible for 100% of the decisions made on behalf of the business and owns all of the business assets. It can employ others but may just be the owner who works for the business.

**Square-Foot Method Estimate:** An estimate based on a calculation of the square footage of the project multiplied by a unit cost.

**Statement of Cash Flows:** A financial statement that summarizes current cash position, cash sources, and use of these funds over a given period of time.

**Statute of Limitations:** Laws that set a maximum period of time within which a lawsuit or claim may be filed.

**Straight Line Depreciation:** A method of depreciation where the salvage cost is subtracted from the initial cost of the item.

**Subcontractor:** An individual or business that contracts with the general contractor or other subcontractors to complete a portion of a larger project.

**Subcontractor's Bond**: A type of bond that protects the general contractor in the event that the subcontractor does not fully perform the contract and/or pay for labor and materials.

**Superintendent:** An onsite supervisor responsible for the daily operations.

**SUTA Dumping:** The transfer of employees between businesses for the purpose of obtaining a lower unemployment compensation tax rate. SUTA dumping is illegal and subject to criminal and/or civil penalties.

# T

**Taxpayer Identification Number:** See Federal Employer Identification Number.

**Tax Provision Expenses:** Tax liabilities owed for federal, state, and local taxes.

**Title III of the Consumer Credit Protection Act (CCPA):** A federal law that protects employees from being discharged by their employers because their wages have been garnished for any one debt and limits the amount of employees' earnings that may be garnished in any one week.

**Title VII of the Civil Rights Act of 1964:** A federal law that prohibits discrimination on the basis of race, color, religion, national origin, and sex.

**Transportation Floater Insurance:** A type of inland marine insurance protecting the transporter against damage that occurs to freight during transport.

**Turnkey Construction:** Similar to the design/build model, the contractor puts together and manages the construction and design team but also obtains financing and land.

# U

**Unemployment Insurance:** A type of insurance that provides unemployment benefits to eligible workers who become unemployed through no fault of their own and meet certain other eligibility requirements. This program is jointly financed through federal and state employer payroll taxes.

**Uniformed Services Employment and Reemployment Rights Act (USERRA):** A federal law that protects service members' reemployment rights when returning from a period of service in the uniformed services, including those called up from the reserves or National Guard, and prohibits employer discrimination based on military service or obligation.

**Unit-Price Contract:** A type of contract where a price per unit is calculated for each item and the contractor is paid according to the actual quantities used.

**Unit Price Estimating Method**: A method of estimating that bundles all of the cost factors such as labor, materials, equipment, and subcontractors to come up with a unit price for the entire task.

# V

**Value Engineering:** A project management approach with the primary objective of understanding the owner's cost, quality, and time priorities to deliver a product of the highest value.

# W

**Wage Garnishment Law:** A federal law that limits the amount an individual's income may be legally garnished and prohibits firing an employee whose pay is garnished for payment of a single debt.

**Walsh-Healey Public Contracts Act:** A federal law that requires payment of minimum wage rates and overtime pay on contracts that provide goods to the federal government.

**Willful Violation:** A safety violation that the employer knowingly commits or commits with plain indifference to the law.

**Work Hours:** As defined under FLSA, hours that ordinarily include all time during which an employee is required to be on the employer's premises, on duty, or at a prescribed work place.

**Worker Adjustment and Retraining Notification Act (WARN)**: A federal law that offers protection to workers, their families, and communities by requiring employers to provide notice 60 days in advance of covered plant closings and covered mass layoffs.

**Workers' Compensation Insurance:** A type of insurance providing monetary compensation to employees who are injured or disabled on the job and benefits for dependents of those workers who are killed because of work-related accidents or illnesses. The insurance is purchased by the employer; no part of it should be paid for by employees or deducted from their pay.

**Working Capital:** The amount of cash available after liabilities or debts are paid. Working capital measures the liquidity of the company's assets.

**Workweek:** As defined under FLSA, it is a period of 168 hours during seven consecutive 24-hour periods. It may begin on any day of the week and at any hour of the day established by the employer.

# Appendix B: Business Plan Template

The following business plan template can be customized for your company. These forms are also located at **NASCLAforms.org** using access code **LA129354** in case you need to modify them on your computer. You may want to work through this plan as you review each chapter, as some of the business plan section topics are covered in more depth.

---

## Business Plan Outline

**Section 1: Cover Sheet**

  1a.  Name of Business

  1b.  Contact Information

**Section 2: Executive Summary**

  2a.  Plan Highlights

  2b.  Keys to Success

**Section 3: Company Summary**

  3a.  Vision

  3b.  Mission

  3c.  Legal Structure

  3d.  Management and Personnel Plan

  3e.  Proposed Location

  3f.  Facilities Requirements

  3g.  Operational Hours

**Section 4: Products and/or Service**

  4a.  Product and/or Service Description

  4b.  Vendors

  4c.  Technology

  4d.  Expansion Opportunities

**Section 5: Market Analysis**

  5a.  Target Market Definition

  5b.  Market Needs

  5c.  Market Trends

  5d.  Market Growth

  5e.  Competitive Comparison

**Section 6: Marketing Strategy**

  6a.  Value Proposition

  6b.  Competitive Edge

  6c.  Pricing Strategy

  6d.  Promotion Strategy

  6e.  Marketing Programs

**Section 7: Financial Plan**

  7a.  Sales Forecast and Assumptions

  7b.  Profit and Loss Pro Forma

  7c.  Source of Financing

---

**Note:** You may also refer to the Financial Management chapter for additional financial documents such as a balance sheet, income statement, and statement of cash flows. The profit and loss pro forma is a good tool for newly-established businesses to determine how much revenue is needed to break even.

# Section 1: Cover Sheet

The cover sheet should contain the name of the business, address, phone number, fax number, e-mail address, and contact name. Some cover sheets also contain a confidentiality statement.

# Section 2: Executive Summary

A business plan normally starts with an executive summary, which should be concise and interesting. This summary includes the highlights of your plan and serves as an introduction to the rest of your plan. Topics in your executive summary should include, but not be limited to, the following:

✓ Business name
✓ Business location
✓ Product or service offered
✓ Purpose of the plan
✓ Projected sales
✓ Profitability
✓ Keys to success

The executive summary should only be a page or two long. Although the executive summary appears first in the printed document, most business plan developers do not write it until after the plan is complete.

# Section 3: Company Summary

1.  **Vision and Mission:** Include a vision and mission statement for your company. The vision should be a short statement about the company's aspirations for the future. The mission describes the company's primary business purpose or goal. These statements outline the business concept and provide a concise definition of where your company fits in the market.

2.  **Legal Structure:** Define the legal structure of your company (i.e., sole proprietorship, partnership, corporation, or limited liability company). Explain why you chose this structure and the benefits it will provide to you and your company. Legal structure is covered in Chapter 2.

3.  **Management:** Outline the key management personnel needed to run your business. Can you run the business yourself or do you need to hire managers to help run the operations? What are the job responsibilities of these managers?

4.  **Employees:** How many employees do you require? What are the job responsibilities of the employees?

5.  **Location:** Describe the location of your business. You do not need to provide a specific address if you do not have one, but identify the area (e.g., downtown location, at home, in a rural area). Explain why this location will provide you with the best opportunity for success.

6.  **Facility Requirements:** Identify your facility requirements. Do you need office space, a production area, storage space, or mobile storage? You may want to draw a diagram of the space.

7.  **Hours of Operation:** What are your hours of operation? Explain how these hours will provide the maximum benefit to your customer. How will you handle emergency situations that arise outside of normal working hours?

# Section 4: Product or Service Description

Defining your product or service (or both) may seem simple. You must describe not only your product or service but how you will provide it to your customers. For example, you may be a general contractor, but without reliable subcontractors and suppliers, you may not be able to complete your projects in the time frame promised to the customer.

Appendix B: Business Plan Template

1. **Product or Service Description:** Write a summary explaining your specialty. For example, are you a general contractor, plumbing contractor, etc.?

2. **Legal Requirements:** Do you have any licensing or registration requirements? Are there any legal requirements for practicing your trade or running your business?

3. **Subcontractors and Suppliers:** Who will be your primary subcontractors and suppliers? What process will you use to evaluate subcontractors and suppliers?

4. **Technology Trends:** Summarize how technology will affect your business. Are there efficiencies that can be gained through technology? For example, can you integrate scheduling or estimating systems into your business processes?

5. **Growth Opportunities:** What expansion opportunities exist in the future after your company is established? Can you offer additional products or services, or expand your customer base to other locations?

## Section 5: Market Analysis

A market analysis is often performed as one of the first tasks in researching and formulating a business plan. Understanding your customers, the demand for your work, and your competition is important to the future success of your business.

1. **Target Market:** Define the target market for your product or service. Describe the key characteristics of your customers. For example, do your primary customers include families, retired adults, or businesses?

2. **Product or Service Description:** Describe the need your product or service will be filling for your customers. If you will provide both products and services, describe how these will benefit your customers.

3. **Trends:** Describe how your product or service aligns with the consumer trends of your customers. What are the construction trends for your trade and how do these fit your customer's needs?

4. **Growth Opportunities:** Outline growth opportunities that exist within your target market. For example, if you are a pool builder and your target market is young families, you may want to concentrate on single-family homes rather than commercial projects.

5. **Competition:** List your major competitors. Are they local, regional, or national?

## Section 6: Marketing Strategy

A marketing strategy is easily formulated by using the "4 P's:" Product, Price, Promotion, and Place. Product is not just your product or service, but how it will benefit your customer. Price refers to your pricing strategy, which can vary based on the market, your goals, and your competition. Promotion deals with marketing in a traditional sense. Your customers will find out about your business through your promotional efforts. Place defines your distribution strategy. In the construction industry, distribution defines the type of customers you want to target. For example, you may decide to differentiate yourself by specializing in certain types of construction.

1. **Value Proposition:** Describe the value that your company will provide your customers. What benefits of using your company will you promote to your customers? For example, you may promote your level of quality or service.

2. **Competitive Edge:** Describe what makes your product or service unique and how you have differentiated yourself from your competitors.

3. **Pricing Strategy:** What pricing strategy will you use? Some options include:

   ✓ Cost-plus pricing, where you determine a markup percentage and add it to the cost of the job.
   ✓ Consistency with competition, where your pricing reflects what the competition is charging.
   ✓ Value pricing, where you try to undercut your competition with lower prices.

4. **Promotion:** How will you familiarize potential customers with your business? Will you promote your product in special venues (i.e., trade shows or special events)? Are there any businesses you can build a co-op relationship with so you can cross-promote each other? For example, you might partner with another trade or supplier to promote each other.

5. **Advertising:** How will you advertise? Will you use media such as radio, TV, newspapers, and the Internet? How often will you advertise?

6. **Sales:** Will you hire sales representatives to promote your company? If so, how many? How will the sales force be divided up? By area or region?

# Section 7: Financial Plan

A financial plan can include several aspects of the potential financial health of the company. At a minimum, it should include projected profits over a specific period. This template, for example, shows the first three years of operation. The financial plan should also explain projected cash flow and identify any additional capital required from outside investors or loans.

The profit-and-loss statement is a tabulation of the gross sales income for the company from which all attributed costs must be deducted. A *pro forma* is a "best guess" at these sales numbers and the associated costs. From this pro forma, you can see your profit or loss based on the numbers you projected and adjust your budget accordingly. A blank profit-and-loss form is located at the end of this section, if you are unable to use the form on the **NASCLAforms.org** website. If you use the spreadsheet located on the website, it will automatically calculate gross profit and net income. These calculations were derived from the following formulas:

**Income – Cost of Goods Sold = Gross Profit**

**Gross Profit – Expenses = Net Income**

You will learn more about financial calculations in the financial management chapter.

## Sales/Income

Use the following points to help you make your sales and expense projections.

You need to determine the average price of the jobs you perform and the number of customers you are projecting for the year. This is your "best guess," but if you have any historical sales data, you may want to use this information in your calculations to determine how your business sales will grow over time.

However you determine your sales, you must list your assumptions so the person reviewing your business plan will understand the numbers presented in your plan.

**Projected sales numbers**

|        | Sales (in dollars) |
|--------|--------------------|
| Year 1 |                    |
| Year 2 |                    |
| Year 3 |                    |

Transfer sales numbers into the profit-and-loss worksheet.

# Appendix B: Business Plan Template

## Cost of Goods Sold (COGS)

Cost of goods sold shows the cost of materials and production of the goods a business sells. For each year, enter your inventory cost and the cost to produce the final product for the customer and add together to show the totals. This total represents the cost of goods sold.

|  | Year 1 | Year 2 | Year 3 |
|---|---|---|---|
| Inventory |  |  |  |
| Production Payroll |  |  |  |
| Total |  |  |  |

Transfer COGS numbers into the profit-and-loss worksheet.

## Management Salaries

Determine how many managers or supervisors you will need to operate your business. A published salary survey will help you estimate what they earn in your type of business and in your region. Determine if you will need to add managers or supervisors in years two and three if you have an increase in business.

|  | Number of Managers | Manager Annual Salary | Total Management Salaries |
|---|---|---|---|
| Year 1 |  |  |  |
| Year 2 |  |  |  |
| Year 3 |  |  |  |

Enter the total management salaries in the respective boxes on your spreadsheet.

## Payroll Taxes

Payroll taxes are calculated at approximately 13% of the salaries listed on your spreadsheet. A formula has been entered to calculate that amount automatically.

Payroll taxes include the following items:

- ✓ Social Security, also known as FICA (a set percentage deducted from an employee's check and EMPLOYER MATCHED)
- ✓ Medicare, also called FICA Medicare (a set percentage deducted from an employee's check and EMPLOYER MATCHED)
- ✓ FUTA - Federal Unemployment Tax Act, authorizes the IRS to use monies for job service and training funded through the federal employment agency; EMPLOYER PAID ONLY
- ✓ SUTA - State Unemployment Tax Act, authorizes the state to use monies for job service/training and retraining of displaced workers; EMPLOYER-PAID ONLY
- ✓ FUI - Federal Unemployment Insurance; EMPLOYER-PAID ONLY
- ✓ SUI - State Unemployment Insurance; EMPLOYER-PAID ONLY

More details on payroll taxes are provided in Chapter 15.

## Outside Services

These services apply to people or businesses who provide services to your company not directly related to the sales or income of the company. They would not appear on your payroll. Estimate your annual expenses for the following outside services. Keep in mind that the cost may be higher in the first year due to start-up needs. The cost may drop in the second year and then level off in the third year.

|  | Year 1 | Year 2 | Year 3 |
|---|---|---|---|
| Lawyer |  |  |  |
| Accountant |  |  |  |
| Technology Consultant |  |  |  |
| Total |  |  |  |

Enter the year totals into the spreadsheet.

## Advertising and Promotion

Consider the type of marketing you will need. If you are creating a radio, newspaper or TV ad, get an estimate on what that would cost. Don't forget to calculate the frequency of advertising you will do. For example, let's say a magazine ad costs $1,000 for a quarter-page ad and the magazine comes out monthly. Your advertising cost would be $12,000 a year. You may want to advertise by printing flyers and mailing them out. Calculate the printing costs as well as the postage to send out the flyers.

|  | Year 1 | Year 2 | Year 3 |
|---|---|---|---|
| Radio |  |  |  |
| TV |  |  |  |
| Newspaper |  |  |  |
| Magazine |  |  |  |
| Flyers |  |  |  |
| Direct Mail |  |  |  |
| Special Events |  |  |  |
| Online Ads |  |  |  |
| Other Please Specify: |  |  |  |
| Total |  |  |  |

Enter the year totals into the spreadsheet.

## Rent

If you rent a facility, determine the rental costs per year. If you have not decided on a location, you may want to look at a few locations and calculate an average rent cost to determine a figure for this category. Keep in mind the square footage requirements that you have set out.

# Appendix B: Business Plan Template

B-7

|  | Annual Rent |
|---|---|
| Location #1 | |
| Location #2 | |
| Location #3 | |
| Average of all three locations | |

If you are going to stay in one location, your rent should remain fixed over three years. If you plan on expanding in years two and three, you may want to increase rent accordingly.

Enter the average of all three locations in the rent column on your spreadsheet.

## Office Supplies

Office supplies include items such as paper, pens, printer cartridges, tape, and other materials as well as cleaning supplies. As your business increases, the consumption of these supplies may increase accordingly.

|  | Year 1 | Year 2 | Year 3 |
|---|---|---|---|
| Office Supplies | | | |
| Cleaning Supplies | | | |
| Total | | | |

Enter the year totals into the spreadsheet.

## Dues, Subscriptions, and Licenses

You may want to join a Chamber of Commerce or trade group or subscribe to trade publications. Your business may also need a license to operate. For example, if you are starting a plumbing company, you may be required to get a contractor's license.

|  | Year 1 | Year 2 | Year 3 |
|---|---|---|---|
| Chamber of Commerce Membership | | | |
| Business Organization Membership (i.e., National Homebuilders Association) | | | |
| Magazine/Newspaper Subscriptions | | | |
| Business License Fees | | | |
| Total | | | |

Enter the year totals into the spreadsheet.

## Travel

Does your business require you to travel to meet with customers? Will you travel locally, regionally, or nationally? What are the air travel, rental car, and hotel costs for this travel requirement? Note that the spreadsheet has a separate section for automobile expenses, where you enter costs such as gasoline or repairs. Use the automobile expense section for trips that will be taken in a company or personal vehicle.

|  | Year 1 | Year 2 | Year 3 |
|---|---|---|---|
| Air Travel |  |  |  |
| Rental Cars |  |  |  |
| Hotel |  |  |  |
| Other |  |  |  |
| Please Specify: |  |  |  |
| Total |  |  |  |

Enter the year totals into the spreadsheet.

## Meals and Entertainment

Determine if you will be providing meals or taking your clients and vendors out for entertainment.

Keep in mind that the IRS allows you to take only a 50 percent deduction on meals and entertainment. It is not considered a 100 percent business expense. Although you enter the full amount on your profit-and-loss statement, your tax accountant will make the proper adjustments on your tax return at the end of the year.

|  | Year 1 | Year 2 | Year 3 |
|---|---|---|---|
| Meals |  |  |  |
| Entertainment |  |  |  |
| Total |  |  |  |

Enter the year totals into the spreadsheet.

## Automobile Expense

Determine if you will need one or more automobiles or trucks to operate your business. The cost to purchase each vehicle appears under "Assets" on your balance sheet, and the cost to operate the vehicles appears under automobile expense on the profit-and-loss statement.

|  | Year 1 | Year 2 | Year 3 |
|---|---|---|---|
| Gasoline |  |  |  |
| Oil Changes |  |  |  |
| Car Washes |  |  |  |
| Other |  |  |  |
| (Repairs) Please Specify: |  |  |  |
| Total |  |  |  |

Enter the annual totals into the spreadsheet.

## Appendix B: Business Plan Template

## Utilities and Telephone

Determine what your utilities and telephone costs will be for the first three years your business is operational. To arrive at this estimate, you will need to determine how many telephone lines and cell phones you need. You should also itemize Internet service and record these totals under this line item.

|  | Year 1 | Year 2 | Year 3 |
|---|---|---|---|
| Electric |  |  |  |
| Water |  |  |  |
| Garbage |  |  |  |
| Telephone |  |  |  |
| Internet Service |  |  |  |
| Other Please Specify: |  |  |  |
| Total |  |  |  |

Enter the annual totals into the spreadsheet.

## Auto Insurance

If you have business vehicles, you will need to carry insurance on them. If you increase the number of vehicles in years two and three, insurance expenses will increase as well. Certain vehicles may also cost more to insure than others. For example, if you have delivery trucks, the insurance will probably be more expensive than a mid-size car.

|  | Year 1 | Year 2 | Year 3 |
|---|---|---|---|
| Vehicle #1 |  |  |  |
| Vehicle #2 |  |  |  |
| Vehicle #3 |  |  |  |
| Total |  |  |  |

Enter the annual totals into the spreadsheet.

## Group Medical Insurance

You may want to carry medical, dental, or life insurance for your employees as a benefit and to increase employee retention.

|  | Year 1 | Year 2 | Year 3 |
|---|---|---|---|
| Medical |  |  |  |
| Dental |  |  |  |
| Life |  |  |  |
| Total |  |  |  |

Enter the annual totals into the spreadsheet.

## Business Insurance

By law, businesses are required to carry workers' compensation insurance. Business liability insurance protects your business against accidents such as fire, flooding, burglary, etc. Business liability insurance is not required by law but by contract. For example, most landlords require you to carry business liability insurance, as do banks and governmental agencies with which you have a contract. Insurance and risk management are covered in more detail in the managing risk chapter.

|  | Year 1 | Year 2 | Year 3 |
|---|---|---|---|
| Workers' Compensation |  |  |  |
| Business Liability |  |  |  |
| Total |  |  |  |

Enter the annual totals into the spreadsheet.

# Worksheet

This is a scratch sheet for entering estimates and data that can then be entered in the spreadsheet.

|  | Year 1 | Year 2 | Year 3 |
|---|---|---|---|
| **Income** | | | |
| Sales | | | |
| **Total Income** | 0.00 | 0.00 | 0.00 |
| | | | |
| **Cost of Goods Sold** | | | |
| Inventory Cost | | | |
| Production Payroll Cost | | | |
| **Total COGS** | 0.00 | 0.00 | 0.00 |
| | | | |
| **Gross Profit** | 0.00 | 0.00 | 0.00 |
| | | | |
| **Expense** | | | |
| Management Salaries | | | |
| Payroll Taxes | 0.00 | 0.00 | 0.00 |
| Outside Services | | | |
| Advertising and Promotion | | | |
| Rent | | | |
| Office Supplies | | | |
| Dues, Subscriptions, and Licenses | | | |
| Travel | | | |
| Meals and Entertainment | | | |
| Automobile Expense | | | |
| Utilities/Telephone | | | |
| Insurance Auto | | | |
| Insurance Group Medical | | | |
| Business Insurance | | | |
| **Total Expense** | 0.00 | 0.00 | 0.00 |
| | | | |
| **Net Income** | 0.00 | 0.00 | 0.00 |

# Appendix C: Useful Links

Listed below are website links that relate to each of the chapters. These websites are provided for your reference for more in-depth searches of the topic areas contained in this book. Internet links to these websites are provided at NASCLAforms.org using access code LA129354.

## Chapter 1 - The Plan

| | | |
|---|---|---|
| **American Express Small Business** | American Express offers business planning links and an area where you can post questions for a small business advisor. | www.americanexpress.com/us/small-business/openforum/explore |
| **Business Plan Pro** | This site offers tools on how to write a business plan including samples and tips to starting a business. | www.bplans.com |
| **Sample Business Plans** | These sites provide sample business plans and other valuable business management materials. | www.allbusiness.com <br><br> www.inc.com <br><br> www.bizmove.com/small-business/business-plan.htm <br><br> www.bizmove.com/starting/m1e2.htm |
| **SBA Business Planning** | The SBA has several different links on writing and using your business plan. | www.sba.gov/category/navigation-structure/starting-managing-business |

## Chapter 2 - Choosing Your Business Structure

| | | |
|---|---|---|
| **IRS Business Structures** | The IRS provides a summary of tax considerations by business structure. | www.irs.gov/businesses/small/article/0,,id=98359,00.html |
| **Louisiana Secretary of State** | The Louisiana Secretary of State Corporations Division has information on business filings and a link to an online business name reservation form. | www.sos.louisiana.gov |
| **SBA Legal Aspects** | The SBA has several different links on forms of ownership and licenses. | www.sba.gov/category/navigation-structure/starting-managing-business/managing-business |
| **Louisiana Economic Development** | The Louisiana Department of Economic Development has information on business filings. | www.opportunitylouisiana.com |

## Chapter 3 – Becoming a Licensed Contractor

| | | |
|---|---|---|
| **Louisiana Licensing Board for Contractors** | The Louisiana Licensing Board for Contractors regulates commercial and residential contractors. Their website has useful information on the licensing process, laws and regulations, and licensing forms. | www.lslbc.louisiana.gov |

## Chapter 4 – Managing Risk

| | | |
|---|---|---|
| **Entrepreneur.com** | Entrepreneur.com has links to insurance resources. | www.entrepreneur.com |
| **Louisiana Department of Labor, Office of Regulatory Services** | The Louisiana Department of Labor, Office of Regulatory Services website gives information on state unemployment. | www.laworks.net/UnemploymentInsurance/UI_Employers.asp |
| **Louisiana Office of Workers' Compensation** | The Louisiana Office of Workers' Compensation website provides information on the state workers' compensation program. | www.laworks.net/WorkersComp/OWC_EmployerMenu.asp |
| **Surety Information Office** | This site has resources related to bonding, bank letters of credit and publishes the "Construction Project Owners Guide to Surety Bond Claims." | www.sio.org |

## Chapter 5 – Your Business Toolbox

| | | |
|---|---|---|
| **Louisiana Economic Development Department** | The Louisiana Economic Development Department website has information about assistance programs and an online business resource guide. | www.led.louisiana.gov |
| **Louisiana Minority Supplier Development Council** | The Louisiana Minority Supplier Development Council website has information on minority business certifications. | www.lamsdc.org |
| **Louisiana Secretary of State, GeauxBiz** | The GeauxBiz website provides information on the licenses and permits needed to start your business in Louisiana. | www.geauxbiz.com |
| **Louisiana Small Business Development Center** | The Louisiana Small Business Development Center website has information about assistance programs and a resource center with useful links. | www.lsbdc.org |
| **SBA Special Interests** | The SBA has several different links for women and minority entrepreneurs. | www.sba.gov/content/minority-owned-businesses |

# Appendix C: Useful Links

| | | |
|---|---|---|
| **Service Corps of Retired Executives (SCORE)** | The SCORE website has useful links for small business and a listing of local SCORE centers. | www.score.org |
| **Small Business Administration (SBA)** | The SBA website has resources for small businesses and a link to the Connecticut District Office website. | www.sba.gov/la |
| **Small Business Administration (SBA) Small Disadvantaged Business Certification** | The SBA website has resources for small disadvantaged business certifications. | www.sba.gov/sdb |
| **U.S. Minority Business Development Agency (MBDA)** | The U.S. MBDA website has links on starting, managing, and financing your business. | www.mbda.gov |
| **U.S. Department of Commerce, Economic Development Administration (EDA)** | The U.S. Department of Commerce, EDA division has information on funding opportunities and additional resources. | www.eda.gov |

## Chapter 6 - Marketing and Sales

| | | |
|---|---|---|
| **Entrepreneur.com Marketing** | Entrepreneur.com has several articles on small business marketing. | www.entrepreneur.com/marketing/index.html |
| **KnowThis.com Sample Marketing Plans** | KnowThis.com has information on writing marketing plans and sample plans. | www.knowthis.com/how-to-write-a-marketing-plan |
| **SBA Marketing Basics** | The SBA has several different links on marketing research and writing your marketing plan. | www.sba.gov/content/developing-marketing-plan |

## Chapter 7 - Bidding and Estimating

| | | |
|---|---|---|
| **Bidshop.com Estimating Software** | This site gives a list of software by type of estimating program. | www.bidshop.org |
| **DMOZ.com Estimating Software** | This site gives a comprehensive list of estimating software. | www.dmoz.org/Computers/Software/Industry-Specific/Construction/Project_Management/Estimating |
| **U.S. Department of Labor, Bureau of Labor Statistics** | The Bureau of Labor Statistics site has helpful information on wages, earnings, and business costs. | www.bls.gov |

## Chapter 8 - Contract Management

| | | |
|---|---|---|
| **B4UBuild.com** | B4UBuild.com has articles on contract law for residential builders. | www.b4ubuild.com/resources/contract/index.shtml |
| **FreeAdvice.com** | Free Advice.com has links to different contract topics. | www.law.freeadvice.com/general_practice/contract_law |
| **Nolo.com** | Nolo.com has articles about contract law. | www.nolo.com |

## Chapter 9 - Scheduling and Project Management

| | | |
|---|---|---|
| **Construction place.com** | Constructionplace.com has an informative glossary of terms focused on construction management. | www.constructionplace.com |
| **FreeDownload Center.com** | Free Download Center.com has project management software downloads. | www.freedownloadscenter.com/Business/Project_Management |

## Chapter 10 - Customer Relations

| | | |
|---|---|---|
| **Microsoft Small Business Center** | The Microsoft site offers helpful customer relations links. | www.microsoft.com/en-us/business/ |
| **Quicken Small Business Center** | The Quicken site offers articles on building excellent customer relations. | www.quicken.intuit.com/all-videos-and-articles.jsp |

## Chapter 11 - Employee Management

| | | |
|---|---|---|
| **Construction Employee Interview Sample Questions** | These sites provide sample employee interview questions for the construction industry. | www.interviewquestionsandanswers.biz/construction-interview-questions-and-answers<br><br>www.constructionarticle.com/common-job-interview-questions |
| **DOL Employment Law Guide** | The Department of Labor has several links on employment law compliance, a compliance guide, and a compliance advisor. | www.dol.gov/compliance/guide/index.htm<br><br>www.dol.gov/elaws/ |
| **IRS Forms** | This site contains IRS forms, such as the W-4 and W-5 that you can download. | www.irs.gov/Forms-&-Pubs |
| **Louisiana New Hire Reportings** | The Louisiana DOL site gives information on employment laws and resources for employers. | www.laworks.net |
| **Louisiana Department of Labor (LDOL)** | The Louisiana Department of Labor, Office of Regulatory Services website gives information on state unemployment. | www.laworks.net/UnemploymentInsurance/UI_Employers.asp |
| **Louisiana Office of Workers' Compensation** | The Louisiana Office of Workers' Compensation website provides information on the state workers' compensation program. | www.laworks.net/WorkersComp/OWC_EmployerMenu.asp |

Appendix C: Useful Links

| | | |
|---|---|---|
| **SBA Employment Law** | The SBA has several different links on employment law. | www.sba.gov/content/employment-labor-law |
| **U.S. Citizenship and Immigration Services** | The I-9 form can be downloaded from this site. | www.uscis.gov |
| **U.S. Equal Employment Opportunity Commission (EEOC)** | The EEOC website has information about the Americans with Disabilities Act (ADA). | www.eeoc.gov |

## Chapter 12 - Jobsite Safety and Environmental Factors

| | | |
|---|---|---|
| **Common Ground Alliance (CGA)** | The Common Ground Alliance is available by calling 811. CGA can connect contractors to One Call Centers to locate underground utilities. | www.call811.com |
| **Construction Industry Compliance Center** | The Construction Industry Compliance Center website has information available on environmental regulations including hazardous and non-hazardous waste. | www.cicacenter.org |
| **Environmental Protection Agency** | The Environmental Protection Agency provides a publication called Managing Your Environmental Responsibilities. | www.epa.gov/Compliance/resources/publications/assistance/sectors/constructmyer/myerguide.pdf |
| **Environmental Protection Agency-Asbestos-Containing Materials List** | The Environmental Protection Agency website provides a list of asbestos-containing materials. | www.epa.gov/asbestos |
| **Environmental Protection Agency-Green Building** | The Environmental Protection Agency website provides information on components of green building, national, state and local funding opportunities, and publications on various environmental topics. | www.epa.gov/greenbuilding |
| **Environmental Protection Agency-Lead in Paint, Dust, and Soil** | The Environmental Protection Agency website provides information on lead hazards. | www.epa.gov/lead |
| **Louisiana Department of Environmental Quality (LDEQ)** | The Louisiana Department of Environmental Quality website has information on environmental services, permitting resources, environmental compliance, and assessment services. | www.deq.louisiana.gov/portal |
| **Louisiana Department of Labor** | The Louisiana Department of Labor website has links to workplace health and safety. | www.laworks.net |

| | | |
|---|---|---|
| **Louisiana One Call 811** | Louisiana's digging safety website and hotline. This site provides information on underground safety law and procedures. | www.laonecall.com |
| **OSHA** | The OSHA website has links regarding safety on the job and safety laws and programs. | www.osha.gov |
| **OSHA Compliance Assistance for Construction** | The OSHA website has a page with numerous construction compliance assistance links. | www.osha.gov/doc |
| **OSHA Construction Resource Manual** | OSHA publishes a construction resource manual online with safety rules and regulations. | www.osha.gov/Publications/Const_Res_Man |

# Chapter 13 - Working with Subcontractors

| | | |
|---|---|---|
| **IRS Publication 1779** | This IRS publication provides criteria to determine employee versus independent contractor status. | www.irs.gov/pub/irs-pdf/p1779.pdf |

# Chapter 14 - Financial Management

| | | |
|---|---|---|
| **IRS Publication 15: Circular E** | The Circular E, used for federal income tax withholding, is available on the IRS website. | www.irs.gov/publications/p15/index.html |
| **SBA Balance Sheet Template** | The SBA has a balance sheet template that you can customize. | www.sba.gov/library/balsheet.xls |
| **SBA Income Statement Template** | The SBA has an income statement template that you can customize. | www.sba.gov/library/incstmt.xls |
| **SBA Financing Basics** | The SBA has several different links on financing and financial statements. | www.sba.gov/category/navigation-structure/starting-managing-business/starting-business/preparing-your-finances/understanding-basics |
| **Social Security Administration** | The Social Security Administration website has information on the current social security tax rate. | www.ssa.gov |

# Chapter 15 - Tax Basics

| | | |
|---|---|---|
| **How to Apply for an EIN** | There are several ways to apply for an EIN. The IRS outlines the procedure on their website. | www.irs.gov/Businesses/Small-Businesses-&-Self-Employed/How-to-Apply-for-an-EIN |
| **IRS Service** | The IRS site has tax forms, publications, and useful information for small businesses. | www.irs.gov |
| **Louisiana Department of Revenue** | The Louisiana Department of Revenue site provides helpful information on state taxes. | www.rev.state.la.us |

Appendix C: Useful Links

| Tax Basics | The SBA has several different links on federal, state, and local taxes. | www.sba.gov/category/navigation-structure/starting-managing-business/starting-business/establishing-business/taxes |

## Chapter 16 - Louisiana Mechanics' Lien Law

| FindLaw.com | FindLaw.com has useful articles on lien law. | www.findlaw.com |
| Statutes Governing Louisiana Mechanics' Lien Law | Legislation governing the Louisiana Mechanics' Lien Law can be found on the Louisiana State Legislature website. Search under Title 9. | www.legis.state.la.us |

## Trade Links

| American Institute of Architects (AIA) | This site has information about the organization and contract documents for purchase. | www.aia.org |
| American National Standards Institute (ANSI) | The ANSI website has information on membership, accreditation services, and educational resources. | www.ansi.org |
| American Society of Plumbing Engineers (ASPE) | The ASPE website has information on membership, certifications, and useful resources. | www.aspe.org |
| American Society of Civil Engineers (ASCE) | The ASCE website has information on membership, conferences, publications, and continuing education. | www.asce.org |
| American Subcontractors Association (ASA) | This site has information for subcontractors and suppliers in the construction industry. | www.asaonline.com |
| American Water Works Association (AWWA) | The AWWA website has information on membership, accreditation services, and educational resources. | www.awwa.org |
| Associated Builders and Contractors (ABC) | The ABC website has information on membership, training, a list of contractors, and links to business development, safety, insurance, and legal resources. | www.abc.org |
| Associated General Contractors (AGC) | This site has information for construction contractors and industry related companies. | www.agc.org |
| International Association of Plumbing and Mechanical Officials (IAPMO) | The IAPMO website has information on membership, certification, and educational resources. | www.iapmo.org |

| | | |
|---|---|---|
| **Louisiana Home Builders Association (LHBA)** | The LHBA website has information on membership, industry news, and legislative issues | www.lhba.org |
| **National Association of Home Builders (NAHB)** | This site is for people interested in homebuilding and the industry. | www.nahb.org |
| **National Association of the Remodeling Industry (NARI)** | This site is for people interested in the remodeling industry. | www.nari.org |
| **National Association of State Contractor Licensing Agencies (NASCLA)** | This site contains useful information about state licensing agencies and information about the organization. | www.nascla.org |
| **National Association of Women in Construction (NAWIC)** | This site has information for women in the construction industry. | www.nawic.org |
| **National Electrical Contractors Association (NECA)** | The NECA website has information on membership, codes and standards, industry news, and educational resources. | www.necanet.org |
| **Plumbing, Heating and Cooling Contractors Association (PHCC)** | The PHCC website has information on membership, educational resources, and a list of contractors. | www.phccweb.org |
| **Water Quality Association (WQA)** | The WQA website has information on membership, certifications, educational resources, and a list of contractors. | www.wqa.org |

# Appendix D: New Business Checklist

The following is a checklist of steps to starting your business. These steps provide a general overview, but you should check with a professional to determine the legal, financial, and tax obligations specific to your business.

**Complete Your Business Plan (covered in Chapter 1 and Appendix A)**

✓ Establish your business vision and mission.

✓ Determine your management structure.

✓ Identify your facility requirements and location.

✓ Research your market and identify your competitors.

✓ Establish a marketing plan and expansion goals.

✓ Determine your break-even point and your financial goals.

**Choose Your Form of Organization (covered in Chapter 2)**

✓ Hire a lawyer to prepare organization documents and give legal advice on business issues.

✓ Choose a form of organization (i.e., sole proprietorship, partnership, or corporation).

✓ Prepare and file business organization documents (i.e., Partnership Agreement, Articles of Organization, Articles of Incorporation, etc.).

✓ Register any fictitious names with the proper state and local municipalities.

✓ Obtain the required business licenses from state and local municipalities.

**Set Up Business Finances**

✓ Select an accountant to prepare financial documents and give business financial advice.

✓ Select a banker and open a business checking account.

✓ Apply for business loans (if applicable).

✓ Apply for business credit cards and establish a line of credit.

**Obtain the Proper Contractor's Licensure (covered in Chapter 3)**

✓ Obtain the proper application materials and review the process for obtaining licensure.

✓ Complete application materials with required documentation.

✓ Understand the requirements for maintaining proper licensure.

## Assess Your Areas of Risk and Obtain the Proper Insurance Coverage (covered in Chapter 4)

✓ Select an insurance company and agent to help assess your risk and coverage requirements.

✓ Obtain business insurance (liability, workers' compensation, automobile, etc.).

✓ Obtain required bonds.

✓ Obtain unemployment insurance registration materials from the proper state agency.

## Obtain the Proper Tax Documentation (covered in Chapter 15)

✓ Apply for a federal employer identification number (if applicable).

✓ Obtain a state employer identification number (if applicable).

✓ Obtain the proper federal and state tax forms (i.e., sales and use tax, withholding tax, etc.).

# Appendix E: Louisiana Contractors Licensing Law

## FOREWORD

Appendices E and F present the Louisiana Contractors Licensing Laws, current through the 2014 Regular Legislative Session, and the Rules and Regulations adopted by the Louisiana State Licensing Board for Contractors.

Commercial projects of $50,000 or more require a license. A license is required for residential building contractors when the cost of the undertaking exceeds $75,000. Residential building contractors are required to submit certificates evidencing workers' compensation coverage in compliance with Title 23 of the Louisiana Revised Statutes of 1950, and general liability insurance in a minimum amount of one hundred thousand dollars ($100,000).

Commercial and residential licenses expire on the anniversary of the date on which the license was originally issued. Licensees may elect one, two, or three-year license renewal terms. A business or personal check is acceptable for license or registration renewal fees, if received by the State Licensing Board office on or before the expiration date of the license or registration. Renewals can also be made online at www.lslbc.louisiana.gov.

Home improvement contractors are required to register with the Board in order to perform services in an amount between seven thousand five hundred dollars ($7,500) and seventy-five thousand dollars ($75,000). Contractors who hold valid commercial or residential licenses with the Board are exempt from this registration requirement. Home improvement contractors are required to submit certificates evidencing workers' compensation coverage in compliance with Title 23 of the Louisiana Revised Statutes of 1950 and general liability insurance in a minimum amount of one hundred thousand dollars ($100,000). Home improvement contractors performing work in excess of $75,000, including all labor and materials, are required to be licensed as a residential building contractor. All home improvement registrations expire on the anniversary of the date on which the registration was originally issued, and become invalid on the expiration date unless renewed annually.

It is the duty of the awarding authority to ascertain if a contractor is duly licensed under the provisions of R.S. 37:2150-2192 before permitting the contractor to obtain plans and specifications, submit a bid or offer to construct a commercial project involving fifty thousand dollars ($50,000) or more, one dollar ($1) or more for hazardous materials or mold remediation, or ten thousand dollars ($10,000) or more for Plumbing, Electrical or Mechanical.

## Contractors Licensing Law

Act No. 233 of 1956 created the State Licensing Board for Contractors as it exists today. That law was amended by Act Nos. 192 and 455 of 1960; Act No. 184 of 1962; Act No. 113 of 1964; Act No. 292 of 1666; Act No. 212 of 1968; Act No. 684 of 1974; Act No. 702 of 1975; Act Nos. 82, 271 and 377 of 1976; Act Nos. 430, 488, 544 and 782 of 1979; Act Nos. 606 and 771 of 1980; Act No. 688 of 1981; Act No. 832 of 1982; Act No. 295 and 296 of 1983; Act No. 51, 915 and 916 of 1984; Act Nos. 599, 645 and 932 of 1985; Act Nos. 501 and 635 of 1988; Act No. 559 of 1989; Act Nos. 649 and 865 of 1991; Act Nos. 344, 681 and 1016 of 1992; Act Nos. 473, 478, 638 and 808 of 1995; Act Nos. 146, 147, 148, 380, 769, 770, 771, 772, 773, 925 and 1299 of 1997; Act No. 65 of 1998; Act No. 1175 of 1999; Act No. 21 of 2000; Act Nos. 8, 659, 711, 802, 968 and 1072 of 2001; Act Nos. 643, 880, 902 and 1146 of 2003; Act Nos. 352 and 724 of 2004; Act No. 240 of 2005; Act No. 398 of 2007; Act Nos. 387, 576 and 725 of 2008; Act No. 156 of 2009; Act No. 67 of 2010; Act No. 107 of 2011; Act Nos. 163, 193 and 803 of 2012; Act Nos. 60 and 195 of 2013; and Act Nos. 791 and 862 of 2014. The following is a complete text of the present law in its statutory form.

# Appendix E: Louisiana Contractors Licensing Law

Title 37 of the Louisiana Revised Statutes, Chapter 24, reads as follows:

## Chapter 24. CONTRACTORS

## Part I. GENERAL

### LA R.S. 37:2150, Purpose; legislative intent

#### §2150. Purpose; legislative intent

The purpose of the legislature in enacting this Chapter is the protection of the health, safety, and general welfare of all those persons dealing with persons engaged in the contracting vocation, and the affording of such persons of an effective and practical protection against the incompetent, inexperienced, unlawful, and fraudulent acts of contractors with whom they contract. Further, the legislative intent is that the State Licensing Board for Contractors shall monitor construction projects to ensure compliance with the licensure requirements of this Chapter.

*Added by Acts 1976, No. 82, §2, eff. July 8, 1976. Acts 1989, No. 559, §1.*

#### §2150.1. Definitions

As used in this Chapter, the following words and phrases shall be defined as follows:

(1) "Board" means the State Licensing Board for Contractors.

(2) "Commercial purposes" means any construction project other than residential homes, a single residential duplex, a single residential triplex, or a single residential fourplex. A construction project consisting of residential homes where the contractor has a single contract for the construction of more than two homes within the same subdivision shall be deemed a commercial undertaking.

(3) "Contract" means the entire cost of the construction undertaking, including labor, materials, rentals, and all direct and indirect project expenses.

(4) (a) "Contractor" means any person who undertakes to, attempts to, or submits a price or bid or offers to construct, supervise, superintend, oversee, direct, or in any manner assume charge of the construction, alteration, repair, improvement, movement, demolition, putting up, tearing down, or furnishing labor, or furnishing labor together with material or equipment, or installing the same for any building, highway, road, railroad, sewer, grading, excavation, pipeline, public utility structure, project development, housing, or housing development, improvement, or any other construction undertaking for which the entire cost of same is fifty thousand dollars or more when such property is to be used for commercial purposes other than a single residential duplex, a single residential triplex, or a single residential fourplex. A construction project which consists of construction of more than two single residential homes, or more than one single residential duplex, triplex, or fourplex, shall be deemed to be a commercial undertaking.

(b) The term "contractor" includes general contractors, subcontractors, architects, and engineers who receive an additional fee for the employment or direction of labor, or any other work beyond the normal architectural or engineering services.

(c) A contractor holding a license in the major classification of hazardous materials, or any subclassifications thereunder, shall be defined in terms of work performed for which the cost is one dollar or more.

(d) "Contractor" shall not mean any person, supplier, manufacturer, or employee of such person who assembles, repairs, maintains, moves, puts up, tears down, or disassembles any patented, proprietary, or patented and proprietary environmental equipment supplied by such person to a contractor to be used solely by the contractor for a construction undertaking.

(4.1) "Electrical contractor" means any person who undertakes to, attempts to, or submits a price or bid or offers to construct, supervise, superintend, oversee, direct, or in any manner assume charge of the

## Appendix E: Louisiana Contractors Licensing Law                                                  E-3

construction, alteration, repair, improvement, movement, demolition, putting up, tearing down, or furnishing labor together with material and equipment, or installing the same for the wiring, fixtures, or appliances for the supply of electricity to any residential, commercial, or other project, when the cost of the undertaking exceeds the sum of ten thousand dollars. This Paragraph shall not be deemed or construed to limit the authority of a contractor, general contractor, or residential building contractor, as those terms are defined in this Section, nor to require such individuals to become an electrical contractor.

(5) "Executive director" means the person appointed by the board to serve as the chief operating officer in connection with the day-to-day operation of the board's business.

(6)  (a) "General contractor" means a person who contracts directly with the owner. The term "general contractor" shall include the term "primary contractor" and wherever used in this Chapter or in regulations promulgated thereunder "primary contractor" shall mean "general contractor".

(b) "General contractor" shall not mean any person, supplier, manufacturer, or employee of such person who assembles, repairs, maintains, moves, puts up, tears down, or disassembles any patented, proprietary, or patented and proprietary environmental equipment supplied by such person to a contractor to be used solely by the contractor for a construction undertaking.

(7) "Home improvement contracting" means the reconstruction, alteration, renovation, repair, modernization, conversion, improvement, removal, or demolition, or the construction of an addition to any pre-existing owner occupied building which building is used or designed to be used as a residence or dwelling unit, or to structures which are adjacent to such residence or building. "Home improvement contracting" shall not include services rendered gratuitously.

(8) "Home improvement contractor" means any person, including a contractor or subcontractor, who undertakes or attempts to, or submits a price or bid on any home improvement contracting project.

(8.1) "Mechanical contractor" means any person who undertakes to, attempts to, or submits a price or bid or offers to construct, supervise, superintend, oversee, direct, or in any manner assume charge of the construction, alteration, repair, improvement, movement, demolition, putting up, tearing down, or furnishing labor, or furnishing labor together with material and equipment, or installing the same for the construction, installation, maintenance, testing, and repair of air conditioning, refrigeration, heating systems, and plumbing for all residential, commercial, and industrial applications as well as ventilation systems, mechanical work controls, boilers and other pressure vessels, steam and hot water systems and piping, gas piping and fuel storage, and chilled water and condensing water systems and piping, including but not limited to any type of industrial process piping and related valves, fittings, and components, when the cost of the undertaking exceeds the sum of ten thousand dollars. This Paragraph shall not be deemed or construed to limit the authority of a contractor, general contractor, or residential building contractor, as those terms are defined in this Section, nor to require such individuals to become a mechanical contractor.

(9) "Person" means any individual, firm, partnership, association, cooperative, corporation, limited liability company, limited liability partnership, or any other entity recognized by Louisiana law; and whether or not acting as a principal, trustee, fiduciary, receiver, or as any other kind of legal or personal representative, or as a successor in interest, assignee, agent, factor, servant, employee, director, officer, or any other representative of such person; or any state or local governing authority or political subdivision performing a new construction project which exceeds the contract limits provided in R.S. 38:2212 and which does not constitute regular maintenance of the public facility or facilities which it has been authorized to maintain.

(10) "Qualifying party" means a natural person designated by the contractor to represent the contractor for the purpose of complying with the provisions of this Chapter including without limitation meeting the requirements for the initial license and/or any continuation thereof.

(11) "Residential building contractor" means any corporation, partnership, or individual who constructs a fixed building or structure for sale for use by another as a residence or who, for a price, commission, fee, wage, or other compensation, undertakes or offers to undertake the construction or superintending of the construction of any building or structure which is not more than three floors in height, to be used by another as a residence, when the cost of the undertaking exceeds seventy-five thousand dollars. The term "residential building contractor" includes all contractors, subcontractors, architects, and engineers who receive an additional fee for the employment or direction of labor, or any other work beyond the normal architectural or engineering services. "Residential building contractor" also means any person performing home improvement contracting as provided for in Paragraph (7) of this Section when the cost of the undertaking exceeds seventy-five thousand dollars. It shall not include the manufactured housing industry or those persons engaged in building residential structures that are mounted on metal chassis and wheels.

(12) "Subcontract" means the entire cost of that part of the contract which is performed by the subcontractor.

(13) (a) "Subcontractor" means a person who contracts directly with the primary contractor for the performance of a part of the principal contract or with another contractor for the performance of a part of the principal contract.

(b) "Subcontractor" shall not mean any person, supplier, manufacturer, or employee of such person who assembles, repairs, maintains, moves, puts up, tears down, or disassembles any patented, proprietary, or patented and proprietary environmental equipment supplied by such person to a contractor to be used solely by the contractor for a construction undertaking.

*Acts 1992, No. 681, §1, eff. July 6, 1992; Acts 1995, No. 638, §1, eff. Feb. 1, 1996; Acts 1997, No. 146, §1; Acts 1997, No. 770, §1; Acts 2003, No. 643, §1; Acts 2003, No. 1146, §2; Acts 2007, No. 398, §1; Acts 2008, No. 725, §1, eff. Jan. 1, 2009.*

### §2151. State licensing board for contractors; membership; qualifications; tenure; vacancies

A. There is hereby created the State Licensing Board for Contractors within the office of the governor that shall consist of fifteen members appointed by the governor as hereinafter set forth and who shall serve without compensation and shall possess the following qualifications:

(1) Each member shall be of full age of majority and shall have been a resident of the state of Louisiana for the last five successive years.

(2) All members shall have been actively engaged as a responsible contractor in the construction classification that they represent for the five-year period prior to their appointment as a board member, except for any member appointed pursuant to Paragraph (8) of this Subsection if he represents the public at large.

(3) At least four members shall have had the greater part of their experience as a licensed contractor in the field of highway and street construction.

(4) At least four members shall have had the greater part of their experience as a licensed contractor in the fields of building or industrial construction, or both fields.

(5) At least one member shall have had the greater part of his experience as a licensed contractor in the field of mechanical construction.

(6) At least one member shall have had the greater part of his experience as a licensed contractor in the field of electrical construction.

(7) At least two members shall have had the greater part of their experience as a subcontractor in the construction industry in fields other than electrical or mechanical construction.

(8) At least two members shall be from and represent the public at large and neither shall earn his livelihood in a construction-related industry.

# Appendix E: Louisiana Contractors Licensing Law E-5

(9) At least one member shall have had the greater experience as a licensed contractor in the field of oil field construction.

(10) There shall be at least one board member from each congressional district in the state of Louisiana.

B. All vacancies that shall occur shall be filled within ninety days of the vacancy, by appointment of the governor within the classification of area and qualification where the vacancy shall occur.

C. On and after January 1, 1996, the members shall serve terms of six years; however, initially four members shall serve terms of two years, four members shall serve terms of four years, and four members shall serve terms of six years.

*Added by Acts 1956, No. 233, §1; Amended by Acts 1964, No. 113, §1; Acts 1976, No. 377, §1; Acts 1981, No. 668, §1; Acts 1984, No. 916, §1, eff. July 20, 1984; Acts 1985, No. 645, §1, eff. July 16, 1985; Acts 1991, No. 649, §§1 and 2, eff. Jan. 1, 1992; Acts 1992, No. 344, §1; Acts 1992, No. 681, §1, eff. July 6, 1992; Acts 2001, No. 8, §12, eff. July 1, 2001. {{NOTE: SEE ACTS 1984, NO. 916, §2.}}*

## §2152. Initial appointments; oaths; panel of names; domicile; officer; bond

A. Each member of the board shall serve at the pleasure of the governor. Each appointment by the governor shall be submitted to the Senate for confirmation. Each member shall take and file with the secretary of state the constitutional oath of office before entering upon the discharge of his duties. Any member appointed to fill a vacancy occurring prior to the expiration of the term of his predecessor shall be appointed for the remainder of the unexpired term from among residents of the same congressional district as that of the member whose office was vacated. However, if there are no qualified applicants from the congressional district of the member whose office was vacated, the governor shall appoint a qualified applicant from any congressional district to fill the vacancy. In making the appointments provided for in this Section, the governor shall appoint at least one person who is nominated by the National Association for the Advancement of Colored People, and at least one person who is nominated by the Louisiana Business League.

(1) Original appointments to the board and appointments to fill vacancies by reason of the expiration of the term for which appointed or by reason of death, resignation, or otherwise, to fill that qualification of board membership who is experienced in the field of highway and street construction, shall be made by the governor as follows:

(a) The board of directors of the Louisiana Associated General Contractors, Inc. shall submit a list of not less than ten names, by certification of its president and secretary, to the secretary of state at the state capitol within fifteen days from the effective date of this Section. Annually between June first and June thirtieth, the organization shall be authorized to make a new certification to the secretary of state; however, after one certificate is made, the list originally submitted shall be included on the panel hereinafter established by the secretary of state until changed by the group submitting the same. It shall be the duty of the secretary of state to compile a panel of names so submitted and to keep same on file in his office as a public record for use as contemplated herein.

(b) From this list of names, the governor shall appoint the board member or board members to fill that class of board members who are experienced in the field of highway and street construction.

(2) Original appointments to the board and appointment to fill any vacancies that may occur to fill that qualification of board membership who is experienced in the field of building construction shall be made by the governor as follows:

(a) (i) The Board of Directors of the Louisiana A.G.C., Inc., shall submit a list of not less than ten names by certification of its president and secretary to the secretary of state at the state capitol within fifteen days from September 9, 1988.

(ii) Annually between June first and June thirtieth, the organization shall be authorized to make new certification to the secretary of state; provided that after one certification is made, the list originally submitted shall be included on the panel hereinafter established by the secretary of state until changed by the group submitting the same.

(iii) It shall be the duty of the secretary of state to compile a panel of names so submitted and to keep same on file in his office as a public record for use as contemplated herein.

(b) (i) The board of directors of the Louisiana Associated General Contractors Inc., shall submit a list of not less than ten names by certification of its president and secretary to the secretary of state at the state capitol within fifteen days from September 9, 1988.

(ii) Annually between June first and June thirtieth, the organization shall be authorized to make new certification to the secretary of state; provided that after one certification is made, the list originally submitted shall be included on the panel hereinafter established by the secretary of state until changed by the group submitting the same.

(iii) It shall be the duty of the secretary of state to compile a panel of names so submitted and to keep same on file in his office as public record for use as contemplated herein.

(c) (i) The board of directors of the Louisiana Associated Builders and Contractors, Inc., shall submit a list of no less than ten names certified by its president and secretary to the secretary of state at the state capitol within fifteen days from September 9, 1988.

(ii) Annually between June first and June thirtieth, the organization shall be authorized to make new certification to the secretary of state; provided that after one certification is made, the list originally submitted shall be included on the panel hereinafter established by the secretary of state until changed by the group submitting the same.

(iii) It shall be the duty of the secretary of state to compile a panel of names so submitted and to keep same on file in his office as public record for use as contemplated herein.

(d) The governor shall appoint one board member from the list submitted pursuant to Subparagraph (a), one board member from the list submitted pursuant to Subparagraph (b), and two board members from the list submitted pursuant to Subparagraph (c), to fill that class of board members who are experienced in the fields of building or industrial construction, or both.

(3) Original appointments to the board and appointments to fill any vacancies that may occur by reason of expiration of the term for which appointed or by reason of death, resignation, or otherwise in the office of the member required to be experienced in the field of mechanical construction shall be made by the governor as follows:

(a) The president and secretary of the Mechanical Contractors Association of Louisiana, Inc. shall submit a list of not less than three names by certification to the secretary of state at the state capitol annually between June first and June thirtieth. It shall be the duty of the secretary of state to compile a panel of the names so submitted and to keep same on file in his office as a public record for use as contemplated herein.

(b) From this list of names the governor shall appoint the board member to fill that class of board member who is required to be experienced in the field of mechanical construction.

(4) Original appointments to the board and appointments to fill any vacancies that may occur by reason of expiration of term for which appointed or reason of death, resignation, or otherwise in the office of the member required to be experienced in the field of the electrical construction shall be made by the governor as follows:

# Appendix E: Louisiana Contractors Licensing Law

(a) The board of directors of the Louisiana Council of the National Electrical Contractors Association, Inc., acting through that organization's duly elected president, shall submit a list of not less than three names by certification to the secretary of state at the state capitol annually between June first and June thirtieth. It shall be the duty of the secretary of state to compile a panel of names so submitted and to keep same on file in his office as a public record for use as contemplated herein.

(b) From this list of names the governor shall appoint the board member to fill that class of board member who is required to be experienced in the field of electrical construction.

(5) Original appointments to the board and appointments to fill any vacancies that may occur by reason of expiration of the term for which appointed or by reason of death, resignation, or otherwise in the office of the members the greater part of whose experience is required to be as a licensed subcontractor in a field other than electrical or mechanical construction shall be made by the governor as follows:

(a) The presidents and secretaries of the chartered American Subcontractors Associations of the state of Louisiana shall submit a list of not less than three names by certification to the secretary of state at the State Capitol within fifteen days from July 26, 1976. Annually thereafter, between June 1 and June 30, that organization shall certify a new list to the secretary of state provided, however, that after one certification is made, the list originally submitted shall be included on the panel hereinafter required to be established by the secretary until changed by the associations submitting the same. It shall be the duty of the secretary of state to compile a panel of the names so submitted and to keep same on file in his office as a public record for use as contemplated herein.

(b) From this list of names the governor shall appoint the two board members who are required to be experienced as licensed subcontractors in a field other than electrical or mechanical construction.

(6) Original appointments to the board and appointments to fill any vacancies that may occur by reason of expiration of the term for which appointed or by reason of death, resignation, or otherwise in the office of the member the greater part of whose experience is required to be a licensed contractor in the field of oil field construction shall be made by the governor as follows:

(a) The board of directors of the Louisiana Oil Field Contractors Association, Inc. shall submit a list of not less than ten names by certification to the secretary of state at the state capitol within fifteen days from July 26th, 1985. Annually thereafter, between June 1st and June 30th, that organization shall certify a new list to the secretary of state provided, however, after one certificate is made, the list originally submitted shall be included on the panel hereinafter established by the secretary of state until changed by the group submitting the same. It shall be the duty of the secretary of state to compile a panel of names so submitted and to keep same on file in his office as a public record for use as contemplated herein.

(b) From the list of names, the governor shall appoint the board member to fill that class of board members who is required to be experienced as a licensed contractor in the field of oil field construction.

(7) Original appointments to the board and appointments to fill any vacancy that may occur by reason of expiration of the term for which appointed or by reason of death, resignation, or otherwise in the office of the member the greater part of whose experience is required to be a licensed contractor in the field of highway and street construction and whose experience is in the field of asphalt pavement shall be made by the governor as follows:

(a) The Board of Directors of the Louisiana Asphalt Pavement Association, Inc. shall submit a list of not less than three names for certification to the secretary of state at the capitol within fifteen days from January 1, 1992. Annually thereafter, between June first and June thirtieth, that organization shall certify two new lists to the secretary of state provided, however, after the certification is made, the list originally submitted shall be included in the panel hereinafter established by the secretary of state until changed by the group submitting the same. It shall be the duty of the secretary of state to compile a panel of names so submitting the same. It shall be the duty of the secretary of state to compile a panel of names so submitting the same. It shall be the duty of the secretary of state to compile a panel of names so submitting the same. It shall be the duty of the secretary of state to compile a panel of names so submitted and to keep same on file in his office as a public record for use as contemplated herein.

(b) From the list of names, the governor shall appoint the board member to fill that class of board member who is required to be experienced as a licensed contractor in the field of highway and street construction.

(8) Appointments to the board, both original and to fill any vacancy which may occur, in the offices of the members whose qualifications are provided for in R.S. 37:2151(A)(8) shall be made by the governor at his discretion.

B. (1) (a) If at any time appointment is to be made to fill a vacancy and the panel of names kept by the secretary of state does not contain names of qualified and recommended persons from which the appointment is to be made, the appointment shall be delayed for a period of fifteen days.

(b) The secretary of state shall contact the organization concerned which shall submit, within ten days after such notice, the names of qualified and recommended persons to be included on the list from which the governor shall select the board members to be appointed.

(2) A person shall be eligible for appointment as a member of the board only if he holds an unexpired license as a contractor under the provisions of this Chapter; however, this provision shall not apply to the person pursuant to R.S. 37:2151(A)(8) if he represents the public at large.

(3) After the board shall have qualified, it shall meet in the city of Baton Rouge which place is hereby fixed as the domicile of the board.

(4) (a) The governor shall designate one member of the board to serve as chairman.

(b) The members shall, by a majority vote, designate a member as vice chairman and a member as secretary-treasurer.

(c) The secretary-treasurer and any administrative employee who shall handle the funds of the board shall furnish bond, in such amount as is fixed by the board, of a surety company qualified to do and doing business in the state of Louisiana. The bond shall be conditioned upon the faithful performance of the duties of office and of the proper accounting of funds coming into his possession.

*Acts 1988, No. 501, §1; Acts 1991, No. 649, §1, eff. Jan. 1, 1992; Acts 1992, No. 344, §1; Acts 1992, No. 1016, §1; Acts 1997, No. 771, §1; Acts 2001, No. 968, §1.*

### §2153. Powers of the board

A. The board shall have the power to make by-laws, rules and regulations for the proper administration of this Chapter; to employ such administrative assistants as are necessary; and to fix their compensation. The board is hereby vested with the authority requisite and necessary to carry out the intent of the provisions of this Chapter.

B. Any bylaws or rules or regulations enacted by the Board shall be adopted and promulgated pursuant to the provisions of R.S. 49:951 et seq.

C. (1) All legal services for the board shall be under the supervision, control, and authority of the attorney general, and no special attorney or counsel shall be employed to represent it except in accordance with the provisions of R.S. 42:262.

(2) (a) However, notwithstanding the provisions of Paragraph (1) of this Subsection and the provisions of R.S. 42:262, the board may contract with outside counsel or collection agencies on a contingency- fee basis to enforce judgments that may arise under this Chapter.

(b) Any such attorney shall be selected pursuant to a request for proposals in accordance with Chapter 16 of Title 39 of the Louisiana Revised Statutes of 1950, and any such collection agency shall be selected

# Appendix E: Louisiana Contractors Licensing Law

pursuant to a request for proposals in accordance with Chapter 17 of Title 39 of the Louisiana Revised Statutes of 1950.

(c) Any contingency fee contract entered into pursuant to this Subsection shall mandate that all collected funds be deposited directly with the board, and, thereafter, the contingency fee shall be paid by the board to the collection agency or attorney.

D. (1) The board is hereby authorized to select, lease, purchase, maintain, own, expand, and sell an office building and the land on which said building is situated. Any building so owned or so acquired shall be used by the board to house the offices of the board and to conduct the affairs of the board. The board is hereby authorized to expend the funds of the board for the purchase of the land and improvements thereon. The board is further authorized to sell the land and improvements thereon. Revenue derived from the sale shall be retained by the board.

(2) The board may lease or sell portions of the land and improvements under such terms and conditions which are consistent with law. All revenue derived from such leases or sales shall be retained by the board.

(3) Prior to a sale authorized by this Subsection, the commissioner of administration shall review the terms of the sale to ascertain that the sale amount constitutes fair market value or greater for the property.

E. In addition to any other duties and powers granted by this Chapter, the board shall:

(1) Grant licenses to qualified contractors pursuant to this Chapter.

(2) Make, amend, or repeal such rules and regulations as it may deem proper fully to effectuate this Chapter and carry out the purposes thereof, in accordance with the Administrative Procedure Act. The enumeration of specific matters which may be made and the subject of rules and regulations shall not be construed to limit general powers of the board to make all rules and regulations necessary fully to effectuate the purpose of this Chapter.

(3) Enforce this Chapter and rules and regulations adopted pursuant thereto.

(4) Suspend or revoke any license for any cause described in this Chapter, or for any cause prescribed by the rules and regulations, and refuse to grant any license for any cause which would be grounds for revocation or suspension of a license.

(5) Publish and distribute materials containing such information as it deems proper to further the accomplishment of the purpose of this Chapter.

F. Notwithstanding any other provisions to the contrary and to the extent deemed necessary or appropriate by the board for the efficient implementation of its responsibilities under this Chapter, the board may delegate its powers and duties to its staff by specific resolution of the board.

*Added by Acts 1956, No. 233, §3. Amended by Acts 1964, No. 113, §3; Acts 1979, No. 430, §1, eff. July 11, 1979; Acts 1981, No. 668, §1; Acts 1983, No. 296, §1; Acts 1992, No. 681, §1, eff. July 6, 1992; Acts 1997, No. 147, §1; Acts 1998, 1st Ex. Sess., No. 65, §1, eff. May 1, 1998; Acts 2001, No. 968, §1.*

## §2154. Meetings; compensation; quorum; license application and issuance procedure

A. (1) The board shall have at least one regular meeting per month on dates and times designated by the chairman. Notice of such board meetings shall be posted at the board office at least ten days prior to the date when the board is to meet. Further, any person desiring actual notice of the board meeting may request in writing that the board send notification through the United States mail at least ten days prior to the board meeting date.

(2) The board may receive applications for licenses under this Chapter at any time. Upon initial application, the license of a contractor domiciled in the state of Louisiana shall be issued after all requirements have been met and approved by the board at its next regularly scheduled meeting. Upon the initial application of a contractor domiciled outside of the state of Louisiana, except as provided herein, a period of at least sixty days

must elapse between the date the application is filed and the license is issued. The executive director shall compile a list of all applicants for licensure that are to be considered at a board meeting and mail such list to each board member at least ten days prior to the meeting. The executive director shall certify that the list contains only the names of applicants who have fulfilled all licensure requirements and the board shall only consider applications on such list.

 (a) For purposes of this Paragraph a contractor shall be considered "domiciled in the state" if he is either of the following:

  (i) An individual who has been a resident of the state of Louisiana for at least one year prior to his filing an application with the board of licensing.

  (ii) Any partnership, association, corporation, or other legal entity whose majority interest is owned by and controlled by one or more residents of the state of Louisiana.

 (b) For purposes of this Paragraph "majority interest" shall be determined in either of the following ways:

  (i) In the case of corporations, on the basis of all stock, common and preferred, whether voting or nonvoting, and on the basis of all debentures, warrants, or other instruments convertible into common stock, preferred stock, or both.

  (ii) In the case of partnerships, on the basis of all capital accounts together with any and all capital advances, loans, and debentures, whether or not convertible into capital accounts.

(3) No application may be considered at special meetings of the board.

(4) No application may be considered from any state or local governmental body including, without limitation, any agency of any such state or local governmental body including any corporation or other entity owned, controlled, or owned and controlled by any such state or local governing body.

(5) All meetings of the board shall be held in the city of Baton Rouge, Louisiana, unless otherwise provided for in the bylaws of the board. Before a special meeting may be held, notice thereof stating time, place, and purpose of said meeting shall be sent by the chairman or vice chairman of the board by registered mail or telegram to the members thereof, addressed to their mailing addresses on file with the board, at least three days before the date of the meeting. No board meeting shall be recessed from one calendar day to another.

B. Each member of the board shall be reimbursed when actually in attendance of a board meeting or when he is required to travel for the official authorized business of the board, not more than seventy-five dollars per day plus actual expenses and mileage to and from his domicile to the place of meeting at the same rate of reimbursement set by the division of administration for state employees under the provisions of R.S. 39:231.

C. Eight members of the board shall constitute a quorum for the conduct of business.

D. There shall be no voting by proxy.

*Added by Acts 1956, No. 233, §4; Amended by Acts 1960, No. 455, §1; Acts 1962, No. 184, §1; Acts 1964, No. 113, §4; Acts 1974, No. 684, §1; Acts 1981, No. 668, §1; Acts 1984, No. 51, §1; Acts 1984, No. 915, §1; Acts 1984, No. 916, §1, eff. July 20, 1984; Acts 1985, No. 599, §1; Acts 1989, No. 559, §1; Acts 1992, No. 344, §1; Acts 1992, No. 681, §1, eff. July 6, 1992. {{NOTE: SEE ACTS 1984, NO. 916, §2.}}*

## §2155. Books and records; evidence; reports

A. The secretary-treasurer shall be responsible for receiving and accounting for all money derived from the operation of this Chapter. He shall register all applicants for licenses, showing for each the date of application, the name, qualifications, place of business, place of residence, and whether license was granted or refused and the date on which such license was granted or refused.

# Appendix E: Louisiana Contractors Licensing Law

B. The book and register of this board shall be prima facie evidence of all matters recorded therein; and a certified copy of such book or register, or any part thereof, attested by the secretary-treasurer, shall be received in evidence in all courts of this state in lieu of the original.

C. The secretary-treasurer thereof shall keep a roster, showing the names and places of business of all licensed contractors, and shall file same with the secretary of state on or before the first day of March of each year.

D. The secretary-treasurer of the board shall keep full and complete minutes of each board meeting whether regular or special, including full information as to each application for license considered and the board's action thereon as well as all expenditures of the board that are approved. These board minutes shall be typed and attested to by the secretary-treasurer and copies thereof shall be made available to each board member and to the public within a period of twenty-one days after the adjournment of said meeting.

E. Within one hundred fifty days of the last day of each calendar year, a certified public accounting firm approved by the state official charged with the auditing of public records and accounts shall audit the financial records of the board and submit the report of his audit to the legislative auditor and shall file a copy of his audit with the secretary of state to be attached to the report of the board on file.

*Added by Acts 1956, No. 233, §5. Amended by Acts 1964, No. 113, §5; Acts 1992, No. 681, §1, eff. July 6, 1992.*

## §2156. Unexpired licenses; fees; renewals

A. Licenses and renewals issued under the provisions of this Chapter shall expire on the anniversary of the date on which the license was originally issued. Licensees shall elect upon renewal one-, two-, or three-year license renewal terms, and licenses may be issued by the board on a multiple-year basis, not to exceed a three-year renewal term for any license. The license becomes invalid on the last day of the term for which it was issued unless renewed; however, after a license has expired, the person to whom such license was issued shall have fifteen days following the expiration date to file an application for the renewal of such license without the payment of a penalty and without further examination, and any person who makes an application for the renewal of a license after fifteen days following the expiration date of the license may, at the discretion of the board, have his license renewed after paying the required license fees and such penalty, not exceeding the sum of fifty dollars, that the board may impose. New applicants for licensing may elect upon application the renewal term of their license.

B. If a license is not renewed within a period of one year from the date of its expiration, any application for renewal shall be considered and treated as a new application.

C. (1) To defray the cost of issuing licenses and of administering this Chapter, the board shall fix reasonable fees to be assessed under this Chapter, and reasonable penalties to be assessed for late applications for renewal of licenses and other administrative infractions; however, the basic license fee shall be the sum of not more than one hundred dollars and the fee for additional classifications shall be such lesser amount as set by the board.

(2) The board shall have the authority to assess an additional surcharge of no more than four hundred dollars in connection with the application for and issuance of a contractor's license to a contractor not domiciled in the state of Louisiana, to be utilized to defray the additional cost of the investigation of the application of the non-Louisiana contractor, including references supplied by the contractor, work history supplied by the work contractor, and other pertinent information required by the board in connection with an application for a contractor's license.

(3) (a) The board shall assess on each license renewal issued to a contractor an additional fee of one hundred dollars per year to be dedicated and allocated as provided in this Paragraph to any public university in this state or any community college school of construction management or construction technology in this state that is accredited by either the American Council for Construction Education or the Accreditation Board for Engineering and Technology. The board shall include on each license renewal form issued to a contractor an optional election whereby the contractor may choose to not participate in the remission of the additional one hundred dollar dedication fee.

(b) Each January, each accredited public university or community college school of construction management or construction technology shall report to the board the number of graduates from its school of construction management or construction technology from the previous calendar year.

(c) Any and all funds collected pursuant to this Paragraph shall be disbursed to the accredited public university or community college schools of construction management or construction technology by August first of each year upon completion of the annual audit of the board. The funds shall be used by the accredited public university or community college schools of construction management or construction technology solely for the benefit of their program and the expenditure of such funds shall be approved by the industry advisory council or board for the program. The funds collected pursuant to this Paragraph shall be in addition to any other monies received by such schools and are intended to supplement and not replace, displace, or supplant any other funds received from the state or from any other source. Any school of construction management or construction technology that experiences a decrease in the funding appropriated to them by the accredited public university or community college as determined by the industry advisory council or board for the program shall be ineligible for participation under the provisions of this Paragraph, and the monies from the fund for such school of construction management or construction technology shall be redistributed on a pro rata basis to all other accredited and eligible schools.

(d) The funds collected pursuant to this Subsection shall be distributed as follows:

(i) One-half on a pro rata basis to each accredited public university or community college school of construction management or construction technology.

(ii) One-half pro rata to each accredited public university school of construction management or construction technology based on the total number of graduates from the previous calendar year from each school as reported to the board.

(e) No funds shall be allocated to any public university or community college school of construction management or construction technology that does not maintain current and active accreditation as required by this Paragraph.

D. The licenses issued under the provisions of this Chapter are not transferable.

E. Any other provisions of this Chapter notwithstanding, no license shall be issued to any foreign corporation which has not obtained from the secretary of state a certificate of authority to do business, as provided in Chapter 3 of Title 12 of the Louisiana Revised Statutes of 1950.

F. Except for the licenses, fees, and assessments authorized by this Chapter, and except for the occupational license taxes authorized by the constitution and laws of this state, and except for permit fees charged by parishes and municipalities for inspection purposes, and except for licenses required by parishes and municipalities for the purpose of determining the competency of mechanical or plumbing contractors, or both, and electrical contractors, no contractor shall be liable for any fee or license as a condition of engaging in the contracting business.

G. No license shall be issued for the subclassification of asbestos removal and abatement under the major classification of hazardous materials as provided in R.S. 37:2156.2(VIII) until the applicant furnishes satisfactory evidence that he or his qualifying party has received certification from the Louisiana Department of Environmental Quality to perform asbestos removal and abatement work.

*Added by Acts 1956, No. 233, §6. Amended by Acts 1960, No. 192, §1; Acts 1962, No. 184, §1; Acts 1964, No. 113, §6; Acts 1975, No. 702, §1; Acts 1976, No. 82, §1, eff. July 8, 1976; Acts 1981, No. 668, §1; Acts 1984, No. 915, §1; Acts 1988, No. 635, §1, eff. Jan. 1, 1989; Acts 1992, No. 681, §1, eff. July 6, 1992; Acts 1995, No. 473, §1; Acts 2001, No. 968, §1; Acts 2004, No. 352, §1; Acts 2005, No. 240, §1; Acts 2008, No. 576, §1, Acts 2013, No. 195 §1; Acts 2014, No. 791 §11.*

# Appendix E: Louisiana Contractors Licensing Law

## §2156.1. Requirements for issuance of a license

A. All persons who desire to become licensed as a contractor shall make application to the board on a form adopted by the board and shall state the classification of work the applicant desires to perform from a list of major classifications as follows:

(1) Building construction.

(2) Highway, street, and bridge construction.

(3) Heavy construction.

(4) Municipal and public works construction.

(5) Electrical work.

(6) Mechanical work.

(7) Plumbing work.

(8) Hazardous materials.

(9) Specialty classifications.

(10) Residential construction.

B. The board shall classify contractors according to the type or types of contracts which they may perform.

C. The applicant shall furnish the board with a financial statement, current to within twelve months of the date of filing, prepared by an independent auditor and signed by the applicant and auditor before a notary public, stating the assets of the applicant, to be used by the board to determine the financial responsibility of the applicant to perform work on a construction undertaking, the entire cost of which is fifty thousand dollars or more. Such assets shall include a net worth of at least ten thousand dollars. An applicant without the net worth required herein may furnish the board a bond, letter of credit, or other security acceptable to the board in the amount of such net worth requirement plus the amount of the applicant's negative net worth if any, and the furnishing of such bond, letter of credit, or other security shall be deemed satisfaction of such net worth requirement for all purposes. The financial statement and any information contained therein, as well as any other financial information required to be submitted by a contractor, shall be confidential and not subject to the provisions of R.S. 44:1 through 37, inclusive. Nothing contained in this Subsection shall be construed to require a licensed contractor to provide a financial statement in connection with the renewal of an existing license.

D. (1) The applicant for licensure shall designate a qualifying party who shall be the legal representative for the contractor relative to the provisions of this Chapter. The designated qualifying party shall complete an application supplied by the board. The board may deny approval of the qualifying party for good cause, which may include the ability of the proposed principal owner or owners, principal shareholder or shareholders, or qualifying party to engage in the business of contracting as demonstrated by his prior contracting business experience. Evidence which may be considered by the board shall be limited to any legal proceedings against the qualifying party or businesses where the qualifying party was in a position of control at the time a problem arose and the ultimate disposition of such proceedings, any financial history of bankruptcies, unpaid judgments, insolvencies, or any similar evidence. When the qualifying party terminates employment with the licensee, the board shall be notified in writing within thirty days of the disassociation and another qualifying party must qualify within sixty days. The qualifying party or parties are:

(a) Any individual contractor or copartner.

(b) Any employee of said applicant who has been in full-time employment for one hundred twenty consecutive days immediately preceding the application. Such employee shall not be allowed to be the qualifying party for more than one company and two subsidiaries.

# E-14                                                    Appendix E: Louisiana Contractors Licensing Law

(c) Any stockholder of a corporation who was an original incorporator or original stockholder as shown in the articles of incorporation.

(2) Upon good showing, the board may waive the required examinations for any person.

(3) Upon the determination that a person has engaged in deceptive practices when taking or attempting to take any board examination, such person shall be ineligible to serve as a qualifying party for a licensee for a period of one year.

E. Notwithstanding any other law of this state to the contrary, a mechanical, plumbing, or electrical contractor may obtain a license to bid and perform work statewide provided such contractor has successfully passed a written examination which is administered or approved by the State Licensing Board for Contractors, which examination shall be a standardized, nationally recognized test.

F. Upon completion of the above, and issuance of a state license for the classification of work for which the contractor desires to perform and contract, mechanical, plumbing, or electrical contractors licensed under this Section are excluded from local, municipal, or parish regulatory authority examination procedures and may bid and perform work within any local jurisdiction upon paying all appropriate fees. The purpose of this Subsection is preemption of local, municipal, or parish regulatory examination authority for statewide-licensed mechanical, plumbing, or electrical contractors bidding and performing work in multiple jurisdictions. Furthermore, this preemption shall further exclude the employees of statewide-licensed electrical and mechanical contractors from local, municipal, or parish regulatory examination or certification authority as a condition to performing work for the statewide-licensed electrical or mechanical contractor.

G. The board shall prepare and maintain a list of local equivalent examinations. Each such local equivalent examination shall be a standardized, nationally recognized test similar to the Block test, which is administered by a local regulatory authority.

H. Any mechanical or electrical contractor who has, prior to July 1, 1985, successfully passed both a state licensing examination administered or approved by the board and a local licensing examination in the same license classification, and who has continuously held such state and local licenses since July 1, 1985, shall be exempted from any requirement herein for passage of an additional test in that license classification. A mechanical or electrical contractor shall make application to the board for such exemptions on a form prepared by the board. The board shall provide for a date by which application for exemption forms must be filed.

I. Any plumbing contractor who currently holds a state license shall be exempt from any requirement herein for passage of an additional examination in that license classification and may bid and perform plumbing work statewide after making application to the board for such exemption on a form prepared by the board.

J. Nothing herein shall be construed to permit plumbing contractors to perform plumbing work without first complying with the licensure provisions of Chapter 16 of this Title, R.S. 37:1361 et seq.

K. Each applicant shall pay all fees required for issuance of the license as provided for in this Chapter.

L. Upon completion of the above requirements, the application shall be submitted to the board for review at its next regularly scheduled meeting.

M. The board shall waive the examination required and grant a mechanical contractor or an electrical contractor license to any person working in the electrical or mechanical construction industry who meets at least one of the following requirements:

(1) Holds either a mechanical or an electrical contractor's license which was issued prior to July 1, 2008, by a local municipality after having passed an examination administered or written by a national testing company approved by the board.

# Appendix E: Louisiana Contractors Licensing Law                                    E-15

(2) Submits five original building permits, issued within the last three years, as proof that he has actually been engaged in either the mechanical or electrical construction building industry prior to July 1, 2008.

(3) Has completed six mechanical or electrical construction projects within the ten-year period prior to July 1, 2008, or has constructed one such project for another person within the five-year period prior to July 1, 2008.

N. (1) Any arborist who currently holds a valid state license issued pursuant to R.S. 3:3804 shall be exempt from any requirement herein for passage of an additional examination in the landscaping, grading, and beautification subclassification and may bid and perform the arborist work described in R.S. 3:3808(A)(1)(a) statewide after making application to the board for such exemption on a form prepared by the board.

(2) Nothing in this Subsection shall be construed to permit arborists to recommend or execute arborist work without first complying with the licensure provisions of Chapter 24 of Title 3 of the Louisiana Revised Statutes of 1950, R.S. 3:3801 et seq.

*Added by Acts 1976, No. 82, §2, eff. July 8, 1976. Amended by Acts 1981, No. 668, §1; Acts 1983, No. 295, §1; Acts 1988, No. 635, §1, eff. Jan. 1, 1989; Acts 1989, No. 559, §1; Acts 1992, No. 681, §1, eff. July 6, 1992; Acts 1997, No. 148, §1; Acts 1997, No. 769, §1; Acts 1999, No. 1175, §1; Acts 2008, No. 725, §1, eff. Jan. 1, 2009; Acts 2012, No. 163, §1. NOTE: See Acts 1988, No. 635, §§2, 3.*

## §2156.2. Major categories; subclassifications; specialty classifications; requirements for contractors holding major classification to perform mechanical, electric, or plumbing work

A. Under each major category is a list of subclassifications that a specialty contractor may obtain, as follows:

I.  Building construction

Subclassifications:

1.  Acoustical treatments
2.  Air conditioning work, ventilation, refrigeration, and duct work
3.  Electrical construction for structures
4.  Fire sprinkler work
5.  Foundations for buildings, equipment, or machinery
6.  Incinerator construction
7.  Installation of equipment, machinery, and engines
8.  Installation of pneumatic tubes and conveyors
9.  Insulation for cold storage and buildings
10. Insulation for pipes and boilers
11. Landscaping, grading, and beautification
12. Lathing, plastering, and stuccoing
13. Masonry, brick, stone
14. Ornamental iron and structural steel erection, steel buildings
15. Painting and interior decorating, carpeting
16. Pile driving
17. Plumbing
18. Residential construction
19. Rigging, house moving, wrecking, and dismantling
20. Roof decks
21. Roofing and sheet metal, siding
22. Sheet metal duct work

23. Steam and hot water heating in buildings or plants
24. Stone, granite, slate, resilient floor installations
25. Swimming pools
26. Tile, terrazzo, and marble
27. Water cooling towers and accessories
28. Drywalls
29. Driveways, parking areas, etc., asphalt and/or concrete exclusive of highway and street work
30. Fencing

II. Highway, street, and bridge construction

Subclassifications:

1. Driveways, parking areas, etc., asphalt and/or concrete
2. Highway and street subsurface drainage and sewer work
3. Permanent or paved highways and streets (asphalt hot and cold plant mix)
4. Permanent or paved highways and streets (asphalt surface treatment)
5. Permanent or paved highways and streets (concrete)
6. Permanent or paved highways and streets (soil cement)
7. Secondary roads
8. Undersealing or leveling of roads
9. Earthwork, drainage, and levees
10. Clearing, grubbing, and snagging
11. Culverts and drainage structures
12. Concrete bridges, over and underpasses
13. Steel bridges, over and underpasses
14. Wood bridges, over and underpasses
15. Landscaping, grading, and beautification
16. Fencing
17. Furnishing and installation of movable structures or machinery, excluding electrical and mechanical work

III. Heavy construction

Subclassifications:

1. Clearing, grubbing, and snagging
2. Dams, reservoirs, and flood control work other than levees
3. Dredging
4. Electrical transmission lines
5. Foundations and pile driving
6. Industrial piping
7. Industrial plants
8. Industrial ventilation
9. Oil field construction
10. Oil refineries
11. Railroads
12. Transmission pipeline construction

# Appendix E: Louisiana Contractors Licensing Law

13. Tunnels
14. Wharves, docks, harbor improvements, and terminals
15. Landscaping, grading, and beautification
16. Fencing

IV. Municipal and public works construction

Subclassifications:

1. Filter plants and water purification
2. Pipe work (gas lines)
3. Pipe work (sewer)
4. Pipe work (storm drains)
5. Pipe work (waterlines)
6. Power plants
7. Sewer plant or sewer disposal
8. Underground electrical conduit installation
9. Landscaping, grading, and beautification
10. Fencing

V. Electrical work

Subclassifications:

1. Electrical transmission lines
2. Electrical work for structures
3. Underground electrical conduit installation
4. Electrical controls

VI. Mechanical Work

Subclassifications:

1. Heat, air conditioning, ventilation, duct work, and refrigeration
2. Industrial pipe work and insulation
3. Plumbing
4. Controls for mechanical work

VII. Hazardous materials

Subclassifications:

1. Asbestos removal and abatement
2. Hazardous materials cleanup and removal
3. Hazardous materials site remediation
4. Any other classification for which the Department of Environmental Quality requires certification pursuant to law or regulation.

VIII. Plumbing

Subclassifications:

1. Potable and nonpotable water systems; construction, removal, repair, and maintenance for buildings and premises.
2. Sanitary and nonsanitary waste and sewerage construction; removal, repair, and maintenance for buildings and premises.

IX. Specialty classifications

A. A person may obtain a specialty classification under any of the above listed subclassifications or under any other specialty work not so listed for which he desires to be licensed.

B. Any contractor who holds a major classification which permits that contractor to bid mechanical or electrical work, prior to the performance of such work under his license, shall designate a qualifying party to successfully pass the standardized nationally recognized test administered by the board for the work to be performed. All time limitations shall be waived and any designated qualifying party who has successfully completed the examination shall not be required to retake the examination.

C. Any contractor who holds a major classification which permits the contractor to bid and perform plumbing work, prior to the performance of such work, shall comply with the provisions of Chapter 16 of this Title, R.S. 37:1361 et seq. All time limitations shall be waived.

D. The board may grant or renew licenses for mechanical, electrical, or plumbing contractors and restrict such licenses to the bidding and performance of work within specified areas of this state as the board shall designate. Such license shall be issued with a notation of the applicable restriction.

*Added by Acts 1976, No. 82, §2, eff. July 8, 1976; Acts 1988, No. 635, §1, eff. Jan. 1, 1989; Acts 1992, No. 681, §1, eff. July 6, 1992; Acts 2001, No. 968, §1. {{NOTE: SEE ACTS 1988, NO. 635, §§2, 3.}}*

### §2156.3. Installation of solar energy equipment and systems

A. No licensed contractor shall install solar energy equipment or solar energy systems on or after February 1, 2015, unless he is in compliance with the provisions of this Section and any rules adopted by the board in accordance with the provisions of this Section.

B. (1) Notwithstanding any provision of law to the contrary, no later than January 1, 2015, the board shall adopt rules in accordance with the Administrative Procedure Act regulating the installation of solar energy equipment or solar energy systems by licensed contractors. Such rules shall, at a minimum, include the requirement of passage of a separate written examination that evidences the contractor's knowledge and understanding of best practices as related to the installation and maintenance of solar energy equipment or solar energy systems by any contractor who does not hold a current Solar PV Installer certification for solar electric systems, or a current Solar Heating Installer certification for solar thermal hot water systems as issued by the North American Board of Certified Energy Practitioners.

(2) Any contractor licensed in this state as of August 1, 2014, holding the major classification of Building Construction, Electrical Work (Statewide), or Mechanical Work (Statewide), shall be deemed to have met the examination requirement pursuant to this Subsection.

C. Contractors applying for the classification of Solar Energy Equipment, shall, in addition to all other application or licensing requirements, meet the following requirements prior to issuance of this classification:

(1) Hold one or more of the following major classifications:

(a) Building Construction.

(b) Electrical Work.

(c) Mechanical Work.

(d) Residential Building Contractor.

(2) Complete training in the design of solar energy systems by an entity and course approved by the board.

D. Any work performed to connect wiring or hookups for any photovoltaic panel or system wherein the panel or system is of a value, including labor, materials, rentals, and all direct and indirect project expenses, of ten thousand

Appendix E: Louisiana Contractors Licensing Law  E-19

dollars or more shall be performed only by a contractor or subcontractor who holds the classification of Electrical Work or who may perform electrical work pursuant to the provisions of R.S. 37:2156.2(B).

E. Any work performed to connect piping or equipment for any solar thermal system wherein the system is of a value, including labor, materials, rentals, and all direct and indirect project expenses, of ten thousand dollars or more shall be performed only by a contractor or subcontractor who holds the classification of Mechanical Work or who may perform mechanical work pursuant to the provisions of R.S. 37:2156.2(B).

F. The provisions of this Section shall be applicable to entities engaging in the business of selling, leasing, installing, servicing, or monitoring solar energy equipment. Nothing in this Section shall be construed to impose civil or criminal liability on homeowners or on any third party whose involvement is financing to the homeowner, financing for installation, or purchasing the tax credits described in this Section from any homeowner or contractor. Entities engaged in the business of arranging agreements for the lease or sale of solar energy systems or acquiring customers for financing entities shall not be exempt from the provisions of this Section.

*Added by Act 2014, No. 862, §1.*

## §2157. Exemptions

A. There are excepted from the provisions of this Chapter:

(1)  Any public utility providing gas, electric, or telephone service which is subject to regulation by the Louisiana Public Service Commission or the council of the city of New Orleans, or to any work performed by such public utility in furnishing its authorized service.

(2)  Owners of property who supervise, superintend, oversee, direct, or in any manner assume charge of the construction, alteration, repair, improvement, movement, demolition, putting up, tearing down, or maintenance of any building, railroad excavation, project, development, improvement, plan facility, or any other construction undertaking, on such property, for use by such owner and which will not be for sale or rent, and the control of access to which shall be controlled by the owner so that only employees and nonpublic invitees are allowed access.

(3)  Persons donating labor and services for the supervision and construction of or for the maintenance and repair of churches.

(4)  Farmers doing construction for agricultural purposes on leased or owned land.

(5)  Persons bidding or performing work on any project totally owned by the federal government.

(6)  Repealed by Acts 2011, No. 107, §2.

(7)  Persons engaged in the rail or pipeline industry with respect to rail or pipeline construction activities performed on property owned or leased by such persons.

(8)  Citizens volunteering labor for the construction of a project which is funded by the Louisiana Community Development Block Grant, Louisiana Small Towns Environment Program.

(9)  Persons, suppliers, manufacturers, or employees of such persons who assemble, repair, maintain, move, put up, tear down, or disassemble any patented, proprietary, or patented and proprietary environmental equipment supplied by such persons to a contractor to be used solely by the contractor for a construction undertaking.

(10)  The manufactured housing industry or those persons engaged in any type of service, warranty, repair, or home improvement work on factory-built, residential dwellings that are mounted on chassis and wheels.

B. However, the provisions of this Chapter shall apply to any contractor employed by persons exempted hereinabove. Further, nothing herein shall be construed to waive local and state health and life safety code requirements.

Added by Acts 1956, No. 233, §7. Amended by Acts 1962, No. 184, §1; Acts 1964, No. 113, §7; Acts 1966, No. 292, §1; Acts 1968, No. 212, §1; Acts 1976, No. 377, §1; Acts 1979, No. 544, §1; Acts 1979, No. 782, §1; Acts 1980, No. 606, §1, eff. July 23, 1980; Acts 1981, No. 668, §1; Acts 1982, No. 832, §1; Acts 1985, No. 982, §1; Acts 1988, No. 635, §1, eff. Jan. 1, 1989; Acts 1989, No. 559, §1; Acts 1992, No. 681, §1, eff. July 6, 1992; Acts 2000, 1st Ex. Sess., No. 21, §1; Acts 2003, No. 643, §1; Acts 2003, No. 902, §1; Acts 2003, No. 1146, §2; Acts 2011, No. 107, §2.

### §2158. Revocation, suspension, and renewal of licenses; issuance of cease and desist orders; debarment; criminal penalty.

A. The board may revoke any license issued hereunder, or suspend the right of the licensee to use such license, or refuse to renew any such license, or issue cease and desist orders to stop work, or debar any person or licensee, for any of the following causes:

(1) Any dishonest or fraudulent act as a contractor which has caused substantial damage to another, as adjudged by a court of competent jurisdiction.

(2) Willful misrepresentation of material fact by an applicant in obtaining a license.

(3) Willful failure to comply with this Chapter or the rules and regulations promulgated pursuant thereto.

(4) Entering into a contract with an unlicensed contractor involving work or activity for the performance of which a license is required under this Chapter.

(5) Permitting the contractor's license to be used by another when the other contractor does not hold a license for the classification of work for which the contract is entered.

(6) Failure to maintain a qualifying party to represent the licensee.

(7) Insolvency or involuntary cessation of business operation.

(8) Failure to continue to fulfill any of the requirements for original licensure.

(9) Problems relating to the ability of the contractor, its qualifying party, or any of its principal owners or principal shareholders to engage in the business of contracting, as demonstrated by their prior contracting business experience.

(10) Disqualification or debarment by any public entity.

(11) Failing to possess any insurance required by federal law.

B. (1) In order to enforce the provisions of this Chapter, the board may conduct hearings in accordance with the provisions of R.S. 49:951 et seq. The board shall maintain and make available a record of all persons or licensees who have been disqualified by any public entity pursuant to R.S. 38:2212(J). If any person or licensee has been disqualified more than once in a twelve-month period, the board shall hold a debarment hearing.

(2) After the hearing, if the board rules that a person has violated any provision of this Chapter, or that a person or licensee has been appropriately disqualified more than once in a twelve-month period, in lieu of revoking or suspending the license, the board may order said person to discontinue immediately all work of every type and nature whatsoever on the construction project which is the subject of the hearing, and/or the board may debar a person or licensee from bidding on projects for any public entity for up to three years. Additionally, the board may require the licensee to pay the actual costs incurred by the board in connection with the investigation and conduction of the hearing. In accordance with R.S. 49:964, the board may grant a stay of the enforcement of its order for good cause.

(3) Any party to the proceeding who is aggrieved by the action of the board may appeal the decision in accordance with law.

# Appendix E: Louisiana Contractors Licensing Law E-21

C. The board may sue and be sued and, to that end, shall have the authority to apply to a court of competent jurisdiction for a temporary restraining order and a writ of injunction to restrain and prohibit any violation of this Chapter and the performance of any work then being done or about to commence.

D. Any contractor who applies for and is denied a license by the board, or whose license has been revoked, rescinded, or suspended, may within six months after the action of the board denying, revoking, rescinding, or suspending the said license, apply to the Nineteenth Judicial District Court in and for the parish of East Baton Rouge, state of Louisiana, and there have determined whether or not the board has abused its discretion and judgment in failing to abide by the intent of this Chapter, and have rendered such judgment as will do justice between the parties.

E. In addition to actions taken by the board, it shall be unlawful for any person to engage in the business of contracting without authority as provided for in R.S. 37:2160.

*Added by Acts 1956, No. 113, §8. Amended by Acts 1964, No. 113, §8; Acts 1992, No. 681, §1, eff. July 6, 1992; Acts 1997, No. 773, §1; Acts 2009, No. 156, §1; Acts 2012, No. 163, §1.*

## §2159. Classification; bidding and performing work within a classification

A. The board before issuing a license to any contractor, shall state the contractor's classification on such license, according to the classification requested by said contractor and for which he has completed all of the requirements.

B. After classification, the licensee shall not be permitted to bid or perform any type or types of work not included in the classification under which his license was issued.

C. After classification as above provided for, the licensee may apply for and receive additions to or changes in his classification by making application therefor, successfully completing the written examination, and paying the required fees. Additions or changes to an existing license shall become effective after completion of the above requirements, and upon board approval at the next regularly scheduled meeting.

D. Nothing in this Chapter is to be construed to mean that the board has any authority to determine or fix or suggest the amount of a contractor's bid limit.

*Added by Acts 1956, No. 233, §9; Amended by Acts 1964, No. 113, §9; Acts 1976, No. 82, §1, eff. July 8, 1976; Acts 1984, No. 915, §1; Acts 1985, No. 599, §2; Acts 1988, No. 635, §1, eff. Jan. 1, 1989; Acts 1992, No. 681, §1, eff. July 6, 1992.*

## §2160. Engaging in business of contracting without authority prohibited; penalty

A. (1) It shall be unlawful for any person to engage or to continue in this state in the business of contracting, or to act as a contractor as defined in this Chapter, unless he holds an active license as a contractor under the provisions of this Chapter.

(2) It shall be unlawful for any contractor, licensed or unlicensed, who advertises in any form or in any news medium, to advertise that he is a licensed contractor without specifying the type of license to which he is referring.

B. It shall be sufficient for the indictment, affidavit, or complaint to allege that the accused unlawfully engaged in business as a contractor without authority from the State Licensing Board for Contractors.

C. (1) Anyone violating this Section of this Chapter shall be guilty of a misdemeanor and, upon conviction, shall be fined a sum not to exceed five hundred dollars per day of violation, or three months in prison, or both.

(2) Notwithstanding any action taken by the board, any person, who does not possess a license from the board, and who violates any of the provisions of this Section, and causes harm or damage to another in excess of three hundred dollars, upon conviction, shall be fined not less than five hundred dollars nor more than five

E-22   Appendix E: Louisiana Contractors Licensing Law

thousand dollars, or imprisoned, with or without hard labor, for not less than six months nor more than five years, or both.

(3) Any fine so assessed and collected shall be remitted to the contractor's educational trust fund provided for in R.S. 37:2162(J).

D. The district attorney, in whose jurisdiction the violation occurs, shall have sole authority to prosecute criminal actions pursuant to this Section.

*Added by Acts 1956, No. 233, §10. Amended by Acts 1962, No. 184, §1; Acts 1964, No. 113, §10; Acts 1981, No. 668, §1; Acts 1992, No. 681, §1, eff. July 6, 1992; Acts 2001, No. 802, §1; Acts 2009, No. 156, §1.*

### §2161. Power to sue and be sued; injunction; restraining orders

The board may sue and be sued and, to that end, shall have the right to go into court in the jurisdiction in which the provisions of this Chapter are being violated, and upon affidavit, secure a temporary restraining order and a writ of injunction restraining and prohibiting the violation of this Chapter and the performance of any work then being done or about to be commenced.

*Added by Acts 1956, No. 233, §11. Amended by Acts 1964, No. 113, §11; Acts 1983, No. 296, §1.*

### §2162. Violations; civil penalty

A. Any person who violates any provision of this Chapter shall, after notice and a hearing, be liable to the board for a fine of up to one thousand dollars plus costs and attorney fees for each offense. If the board brings an action against a person pursuant to this Section and fails to prove its case, then it shall be liable to such person for the payment of his reasonable litigation expenses as defined in R.S. 49:965.1(D)(1).

B. In addition to or in lieu of the criminal penalties and administrative sanctions provided in this Chapter, the board is empowered to issue an order to any person or firm engaged in any activity, conduct, or practice constituting a violation of any provision of this Chapter, directing such person or firm to forthwith cease and desist from such activity, conduct, or practice. Such order shall be issued in the name of the state of Louisiana under the official seal of the board.

C. If the person or firm to whom the board directs a cease and desist order does not cease or desist the proscribed activity, conduct, or practice immediately, the board may cause to issue in any court of competent jurisdiction and proper venue, a writ of injunction enjoining such person or firm from engaging in any activity, conduct, or practice prohibited by this Chapter.

D. Upon proper showing by the board that such person or firm has engaged or is engaged in any activity, conduct, or practice prohibited by this Chapter, the courts shall issue a temporary restraining order restraining the person or firm from engaging in such unlawful activity, conduct, or practice pending the hearing on a preliminary injunction, and in due course a permanent injunction shall issue after hearing, commanding the cessation of the unlawful activity, conduct, or practice complained of, all without the necessity of the board having to give bond. A temporary restraining order, preliminary injunction, or permanent injunction issued hereunder shall not be subject to being released upon bond.

E. In the suit for an injunction, the board may demand of the defendant a penalty as provided in Subsection A of this Section. A judgment for penalty, attorney fees, and costs may be rendered in the same judgment in which the injunction is made absolute. If the board brings an action against a person pursuant to this Section and fails to prove its case, then it shall be liable to such person for the payment of his attorney fees and costs.

F. The trial of the proceeding by injunction shall be summary and by the judge without a jury.*

G. Anyone violating this Chapter who fails to cease work, after proper hearing and notification from the board, shall not be eligible to apply for a contractor's license for a period not to exceed one year from the date of official notification to cease work.

# Appendix E: Louisiana Contractors Licensing Law                    E-23

H. It shall be within the power of the board to withhold approval, for up to six months, of any application from anyone who, prior to said application, has been found in violation of this Chapter.

I. In addition to any other penalties provided for in this Chapter, the board may, after notice and hearing, issue an order directing the contractor to cease and desist all actions constituting a violation until such time as a contractor complies with the requirements of this Chapter, and to pay to the board a civil penalty of not more than ten percent of the total contract being performed.

J. All fines or penalties collected by the board pursuant to this Section for violations of any provision of this Chapter shall, annually, at each audit of the board, be transferred to a separate contractor's educational trust fund to be used for educational purposes as determined by the board.

K. Upon the expiration of the delays set forth in the Administrative Procedure Act for an aggrieved party to appeal any fine or penalty assessed by the board, if such an appeal has not been so filed, the board may initiate civil proceedings against such party seeking to obtain a judgment against that party in an amount equivalent to the amount of the fine so assessed, together with legal interest and all reasonable attorney fees incurred by the board in bringing such action. Such proceedings shall be conducted on a summary basis, with the only defenses that may be raised by the defendant being limited to any lack of notice having been afforded to him as to the meeting of the board during which the fine was assessed. Venue for all proceedings brought pursuant to this Subsection shall lie in the Nineteenth Judicial District Court for the parish of East Baton Rouge.

L. In addition to all other authority granted to the board under the provisions of this Chapter, the board shall have the authority to cause to be issued to any person who is alleged to have violated any of the provisions of this Chapter a citation setting forth the nature of the alleged violation, and further providing to that person the option of either pleading no contest to the charge and paying to the board a fine prescribed by any provision of this Chapter or appearing at an administrative hearing to be conducted by the board as to the alleged violation. Such citations may be issued by any authorized employee of the board, and may be issued either in person or via the United States Postal Service, postage prepaid and properly addressed. This Subsection shall not be applicable to any criminal enforcement action brought under the provisions of this Chapter.

M. Any person registered or licensed under the provisions of this Chapter who is the subject of two or more complaints received by the board within a six month period shall have his name and the nature of each complaint received posted on the board's website.

*Acts 1992, No. 681, §1, eff. July 6, 1992; Acts 1995, No. 808, §1; Acts 1997, No. 380, §1; Acts 1997, No. 772, §1; Acts 2001, No. 968, §1; Acts 2007, No. 398, §1; Acts 2009, No. 156, §1.*

> *\*As appears in enrolled bill.*

## §2163. Bid procedures; penalty

A. (1) It is the intent of this Section that only contractors who hold an active license be awarded contracts either by bid or through negotiation. All architects, engineers, and awarding authorities shall place in their bid specifications the requirement that a contractor shall certify that he holds an active license under the provisions of this Chapter and show his license number on the bid envelope. In the case of an electronic bid proposal, a contractor may submit an authentic digital signature on the electronic bid proposal accompanied by the contractor's license number in order to meet the requirements of this Paragraph. Except as otherwise provided herein, if the bid does not contain the contractor's certification and show the contractor's license number on the bid envelope, the bid shall be automatically rejected, shall be returned to the bidder marked "Rejected", and shall not be read aloud.

(2) Any bid that does not require the contractor to hold an active license shall state the exemption on the bid envelope and shall be treated as a lawful bid for the purpose of this Section.

(3) On any project that has been classified by the architect or engineer, prior to the bid, as a plumbing project, bids may only be accepted from those who have as a qualifying party a person who has complied with the provisions of Chapter 16 of this Title, R.S. 37:1361 et seq.

(4) Any contractor who submits a bid for a type of construction for which he does not hold an active license to perform shall be acting in violation of this Section and shall be subject to all provisions for violations and penalties thereof.

(5) Any subcontractor who submits a bid or quotes a price to any unlicensed or inactive prime contractor shall be subject to all provisions for violations and penalties thereof.

B. Where bids are to be received or forms furnished by the awarding authority, no proposal forms or specifications shall be issued to anyone except a licensed contractor who holds an active license or his authorized representatives. In no event shall proposal forms be issued later than twenty-four hours prior to the hour and date set for receiving proposals.

C. Nothing in this Section shall be construed as prohibiting the issuance of plans and specifications to recognized plan rooms, or material suppliers, or both when said plans and specifications will be used only to prepare proposals which will be incorporated in the bid prepared by the contractor or the issuance of plans to the contractor except in connection with federal aid or other projects as set forth in R.S. 37:2157(A)(6).

D. It shall be the obligation of the architect, engineer, or awarding authority to classify public projects. Once the project is classified, any interested person may object by sending a certified letter to both the board and to the architect, engineer, or awarding authority. Said objection shall be received by the board and by the architect, engineer, or awarding authority at least ten working days prior to the date on which bids are to be opened. The objection shall state with particularity the reasons for the objection. The objection shall be submitted to a committee for determination. The chairman of the board shall appoint the committee which shall consist of board members. The committee shall have the power to approve the project classification or add an additional classification by vote of a majority of the members of the committee. The matter shall be resolved and the board shall notify the architect, engineer, and awarding authority no less than five days prior to the time when bids are to be opened, unless all parties agree that a delay will not cause harm to others.

E. (1) Any awarding authority or its agent who violates the provisions of this Section shall be deemed guilty of a misdemeanor and, upon conviction, be punished by a fine of not less than one hundred dollars or more than two hundred dollars or imprisonment in the parish jail for not less than thirty days nor more than sixty days, or both, such fine and imprisonment at the discretion of the court.

(2) In addition, the board may, after notice and a hearing, impose a fine upon any awarding authority or its agent who intentionally violates the provisions of this Section. The board may not impose any fine as authorized by this Paragraph on the state, its agencies, boards, or commissions, or any political subdivision thereof.

*Added by Acts 1956, No. 233 §13. Amended by Acts 1962, No. 184, §1; Acts 1964, No. 113, §13; Acts 1976, No. 377, §1; Acts 1980, No. 606, §1, eff. July 23, 1980; Acts 1981, No. 668, §1; Acts 1988, No. 635, §1, eff. Jan. 1, 1989; Acts 1991, No. 865, §1, eff. July 23, 1991; Acts 1992, No. 681, §1, eff. July 6, 1992; Acts 1995, No. 478, §1; Acts 1997, No. 1299, §1; Acts 2001, No. 802, §1; Acts 2001, No. 1072, §1.*

## §2164. Reciprocity

Any applicant holding a license in good standing in a comparable classification in another state recognized by the respective agency as a reciprocity state may have the trade portion of the examination waived upon written certification from that state in which the applicant is licensed. The business law portion of the examination and the provisions of R.S. 37:2156.1 shall not be waived. Applicants shall comply with all other licensing requirements of this state; however, for good cause, the board may waive any other licensing requirement.

*Acts 1989, No. 559, §1; Acts 1992, No. 681, §1, eff. July 6, 1992.*

# Appendix E: Louisiana Contractors Licensing Law

E-25

## §2165. Residential Building Contractors Subcommittee; membership; terms

A. There is hereby established within the State Licensing Board for Contractors the Residential Building Contractors Subcommittee, consisting of five members who shall be residents of the state of Louisiana and who have been actively engaged in residential contracting for at least five years prior to appointment by the governor. Three members of the subcommittee shall be appointed by the governor from a list of not less than ten names submitted by the Louisiana Homebuilders Association as certified by its president and secretary. One member of the subcommittee shall be appointed to represent congressional district one, one member to represent congressional districts four and five, one member to represent congressional district three, one member to represent congressional district two, and one member to represent congressional district six.

B. The terms of office of the initial members appointed to the subcommittee shall be one for a three-year term, one for a two-year term, and one for a one-year term, to be determined by the governor. Thereafter, all members shall be appointed for three-year terms. All terms shall commence thirty days after the appointment and all members shall serve until their successors have been appointed and qualified. Vacancies occurring in the membership of the subcommittee for any reason shall be filled by appointment by the governor for the unexpired term. No person shall be appointed for more than two consecutive terms. The governor may remove a member for cause.

C. The executive director of the State Licensing Board for Contractors shall serve as executive director of the subcommittee and shall not have voting privileges.

D. (1) An ex officio member of the State Licensing Board for Contractors shall serve on the subcommittee and shall serve as the liaison between the subcommittee and the board. He shall be appointed by the chairman of the State Licensing Board for Contractors and shall serve as the chairman of the subcommittee. His presence at a meeting of the subcommittee may be counted toward establishing a quorum of the subcommittee, and he shall only have voting privileges if either of the following circumstances exists:

(a) His presence is necessary to establish a quorum of the subcommittee and there is a tie vote between the appointed members of the subcommittee.

(b) His presence is necessary to establish a quorum of the subcommittee, only one appointed member of the subcommittee is present, and an additional ex officio member has been appointed pursuant to Paragraph (2) of this Subsection.

(2) An additional ex officio member of the State Licensing Board for Contractors shall serve on the subcommittee only if his presence, along with the ex officio member serving pursuant to Paragraph (1) of this Subsection, is required to establish a quorum of the subcommittee. This additional ex officio member shall be appointed by the chairman of the State Licensing Board for Contractors and shall serve as the vice chairman of the subcommittee. He shall only have voting privileges if there is a tie vote between an appointed member of the subcommittee and the ex officio member serving as chairman of the subcommittee.

(3) The State Licensing Board for Contractors shall pay per diem and travel expenses for ex officio members.

E. A quorum of the subcommittee shall consist of a majority of its members and the subcommittee shall meet at least once every other month to conduct its business. The executive director shall give written notice to each member of the time and place of each meeting at least ten days prior to the scheduled date of the meeting.

F. Each member of the subcommittee shall be entitled to a per diem allowance of seventy-five dollars for each meeting they attend and be reimbursed for all travel expenses necessarily incurred in attending meetings.

*Acts 1995, No. 638, §1, eff. Feb. 1, 1996; Acts 1999, No. 1175, §1; Acts 2001, No. 659, §1; Acts 2012, No. 803, §9.*

## §2166. Powers and duties

Subject to the approval of the State Licensing Board for Contractors, the subcommittee shall have the following powers and duties:

# E-26 Appendix E: Louisiana Contractors Licensing Law

(1) To adopt rules and regulations to govern residential building contractors in the state of Louisiana.

(2) To issue, suspend, modify, or revoke licenses to do business in the state of Louisiana pursuant to the provisions of R.S. 37:2158.

(3) To prescribe and adopt regulations and policies for continuing education. However, notwithstanding any other law to the contrary, the subcommittee shall not approve for use by licensees any continuing education courses or written training programs provided by a member of the subcommittee or legal entity in which he has a controlling interest.

(4) To cause the prosecution and enjoinder of all persons violating provisions of this Chapter, and incur necessary expenses therefor.

*Acts 1995, No. 638, §1, eff. Feb. 1, 1996; Acts 1999, No. 1175, §1.*

## §2167. Licensure required; qualifications; examination; waivers

A. No person shall work as a residential building contractor, as defined in this Chapter, in this state unless he holds an active license in accordance with the provisions of this Chapter.

B. In order to obtain a license as a residential building contractor an applicant shall demonstrate to the subcommittee that he:

(1) Has submitted certificates evidencing workers' compensation coverage in compliance with Title 23 of the Louisiana Revised Statutes of 1950, and liability insurance in a minimum amount of one hundred thousand dollars or liability protection provided by a liability trust fund as authorized by R.S. 22:46(9)(d) in a minimum amount of one hundred thousand dollars.

(1) Has passed the examination administered by the State Licensing Board for Contractors.

(1) Has submitted a financial statement prepared by an independent auditor and signed by the applicant and auditor before a notary public, stating that the applicant has a net worth of at least ten thousand dollars.

C. The State Licensing Board for Contractors shall administer an examination for licensure of residential building contractors at such times and places as it shall determine in accordance with the testing procedures of the board. The examination shall test the applicant's knowledge of such subjects as the subcommittee may consider useful in determining the applicant's fitness to be a licensed residential building contractor. The subcommittee shall determine the criteria for satisfactory performance.

D. The subcommittee shall waive the examination and grant a residential building contractor's license to any person working in the residential building industry who meets at least one of the following requirements:

(1) Holds a builder construction license issued by the State Licensing Board for Contractors prior to February 1, 1996.

(2)-(4) Terminated by Acts 1997, No. 925, §1, eff. Jan. 1, 1998.

E. The provisions of Paragraphs D(2), (3), and (4) shall terminate on January 1, 1998.

*Acts 1995, No. 638, §1, eff. Feb. 1, 1996; Acts 1997, No. 925, §1, eff. Jan. 1, 1998; Acts 2001, No. 802, §1; Acts 2003, No. 1146, §1; Acts 2008, No. 415, §2, eff. Jan. 1, 2009.*

## §2167.1. Inactive license

A. Notwithstanding any other provision of law to the contrary, any residential building contractor licensee in good standing with the board who has held a license to engage in residential building construction issued pursuant to this Chapter for not less than one consecutive year may elect to place his license in an inactive license status with the board, provided he applies for a transfer to inactive status.

# Appendix E: Louisiana Contractors Licensing Law

B. During the period a license is in inactive status, the licensee shall be prohibited from engaging in any activity requiring a residential building contractor license.

C. An inactive licensee shall be required to renew his inactive license on a yearly basis in the same manner as provided in R.S. 37:2168 and by paying an annual renewal fee, which shall not exceed the annual renewal fee paid by active licensees. However, an inactive licensee shall not be required to submit insurance certificates pursuant to R.S. 37:2167(B)(1) or fulfill any other additional requirements that an active licensee would not be required to fulfill when renewing his license.

D. An inactive licensee shall be required to fulfill all prescribed continuing education requirements established for active licensees.

E. A licensee may request transfer from inactive status to active status at any time, provided all of the following conditions exist:

(1) The inactive license has been renewed as provided for in this Section.

(2) The inactive license is current at the time the request is received by the board.

(3) The licensee submits the required insurance certificates as provided in R.S. 37:2167(B)(1).

*Acts 2001, No. 802, §1; Acts 2011, No. 107, §1.*

## §2168. Term of license; renewal of license

A. The term of a license issued pursuant to the provisions of this Chapter shall be for a term not to exceed three years, as determined by the board.

B. Licenses and renewals issued under the provisions of this Chapter shall expire on the anniversary of the date on which the license was originally issued. Licensees shall elect upon renewal one-, two-, or three-year license renewal terms, and licenses may be issued by the board on a multiple-year basis, not to exceed a three-year term for any license. The license becomes invalid on the last day of the term for which it was issued unless renewed; however, after a license has expired, the person to whom such license was issued shall have fifteen days following the expiration date to file an application for the renewal of such license without the payment of a penalty and without further examination, and any person who makes an application for renewal of a license after fifteen days following the expiration date of the license may, at the discretion of the subcommittee, have his license renewed after paying the required license fees and such penalty, not exceeding the sum of fifty dollars, that the board may impose. New applicants for licensing may elect upon application the renewal term of their license.

*Acts 1995, No. 638, §1, eff. Feb. 1, 1996; Acts 2008, No. 576, §1.*

## §2169. Fees

A. The subcommittee shall fix fees in a manner established by its rules. Initial fees for residential building contractors shall not exceed the following amounts:

(1) Examination fee $50.00

(2) License fee $100.00

(3) Renewal fee $100.00

(4) Delinquent fee $50.00

B. All fees shall be paid into the account of the State Licensing Board for Contractors.

*Acts 1995, No. 638, §1, eff. Feb. 1, 1995.*

## §2170. Exceptions

A. There are excepted from the provisions of this Chapter:

(1) Owners of property who supervise, superintend, oversee, direct, or in any manner assume charge of the construction, alteration, repair, improvement, movement, demolition, putting up, tearing down, or maintenance of their personal residences, provided the homeowner does not build more than one residence per year. The one-year period shall commence on the date of occupancy of the residence. However, an owner of property may build more than one personal residence in a one-year period if the construction of an additional residence occurs as a result of a change in the legal marital status of the owner or change in the employment status of the owner whereby the owner must relocate to another employment location, which is located in excess of fifty miles from his personal residence.

(2) Persons performing the work of a residential building contractor in areas or municipalities that do not have a permitting procedure.

(3) Farmers doing construction for agricultural or related purposes on leased or owned land.

B. However, the provisions of this Chapter shall apply to any contractor employed by persons exempted in Subsection A except those contractors employed for remodeling purposes. Further, nothing in this Section shall be construed to waive local and state health and life safety code requirements.

*Acts 1995, No. 638, §1, eff. Feb. 1, 1996; Acts 1999, No. 1175, §1; Acts 2001, No. 711, §1.*

## §2171. Prohibited activities

No person shall hold himself out as a Louisiana licensed residential building contractor unless he holds an active license as such pursuant to the provisions of this Chapter, and possesses any insurance required by federal law.

*Acts 1995, No. 638, §1, eff. Feb. 1, 1996; Acts 2001, No. 802, §1; Acts 2012, No. 163, §1.*

## §2171.1. Inspection of local building permits

Each month the board or its staff shall inspect the list of residential building permits issued by each local building permit official in this state to ensure that no person is working as a residential building contractor without an active license.

*Acts 2001, No. 802, §1.*

## §2171.2. Requirements; building permit

A. Prior to the issuance of any building permit, the local building permit official shall require that the applicant for such permit produce proof that the applicant possesses an active, applicable contractors license issued by the board, or that the applicant's proposed building activity is exempt from such licensure under this Chapter. The local building permit official shall require any applicant claiming an exemption for residential construction activities to execute an affidavit attesting to the claimed exemption. Such affidavit shall be submitted to the local building permit official prior to the issuance of a permit. Such affidavit shall be executed on a form provided by the board.

B. In addition to and notwithstanding requirements set forth in Subsection A of this Section, a nonresident commercial, residential, or home improvement contractor applicant shall provide its federal taxpayer identification number to the local building permit official, as well as proof of registration to do business in the state of Louisiana.

C. Liability shall not be imposed on a political subdivision or its officers or employees based upon the exercise or performance of, or the failure to exercise or perform any act or duty provided for in this Section.

*Acts 2004, No. 724, §1; Acts 2010, No. 67, §1.*

Appendix E: Louisiana Contractors Licensing Law                                                    E-29

### §2172. Repealed by Acts 2001, No. 1137, §1.

### §2173. Effect on local regulatory examination authority

This Chapter shall preempt municipal or other local regulatory examination authority over residential builders. In the event that the governing authority or any municipality or parish finds that the state minimum standards do not meet its needs, the local government may provide requirements not less stringent than those specified by the state.

*Acts 1995, No. 638, §1, eff. Feb. 1, 1996.*

### §2175.1. Home improvement contracting; written contract required; right to cancel

A. Every agreement to perform home improvement contracting services, as defined by this Part, in an amount in excess of one thousand five hundred dollars, but not in excess of seventy-five thousand dollars, shall be in writing and shall include the following documents and information:

(1) The complete agreement between the owner and the contractor and a clear description of any other documents which are or shall be incorporated into the agreement.

(2) The full names, addresses, and the registration number of the home improvement contractor.

(3) A detailed description of the work to be done and the materials to be used in the performance of the contract.

(4) (a) The total amount agreed to be paid for the work to be performed under the contract including all change orders and work orders.

(b) An approximation of the cost expected to be borne by the owner under a cost-plus contract or a time-and-materials contract.

(5) The signature of all parties.

(6) If the contract is for goods or services in connection with the repair or replacement of a roof system to be paid from the proceeds of a property or casualty insurance policy, a statement in boldface type of a minimum size of ten points, in substantially the following form:

"You may cancel this contract in connection with the repair or replacement of a roof system at any time within seventy-two hours after you have been notified that your insurer has denied all or any part of your claim to pay for the goods and services to be provided under this contract. See attached notice of cancellation form for an explanation of this right."

(7) If the contract is for goods or services in connection with the repair or replacement of a roof system to be paid from the proceeds of a property or casualty insurance policy, a fully completed form in duplicate, captioned "NOTICE OF CANCELLATION", which shall be attached to the contract but easily detachable, and which shall contain, in boldface type of a minimum size of ten points, the following statement:

"NOTICE OF CANCELLATION

If your insurer denies all or any part of your claim to pay for goods and services in connection with the repair or replacement of a roof system to be provided under this contract, you may cancel the contract by mailing or delivering a signed and dated copy of this cancellation notice or any other written notice to (name of home improvement contractor) at (address of contractor's place of business) at any time within seventy-two hours after you have been notified that your claim has been denied. If you cancel, any payments made by you under the contract, except for certain emergency work already performed by the contractor, shall be returned to you within ten business days following receipt by the contractor of your cancellation notice.

I HEREBY CANCEL THIS TRANSACTION

_____

(Date)

_____

(Insured's Signature)

B. At the time of signing, the owner shall be furnished with a copy of the contract signed by both the home improvement contractor and the owner. No work shall begin prior to the signing of the contract and transmittal to the owner of a copy of the contract.

C. Contracts which fail to comply with the requirements of this Section shall not be invalid solely because of noncompliance.

D. (1) A person who has entered into a written contract with a home improvement contractor to provide goods or services in connection with the repair or replacement of a roof system to be paid from the proceeds of a property or casualty insurance policy may cancel the contract within seventy-two hours after the insured party has been notified by the insurer that all or any part of the claim has been denied. Cancellation shall be evidenced by the insured party giving written notice of cancellation to the home improvement contractor at the address stated in the contract. Notice of cancellation, if given by mail, shall be by certified mail, return receipt requested, and shall be effective upon deposit into the United States mail, postage prepaid, and properly addressed to the home improvement contractor. Notice of cancellation need not take a particular form and shall be sufficient if it indicates, by any form of written expression, the intention of the insured party not to be bound by the contract.

(2) Within ten days after a contract referred to in this Subsection has been cancelled, the home improvement contractor shall tender to the owner or possessor of the residential real estate any payments, partial payments, or deposits made by the insured party and any note or other evidence of indebtedness. If, however, the home improvement contractor has performed any emergency services, acknowledged by the insured in writing to be necessary to prevent damage to the premises, the home improvement contractor shall be entitled to the reasonable value of such services.

E. For the purposes of this Part, "roof system" means the components of a roof, including but not limited to covering, insulation, and ventilation.

_Acts 2003, No. 1146, §2; Acts 2007, No. 398, §1; Acts 2012, No. 193, §1._

### §2175.2. Home improvement contracting; registration required

A. (1) No person shall undertake, offer to undertake, or agree to perform home improvement contracting services unless registered with and approved by the Residential Building Contractors Subcommittee of the State Licensing Board for Contractors as a home improvement contractor.

(2) Any home improvement contractor who possesses a certificate of registration from the subcommittee as of October 1, 2007, shall be entitled to complete any preexisting contracts he has entered into in excess of seventy-five thousand dollars without having to obtain a residential contractor's license as provided for in this Chapter. However, such home improvement contractor shall be required to obtain a residential contractor's license prior to bidding or entering into any contracts in excess of seventy-five thousand dollars after October 1, 2007.

B. In order to be registered as a home improvement contractor, an applicant must make a written application under oath to the subcommittee. The application shall set forth information that includes the following:

(1) The applicant's name, home address, business address, and social security number.

# Appendix E: Louisiana Contractors Licensing Law

(2) The names and addresses of any and all owners, partners, or trustees of the applicant including, in case of corporate entities, the names and addresses of any and all officers, directors, and principal shareholders. This Section shall not apply to publicly traded companies.

(3) A statement whether the applicant has ever been previously registered in the state as a home improvement contractor, under what other names he was previously registered, whether there have been previous judgments or arbitration awards against him, and whether his registration has ever been suspended or revoked.

C. The applicant shall furnish the board proof of general liability insurance in a minimum amount of one hundred thousand dollars, proof of workers' compensation insurance, and proof of registration with the Department of Revenue by providing a certificate of resident/nonresident status.

D. The subcommittee shall fix fees, in an amount not to exceed fifty dollars, in a manner established by its rules for the registration and renewal for home improvement contractors.

E. No application for registration or renewal conforming to the requirements of this Section may be denied or revoked except for a finding by the subcommittee that the applicant has done one or more of the following acts which are grounds for denial:

(1) Made material omissions or misrepresentations of fact on their application for registration or renewal.

(2) Failed to pay either the registration fee or renewal fee.

(3) Failed consistently to perform contracts or has performed contracts in an unworkmanlike manner or has failed to complete contracts with no good cause or has engaged in fraud or bad faith with respect to such contracts.

F. The subcommittee shall issue and deliver a certificate of registration to all applicants who have been approved for registration. Each certificate of registration issued by the subcommittee shall bear a number which shall be valid for one year from the date of its issuance and may be renewed upon approval of the subcommittee. The certificate shall not be transferable.

*Acts 2003, No. 1146, §2; Acts 2004, No. 724, §1; Acts 2007, No. 398, §1; Acts 2012, No. 193, §1.*

## §2175.3. Home improvement contracting; prohibited acts; violations

A. The following acts are prohibited by persons performing home improvement contracting services:

(1) Operating without a certificate of registration issued by the subcommittee.

(2) Abandoning or failing to perform, without justification, any contract or project engaged in or undertaken by a registered home improvement contractor, or deviating from or disregarding plans or specifications in any material respect without the consent of the owner.

(3) Failing to credit the owner any payment they have made to the home improvement contractor in connection with a home improvement contracting transaction.

(4) Making any material misrepresentation in the procurement of a contract or making any false promise likely to influence, persuade, or induce the procurement of a contract.

(5) Violation of the building code of the state or municipality.

(6) Failing to notify the subcommittee of any change of trade name or address, or conducting a home improvement contracting business in any name other than the one in which the home improvement contractor is registered.

(7) Failing to pay for materials or services rendered in connection with his operating as a home improvement contractor where he has received sufficient funds as payment for the particular construction work, project, or operation for which the services or material were rendered or purchased.

(8) Making a false representation that the person is a state licensed general contractor.

(9) Failing to possess any insurance required by federal law.

(10) Advertising or promising to pay or rebate all or any portion of an applicable insurance deductible as an inducement to the sale of goods or services in connection with the repair or replacement of a roof system. For the purposes of this Section, a promise to pay or rebate the insurance deductible shall include granting any allowance or offering any discount against the fees to be charged or paying the insured party any form of compensation for any reason, including but not limited to permitting the home improvement contractor to display a sign or any other type of advertisement at the insured party's premises, or paying an insured party for providing a letter of referral or recommendation. If a home improvement contractor violates this Paragraph:

(a) The insurer to whom the insured party tendered the claim shall not be obligated to consider the estimate prepared by the home improvement contractor.

(b) The insured party or the applicable insurer may bring an action against the home improvement contractor in a court of competent jurisdiction for damages sustained as a result of the home improvement contractor's violation.

(11) Failing to obtain any insurance required by federal law.

B. (1) Violations of this Section shall subject the violator to the administrative sanctions as prescribed in this Part.

(2) A violation of Paragraph (A)(10) of this Section shall constitute a prohibited practice under the Unfair Trade Practices and Consumer Protection Law, R.S. 51:1401 et seq., and shall be subject to the enforcement provisions of that Chapter.

*Acts 2003, No. 1146, §2; Acts 2012, No. 163, §1; Acts 2012, No. 193, §1.*

### §2175.4. Home improvement contracting; administrative penalties

A. If the subcommittee determines that any registrant is liable for violation of any of the provisions contained in this Part, the subcommittee may suspend the registrant's certificate of registration for such period of time as shall be determined by the subcommittee, revoke the registrant's certificate of registration, or reprimand the registrant.

B. The subcommittee may assess an administrative penalty not to exceed one hundred dollars or twenty-five percent of the total contract price, whichever is greater, payable within thirty days of their order, for each violation of any of the provisions of this Part, committed by the home improvement contractor who is registered or who is required to be registered, plus any administrative costs incurred by the subcommittee.

C. In determining whether to impose an administrative penalty, the administrator shall consider the seriousness of the violation, the effect of the violation on the complainant, any good faith on the part of the home improvement contractor, and the home improvement contractor's history of previous violations.

*Acts 2003, No. 1146, §2.*

### §2175.5. Home improvement contracting; exceptions

A. The following persons are excepted from the provisions of this Part:

(1) The state or any of its political subdivisions.

# Appendix E: Louisiana Contractors Licensing Law

(2) (a) A homeowner who physically performs the home improvement work on his personal residence.

(b) An individual who physically performs home improvement work on other property owned by him when the home improvement work has a value of less than seven thousand five hundred dollars.

(3) Persons licensed as a contractor, subcontractor, or residential building contractor pursuant to Chapter 24 of this Title.

(4) Electricians, plumbers, architects, or other persons who are required by law to attain standards of competency or experience as a prerequisite to licensure for and engaging in such profession who are acting exclusively within the scope of the profession for which they are currently licensed pursuant to such other law.

(5) Any person who performs labor or services for a home improvement contractor for wages or salary and who does not act in the capacity as a home improvement contractor.

(6) Any person who works exclusively in any of the following home improvement areas:

(a) Landscaping.

(b) Interior painting or wall covering.

B. Nothing in this Section shall be construed to waive local and state health and life safety code requirements.

*Acts 2003, No. 1146, §2, Acts 2013, No. 60, §1.*

## § 2175.6. **Home improvement contracting; claims of unregistered persons.**

No home improvement contractor who fails to obtain a certificate of registration as provided for in this Part shall be entitled to file a statement of claim or a statement of lien or privilege with respect to monetary sums allegedly owed under any contract, whether express, implied, or otherwise, when any provision of this Part requires that the home improvement contractor possess a certificate of registration issued by the subcommittee in order to have properly entered into such a contract.

*Acts 2007, No. 398, §1.*

## §2181. Purpose

The legislature hereby declares that it is in the best interest of the citizens of the state to require the licensure and regulation of those persons who perform mold remediation. The purpose of this Chapter is to require qualifying criteria in a professional field in which unqualified individuals may injure or mislead the public. The provisions of this Chapter shall contribute to the safety, health, and welfare of the people of this state.

*Acts 2003, No. 880, §1.*

## §2182. Definitions

As used in this Chapter, the following words shall have the following meanings unless the context clearly indicates otherwise:

(1) "Applicant" means a person who seeks to be examined for licensure by the board.

(2) "Board" means the State Licensing Board for Contractors, as provided for in R.S. 37:2150 et seq.

(3) "Licensee" means any person who has been issued a license by the board in accordance with the provisions of this Chapter.

(4) "Mold remediation" means the removal, cleaning, sanitizing, demolition, or other treatment, including preventive activities, of mold or mold-contaminated matter that was not purposely grown at that location.

*Acts 2003, No. 880, §1.*

## §2183. Scope

This Chapter applies only to the regulation of mold-related activities that affect indoor air quality and does not apply to routine cleaning when not conducted for the purpose of mold remediation.

*Acts 2003, No. 880, §1.*

## §2184. Powers and duties of the board

In addition to the powers and duties allocated to the board pursuant to Chapter 24 of this Title, the board shall also:

(1) Adopt rules and regulations, in accordance with the Administrative Procedure Act, as the board deems necessary to administer and implement the provisions of this Chapter or to govern the practice of mold remediation in the state.

(2) Issue, suspend, modify, and revoke licenses to practice mold remediation.

(3) Report to the attorney general all persons who violate the provisions of this Chapter.

(4) Maintain an up-to-date list of all licensees.

(5) Adopt minimum standards of practice for persons licensed to conduct mold remediation.

*Acts 2003, No. 880, §1.*

## §2185. Licensing required

A. Beginning July 1, 2004, no person shall engage in or conduct, or advertise or hold himself out as engaging in or conducting the business of, or acting in the capacity of a person who conducts mold remediation unless such person holds a mold remediation license as provided for in this Chapter.

B. The following persons shall not be required to obtain a license issued pursuant to this Chapter:

(1) A residential property owner who performs mold remediation on his own property.

(2) A nonresidential property owner, or the employee of such owner, who performs mold remediation on an apartment building owned by that person that has more than four dwelling units.

(3) An owner or tenant, or a managing agent or employee of an owner or tenant, who performs mold remediation on property owned or leased by the owner or tenant. This exemption does not apply if the managing agent or employee engages in the business of performing mold remediation for the public.

(4) An employee of a licensee who performs mold remediation while supervised by the licensee.

(5) A licensed residential building contractor who performs mold assessment or mold remediation services no more than twenty square feet when acting within the scope of his license.

*Acts 2003, No. 880, §1.*

## §2186. Qualifications for licensure; application; fees

A. The board shall, by rule adopted in accordance with the Administrative Procedure Act, establish minimum qualifications for licensing. Applications for licenses and for renewal licenses shall be made in writing to the board on forms provided by the board.

Appendix E: Louisiana Contractors Licensing Law                                                                    E-35

B. An applicant for a license to perform mold remediation shall meet the following requirements:

(1) Attainment of eighteen years of age.

(2) Successful completion of high school or its equivalent.

(3) Present evidence to the board that he has satisfactorily completed at least the following board-approved course work:

(a) Twenty-four hours of training in mold remediation and basic mold assessment.

(b) Four hours of instruction in Louisiana's "Unfair Trade Practices and Consumer Protection Law".

(4) Payment of the appropriate fees.

(5) Submission of a license application as prescribed by the board.

(6) Has submitted insurance certificates evidencing workers' compensation coverage in compliance with Title 23 of the Louisiana Revised Statutes of 1950 and liability insurance in a minimum amount of fifty thousand dollars.

C. An applicant shall furnish the board with a financial statement, current to within twelve months of the date of filing, prepared by an independent auditor and signed by the applicant and auditor before a notary public, stating the assets of the applicant, to be used by the board to determine the financial responsibility of the applicant to perform mold remediation services. Such assets shall include a net worth of at least ten thousand dollars. An applicant without the net worth required herein may furnish the board a bond, letter of credit, or other security acceptable to the board in the amount of such net worth requirement plus the amount of the applicant's negative net worth if any, and the furnishing of such bond, letter of credit, or other security shall be deemed satisfaction of such net worth requirement for all purposes.

D. The board may charge and collect fees not in excess of the following:

(1) Application for license $100.00

(2) License renewal $100.00

(3) Delinquent renewal $ 50.00

(4) The fee provided for in this Subsection shall not be charged to a licensed residential building contractor who performs mold remediation services when acting within the scope of his license.

*Acts 2003, No. 880, §1.*

### §2187. Written reports; prohibited activities

A. A person who performs mold assessment services shall provide a written report to each person for whom he performs such services for compensation.

B. (1) No licensee shall perform both mold assessment and mold remediation on the same property.

(2) No person shall own an interest in both the entity which performs mold assessment services and the entity which performs mold remediation services on the same property.

*Acts 2003, No. 880, §1.*

### §2188. License issuance and renewal

A. Licenses and renewals issued under the provisions of this Chapter shall expire on the anniversary date on which the license was originally issued. Licensees shall elect upon renewal one-, two-, or three-year license renewal terms, and licenses may be issued by the board on a multiple-year basis, not to exceed a three-year term for any license. The license becomes invalid on the last day of the term for which it was issued, unless renewed; however, after a license has expired, the person to whom such license was issued shall have fifteen days following the expiration date to file an application for the renewal of such license without the payment of a penalty and without further examination, and any person who makes an application for renewal of a license after fifteen days following the expiration date of the license may, at the discretion of the board, have his license renewed after paying the required license fees and such penalty, not exceeding the sum of fifty dollars, that the board may impose. New applicants for licensing may elect upon application the renewal term of their license.

B. Any licensee who fails to timely renew his license may thereafter renew upon payment of the appropriate renewal and delinquent fees and upon filing of a renewal application. The period for delinquent renewal of an expired license shall be limited to the six-month period immediately following the expiration date of the active license. Failure to renew an expired license during such six-month period shall result in forfeiture of renewal rights and shall require the former licensee to apply as an initial applicant and meet all requirements of an initial applicant.

C. Licenses shall be in a form prescribed by the board.

*Acts 2003, No. 880, §1; Acts 2008, No. 576, §1.*

### §2189. Prohibited acts; penalties

A. The board may suspend or revoke any license, or censure, fine, or impose probationary or other restrictions on any licensee for good cause shown which shall include but not be limited to the following:

(1) Conviction of a felony or the entering of a plea of guilty or nolo contendere to a felony charge under the laws of the United States or any other state.

(2) Deceit or misrepresentation in obtaining a license.

(3) Providing false testimony before the board.

(4) Efforts to deceive or defraud the public.

(5) Professional incompetence or gross negligence.

(6) Rendering, submitting, subscribing, or verifying false, deceptive, misleading, or unfounded opinions or reports.

(7) Violating any rule or regulation adopted by the board or any provision of this Chapter.

(8) Aiding or abetting a person to evade the provisions of this Chapter or knowingly combining or conspiring with an unlicensed person with the intent to evade the provisions of this Chapter.

(9) Violating any standard of conduct adopted by the board.

(10) Engaging in conduct, advertising or holding oneself out as engaging in or conducting the business of, or acting in the capacity of a person who performs mold remediation services without possessing a valid license.

(11) Falsely representing oneself as being the holder of a valid license by using the title "licensed mold remediator" or any title, designation, or abbreviation deceptively similar or likely to create the impression that such person is licensed.

B. Violators of any of the provisions of this Section may be fined by the board in an amount not to exceed two thousand dollars per violation and ten thousand dollars for each subsequent violation.

C. All fines collected pursuant to this Section for violations shall annually, at each audit of the board, be transferred to a separate contractor's educational trust fund to be used for educational purposes as determined by the board.

*Acts 2003, No. 880, §1.*

# Appendix E: Louisiana Contractors Licensing Law

## §2190. Revocation or suspension; payment of costs of proceedings

A. Revocation of a license as a result of disciplinary action by the board may prohibit the reissuance of a license to such licensee for a period of up to one year from the date of revocation. The license of an applicant whose license has been revoked may be reissued by the board upon the submission of evidence by the applicant of satisfactory completion of the board-approved course work required for new applicants pursuant to R.S. 37:2186(B)(3).

B. The board, as a probationary condition or as a condition of a revocation or suspension, may require a licensee to pay all costs of the board proceedings, including but not limited to investigators', stenographers', and attorney fees, and costs.

*Acts 2003, No. 880, §1.*

## §2191. Cease and desist orders; injunctive relief

A. In addition to or in lieu of the criminal penalties and administrative sanctions provided for in this Chapter, the board may issue an order to any person engaged in any activity, conduct, or practice constituting a violation of any provision of this Chapter or any rule or regulation adopted pursuant to this Chapter directing such person to cease and desist from such activity, conduct, or practice. Such order shall be issued in the name of the state under the official seal of the board.

B. If the person to whom the board directs a cease and desist order does not cease and desist the prohibited activity, conduct, or practice within two days of service of such order by certified mail, the board may seek a writ of injunction in any court of competent jurisdiction and proper venue enjoining such person from engaging in the activity, conduct, or practice.

*Acts 2003, No. 880, §1.*

## §2192. Fees and other funds received

All fees and fines received by the board under this Chapter shall be used solely to effectuate the provisions of this Chapter and Chapter 24 of this Title.

*Acts 2003, No. 880, §1.*

# Appendix F: Rules and Regulations of the Louisiana Licensing Board for Contractors

## CHAPTER ONE.

### GENERAL PROVISIONS

### §101. Contractor's Recordkeeping

A. It shall be the responsibility of each licensed contractor, residential building contractor, home improvement contractor, mechanical contractor, and electrical contractor to maintain adequate records at all times to show compliance with the licensure requirements of all subcontracts and subcontractors. Such records shall be made available to the board's inspectors at all reasonable times. The failure to maintain adequate records or the failure to furnish copies of such records within 72 hours notice thereof shall constitute a violation of this rule.

*AUTHORITY NOTE: Promulgated in accordance with R.S. 37:2150-2192.*

*HISTORICAL NOTE: Adopted by the Department of Commerce, Licensing Board for Contractors, November 1974, amended and promulgated LR 8:135 (March 1982), amended LR 12:761 (November 1986), amended by the Department of Economic Development, Licensing Board for Contractors, LR 16:601 (July 1990), LR 19:1125 (September 1993), amended by the Office of the Governor, Licensing Board for Contractors, LR 38:149 (January 2012).*

### §103. Disassociation of a Qualifying Party

A. When a qualifying party terminates his or her employment or association with the licensee, the licensee must notify the board in writing within 30 days of the disassociation. Failure by the licensee to cause a new person to qualify as its qualifying party within 60 days of the disassociation will subject the licensee to suspension or revocation of the license.

B. Failure to notify the board of the disassociation of a qualifying party constitutes a violation pursuant to R.S. 37:2158.

*AUTHORITY NOTE: Promulgated in accordance with R.S. 37:2150-2192.*

*HISTORICAL NOTE: Adopted by the Department of Commerce, Licensing Board for Contractors, November 1974, amended and promulgated LR 8:137 (March 1982), amended by the Department of Economic Development, Licensing Board for Contractors, LR 19:1126 (September 1993), amended by the Office of the Governor, Licensing Board for Contractors, LR 38:149 (January 2012).*

### §105. Report of Changes

A. A licensee shall notify the board in writing of any change to the following information and shall provide any and all documentation and fees required by the board within 15 days after such change:

1. the licensee's type of business structure (sole proprietorship, partnership, limited liability company, corporation, etc.);

2. the licensee's business address;

3. the licensee's name;

4. the identity or address of the licensee's registered agent;

5. the identity, address, or ownership percentage of each shareholder;

6. the identity of each officer and the office held;

7. the identity or address of each partner; and

8. the identity or address of each member.

*AUTHORITY NOTE: Promulgated in accordance with R.S. 37:2153.*

*HISTORICAL NOTE: Adopted by the Department of Commerce, Licensing Board for Contractors, November 1974, amended and promulgated LR 8:137 (March 1982), amended by the Office of the Governor, Licensing Board for Contractors, LR 38:149 (January 2012).*

## §107. Enforcement of Act and Rules

A. The board, pursuant to R.S. 37:2158 and R.S. 37:2161, may bring suit to enjoin violations of this act and the executive director and/or his designated agent and/or the legal counsel for the board is hereby authorized to institute such suit on behalf of the board and to sign the verification of the petition for injunction and to do all things necessary in connection with the institution of such legal proceedings when so directed by the board.

*AUTHORITY NOTE: Promulgated in accordance with R.S. 37:2150-2192.*

*HISTORICAL NOTE: Adopted by the Department of Commerce, Licensing Board for Contractors, November 1974, amended and promulgated LR 8:137 (March 1982), amended by the Department of Economic Development, Licensing Board for Contractors, LR 19:1126 (September 1993), amended by the Office of the Governor, Licensing Board for Contractors, LR 38:149 (January 2012).*

## §109. Name

A. Each contractor, residential building contractor, home improvement contractor, mechanical contractor, and electrical contractor shall bid, contract for, and perform work in the name which appears on the official records of the state Licensing Board for Contractors for the current license.

B. If a licensed contractor, residential building contractor, home improvement contractor, mechanical contractor, or electrical contractor assigns a contract, or any portion of a contract for which a license is required to another contractor, residential building contractor, home improvement contractor, mechanical contractor, or electrical contractor, the person or firm to which it is assigned and who performs the work must possess the proper current license. No unlicensed contractor shall be permitted to assign a contract, or any portion or a contract, in an amount for which a license is required to a licensed contractor, residential building contractor, home improvement contractor, mechanical contractor, or electrical contractor in circumvention of the Contractors Licensing Law.

*AUTHORITY NOTE: Promulgated in accordance with R.S. 37:2150-2192.*

*HISTORICAL NOTE: Adopted by the Department of Commerce, Licensing Board for Contractors, November 1974, amended and promulgated LR 8:137 (March 1982), amended by the Department of Economic Development, Licensing Board for Contractors, LR 19:1126 (September 1993), amended by the Office of the Governor, Licensing Board for Contractors, LR 38:149 (January 2012).*

## §110. Reliance upon Exemption

A. Any contractor, residential building contractor, home improvement contractor, mechanical contractor, or electrical contractor relying on an exemption when bidding shall state such exemption pursuant to R.S. 37:2163(A)(2).

*AUTHORITY NOTE: Promulgated in accordance with R.S. 37:2150-2192.*

*HISTORICAL NOTE: Promulgated by the Office of the Governor, Licensing Board for Contractors, LR 38:149 (January 2012).*

# Appendix F: Rules and Regulations of the Louisiana Licensing Board for Contractors

## §111. Correction without Complaint

A. If a possible violation is known to the board, the board may correct it or take appropriate action without formal complaint.

*AUTHORITY NOTE: Promulgated in accordance with R.S. 37:2153.*

*HISTORICAL NOTE: Adopted by the Department of Commerce, Licensing Board for Contractors, November 1974, amended and promulgated LR 8:137 (March 1982), amended by the Office of the Governor, Licensing Board for Contractors, LR 38:149 (January 2012).*

## §113. Maintenance of Skills

A. As provided by R.S. 37:2150 after granting said license, the licensee shall at all times show its ability to serve the public economically, expediently and properly; shall possess the necessary qualifications of responsibility, skill, experience and integrity so that the licensee will not tear down standards of construction established within the industry, and shall continue to maintain the qualifications established in R.S. 37:2156.1.

B. A residential building contractor shall be required to complete a minimum of six hours of continuing education annually by a board approved provider. Proof of compliance with this requirement shall be filed with the board annually in the format required by the board, as a condition for the maintenance and/or renewal of the license. A contractor who holds a valid, current commercial license in the major classifications of: building construction; highway, street and bridge construction; heavy construction; or municipal and public works construction, shall be deemed to have fulfilled this requirement.

*AUTHORITY NOTE: Promulgated in accordance with R.S. 37:2150-2192.*

*HISTORICAL NOTE: Adopted by the Department of Commerce, Licensing Board for Contractors, November 1974, amended and promulgated LR 8:137 (March 1982), amended by the Office of the Governor, Licensing Board for Contractors, LR 38:150 (January 2012), LR 40:2574 (December 2014).*

## §115. Bankruptcy

A. It shall be the responsibility of any licensed contractor, residential building contractor, home improvement contractor, mechanical contractor, or electrical contractor who, voluntarily or involuntarily, is subjected to any provision of the laws of bankruptcy, to notify this board immediately and to make available to this board any and all information pertinent thereto.

B. Any licensed contractor, residential building contractor, home improvement contractor, mechanical contractor, or electrical contractor who is ordered by a competent court to cease operations or whose operations are closed due to operation of any law, shall notify this board immediately and make available to this board any and all information pertinent thereto.

C. If any licensed contractor, residential building contractor, home improvement contractor, mechanical contractor, or electrical contractor is ordered by a competent court to pay a final and executory judgment awarded against him in the operation of his business, for charges for labor, material, breach of contract, etc., and fails to pay said judgment immediately upon its becoming final and executory, a hearing may be scheduled by the board for the purpose of disciplining the licensee in accordance with La. R.S. 37:2150, et seq.

*AUTHORITY NOTE: Promulgated in accordance with R.S. 37:2150-2192.*

*HISTORICAL NOTE: Adopted by the Department of Commerce, Licensing Board for Contractors, November 1974, amended and promulgated LR 8:138 (March 1982), amended by the Department of Economic Development, Licensing Board for Contractors, LR 19:1126 (September 1993), amended by the Office of the Governor, Licensing Board for Contractors, LR 38:150 (January 2012).*

## §117. Major Classification

A. Any contractor possessing a major classification is permitted to bid or perform any of the specialty type work listed under its respective major classification in R.S. 37:2156.2 or any other work that might not be listed which is directly related to the major classification it may hold as long as it is not prohibited by any rule, except as provided in R.S. 37:2156.2(A)(IX)(B), (C), and (D).

*AUTHORITY NOTE: Promulgated in accordance with R.S. 37:2150-2164.*

*HISTORICAL NOTE: Promulgated by the Department of Commerce, Licensing Board for Contractors, LR 11:340 (April 1985), amended by the Department of Economic Development, Licensing Board for Contractors, LR 19:1126 (September 1993), amended by the Office of the Governor, Licensing Board for Contractors, LR 38:149 (January 2012).*

## §119. Construction Management

A. Any person, company or entity who undertakes, attempts to, or submits a price or bid or offer to perform work in construction management or program management whose scope of authority and responsibility includes supervision, oversight, direction, or in any manner assuming charge of the construction services provided to an owner by a contractor or contractors in excess of $50,000 must possess a license from this board in the major classification of building construction or heavy construction or highway, street, and bridge construction or municipal and public works construction. Any licensed contractor with any of these major classifications shall be able to bid and perform any such project specified for construction and/or program management within the scope of the classification(s) they hold. If a program manager whose scope of authority and responsibilities does not include any of the above stated tasks, and who does not subcontract actual construction work, that program manager does not need a contractor's license.

*AUTHORITY NOTE: Promulgated in accordance with R.S. 37:2150-2192.*

*HISTORICAL NOTE: Promulgated by the Office of the Governor, Licensing Board for Contractors, LR 41:536 (March 2015).*

## CHAPTER THREE.

## LICENSE

### §301. Requirements

A. All applications for a license or registration shall contain the information required on the forms which are available at the offices of the State Licensing Board for Contractors, 2525 Quail Drive, Baton Rouge, LA 70808. Each application shall be time dated when received. Licensure may occur once the following minimum conditions are met:

1.  the application is complete, including the required financial statement, references, and federal employer identification number;

2.  all applicable fees, fines, or other sums due to the board are paid in full;

3.  all examination requirements have been met; and

4.  approval by the board.

*AUTHORITY NOTE: Promulgated in accordance with R.S. 37:2153.*

*HISTORICAL NOTE: Adopted by the Department of Commerce, Licensing Board for Contractors, November 1974, amended and promulgated LR 1:401 (September 1975), amended LR 3:11 (January 1977), LR 8:137 (March 1982), amended by the Department of Economic Development, Licensing Board for Contractors, LR 16:602 (July 1990), amended by the Office of the Governor, Licensing Board for Contractors, LR 38:150 (January 2012).*

# Appendix F: Rules and Regulations of the Louisiana Licensing Board for Contractors

### §307. Ownership of License

A. The license for which a person becomes the qualifying party belongs to the licensee, as: a corporate license belongs to the corporation; a partnership license belongs to the partnership; a limited liability company license belongs to the limited liability company, etc.; and an individual license belongs to the individual, regardless of the status of the qualifying party of the entity.

B. A domestic business entity licensed or registered by the board as a limited liability company, business corporation, partnership in commendam, or partnership, that converts under the provision of R.S. 12:1601 et seq., or is a surviving entity following a merger pursuant to 26 U.S.C. 368(a)(1)(f) where ownership of the entity does not change, shall be recognized by the board without having to file a new application for a license or registration. However, prior to updating a license or registration of the converted entity or surviving entity, the converted entity or surviving entity must furnish the following information to the board:

1. a copy of the conversion application or act of merger filed with the Secretary of State;

2. a copy of the certificate of conversion or certificate of merger issued by the Secretary of State;

3. the current license or registration issued by the board;

4. a copy of the revised certificate(s) of insurance in the new name of the converted entity or surviving entity for any coverage required for the issuance of the updated license or registration;

5. any revised contract or other agreement required for the issuance of the license or registration in the name of the converted entity or surviving entity.

C. An updated license or registration issued pursuant to Subsection B of this Section shall have an effective date retroactive to the effective date of the conversion as stated on the certificate of conversion, or the merger as stated on the certificate of merger.

*AUTHORITY NOTE: Promulgated in accordance with R.S. 37:2153 and R.S. 12:1308.*

*HISTORICAL NOTE: Adopted by the Department of Commerce, Licensing Board for Contractors, November 1974, amended and promulgated LR 8:136 (March 1982), ), amended by the Office of the Governor, Licensing Board for Contractors, LR 38:150 (January 2012), LR 40:2575 (December 2014).*

### §309. Application of Subsidiary

A. Any application for a license for a subsidiary shall be considered as a new application and subject to all laws and rules and regulations governing same.

*AUTHORITY NOTE: Promulgated in accordance with R.S. 37:2154.*

*HISTORICAL NOTE: Adopted by the Department of Commerce, Licensing Board for Contractors, November 1974, amended and promulgated LR 8:137 (March 1982), amended by the Office of the Governor, Licensing Board for Contractors, LR 38:151 (January 2012).*

### §311. Reciprocity

A. Any applicant applying for a license who desires that any portion of the law regarding time limitations or trade examinations be waived shall cause the applicable licensing board of its domiciliary state to certify in writing that such board shall grant a Louisiana domiciliary that same waiver of such laws in that state.

*AUTHORITY NOTE: Promulgated in accordance with R.S. 37:2150-2192.*

*HISTORICAL NOTE: Promulgated by the Department of Economic Development, Licensing Board for Contractors, LR 16:602 (July 1990), amended LR 19:1126 (September 1993), amended by the Office of the Governor, Licensing Board for Contractors, LR 38:151 (January 2012).*

## §315. License Revocation and Suspension

A. Any person, firm or corporation duly licensed under the provision of R.S. 37:2150 et seq., who violates any provisions of the said Louisiana Contractors Licensing Law or any rule or regulation of the board may, after due and proper hearing, have its license suspended or revoked by this board. Prior to the board's action on suspension or revocation of licenses as aforesaid, the licensee shall be given a hearing in accordance with §701 of these Rules.

*AUTHORITY NOTE: Promulgated in accordance with R.S. 37:2150-2192.*

*HISTORICAL NOTE: Promulgated by the Department of Commerce, Licensing Board for Contractors, LR 8:138 (March 1982), amended by the Department of Economic Development, Licensing Board for Contractors, LR 19:1126 (September 1993), amended by the Office of the Governor, Licensing Board for Contractors, LR 38:151 (January 2012).*

## §317. Approval Withheld

A. In any instance where approval of an application has been withheld under the terms of R.S. 37:2156(D), the applicant shall have the right to apply to the board for a hearing following which the board may continue to withhold approval or grant its approval at its discretion.

*AUTHORITY NOTE: Promulgated in accordance with R.S. 37:2153 and R.S. 37:2157(D).*

*HISTORICAL NOTE: Promulgated by the Department of Commerce, Licensing Board for Contractors, LR 8:138 (March 1982), amended LR 11:341 (April 1985), amended by the Office of the Governor, Licensing Board for Contractors, LR 38:151 (January 2012).*

## §319. Solar Energy Equipment

A. Contractors applying for the classification of solar energy equipment, must, in addition to all other application or licensing requirements, meet the following requirements prior to issuance of this classification:

1. hold one or more of the following major classifications:

   a. building construction;

   b. electrical work;

   c. mechanical work;

   d. residential building contractor;

2. complete training in the design of solar energy equipment by an entity and course approved by the board;

3. pass a written examination approved by the Licensing Board for Contractors on the installation and maintenance of solar energy equipment.

   a. Any contractor licensed by the state Licensing Board as of August 1, 2014, holding the major classification of building construction, electrical work (statewide) and/or mechanical work (statewide) shall be deemed to have met this examination requirement.

   b. An applicant who holds a current solar pv installer certification for solar electric systems or a current solar heating installer certification for solar thermal hot water systems issued by the North American Board of Certified Energy Practitioners shall be deemed to have met both this examination requirement and the training requirement in §1115.A.2.

B. Any work performed to connect wiring or hookups for any photovoltaic panel or system wherein the panel or system is of a value, including labor, materials, rentals, and all direct and indirect project expenses of $10,000 or more shall be performed only by a contractor or subcontractor who holds the classification of electrical work or who may perform electrical work under the provisions of R.S. 37:2156.2(IX)(B).

# Appendix F: Rules and Regulations of the Louisiana Licensing Board for Contractors

C. Any work performed to connect piping or equipment for any solar thermal system wherein the system is of a value, including labor, materials, rentals, and all direct and indirect project expenses of $10,000 or more shall be performed only by a contractor or subcontractor who holds the classification of mechanical work or who may perform mechanical work under the provisions of R.S. 37:2156.2(IX)(B).

D. Entities engaging in the business of selling or leasing solar energy equipment wherein such entities enter into agreements for installing, servicing, or monitoring solar energy equipment, including entities engaged in the business of arranging agreements for the lease or sale of solar energy systems or acquiring customers for financing entities, must possess a state contractor's license with the classification of solar energy equipment.

*AUTHORITY NOTE: Promulgated in accordance with R.S. 37:2156.3.*

*HISTORICAL NOTE: Promulgated by the Office of the Governor, Licensing Board for Contractors, LR 40:2575 (December 2014).*

## §321. Licensure for Individuals with Military Training and Experience, and Military Spouses

A. The board shall issue a license or registration to a military-trained applicant to allow the applicant to lawfully act as a contractor, residential building contractor, home improvement contractor, mechanical contractor, electrical contractor in this state if, upon application to the board, the applicant satisfies all of the following conditions:

1.  has completed a military program of training, been awarded a military occupational specialty, and performed in that specialty, and performed in that specialty at a level that is substantially equivalent to or exceeds the requirements for licensure or registration as a contractor, residential building contractor, home improvement contractor, mechanical contractor, or electrical contractor in this state;

2.  has engaged in the active practice of contracting in the classification or subclassification for which a license or registration is sought;

3.  has not been disciplined in any jurisdiction for an act that would have constituted grounds for refusal, suspension, or revocation of a contractor's license or registration in this state at the time the act was committed.

B. The board shall issue a license or registration to a military trained applicant, if, upon application to the board, the applicant holds a current license, certification, or registration from another jurisdiction and that jurisdiction's requirements for licensure, certification, or registration are substantially equivalent to or exceed the requirements for licensure or registration in this state.

C. The board shall issue a license or registration to a military spouse to allow the military spouse to act as a contractor in this state if, upon application to the board, the military spouse satisfies all of the following conditions:

1.  holds a current license, certification, or registration from another jurisdiction, and that jurisdiction's requirements for licensure, certification or registration are substantially equivalent to or exceed the requirements for licensure or registration in this state;

2.  can demonstrate competency to act as a contractor through methods determined by the board such as, but not limited to, having completed continuing education units or having had recent experience in the classification or subclassification for which a license or registration is being sought;

3.  has not been disciplined in any jurisdiction for an act that would have constituted grounds for refusal, suspension, or revocation of a license or registration to act as a contactor in this state at the time the act was committed;

4.  is in good standing and has not been disciplined by the agency that issued the license, certification, or permit.

D. The board shall issue a temporary practice permit to a military-trained applicant or military spouse licensed, certified, or registered in another jurisdiction while the military-trained applicant or military spouse is satisfying the requirements for licensure or registration, if that jurisdiction has licensure, certification, or registration standards substantially equivalent to the standards for licensure or registration in this state. The military-trained applicant or military spouse may practice under the temporary permit until a license or registration is granted, or until a notice to deny a license or registration is issued in accordance with §701.

E. The provisions of this Section shall not apply to any applicant receiving a dishonorable discharge or a military spouse whose spouse received a dishonorable discharge.

AUTHORITY NOTE: Promulgated in accordance with R.S. 37:2156.3.

HISTORICAL NOTE: Promulgated by the Office of the Governor, Licensing Board for Contractors, LR 40:2575 (December 2014).

## CHAPTER FIVE.

## EXAMINATION

### §501. Qualifying Party

A. Any licensee may have more than one qualifying party. Nothing in the law is to be construed so as to prohibit a licensee from having more than one qualifying party per trade.

B. If a qualifying party for a particular trade discontinues employment with a licensee, the licensee will still have a valid license and may bid on jobs in that trade classification, but the licensee must have a qualifying party before commencing work on a new job.

AUTHORITY NOTE: Promulgated in accordance with R.S. 37:2150-2192.

HISTORICAL NOTE: Adopted by the Department of Commerce, Licensing Board for Contractors, November 1974, amended and promulgated LR 8:136 (March 1982), amended by the Department of Economic Development, Licensing Board for Contractors, LR 19:1127 (September 1993), amended by the Office of the Governor, Licensing Board for Contractors, LR 38:151 (January 2012).

### §503. Authorized to Take Examination

A. 1. The qualifying party or parties authorized to take the examination are:

    a. a sole proprietor or spouse of a sole proprietor (individual);

    b. any partner (partnership);

    c. any original stockholder or incorporator (corporation);

    d. any original member (limited liability company);

    e. any employee of said applicant who has been in full-time employment for 120 consecutive days immediately preceding the examination.

2. The employee shall be prepared to execute an affidavit furnished by the board at the time he takes the examination giving his length of employment and social security number. The employee shall be prepared to show evidence of eligibility by furnishing evidence of employment for the four preceding months. The evidence of employment should demonstrate that the employee received an average gross income for the preceding 120 consecutive days at least equal to the federal minimum wage for the number of hours worked, that the employee worked an average of at least 32 hours per week for the preceding 120-day period, and that each payroll check in said period was negotiated within 30 days of the end of the pay period. Further, the employee must demonstrate that he meets the criteria to be classified as an *employee* as defined by the Internal Revenue Service. All such evidence must be submitted in a verifiable format, through records acceptable to the board.

Appendix F: Rules and Regulations of the Louisiana Licensing Board for Contractors          F-9

B. No person qualifying as an employee shall be allowed to be the qualifying party for more than one company and two subsidiaries. If more than two subsidiaries are formed or acquired by a parent company, a separate qualifying party shall be registered with the board for each two additional subsidiary companies. Under no circumstances may an individual qualifying as an employee be the qualifying party for more than three such related entities, or for more than one unrelated entity.

C. An employee who has not been in full-time employment for 120 consecutive days immediately preceding the application due to an absence resulting from deployment in active military service may be considered as a full-time employee if the employee has been re-employed in accordance with R.S. 29:410 and, considering the employee's period of employment immediately preceding the absence resulting from deployment in active military service, the employee otherwise satisfies the requirement of full-time employment.

*AUTHORITY NOTE: Promulgated in accordance with R.S. 37:2153(A).*

*HISTORICAL NOTE: Adopted by the Department of Commerce, Licensing Board for Contractors, November 1974, amended and promulgated LR 8:136 (March 1982), amended by the Department of Economic Development, Licensing Board for Contractors, LR 19:1127 (September 1993), LR 23:1495 (November 1997), amended by the Office of the Governor, Licensing Board for Contractors, LR 38:151 (January 2012).*

## §505. Additional Classifications

A. A licensed contractor may add additional classifications to his license at any time provided:

1. the request for additional classification(s) is in writing;

2. a completed and notarized qualifying party application form is submitted pursuant to R.S. 37:2156.1(D)(1);

3. the required additional fees are paid and the qualifying party successfully passes the examination;

4. additions or changes to an existing license shall become effective after completion of the above requirements and upon board approval at the next regularly scheduled board meeting.

*AUTHORITY NOTE: Promulgated in accordance with R.S. 37:2150-2192.*

*HISTORICAL NOTE: Adopted by the Department of Commerce, Licensing Board for Contractors, November 1974, amended and promulgated LR 8:136 (March 1982), amended LR 11:341 (April 1985), LR 12:760 (November 1986), amended by the Department of Economic Development, Licensing Board for Contractors, LR 16:602 (July 1990), LR 19:1127 (September 1993), amended by the Office of the Governor, Licensing Board for Contractors, LR 38:152 (January 2012).*

## §507. Applicants

A. Except as otherwise provided by law, all initial applicants shall be required to take and successfully pass the business and law portion of the board's examination and the trade portion where there exists an examination for same.

B. The qualifying party shall submit his application, with all supporting documentation for approval. The qualifying party shall list all prior affiliations with a licensed contractor(s) and shall disclose whether or not any sanctions have been levied against such contractor(s). The qualifying party shall also state his and/or the contractor's involvement in such sanctions.

*AUTHORITY NOTE: Promulgated in accordance with R.S. 37:2150-2192.*

*HISTORICAL NOTE: Adopted by the Department of Commerce, Licensing Board for Contractors, November 1974, amended and promulgated LR 8:136 (March 1982), amended by the Department of Economic Development, Licensing Board for Contractors, LR 16:602 (July 1990), LR 19:1127 (September 1993), amended by the Office of the Governor, Licensing Board for Contractors, LR 38:152 (January 2012), LR 40:2576 (December 2014).*

# §509. Exemption from Examination

A. A contractor, residential building contractor, mechanical contractor, or electrical contractor who is a subsidiary of a currently licensed contractor, residential building contractor, mechanical contractor or electrical contractor and who is making application for a license in the same classification(s) as that of the currently licensed contractor, residential building contractor, mechanical contractor, or electrical contractor shall not be required to take an examination on the subject for which said subsidiary contractor, residential building contractor, mechanical contractor, or electrical contractor is seeking a license, with the approval of the board, provided that the holders of a majority of the stock in the subsidiary contractor, residential building contractor, mechanical contractor, or electrical contractor are the same as the holders of the majority of stock in the currently licensed contractor, residential building contractor, mechanical contractor, or electrical contractor, and further provided that the individual who was designated as the qualifying party at the time a license was originally issued to the currently licensed contractor, residential building contractor, mechanical contractor, or electrical contractor remains in the employ of the currently licensed contractor, residential building contractor, mechanical contractor, or electrical contractor at the time of application for license by the subsidiary contractor, residential building contractor, mechanical contractor, or electrical contractor.

B. A qualifying party may be exempt from taking another examination for the same classification for which he has previously taken and passed.

C. Pursuant to R.S. 37:2156.1(M), any applicant seeking an exemption from the examination required for a mechanical contractor or electrical contractor license on the basis that it has worked in the mechanical or electrical construction industry must submit the following documentation:

1. proof that it holds either a mechanical or an electrical contractor's license issued prior to July 1, 2008 by a local municipality, after having passed an examination administered or written by a national testing company approved by the board; or

2. five original building permits, issued within the last three years, proving that it has actually been engaged in either the mechanical or electrical construction building industry prior to July 1, 2008. If the permit does not specify the entity or person performing the mechanical or electrical work, then additional documentation will be required to verify that the applicant actually performed the mechanical or electrical work under the permit, including but not limited to: a job proposal, contract, invoice or receipts, a signed punch list, certification of completion by the owner, and proof of payment by the owner or general contractor; or

3. proof that it has completed six mechanical or electrical construction projects within the ten-year period prior to July 1, 2008, or has constructed one such project for another person within the five-year period prior to July 1, 2008. Evidence for each job shall include, but not be limited to, a combination of at least three of the following:

    a. a job proposal, contract, invoice or receipts, a signed punch list, certification of completion by the owner, proof of payment by the owner or general contractor, permit applications; and

    b. evidence that the applicant operated as a business at the time of each job, including but not limited to, copies of such items as tax documents showing business income from such work, a local occupational license, a local mechanical license, receipts from material supply dealers showing that the applicant purchased sufficient materials for the work performed, state and/or federal tax identification numbers, certificates of good standing from the Secretary of State, and similar business documentation;

    c. at least one project for which sufficient proof is provided must have been in the amount of $10,000 or more.

D. No applicant may be exempted from the required examinations pursuant to R.S. 37:2156.1(M) for more than three parishes.

# Appendix F: Rules and Regulations of the Louisiana Licensing Board for Contractors

E. Proof of plumbing work, including a plumbing license or permit, will be insufficient to exempt an applicant from the examination required for a mechanical contractor's license.

*AUTHORITY NOTE: Promulgated in accordance with R.S. 37:2150-2192.*

*HISTORICAL NOTE: Adopted by the Department of Commerce, Licensing Board for Contractors, November 1974, amended and promulgated LR 8:136 (March 1982), amended by the Department of Economic Development, Licensing Board for Contractors, LR 16:602 (July 1990), LR 19:1127 (September 1993), amended by the Office of the Governor, Licensing Board for Contractors, LR 38:153 (January 2012), LR 40:2576 (December 2014).*

## §511. No Written Examination Given

A. Applicants requesting a specialty class where there is no written examination shall be examined by the board on the experience shown on his application.

*AUTHORITY NOTE: Promulgated in accordance with R.S. 37:2153.*

*HISTORICAL NOTE: Adopted by the Department of Commerce, Licensing Board for Contractors, November 1974, amended and promulgated LR 8:137 (March 1982), amended by the Office of the Governor, Licensing Board for Contractors, LR 38:153 (January 2012).*

## §513. Cheating

A. Anyone found using unauthorized code books, text books, pagers, beepers, cellular telephones, tape recorders, radio transmitters, portable scanning devices, cameras, portable photocopy machines, reference materials, notes, blank writing or note paper, or any other aid or electronic device not specifically provided by the Examination Section for the purpose of examination administration shall have his or her examination confiscated, the exam results invalidated, and shall have his or her name placed on the agenda for the board's next regularly scheduled meeting for consideration and appropriate action. Failure to appear before the board shall result in the imposition of a one year waiting period before the applicant may retake the examination(s).

B. It is the policy of the board that the specific contents of its examinations are considered to be proprietary and confidential. Anyone found in possession of examination questions, answers, or drawings in whole or in part shall have his or her examination confiscated, the exam results invalidated, shall be barred from taking any other examination, and shall not be eligible to become a qualifying party for the licensee for a period of one year.

*AUTHORITY NOTE: Promulgated in accordance with R.S. 37:2150-2192.*

*HISTORICAL NOTE: Promulgated by the Department of Economic Development, Licensing Board for Contractors, LR 21:1214 (November 1995), amended by the Office of the Governor, Licensing Board for Contractors, LR 38:153 (January 2012).*

## §515. Examination Scheduling

A. A qualifying party candidate who has been approved to take an examination shall be given a means to register and schedule the examination.

B. A candidate who fails to appear on the scheduled examination date and time shall forfeit his or her examination fee and be required to submit a new examination fee before a new examination date will be scheduled.

C. A candidate who fails an examination may schedule an additional attempt 30 days or more after the date on which he or she failed an examination.

*AUTHORITY NOTE: Promulgated in accordance with R.S. 37:2150-2192.*

*HISTORICAL NOTE: Promulgated by the Department of Economic Development, State Licensing Board for Contractors, LR 21:1214 (November 1995), amended by the Office of the Governor, Licensing Board for Contractors, LR 38:153 (January 2012), LR 40:2576 (December 2014).*

## §517. Examination Administration Procedures

A. Administrative check-in procedures begin one-half hour before the examinations begin. Candidates must report to the testing center for processing at least 15 minutes prior to the examination's starting time. Any candidate reporting after the 15-minute reporting time may not be allowed admittance to the examination room. Every candidate must present acceptable government-issued photographic identification to be admitted to the examination room.

B. Personal items (e.g., telephones, pagers, calculators, purses, briefcases, etc.) shall not be allowed in the testing room. A candidate shall not have access to these items during examination administration.

C. A candidate wearing bulky clothing or attire which would facilitate concealment of prohibited materials shall be requested to leave said clothing or attire outside the examination room or to remove it and place it in the front of the examination room. Failure to remove the article shall constitute permission to search for contraband materials, or a cancellation of his or her scheduled examination, at the option of the candidate.

D. All examination activities are subject to being filmed, recorded, or monitored.

E. A candidate taking an examination shall not be allowed access to telephones or other communication devices during the course of the examination.

AUTHORITY NOTE: Promulgated in accordance with R.S. 37:2150-2192.

HISTORICAL NOTE: Promulgated by the Department of Economic Development, Licensing Board for Contractors, LR 21:1214 (November 1995), amended by the Office of the Governor, Licensing Board for Contractors, LR 38:153 (January 2012), LR 40:2576 (December 2014).

## §519. Test Item Challenges

A. A candidate who believes that an individual test item may not have a correct answer or may have more than one correct answer shall be afforded an opportunity to challenge the test item. The candidate shall record his or her comments in writing on a form supplied by the test monitor at the candidate's request during the examination. Comments will not be accepted at any other time. Comments should provide a detailed explanation as to why the candidate feels the item is incorrect. General comments (e.g., "This item is wrong.") will not be investigated.

B. Examination comments shall be reviewed.

C. If a test item comment is deemed to be valid, the director of the Examinations and Assessment Section shall have the authority to change a grade based upon test item comment(s).

AUTHORITY NOTE: Promulgated in accordance with R.S. 37:2150-2192.

HISTORICAL NOTE: Promulgated by the Department of Economic Development, Licensing Board for Contractors, LR 21:1214 (November 1995), amended by the Office of the Governor, Licensing Board for Contractors, LR 38:153 (January 2012), LR 40:2576 (December 2014).

## §521. Examination Reviews Prohibited

A. Examinations may not be reviewed.

AUTHORITY NOTE: Promulgated in accordance with R.S. 37:2150-2192.

HISTORICAL NOTE: Promulgated by the Department of Economic Development, Licensing Board for Contractors, LR 21:1215 (November 1995), amended by the Office of the Governor, Licensing Board for Contractors, LR 38:154 (January 2012).

Appendix F: Rules and Regulations of the Louisiana Licensing Board for Contractors                    F-13

## CHAPTER SEVEN.

## HEARINGS; MEETINGS

### §701. Hearings

A. Hearings may be conducted by the board's legal counsel at regular or special meetings whenever deemed necessary and special hearing officers may be hired at the board's discretion. Hearings shall be conducted in accordance with the Administrative Procedure Act.

B. Written notice shall be given to all parties at least five days prior to such hearings or special meetings. The board members shall be notified at least three days prior to such hearings or special meetings. The notice shall include the time, place and purpose of the hearing or special meeting and may be held at any place within the state.

C. Confirmation of the written notice required by this Section may be proved by any one of the following:

1. a signed return receipt of certified or registered mail, confirming delivery and receipt of the required notice;

2. a signed confirmation by a board employee that actual physical delivery was made to the contractor, or left at the address on file with the board for that contractor;

3. a confirmation of facsimile transmission, if the contractor has provided the board with a facsimile number in documents on file with the board;

4. a copy of notice by electronic transmission, if the contractor has provided the board with an electronic address in documents on file with the board;

5. a printed electronic confirmation of delivery and/or confirmation of signature from the U.S. Postal Service;

6. a written, electronic, or facsimile response to the notice or subpoena provided therewith, from the contractor or its representative; or

7. appearance by the contractor or its authorized representative at the hearing.

D. As authorized by R.S. 49:962, the board may hear and decide petitions for declaratory orders and rulings as to the applicability of any statutory authority or of any rule or order of the board. Such orders and rulings shall have the same status as board decisions or orders in adjudicated cases.

*AUTHORITY NOTE: Promulgated in accordance with R.S. 37:2150-2192.*

*HISTORICAL NOTE: Adopted by the Department of Commerce, Licensing Board for Contractors, November 1974, amended and promulgated LR 4:69 (March 1978), LR 8:137 (March 1982), amended by the Department of Economic Development, Licensing Board for Contractors, LR 19:1127 (September 1993), amended by the Office of the Governor, Licensing Board for Contractors, LR 38:154 (January 2012).*

### §703. Disqualification or Debarment by Any Public Entity

A. Pursuant to the requirements of R.S. 37:2158(B), a public entity which disqualifies any person or licensee pursuant to R.S. 38:2212(J) must provide the board with written notification thereof within 30 days of the date of such disqualification. The notice required by this Section shall include the basis for the disqualification, the terms and provisions thereof, and copies of the evidence or basis upon which the disqualification was imposed.

*AUTHORITY NOTE: Promulgated in accordance with R.S. 37:2153(A).*

*HISTORICAL NOTE: Promulgated by the Department of Economic Development, Licensing Board for Contractors, LR 23:1495 (November 1997), amended by the Office of the Governor, Licensing Board for Contractors, LR 38:154 (January 2012).*

# CHAPTER NINE.

## SUBCONTRACTORS

### §901. Subcontractors

A. It shall be the responsibility of a licensed contractor, residential building contractor, mechanical contractor, or electrical contractor to secure the current valid license number of any subcontractor who submits a bid to it or performs work for which a license is required. If any licensed contractor, residential building contractor, mechanical contractor, or electrical contractor awards a contract for which a license is required to any unlicensed subcontractor, the license of the awarding contractor, residential building contractor, mechanical contractor, or electrical contractor may be suspended, revoked or rescinded after a hearing is conducted by the board.

*AUTHORITY NOTE: Promulgated in accordance with R.S. 37:2153.*

*HISTORICAL NOTE: Adopted by the Department of Commerce, Licensing Board for Contractors, November 1974, amended and promulgated LR 8:137 (March 1982), amended by the Office of the Governor, Licensing Board for Contractors, LR 38:154 (January 2012).*

### §903. Subcontractor License; Default

A. It shall be a violation for any general contractor, contractor, owner, awarding authority, subcontractor, or any other person to contract or subcontract all or any portion of work to any other contractor or subcontractor unless said contractor or subcontractor was duly licensed by the board as of the final date fixed for the submission of bids on said work from the primary contractor to the owner or awarding authority. This rule shall be subject to the provisions and limitations established by R.S. 37:2156(B) and (D).

B. If work is subcontracted as per this rule, and the subcontractor should default for any reason, the awarding authority shall have the right to take bids from any subcontractor that is properly licensed at the time of this default.

*AUTHORITY NOTE: Promulgated in accordance with R.S. 37:2150-2192.*

*HISTORICAL NOTE: Promulgated by the Department of Commerce, Licensing Board for Contractors, LR 8:138 (March 1982), amended by the Department of Economic Development, Licensing Board for Contractors, LR 19:1128 (September 1993), amended by the Office of the Governor, Licensing Board for Contractors, LR 38:154 (January 2012).*

# CHAPTER ELEVEN.

## BIDDING

### §1103. Proper Classification

A. All licensed contractors bidding in the amount for which a license is required shall be required to have qualified for the classification in which they bid.

B. The refusal by any licensed contractor, residential building contractor, home improvement contractor, subcontractor, mechanical contractor, or electrical contractor to honor a bid price may be grounds for a finding of a violation of the contractors licensing law.

C. When two or more contractors bid as a joint venture on any project in the amount for which a license is required with R.S. 37:2150 et seq., all parties are required to be licensed at the time the bid is submitted. Each party to the joint venture may only perform within the applicable classifications of the work of which it is properly classified to perform.

*AUTHORITY NOTE: Promulgated in accordance with R.S. 37:2153.*

# Appendix F: Rules and Regulations of the Louisiana Licensing Board for Contractors

*HISTORICAL NOTE: Promulgated by the Department of Commerce, Licensing Board for Contractors, LR 8:137 (March 1982), amended by the Office of the Governor, Licensing Board for Contractors, LR 38:155 (January 2012), LR 40:2577 (December 2014).*

## §1109. Division of Contract

A. Any division of a contract into parts which would avoid the necessity of a license to bid for, contract for, or perform the work, will be disregarded, and the parts of the contract will be treated as one contract totaling the amount of these parts when combined.

B. For the purpose of determining a scope of work, the board should review whether the contract or contracts in question constitute a single scope of work or whether they constitute separate scopes of work. The board may be guided in this interpretation by a review of the drawings, plot plans, blueprints, architectural plans, site maps, technical drawings, engineering designs, sketches, diagrams, black lines, blue lines, drafts or other renderings depicting the total scope of work.

*AUTHORITY NOTE: Promulgated in accordance with R.S. 37:2153.*

*HISTORICAL NOTE: Adopted by the Department of Commerce, Licensing Board for Contractors, November 1974, amended and promulgated LR 8:137 (March 1982), amended by the Office of the Governor, Licensing Board for Contractors, LR 38:155 (January 2012).*

## §1111. Failure to Insure or Bond

A. Whenever a licensed contractor, residential building contractor, home improvement contractor, mechanical contractor or electrical contractor bids a project within the scope of this act and is awarded the contract, the refusal or inability of the contractor, residential building contractor, home improvement contractor, mechanical contractor, or electrical contractor to provide bonding and insurance coverage as required by the bid proposal, may be grounds for a finding of a violation of §113.A.

*AUTHORITY NOTE: Promulgated in accordance with R.S. 37:2150-2192.*

*HISTORICAL NOTE: Adopted by the Department of Commerce, Licensing Board for Contractors, November 1974, amended and promulgated LR 8:137 (March 1982), amended by the Department of Economic Development, Licensing Board for Contractors, LR 19:1128 (September 1993), amended by the Office of the Governor, Licensing Board for Contractors, LR 38:155 (January 2012).*

## §1113. Electrical or Mechanical Work

A. Any person, firm, partnership, co-partnership, association, corporation, or other organization bidding on or performing a job for which a license is required, the majority of which job is classified as V. Electrical Work or VI. Mechanical Work, the licensee shall hold the major classification or subdivision thereunder of electrical work or mechanical work as the case may be.

B. On all jobs involving mechanical or electrical work, the board shall consider the monetary value of the electrical or mechanical material and/or equipment furnished by the owner or builder, if any, in determining the amount of electrical or mechanical work involved.

C. The board takes cognizance of all local ordinances and codes regulating the licensing of electrical and mechanical contractors.

*AUTHORITY NOTE: Promulgated in accordance with R.S. 37:2159 and 37:2153.*

*HISTORICAL NOTE: Adopted by the Department of Commerce, Licensing Board for Contractors, November 1974, amended and promulgated LR 8:137 (March 1982), amended by the Office of the Governor, Licensing Board for Contractors, LR 38:155 (January 2012).*

## CHAPTER THIRTEEN.

## FEES

### §1301. Fee for Licenses

A. The annual fee for licenses for the following year may be set by the board at its July meeting each year. If a new fee is not set, the fee(s) for the prior year shall continue to be in full force and effect until changed by the board.

*AUTHORITY NOTE: Promulgated in accordance with R.S. 37:2150-2192.*

*HISTORICAL NOTE: Adopted by the Department of Commerce, Licensing Board for Contractors, November 1974, amended and promulgated LR 2:271 (September 1976), amended LR 8:136 (March 1982), LR 10:199 (March 1984), LR 11:341 (April 1985), LR 12:761 (November 1986), amended by the Department of Economic Development, Licensing Board for Contractors, LR 19:1128 (September 1993), amended by the Office of the Governor, Licensing Board for Contractors, LR 38:155 (January 2012).*

## CHAPTER FIFTEEN.

## RESIDENTIAL

### §1501. Definitions

A. Anyone bidding or performing the work of a general contractor on a residential project in the amount for which a license is required must be licensed under the classification *residential construction*. This requirement shall not include individuals who build no more than one residence for their own personal use as their principal residence per year.

B. A subcontractor, architect or engineer who acts as a residential building contractor as defined in R.S. 37:2150.1(11) must possess a residential construction license.

C. "Cost of a project" includes the value of all labor, materials, subcontractors, general overhead and supervision. With respect to modular housing, "cost of the project" shall not include the cost of the component parts of the modular home in the condition each part leaves the factory, in accordance with R.S. 40:1730.71.

*AUTHORITY NOTE: Promulgated in accordance with R.S. 37:2150-2192.*

*HISTORICAL NOTE: Promulgated by the Department of Economic Development, Licensing Board for Contractors, LR 22:94 (February 1996), amended by the Office of the Governor, Licensing Board for Contractors, LR 38:155 (January 2012).*

### §1503. Requirements

A. All residential building contractors shall work in the name which appears on the official records of the State Licensing Board for Contractors for the current license.

B. If a licensed general residential contractor assigns a contract, or any portion of a contract, in the amount for which a license is required to another general residential contractor, the person or firm to which it is assigned and/or who performs the work must possess the proper current license. No unlicensed contractor shall be permitted to assign a contract, or any portion of a contract, in the amount for which a license is required to a licensed contractor in circumvention of the laws of the state of Louisiana.

C. All applications for a residential contractors license shall contain the information required on the forms which are available at the offices of the State Licensing Board for Contractors, 2525 Quail Drive, Baton Rouge, Louisiana 70808. The application shall be time dated when received and shall be reviewed by the Residential Contractors Licensing Board Subcommittee prior to being submitted to the Contractors Licensing Board at the next regularly scheduled meeting of the board, provided that:

# Appendix F: Rules and Regulations of the Louisiana Licensing Board for Contractors

1. the application is complete, including the required financial statement, references, federal identification number, certificate of workers compensation insurance, certificate of general liability insurance in the minimum amount of $100,000, and properly notarized;

2. all applicable fees, fines, or other sums due to the board are paid in full;

3. the complete application is received and verified by the board in time to comply with all notice requirements; and

4. all examination requirements have been met.

D. Workers compensation and general liability insurance, obtained from an insurer authorized to sell those forms of insurance coverage in the state, shall be maintained continuously by residential building contractors. Insurance certificates evidencing current workers compensation and general liability insurance shall be submitted with each new application, every renewal application, and upon the renewal date of coverage. In the event of a lapse of insurance coverage, a cease and desist order shall be issued and such lapse shall be grounds for suspension or revocation of the license after proper hearing.

E. The qualifying party for each applicant must pass any examinations required and administered by the state Licensing Board for Contractors.

F. The qualifying party shall be an individual owner, an original incorporator, partner, member or shareholder, or an employee of the applicant who has been in full-time employment for 120 consecutive days immediately preceding the application. Any licensed residential building contractor may have more than one qualifying party.

*AUTHORITY NOTE: Promulgated in accordance with R.S. 37:2150-2192.*

*HISTORICAL NOTE: Promulgated by the Department of Economic Development, Licensing Board for Contractors, LR 22:94 (February 1996), amended by the Office of the Governor.*

## §1505. Exceptions

A. An applicant for a residential building contractor's license who can show written proof that it possessed a contractor's license for building construction as required by R.S. 37:2167(D)(1) prior to February 1, 1996 shall not be required to take the examinations required by the State Licensing Board for Contractors, but shall meet all other requirements for such license.

*AUTHORITY NOTE: Promulgated in accordance with R.S. 37:2150-2192.*

*HISTORICAL NOTE: Promulgated by the Department of Economic Development, Licensing Board for Contractors, LR 22:94 (February 1996), amended by the Office of the Governor, Licensing Board for Contractors, LR 38:156 (January 2012), LR 40:2577 (December 2014).*

## §1507. Violations

A. The Licensing Board for Contractors Residential Subcommittee has the authority to conduct hearings on alleged violations by residential building contractors in accordance with the provisions of R.S. 37:2158.

B. The Licensing Board for Contractors Residential Subcommittee shall make recommendations to the Contractors Board regarding their findings and determinations as a result of the hearings on said alleged violations.

C. Residential building contractors whose alleged violations were heard by the subcommittee and a recommendation rendered, may request to appear at the next regularly scheduled board meeting or at any other board meeting where their alleged violations are brought before the board for final action, and may be given an opportunity to address the board regarding the subcommittee's recommendation.

*AUTHORITY NOTE: Promulgated in accordance with R.S. 37:2150-2192.*

F-18          **Appendix F: Rules and Regulations of the Louisiana Licensing Board for Contractors**

*HISTORICAL NOTE: Promulgated by the Department of Economic Development, Licensing Board for Contractors, LR 22:95 (February 1996), amended by the Office of the Governor, Licensing Board for Contractors, LR 38:156 (January 2012).*

### §1509. Penalties

A. The Subcommittee has the authority to issue, suspend, modify or revoke residential contractors licenses, subject to the final approval of the state Licensing Board for Contractors.

B. In accordance with the provisions of R.S. 37:2162, the subcommittee shall have the authority to issue a fine not to exceed ten percent of the total contract being performed for each violation, for the causes listed in R.S. 37:2158, subject to final approval by the state Contractors Licensing Board.

C. In addition to or in lieu of any of the penalties provided in this Chapter, the subcommittee is empowered to issue a cease and desist order. Further, the subcommittee may seek the other civil remedies provided in R.S. 37:2162 for violations of this Chapter, subject to the final approval of the state Licensing Board for Contractors.

*AUTHORITY NOTE: Promulgated in accordance with R.S. 37:2150-2192.*

*HISTORICAL NOTE: Promulgated by the Department of Economic Development, Licensing Board for Contractors, LR 22:95 (February 1996), amended by the Office of the Governor, Licensing Board for Contractors, LR 38:156 (January 2012), LR 40:2577 (December 2014).*

### §1511. Home Improvement Registration

A. Home improvement contractors are required to register with the board in order to perform services in an amount of $7,500 or more, not to exceed $75,000. Contractors who hold valid commercial or residential licenses with the board are exempt from this registration requirement. Home improvement contractors are required to submit certificates evidencing workers' compensation coverage in compliance with title 23 of the *Louisiana Revised Statutes* of 1950, proof of general liability insurance in a minimum amount of $100,000.

*AUTHORITY NOTE: Promulgated in accordance with R.S. 37:2150-2192.*

*HISTORICAL NOTE: Promulgated by the Office of the Governor, Licensing Board for Contractors, LR 38:813 (March 2012), amended LR 40:2577 (December 2014).*

### §1513. New Home Warranty Act

A. Pursuant to R.S. 9:3145, a builder shall give the owner written notice of the requirements of the New Home Warranty Act.

B. Failure to provide such written notice shall be grounds for the residential subcommittee to suspend, modify, or revoke the license of the contractor who failed to provide the required notice, subject to the final approval of the board.

*AUTHORITY NOTE: Promulgated in accordance with R.S. 37:2150-2192.*

*HISTORICAL NOTE: Promulgated by the Office of the Governor, Licensing Board for Contractors, LR 38:813 (March 2012).*

# Appendix G: Louisiana Underground Utilities and Facilities Damage Prevention Law

**Louisiana Revised Statutes Title 40, Chapter 8, Part VIII.**

### §1749.11. Short title; purpose

A. This Part shall be known and may be cited as the "Louisiana Underground Utilities and Facilities Damage Prevention Law".

B. It is the public policy of this state to promote the protection of property, workmen, and citizens in the immediate vicinity of an underground facility or utility from damage, death, or injury and to promote the health and well-being of the community by preventing the interruption of essential services which may result from the destruction of, or damage to, underground facilities or utilities.

*Acts 1988, No. 923, §1; Acts 1999, No. 506, §1, eff. June 29, 1999.*

### §1749.12. Definitions

As used in this Part, the following terms shall have the meanings ascribed to them in this Section:

(1) "Agricultural excavator" means a person who owns or operates a farm and is directly involved in the cultivation of land or crops or who raises livestock.

(2) "Damage" means any defacing, scraping, gouging, breaking, cutting, or displacement of, impact upon or removal of an underground facility or utility or its means of primary support.

(3) "Demolisher" means any person engaged in the act of demolishing as defined in Paragraph (2) of this Section.

(4) "Demolition" means the total or partial wrecking, razing, rendering, moving, or removing of any building or structure, movable or immovable.

(5) "Emergency" means any crisis situation which poses an imminent threat or danger to life, health, or property, requires immediate action, and immediate action is taken.

(6) "Excavation" or "excavate" means any operation for the purpose of movement or removal of earth, rock, or other materials in or on the ground by the use of powered or mechanical or manual means, including pile driving, digging, blasting, auguring, boring, back filling, dredging, compressing, plowing-in, trenching, ditching, tunneling, land-leveling, grading, and mechanical probing. "Excavation" or "excavate" shall not include manual probing.

(7) "Excavator" means any person who engages in excavation operations.

(8) "Forestry excavator" means an excavator who is a logger, prescribed burner, site preparation operator, or tree planter for commercial forestry operations.

(9) "Inclement weather" means weather that prohibits or impedes a worker's use of his locating equipment or causes undue risk to himself or his equipment such as lightning, heavy rain, tornadoes, hurricanes, floods, sleet, snow, or flooding conditions.

(10) "Mark by time" is the date and time provided by the regional notification center by which the utility or facility operator is required to mark the location or provide information to enable an excavator or demolisher,

using reasonable and prudent means, to determine the specific location of the utility or facility as provided for in R.S. 40:1749.14(D). The mark-by time may be extended if mutually agreed upon and documented between the excavator and operator.

(11) "Operator" means any person who owns or operates a public or private underground facility or utility which furnishes a service or material or stores, transports, or transmits electric energy, steam, oil, gases, natural gas, gas, mixture of gases, petroleum, petroleum products, hazardous or flammable fluids, toxic or corrosive fluids/gases, including telephone or telegraph system, fiber optic electronic communication systems, or water or water systems, or drainage, sewer systems, or traffic control systems or other items of like nature.

(12) "Person" means an individual, firm, partnership, association, limited liability company, corporation, joint venture, municipality, governmental agency, political subdivision, or agent of the state or any legal representative thereof.

(13) "Regional notification center" means any one of the following:

(a) An entity designated as nonprofit by the Internal Revenue Service under Section 501(c) of the Internal Revenue Code and which is organized to protect its members from damage and is certified by the Department of Public Safety and Corrections in accordance with this Part.

(b) An organization of operators, consisting of two or more separate operators who jointly have underground utilities or facilities in three or more parishes in Louisiana, which is organized to protect its own installation from damage and has been certified by the Department of Public Safety and Corrections in accordance with this Part.

(c) An operator who has underground utilities or facilities in a majority of parishes in Louisiana and is organized to protect its own installation from damage, and has been certified by the Department of Public Safety and Corrections in accordance with this Part.

(14) "Service line or lines" means underground facilities or utilities which provide power, gas, natural gas, communication, or water capabilities to a building or structure or buildings or group of structures.

(15) "Underground facility or utility" means any pipe, conduit, duct, wire, cable, valve, line, fiber optic equipment, or other structure which is buried or placed below ground or submerged for use in connection with storage, conveyance, transmission, or protection of electronics communication system, telephone or telegraph system, or fiber optic, electric energy, oil, natural gas, gas, gases, steam, mixture of gases, petroleum, petroleum products, hazardous or flammable fluids/gases, toxic or corrosive fluids/gases, hazardous fluids/gases, or other substances of like nature or water or water systems, sewer systems or traffic, drainage control systems, or other items of like nature.

(16) "Wildfire" means an uncontrolled combustion of natural vegetation.

*Acts 1988, No. 923, §1; Acts 1997, No. 1050, §1, eff. July 11, 1997; Acts 1999, No. 506, §1, eff. June 29, 1999; Acts 2010, No. 249, §1, eff. Sept. 1, 2010; Acts 2011, No. 38, §1, eff. Oct. 1. 2011; Acts 2012, No. 103, §1; Acts 2014, No. 203, eff. Aug. 1, 2014.*

### §1749.13. Excavation and demolition; prohibitions

A. Except as provided in this Section, no person shall excavate or demolish in any street, highway, public place, or servitude of any operator, or near the location of an underground facility or utility, or on the premises of a customer served by an underground facility or utility without having first ascertained, in the manner prescribed in Subsection B of this Section, the specific location as provided in R.S. 40:1749.14(D) of all underground facilities or utilities in the area which would be affected by the proposed excavation or demolition.

B.     (1) Except as provided in R.S. 40:1749.15, prior to any excavation or demolition, each excavator or demolisher shall serve telephonic or electronic notice of the intent to excavate or demolish to the regional

# Appendix G: Louisiana Underground Utilities and Facilities Damage Prevention Law

notification center or centers serving the area in which the proposed excavation or demolition is to take place. Such notice shall be given to the notification center at least forty-eight hours, but not more than one hundred twenty hours, excluding weekends and holidays, in advance of the commencement of any excavation or demolition activity. Holidays shall consist of the following: New Year's Day; Good Friday; Independence Day; Labor Day; Thanksgiving Day; and Christmas Day, or the days on which those holidays are observed by the state.

(2) This notice shall contain the name, address, and telephone number of the person filing the notice of intent, and, if different, the person responsible for the excavation or demolition, the starting date, anticipated duration, and description of the specific type of excavation or demolition operation to be conducted, the specific location of the proposed excavation or demolition and a statement as to whether directional boring or explosives are to be used. If the excavation or demolition is part of a larger project, the notice shall be confined to the actual area of proposed excavation or demolition that will occur during the twenty-day time period under R.S. 40:1749.14(C).

(3) Telephonic notice shall be recorded on tape or stored into an electronic data bank by the regional notification center and a record of the notice shall be retained for a three-year period from the date of notification. A record of an electronic notice shall also be retained by the regional notification center for a three-year period from the date of notification.

(4) Notice shall be given and shall include a specific location request for excavation or demolition work to be performed at least forty-eight hours, but not more than one hundred twenty hours, excluding weekends and holidays, in advance of actual work commencement. Holidays shall consist of the following: New Year's Day; Good Friday; Independence Day; Labor Day; Thanksgiving Day; and Christmas Day, or the days on which those holidays are observed by the state. The marking of an operator's facility or utility shall be provided for excavation or demolition purposes only.

(5) The excavator or demolisher shall wait at least forty-eight hours, beginning at 7:00 a.m. on the next working day, following notification, unless mutually agreed upon and documented by the excavator and operator to extend such time, before commencing any excavation or demolition activity, except in the case of an emergency as defined in the provisions of this Part or if informed by the regional notification center that no operators are to be notified.

C. This Part shall not apply to activities by operators or land owners excavating their own underground utilities or facilities on their own property or operators' exclusive right-of-way provided there is no encroachment on the rights-of-way of any operator.

D. Excavators may use white paint as marking under American Public Works Association guidelines.

E. Repealed by Acts 2010, No. 249, §2, eff. Sept. 1, 2010.

*Acts 1988, No. 923, §1; Acts 1992, No. 883, §1; Acts 1997, No. 1050, §1, eff. July 11, 1997; Acts 1999, No. 506, §1, eff. June 29, 1999; Acts 2006, No. 428, §1, eff. June 15, 2006; Acts 2010, No. 249, §§1, 2, eff. Sept. 1, 2010; Acts 2011, No. 38, §1, eff. Oct. 1, 2011; Acts 2014, No. 203, eff. Aug. 1, 2014.*

## §1749.14. Regional notification center

A. Each operator of an underground utility or facility, including all state agencies and political subdivisions of the state, shall become a member of, participate in, and share the cost of a regional notification center, except as provided for in R.S. 40:1749.19. Each regional notification center shall have the capability to receive emergency locate requests twenty-four hours a day and to disseminate the information as soon as it is received to the appropriate operators and all affected regional notification centers in this state.

B. A regional notification center receiving a notice of intent to excavate shall notify all member operators having underground utilities or facilities in or near the site of the proposed excavation, except for the operator who provided the notice of intent and requested not to receive such notification. All member operators shall furnish the regional notification center with current emergency contact or notification information, including twenty-four hour telephone numbers.

C.  (1) Each operator of an underground facility or utility, after having received the notification request from the regional notification center of an intent to excavate, shall supply, prior to the proposed excavation, the following information to the person responsible for the excavation:

(a) The specific location and type of all of its underground utilities or facilities which may be damaged as a result of the excavation or demolition. If the surface over the buried or submerged line is to be removed, supplemental offset markings may be used. Offset markings shall be on a uniform alignment and shall clearly indicate that the actual facility is a specific distance away.

(b)  (i) Unless otherwise required by federal or state statutes, the specific location and type of underground utility or facility may, at the operator's option, be marked to locate the utilities or facilities. If the utilities or facilities are visibly marked by the operator, they shall be marked by the operator by color coded paint, flags, or stakes or similar means using the American Public Works Association color code.

(ii) The location of underground fiber optic cables shall be identified in accordance with the provisions of this Subparagraph and such identification shall also include an added special marking that is uniquely associated with fiber optic cables.

(iii) When the utility or facility operator has marked the location of underground facilities or utilities, the marking shall be deemed good as long as visible but not longer than twenty calendar days, including weekends and holidays, from the "mark by" time. An additional notice to the regional notification center shall be given by the excavator or demolisher in accordance with the provisions of this Part when the marks are no longer visible or if the excavation or demolition cannot be completed within twenty calendar days from the "mark by" time, whichever occurs first.

(iv) The excavator shall use all reasonable and prudent means, within common industry practice, to protect and preserve all marks of the underground utility or facility.

(v) In the case whereby a forestry excavator or agricultural excavator has requested that the utilities and facilities be marked for location, the operator of a utility or facility shall mark the area of their utilities or facilities. The markings provided by the operator shall be deemed good as long as the markings are visible or up to thirty calendar days from the time the markings were made, whichever is shorter.

(2) If the operator does not visibly mark the location of these utilities or facilities, the operator shall provide information to enable an excavator using reasonable and prudent means to determine the approximate location of the utility or facility. The information provided by the operator shall include a contact person and a specific telephone number for the excavators to call. After the operator has received the notification request, the information on location, size, and type of underground utility or facility must be provided by the operator to the excavator prior to excavation.

(3) In the event of inclement weather as defined in this Part, the mark by time shall be extended by a duration equal to the duration of the inclement weather. The owner or operator shall notify the excavator or demolisher before the expiration of the mark by time of the need for such extension.

# Appendix G: Louisiana Underground Utilities and Facilities Damage Prevention Law

D. For the purpose of this Section, the specific location of the underground facilities is defined as an area not wider than the width of the underground facility or utility as marked plus eighteen inches on either side.

E.     (1) An excavator or demolisher who has given notice and otherwise complied with the provisions of this Part shall be immune from civil liability for damages in the area of the proposed excavation or demolition caused by such excavation or demolition to any owner or operator who:

> (a) Was required by the provisions of this Part to become a member, participate in, or share the cost of a regional notification center, and failed to do so.

> (b) Failed to mark or provide information as required by the provisions of this Part.

(2) The immunity provided by this Subsection shall not apply to civil liability for damages caused by the negligence of the excavator or demolisher.

F. Should an owner or operator file suit against an excavator or demolisher for damages to underground facilities or utilities and the court finds in favor of the owner or operator, in addition to damages provided for by this Part, the owner or operator shall be entitled to recover reasonable attorney fees and costs. If the court finds in favor of the excavator or demolisher, the excavator or demolisher shall be entitled to recover reasonable attorney fees and costs.

*Acts 1988, No. 923, §1, eff. Sept. 9, 1989; Acts 1992, No. 883, §1; Acts 1995, No. 491, §1; Acts 1997, No. 1050, §1, eff. July 11, 1997; Acts 1999, No. 506, §1, eff. June 29, 1999; Acts 2010, No. 249, §1, eff. Sept. 1, 2010; Acts 2011, No. 38, §1, eff. Oct. 1, 2011; Acts 2014, No. 203, eff. Aug. 1, 2014.*

### §1749.15. Emergency excavation; notice required; penalty

A. The notice required pursuant to R.S. 40:1749.13 shall not apply to any person conducting an emergency excavation. Oral notice of the emergency excavation shall be given as soon as practicable to the regional notification center or each operator having underground utilities and facilities located in the area and, if necessary, emergency assistance shall be requested from each operator in locating and providing immediate protection to its underground utilities and facilities.

B. The excavator shall orally certify in the notice required in Subsection A of this Section that the situation poses an imminent threat or danger to life, health, or property and requires immediate action and that the excavator has a crew on site.

C. There is a rebuttable presumption that the excavator failed to give notice as required pursuant to this Section if the excavator failed to give any notice to the regional notification center within the following time periods:

(1) Within four hours of the beginning of the emergency excavation.

(2) In the case of a gubernatorially declared state of emergency due to a tropical storm or hurricane event, within twelve hours of the beginning of the emergency excavation within the parishes to which the emergency declaration applies.

(3) In the case of a wildfire, within twenty-four hours after control of the emergency.

*Acts 1988, No. 923, §1; Acts 1997, No. 1050, §1, eff. July 11, 1997; Acts 1999, No. 506, §1, eff. June 29, 1999; Acts 2011, No. 38, §1, eff. Oct. 1, 2011; Acts 2012, No. 103, §1.*

## §1749.16. Precautions to avoid damage

In addition to the notification requirements in R.S. 40:1749.13 and 1749.14 and the emergency notification requirements in R.S. 40:1749.15, each person responsible for an excavation or demolition operation shall do the following:

(1) Plan the excavation or demolition to avoid damage to or minimize interference with underground facilities in and near the construction area.

(2) Maintain a safe clearance between the underground utilities or facilities and the cutting edge or point of any power or mechanized equipment, taking into account the known limit of control of the cutting edge or point to avoid damage to utilities or facilities.

(3) Provide support for underground facilities or utilities in and near the construction area, during excavation and back filling operations, as may be reasonably necessary to protect the utility or facility.

(4) Dig test pits to determine the actual location of facilities or utilities handling electricity, gas, natural gas, oil, petroleum products, or other flammable, toxic, or corrosive fluids/gases if these facilities or utilities are to be exposed.

*Acts 1988, No. 923, §1; Acts 1997, No. 1050, §1, eff. July 11, 1997; Acts 1999, No. 506, §1, eff. June 29, 1999.*

## §1749.17. Excavation or demolition; repair of damage

A. Each person responsible for any excavation or demolition operations which result in any damage to an underground facility or utility shall, immediately upon discovery of that damage, notify the owner or operator of the utility or facility of the location and nature of the damage and shall allow the owner or operator reasonable time to accomplish necessary repairs before continuing the excavation, demolition, or back filling in the immediate area of damage.

B. Each person responsible for an excavation or demolition operation which results in damage to an underground facility or utility permitting the escape of any flammable, toxic, or corrosive fluids/gases shall, immediately upon discovery of that damage:

(1) Notify the owner or operator of the utility or facility as provided in Subsection A, and all other appropriate emergency response personnel, including 911 and the local law enforcement and fire departments and allow the owner or operator reasonable time to accomplish necessary repairs before continuing the excavation, demolition, or back filling in the immediate area of damage.

(2) Take any other action as may be reasonably necessary to protect persons and property and to minimize hazards until arrival of the owner or operator's personnel and police or fire department.

(3) Comply with any other notification process required by law or regulation.

C. For the purposes of this Part, failure to comply with the provisions of Subsection B shall constitute a single violation, except as provided below by Subsection D.

D. After discovery of the damage, each day that an excavator or demolisher fails to comply with the provisions of Subsection B shall be considered a separate violation.

*Acts 1988, No. 923, §1; Acts 1997, No. 1050, §1, eff. July 11, 1997; Acts 1999, No. 506, §1, eff. June 29, 1999; Acts 2001, No. 160, §1.*

## §1749.18. Certification of a regional notification center by Department of Public Safety and Corrections

A. The Department of Public Safety and Corrections shall promulgate rules and regulations in accordance with the Administrative Procedure Act to establish a certification program for regional notification centers in this state.

# Appendix G: Louisiana Underground Utilities and Facilities Damage Prevention Law
G-7

B. Such rules and regulations shall include but not be limited to requirements that the regional notification center must have and maintain the following:

(1) Ability to accept and timely process and locate requests as required by law, including providing of ticket numbers, copies of tickets, notifications, and other procedures and information.

(2) Ability to accept and timely process short notice, priority, and emergency locate requests.

(3) Voice recording of all incoming calls and retention of voice tapes for at least three years.

(4) Any other requirements that may be necessary for a regional notification center to properly perform the duties and functions required under this Part.

C. The department shall include in the rules and regulations procedures for certification by the department and may charge a fee for the certification process, not to exceed two thousand five hundred dollars. The rules and regulations required by this Section shall be promulgated by the department within six months after June 29, 1999.

D. An entity operating in this state as an authorized regional notification center prior to and upon June 29, 1999, shall have six months from the date of final adoption of the rules and regulations required by this Section to seek and obtain compliance certification from the Department of Public Safety and Corrections. Failure to obtain such certification shall result in the cessation of activities by the regional notification center.

E. An entity not operating in this state as an authorized regional notification center prior to and upon June 29, 1999, shall obtain compliance certification from the Department of Public Safety and Corrections prior to performing the operations of a regional notification center in or for this state.

*Acts 1988, No. 923, §1; Acts 1999, No. 506, §1, eff. June 29, 1999.*

### §1749.19. Voluntary participation by incorporated municipalities and parish governments

A. Each incorporated municipality or parish government which owns or operates, in its own right or through a special district or districts created pursuant to constitutional or statutory authority, a drainage system, a sewer system, drainage, water or water system, traffic control system, an electrical energy system and/or a gas or natural gas system underground facility within its local jurisdiction which would otherwise be included in R.S. 40:1749.14, and which does not desire to be so included, shall adopt an ordinance indicating this desire by December 31, 1998. The ordinance shall be filed with the secretary of state for verification purposes. An incorporated municipality or parish government which fails to adopt the ordinance shall be subject to the provisions of this Part on and after December 31, 1998.

B. Each municipality or parish government which owns or operates in its own right, or through a special district or districts created pursuant to law, a drainage system, a sewer system, water or water system, telephone or telegraph, fiber optic, electronics equipment system, traffic control system, an electrical energy system, natural gas system, and/or a gas system underground facility within its local jurisdiction which would otherwise be included in R.S. 40:1749.17, and which is incorporated or created subsequent to July 1, 1997, and which does not desire to be so included, shall comply with the provisions of Subsection A of this Section within one year of the date of its first municipal elections or within one year of the date of creation of a special district.

*Acts 1988, No. 923, §1; Acts 1997, No. 1050, §1, eff. July 11, 1997.*

### §1749.20. Violations; penalties

A.    (1) A person who is required by this Part to become a member of, participate in, or share the cost of, a regional notification center and who fails to do so shall be subject to a civil penalty of not more than two hundred fifty dollars for the first violation and not more than one thousand dollars for each subsequent violation. A subsequent violation shall be deemed to have occurred if the person fails to become a member of, participate in, or share the cost of, a regional notification center as required within ninety days after issuance of a citation for the previous violation.

(2) A person who participates in a regional notification center and who fails to mark or provide information regarding the location of underground utilities and facilities used to store, transport, or convey that which is not regulated pursuant to Chapter 16 of Subtitle II of Title 30 of the Louisiana Revised Statutes of 1950, otherwise known as the Hazardous Materials Information Development, Preparedness, and Response Act, shall be subject to a civil penalty of not more than one thousand dollars. A subsequent violation shall be deemed to have occurred if a person fails to provide information or markings within two years of the issuance of a prior citation for the same or similar conduct.

(3) A person who is required by law to participate in a regional notification center and who fails to provide information or markings to indicate hazardous material as defined in Title 30 of the Louisiana Revised Statutes of 1950 shall be subject to the following:

  (a) For the first violation, a warning letter shall be given.

  (b) For a second violation, a civil penalty of not more than two hundred fifty dollars.

  (c) For a third violation, a civil penalty of not more than five hundred dollars.

  (d) For a fourth violation, a civil penalty of not more than one thousand dollars.

  (e) For a fifth and each subsequent violation, a civil penalty of not less than two thousand dollars nor more than twenty-five thousand dollars.

B. An excavator or demolisher who violates the provisions of R.S. 40:1749.13, 1749.16, or 1749.17(B) shall be subject to the following:

  (1) For the first violation, a warning letter shall be given.

  (2) For a second violation of a similar nature within a two-year period from the previous violation, a civil penalty of not more than two hundred fifty dollars.

  (3) For a third violation of a similar nature within a two-year period from a previous violation, a civil penalty of not more than five hundred dollars.

  (4) For a fourth violation of a similar nature within a two-year period from the previous violation, a civil penalty of not more than one thousand dollars.

  (5) For a fifth and each subsequent violation of a similar nature within a two-year period from the previous violation, a civil penalty of not less than two thousand nor more than twenty-five thousand dollars.

  (6) For any violation involving hazardous materials as defined in Title 30 of the Louisiana Revised Statutes of 1950, a civil penalty of not less than two thousand dollars nor more than twenty-five thousand dollars.

  (7) An excavator or demolisher who is issued a citation for a violation shall immediately stop all excavation or demolition activity until the requirements of this Part are met. Failure to do so shall subject the excavator or demolisher to an additional citation and civil penalty of not more than twenty-five thousand dollars for each such subsequent citation issued.

C. An excavator or demolisher who violates the provisions of R.S. 40:1749.15 shall be subject to the following:

  (1) For the first violation, a civil penalty of not more than fifty dollars.

  (2) For a second violation of a similar nature within a two-year period from the previous violation, a civil penalty of not more than two hundred dollars.

Appendix G: Louisiana Underground Utilities and Facilities Damage Prevention Law    G-9

(3) For a third violation of a similar nature within a two-year period from a previous violation, a civil penalty of not more than five hundred dollars.

(4) For a fourth and each subsequent violation of a similar nature within a two-year period from the previous violation, a civil penalty of not less than five hundred dollars nor more than five thousand dollars.

D. A person may be cited with a violation and held liable for a civil penalty pursuant to this Section although the commission of the offense did not occur in the presence of a law enforcement officer if the evidence is sufficient to establish that the defendant has committed the offense.

*Acts 1988, No. 923, §1; Acts 1997, No. 1050, §1, eff. July 11, 1997; Acts 1999, No. 506, §1, eff. June 29, 1999; Acts 2001, No. 160, §1; Acts 2010, No. 249, §1, eff. Sept. 1, 2010; Acts 2011, No. 38, §1, eff. Oct. 1, 2011; Acts 2012, No. 103, §1; Acts 2014, No. 203, eff. Aug. 1, 2014.*

## §1749.21. Miscellaneous provisions

A. Except as otherwise specifically provided herein, the provisions of this Part shall not affect any civil remedies for personal injury or property damage, including damage to underground facilities or utilities.

B. Nothing in this Part shall affect any permitting process granted to a parish, municipal, local, or state governing authority. If a permit is issued in conjunction with excavation or demolition subject to the provisions of this Part, upon issuing the permit, the governing authority is encouraged to distribute to the permittee information regarding compliance with the provisions of this Part. The regional notification centers shall provide the information to the governing authority for distribution. The failure of the governing authority to distribute the information shall not for that reason alone create any liability on the part of the governing authority or permittee nor otherwise reduce or limit the duties and responsibilities of excavators or demolishers under this Part.

*Acts 1988, No. 923, §1; Acts 1997, No. 1050, §1, eff. July 11, 1997.*

## §1749.22. Preemption

No parish, municipal, local, or state governing authority may enact any ordinance or promulgate any rules or regulations which are in conflict with the provisions of this Part.

*Acts 1988, No. 923, §1.*

## §1749.23. Enforcement and adjudication; administration; levy of civil penalties

A. The provisions of this Part may be enforced by the Department of Public Safety and Corrections or by any local law enforcement agency. The Department of Public Safety and Corrections or its designee may provide forms, including citation, complaint, and incident report forms, to other law enforcement agencies for use in enforcement of the provisions of this Part.

B. The deputy secretary for the office of public safety services in the Department of Public Safety and Corrections or any local law enforcement agency shall have the right to:

(1) Exclusively monitor excavation or demolition that is subject to the provisions of this Part to ensure compliance with the provisions of this Part, including requesting the production by the excavator or demolisher of the locate request number issued by the regional notification center.

(2) Issue citations for violations of the provisions of this Part in addition to other enforcement powers provided by law.

(3) Seek restraining orders, injunctions, or other civil remedies to halt or prevent violations of the provisions of this Part.

C. Proceedings and adjudications for the levying of civil penalties under this Part shall be conducted by the division of administrative law in accordance with regulations adopted pursuant to the Administrative Procedure Act.

D. The secretary of the Department of Public Safety and Corrections or his designee may promulgate rules and regulations for the implementation and administration of the provisions of this Part relative to enforcement, which shall include developing a procedure for reporting and investigating complaints of violations of this Part that includes the following:

(1) Establishing a centralized complaint reporting point using a toll-free phone number that is available to contractors, utility operators, and the general public.

(2) Establishing a uniform complaint form to record the complainant's name and identifying information, the nature and details of the complaint, the geographic location of the complaint, any information about excavators, the date and time of the complaint, the date and time of the complaint report, and whether any collateral damage or off-site impact occurred including information about that impact or damage.

(3) Establishing a procedure to investigate the validity of the complaint using information provided by but not limited to certified regional notification centers with jurisdiction in the reported geographic area.

(4) Establishing a procedure for determining the appropriate law enforcement agency in the reported geographic area that will be responsible for investigating the complaint and for forwarding the complaint report to that law enforcement agency.

(5) Establishing a procedure for the law enforcement agency to completely investigate a complaint and obtain the information needed to issue a citation and adjudicate the complaint.

(6) Establishing a procedure for receiving citations issued by law enforcement agencies, determining whether the cited party wishes to contest the charge, and transferring contested citations to the division of administrative law for adjudication.

(7) Establishing a procedure for recording the number of citations issued and their disposition.

(8) Establishing procedures for collecting civil penalties for deposit into the Underground Damages Prevention Fund and disbursing those civil penalties according to the provisions of this Part.

*Acts 1997, No. 1050, §1, eff. July 11, 1997; Acts 1999, No. 506, §1, eff. June 29, 1999; Acts 2001, No. 162, §1.*

# National Association of State Contractors Licensing Agencies
## NASCLA Membership Information

## Membership Benefits

**Associate Member**
- Online Access to NASCLA "Members Only" website
- Invitation to the Annual Conference
- Annual Complimentary Copy of the NASCLA Contractor State Licensing Information Directory
- Copy of the NASCLA Membership Directory
- Copy of NASCLA's Quarterly Newsletter
- Networking Opportunities with others associated with the construction industry

**State Member**
- Online Access to NASCLA "Members Only" website
- Invitation to the Annual Conference and Mid Year Meeting
- Annual Complimentary Copy of the NASCLA Contractor State Licensing Information Directory
- Copy of the NASCLA Membership Directory
- Copy of NASCLA's Quarterly Newsletter
- Networking Opportunities with others associated with the construction industry

**International Member**
- Online Access to NASCLA "Members Only" website
- Invitation to the Annual Conference
- Annual Complimentary Copy of the NASCLA Contractor State Licensing Information Directory
- Copy of the NASCLA Membership Directory
- Copy of NASCLA's Quarterly Newsletter
- Networking Opportunities with others associated with the construction industry

**Business Member**
- Online Access to NASCLA "Members Only" website
- Invitation to the Annual Conference
- Annual Complimentary Copy of the NASCLA Contractor State Licensing Information Directory
- Copy of the NASCLA Membership Directory
- Copy of NASCLA's Quarterly Newsletter
- Networking Opportunities with others associated with the construction industry
- Sponsorship and Vendor Opportunities at the Annual Conference

## NASCLA'S MISSION

"Our national association is dedicated to the assistance of contractor licensing and enforcement agencies, trade associations, and members of the construction industry to best promote mutual interests and improve the quality standards and understanding of regulation in order to enhance protection of the general public.

The organization serves as a clearinghouse of information and resources for its membership, while providing valuable educational and licensure publications to the contracting community."

**NASCLA**

NATIONAL ASSOCIATION OF STATE
CONTRACTORS LICENSING AGENCIES

23309 N. 17th Drive
Building 1, Unit 110
Phoenix, Arizona 85027

Phone: (623) 587-9354

Fax: (623) 587-9625

www.nascla.org

## APPLICANT INFORMATION

To become a member, please return this form with a check made payable to NASCLA at the address listed above or you may visit our website at www.nascla.org to register online for membership.

If you have any questions, please call NASCLA at (866) 948-3363.

## MEMBERSHIP CLASSIFICATIONS

Please read the classifications below and check the box that best describes your membership classification.

❏ **Associate Member:** Limited to contractor trade associations, contracting firms, construction material suppliers and regional (county, city or municipal) contractor licensing agencies.

$125.00 Annual Membership Fee.

❏ **State Member:** Limited to states that have enacted laws to regulate the business of contracting.

$475.00 Annual Membership Fee.

❏ **International Member:** Limited to regulatory agencies from other nations, countries or states other than the 50 United States of America and its territories.

$475.00 Annual Membership Fee.

❏ **Business Member:** Limited to firms whose business is related to the construction industry? These members shall not use the name of the association and its logo or in any manner refer to NASCLA in advertising, selling or soliciting.

$750.00 Annual Membership Fee.

❏ **Affiliate Member:** Limited to former employees and board members of state contractor licensing agencies who are not actively engaged in the contracting business.

$50.00 Annual Membership Fee.

Name: _____

Title: _____

Company: _____

City, State, Zip Code: _____

Phone: _____

Email: _____ Website: _____